Why did war break out in the summer of 1914?
This major re-examination of Habsburg decision-
making from 1912 to July 1914 argues that it was
Austria-Hungary, not Germany, that initiated the
military steps which brought about the First World
War. Based on extensive new archival research,
this book describes how the local war of 1914
grew out of the earlier Balkan fighting of 1912-13
and the progressive militarization of the Habsburg
policy elite, and then became readily converted
into a world war. The Habsburg decision for war
is put into the perspective of pre-war European
politics and the unique entanglement of domestic
and foreign policy confronting Habsburg
statesmen in a monarchy embracing eleven
nationalities.

Military strategy, the impact of organizational
structures upon decisions, and the economic life
of the monarchy are discussed, and a fascinating
insight is provided into the world of Realpolitik and
the climactic decisions that took Austria-Hungary
to war.

Samuel R. Williamson, Jr is President and Vice-
Chancellor of The University of the South,
Sewanee, and a member of the International
Institute for Strategic Studies. His study *The
Politics of Grand Strategy: Britain and France
Prepare for War, 1904-1914* (1969) won the
George Louis Beer Prize of the American
Historical Association, and he has published
widely on the origins of the First World War.

D1384203

The Making of the 20th Century

This series of specially commissioned titles focuses attention on significant and often controversial events and themes of world history in the present century. Each book provides sufficient narrative and explanation for the newcomer to the subject while offering, for more advanced study, detailed source-references and bibliographies, together with interpretation and reassessment in the light of recent scholarship.

In the choice of subjects there is a balance between breadth in some spheres and detail in others; between the essentially political and matters economic or social. The series cannot be a comprehensive account of everything that has happened in the twentieth century, but it provides a guide to recent research and explains something of the times of extraordinary change and complexity in which we live. It is directed in the main to students of contemporary history and international relations, but includes titles which are of direct relevance to courses in economics, sociology, politics and geography.

The Making of the 20th Century

Series Editor: GEOFFREY WARNER

Already published:

Forthcoming:

Austria–Hungary and the Origins of the First World War

Samuel R. Williamson, Jr

St Martin's Press   New York

First published in the United States of America in 1991

Printed in Hong Kong

ISBN 0–312–05239–1 (cloth)
ISBN 0–312–05283–9 (paper)

Library of Congress Cataloging-in-Publication Data
Williamson, Samuel R.
    Austria–Hungary and the origins of the First World War / Samuel R.
Williamson, Jr.
        p.   cm.—(The Making of the 20th century)
    Includes bibliographical references and index.
    ISBN 0–312–05239–1 (cloth).—ISBN 0–312–05283–9 (paper)
    1. Austria—History—1867–1918.   2. World War, 1914–1918—Causes.
I. Title.   II. Series.
DB86.W515   1990
943.6′044—dc20
                                                            90–41895
                                                                CIP

Contents

For Joan
and
George, Treeby, and Thaddeus

Acknowledgements

I first visited Vienna at Christmas 1958; immediately, the faded splendour of the Habsburg empire captured my imagination. Subsequently, a graduate course at Harvard on the Habsburgs with William Slottman furthered my interest. Then in the late 1960s Ernest May urged that I consider a short study on Austria–Hungary and the July crisis; both of us thought a quick trip to the Habsburg archives would be enough. We were wrong. I soon found that much of the basic monographic research had not been done and that the archives were a treasure chest. Over the next years I planned a larger, longer, two-volume study on the operation of the Habsburg monarchy from 1910 to 1914. Much of that study is now complete, but significant service first as dean, then provost, and now as a college president have delayed its completion. I have, however, during the years published a series of articles on various aspects of Habsburg decision-making before 1914. This shorter work, first suggested by Zara Steiner, seeks to take advantage of the underlying research from the earlier effort while conforming to the format of the series, 'The Making of the Twentieth Century'.

Many individuals have helped in this lengthy research effort. I now wish to thank them. First to Ernest May for having prompted the investigation; to Zara Steiner for insisting that I finish; to Geoffrey Warner who solicited my participation in the Macmillan series; to Richard E. Neustadt for unflagging interest in Habsburg history; Josef Anderle, Christopher Andrew, Volker Berghahn, Geoffrey Best, John Boyer, Lamar Cecil, Ronald E. Coons, Gordon Craig, Richard Crampton, István Deák, Friedrich Engel-Janosi, Sir Michael Howard, Konrad Jarausch, Robert A. Kann, Paul Kennedy, Béla K. Király, Enno Kraehe, John Leslie, David MacKenzie, Eduard März, Paul Schroeder, Jonathan Steinberg, Norman Stone, Solomon Wank and Gerhard Weinberg.

Professor Gerald Stourzh has given me much encouragement and read one draft of the manuscript. The late Professor Hugo Hantsch

arranged for me to interview Count Berchtold's son, while Dr Curt
de Reininghaus shared with me his impressions of his step-father,
General Franz Conrad von Hötzendorf. Duke Franz von Hohenberg
and Albrecht Hohenberg graciously allowed me access to the papers
of Archduke Franz Ferdinand, while the late Friedrich Würthle
shared with me his extensive knowledge of the assassination plot.

The archival officials in Vienna have been exceptionally patient,
helpful and always understanding. I am especially indebted
to Director General Dr Kurt Peball who, when serving at the
Kriegsarchiv, encouraged me in a variety of ways; so also did
Oberrat Dr Peter Broucek. Dr Richard Blaas, Dr Rudolf Neck, Dr
Anna Coreth, Dr Maria Woinovich, Dr Rainer Egger, Dr Horst
Brettner-Messler and Dr Robert Stropp have assisted me again and
again.

Professor Dragan Živojinović of the University of Belgrade translated some of the Serbian materials for me; Professor Milorad
Ekmečić of the University of Sarajevo has encouraged the study and
assisted with the Bosnian archives in Sarajevo, as has Director Dr
Božidar Madžar of the Bosnian archives.

The librarians at Widener Library, Harvard University; at
Churchill College, Cambridge; at the Cambridge University
Library; at the National Humanities Center; and at The University
of the South have all been most helpful. I owe a special debt to Dr
James Govan and the staff of the Library of the University of North
Carolina at Chapel Hill for their unfailing assistance over many
years.

Financial support for leaves and research assistance has come
from Harvard University, the University of North Carolina at
Chapel Hill, the National Humanities Center, the National Endow-
ment for the Humanities, the American Council of Learned Societies
and Churchill College, Cambridge. This financial backing has made
possible much of the research.

I have benefitted from the assistance of a number of graduate
students and friends, far more than they realize: Thomas Conner,
Peter Coogan, Ronald Maner, Daniel Hughes, Jonathan Randel,
Scott Lackey and especially Russel Van Wyk, who has done yeoman
service.

My administrative colleagues, whether I served as Senior Tutor
at Harvard, or as Dean or Provost at Chapel Hill, or as President
and Vice-Chancellor at Sewanee have all understood my desire to

complete this work; they have done much to assist it. I am especially grateful to Mrs Cathy Young and Mrs Pat Witcher of The University of the South for putting the manuscript into final form. I am most appreciative of the care that Macmillan, through Vanessa Graham and Anne Neville, has taken in the production of this book. Their encouragement has made it easier to mesh academic with administrative responsibilities.

At every stage my wife Joan has sustained the Habsburg enterprise, including a trip to Vienna with three children under the age of five; George, Treeby and Thad have grown up thinking that Franz Joseph was a friendly uncle and daddy's constant companion. I dedicate this book to them, with thanksgiving and joy.

The maps on the Habsburg monarchy (Maps 1 and 2) are reproduced with the gracious permission of Professor and Mrs A. J. P. Taylor from his study, *The Habsburg Monarchy, 1809–1918* (London, 1950). The map of the Balkans from 1912–13 (Map 3) is reprinted from *Europe's Crucial Years: The Diplomatic Background of World War I*, by Dwight E. Lee, by permission of the University Press of New England, copyright 1974 by the Trustees of Dartmouth College. The map on the location of the Habsburg armies in the July crisis (Map 4) is from *West Point Military History Series: Atlas for the Great War* (Wayne, New Jersey, 1986) by permission of the Department of History, The United States Military Academy and General Thomas E. Griess.

The place names on the maps are left as drawn. In the text, I have followed the convention of using the geographical names familiar to the decision-makers in July 1914, followed by the more recent versions of the place names.

Sewanee: The University of the South
July 1989

Maps

Chronology

1848		Franz Joseph becomes emperor/king of Austria and Hungary
1866		Prussia defeats Austria at Sadowa (Königgrätz)
1867		*Ausgleich* settlement between Franz Joseph and the Magyar leadership
1878		Congress of Berlin after the Russo-Turkish war Austria–Hungary assumes administrative supervision of Bosnia–Herzegovina
1879		Andrássy and Bismarck sign the Dual Alliance
1882		Italy joins the Dual Alliance which becomes the Triple Alliance
1883		King Carol of Rumania becomes silent partner of the Triple Alliance
1894		Franco-Russian alliance created
1898		Archduke Franz Ferdinand recognized as heir-apparent
1903		Obrenović dynasty overthrown in Serbia; replaced by King Peter of the Karadjordjević dynasty
1904		Signature of the Anglo-French entente
1904–05		Russo-Japanese War and Russian defeat
1905		First Moroccan Crisis
1906		Aehrenthal appointed foreign minister; Conrad von Hötzendorf appointed chief of the General Staff; Schönaich appointed war minister
1907		Anglo-Russian entente signed; creation of Triple Entente
1908–09		Habsburg monarchy annexes Bosnia–Herzegovina; ensuing crisis with Serbia and Russia
1911	July–October	Second Moroccan Crisis
	September	Start of the Italo-Turkish war in Tripoli (Libya)
	November–December	Auffenberg becomes war minister; Schemua becomes chief of the General Staff
1912	February	Berchtold succeeds Aehrenthal; Biliński becomes common foreign minister
	March–May	Signature of Balkan League between Serbia, Greece, Bulgaria; Montenegro joins later
	September	Delegations meet in Vienna
	October	First Balkan War begins

		Russia keeps third-year troops on duty
		Austria–Hungary mobilizes some troops
	November	Delegations meet in Budapest
		Intensification of crisis with Russia and Serbia
	December	Conrad returns as chief of the General Staff; Krobatin replaces Auffenberg as war minister
		First war–peace crisis with Serbia; Franz Joseph and Berchtold refuse to opt for war with Serbia
		Conferences of ambassadors and ministers in London to end Balkan fighting
		Triple Alliance renewed
1913	February	Germany cautions Austria–Hungary on crisis with Russia and Serbia
	March	Austria–Hungary and Russia reduce troop mobilizations
	April	Scutari falls to Montenegro; ensuing crisis
	May	Second war–peace crisis: Austria–Hungary demands and gets Montenegro to abandon Scutari
		Treaty of London ends First Balkan War
	May–June	Colonel Redl spy scandal and crisis
	June	Tisza becomes Hungarian prime minister
		Bulgaria attacks Serbia; Greece, Turkey, Rumania and Montenegro attack Bulgaria; Second Balkan War starts
	July	Bulgaria asks for peace
	August	Treaty of Bucharest signed
	October	Third war–peace crisis: Austria–Hungary demands and gets Serbian evacuation of Albanian towns
	November	Delegations meet in Vienna
		Ottokar Czernin sent to Rumania as minister
	November–December	Liman von Sandars crisis between Russia and Germany
1914	February	Russia revamps mobilization timetables
	April	Franz Joseph illness
	May	Delegations meet in Budapest
	Late May	Princip, Grabež, Čabrinovič return to Bosnia for the assassination effort
	June	Visit of Czar Nicholas to Rumania
		Visit of Kaiser William with Franz Ferdinand at Konopischt
		Visit of Berchtold with Franz Ferdinand at Konopischt
		Matscheko prepares memorandum on Austro-Hungarian foreign policy
	28 June	Assassination of Archduke Franz Ferdinand and wife Sophie at Sarajevo

5 July	Hoyos mission to Berlin
	Austria–Hungary receives 'blank cheque' for action against Serbia
7 July	Habsburg Common Council favours war with Serbia; Hungarian Prime Minister Tisza opposes
14 July	Tisza agrees to war on stipulation of no additional territory to Habsburg monarchy
19 July	Habsburg Common Council approves terms of ultimatum
20–23 July	French President Poincaré and Premier Viviani in St Petersburg
	French reaffirm their diplomatic support of Russia
23 July	Austria–Hungary gives 48-hour ultimatum to Serbia
25 July	Serbian reply does not accept demand for an outside (Habsburg) investigation of conspiracy
	Serbia orders mobilization; Russia takes some preliminary mobilization steps
26 July	Grey proposes mediation; it is rejected by Vienna
28 July	Austria–Hungary partially mobilizes and declares war on Serbia
	Halt in Belgrade plan suggested; Vienna later rejects it
29 July	Scattered Austro-Hungarian shelling of Serbian territory
	Germany attempts to win British neutrality
30 July	Russia orders general mobilization
	Britain rebuffs German overtures on neutrality
31 July	Germany declares state of threatening danger of war; demands that Russia cease its mobilization
	Austria–Hungary orders general mobilization
1 August	France refuses to bow to German demands of neutrality in event of Russo-German war
	France and Germany mobilize
	Germany declares war on Russia
2 August	British cabinet gives limited assurance to France on defence of its northern coasts
	Germany invades Luxembourg
3 August	Germany invades Belgium
	Germany declares war on France
4 August	Britain declares war on Germany
6 August	Austria–Hungary declares war on Russia

Glossary of Names

Aehrenthal, Alois, Baron (later Count) Lexa: Austro-Hungarian foreign minister, 1906–12

Andrássy, Count Julius: Hungarian prime minister, 1867–71; Austro-Hungarian foreign minister, 1871–9

Auffenberg von Komarów, General Moritz: Austro-Hungarian war minister, 1911–12; inspector general of the army, 1912–14

Apis: nickname of Dragutin Dimitrijević: head of Serbian military intelligence; central figure in the Black Hand

Baernreither, Joseph Maria: Austrian writer and political figure

Bardolff, Colonel Karl (later General): head of Franz Ferdinand's military chancellory, 1911–14

Beck-Rzikowski, General Friedrich: Chief of the Austro-Hungarian General Staff, 1881–1906

Berchtold, Count Leopold: Austro-Hungarian foreign minister, 1912–15

Bethmann Hollweg, Theobald von: German chancellor, 1909–17

Biliński, Leon von: Austro-Hungarian common finance minister, 1912–17

Bolfras, General Arthur: head of Franz Joseph's military chancellory, 1889–1916

Brosch von Aarenau, Colonel Alexander: head of Franz Ferdinand's military chancellory, 1906–11

Burián István: Austro-Hungarian common finance minister, 1903–12; Hungarian emissary to the Austro-Hungarian government, 1913–15

Carol I: Prince, later King of Rumania, 1866–1914

Cartwright, Sir Fairfax: British ambassador to Vienna, 1908–13

Conrad von Hötzendorf, General Franz: Chief of the Austro-Hungarian General Staff, 1906–11, 1912–17

Czernin, Count Ottokar: friend of Franz Ferdinand; Habsburg minister to Bucharest, 1913–16

Ferdinand: Prince, later King of Bulgaria, 1887–1918

Forgách, Count Johann: Section chief of the Austro-Hungarian foreign ministry, 1913–17

Franz Ferdinand: Archduke, heir to Habsburg monarchy, 1898–1914

Franz Joseph: Emperor/King, ruler of Austria and Hungary and Austria–Hungary, 1848–1916

Friedjung, Heinrich: professor and publicist in Vienna

Grey, Sir Edward: British foreign secretary, 1905–16

Hartwig, Nicholas: Russian minister to Serbia, 1909–14

Haus, Vice-Admiral Anton: Chief of the Austro-Hungarian navy, 1913–17

Hoyos, Count Alexander: Chief of the Cabinet of the Austro-Hungarian foreign ministry, 1912–15

Izvolsky, Alexander: Russian foreign minister, 1906–1910, Russian ambassador to France, 1910–17

Jagow, Gottlieb von: German secretary of state for foreign affairs, 1913–16

Kállay, Benjamin: Austro-Hungarian common finance minister, 1882–1903

Kiderlen-Wächter, Alfred von: German secretary of state for foreign affairs, 1910–12

Kokovtsov, Vladimir: Russian prime minister, 1911–14

Krobatin, General Alexander: Austro-Hungarian war minister, 1912–17

Matscheko, Franz von: Section chief in the Austro-Hungarian foreign ministry, 1913–15

Mérey von Kapos-Mére, Kajetan: Austro-Hungarian ambassador to Italy, 1910–15

Moltke, Count Helmut von (the younger): Chief of the German (Prussian) General Staff, 1906–14

Montecuccoli, Admiral Rudolf: chief of the Austro-Hungarian navy, 1904–13

Nikita: Prince, later King of Montenegro, 1860–1918

Nicholas II: Czar of Russia, 1894–1917

Pašić, Nikola: Serbian prime minister, 1906–08, 1909–11; Serbian prime minister and foreign minister, 1912–18

Peter Karadjordjević: King of Serbia, 1903–18

Poincaré, Raymond: French premier, 1912–13; President of France, 1913–20

Potiorek, General Oskar: Governor-General of Bosnia–Herzegovina, 1911–14

Princip, Gavrilo: Bosnian student who shot Franz Ferdinand and his wife Sophie at Sarajevo

Redl, Colonel Alfred: senior Austro-Hungarian intelligence officer and spy for Russia

Redlich, Josef: Austrian professor, jurist, member of the Austrian House of Deputies, 1907–18

Reininghaus, Gina von: wife of Hermann von Reininghaus; second wife of General Conrad von Hötzendorf

San Giuliano, Antonio di: Italian foreign minister, 1910–14

Sazonov, Serge: Russian foreign minister, 1910–16

Schemua, General Blasius: Chief of the Austro-Hungarian General Staff, 1911–12

Schönaich, General Franz von: Austro-Hungarian war minister, 1906–11

Sophie Chotek: Countess, later Princess, later Duchess of Hohenberg, wife of Archduke Franz Ferdinand

Stürgkh, Karl: Austrian prime minister, 1911–16

Szápáry, Count Friedrich: Section chief in the Austro-Hungarian foreign ministry, 1912–13; ambassador to Russia, 1913–14

Szögyény-Marich, Count Ladislaus: Austro-Hungarian ambassador to Germany, 1892–1914

Tisza, István: President, Lower House of the Hungarian parliament, 1912–13; prime minister, 1913–17

Tschirschky, Heinrich von: German ambassador to Vienna, 1907–16

William II: German emperor and king of Prussia, 1888–1918

Introduction

On 28 July 1914 Austria–Hungary declared war on the neighbour-ing kingdom of Serbia. The declaration came precisely one month after the assassination of Archduke Franz Ferdinand, heir to the Austrian throne, and his wife Sophie, in Sarajevo by a Bosnian student educated in Serbia. Thus began the Third Balkan War. Almost immediately, the conflict expanded into the First World War with Russia's decision to mobilize and Germany's response to that step. The war began in eastern Europe; the Habsburg government in Vienna took the pivotal decisions that started the fighting.

Yet Austria–Hungary's role in the outbreak of the war has in recent decades either been ignored or so generally assumed as to be neglected. Rather, the emphasis has been on Germany's actions — for reasons of domestic politics and the legacies of *Weltpolitik* — in plunging Europe into a world war. Seldom have the Triple Entente powers been credited with steps that escalated the crisis. Now, recent works of fundamental importance, based on the archives of the Habsburg monarchy, permit a reassessment of Vienna's foreign policies in the last years before July 1914. In this analysis it is also possible to insert a comparative dimension, with new attention to the incendiary actions of the Serbian and Russian governments, without however diminishing the importance of Berlin's irresponsi-ble behaviour. Because of the linkages in European decision-making, this study on Austria–Hungary is perhaps fittingly focused on the one government that clearly initiated the violence in July 1914.

What led the decision-makers in Vienna to conclude that war would resolve the problem posed by greater Serbian nationalism? How did the tensions of the Balkan Wars of 1912–13 contribute to a set of perceptions that rendered a military solution preferable to further diplomatic efforts? What process led the Emperor/King Franz Joseph, on the Habsburg throne for sixty-six years, to risk both his dynasty and the multinational government which he

1

headed? In seeking to answer these questions, this monograph explores the degree to which the 'unspoken assumptions' of a political and military leadership propel states to war. Confronted with crisis after crisis, the Austro-Hungarian leaders looked to Berlin for assistance, while desperately trying to control their own destinies. The senior leadership of the monarchy often differed over alternatives. Personality clashes and power struggles over the monarchy's future frequently dominated the political landscape. Sometimes the pressure of external factors shaped the content of domestic politics. In the strange, contorted world of Austria–Hungary, in which a single leader linked two separate governments, decisions often came slowly and painfully. But in July 1914 the civilians, the generals and the public favoured a policy of force over diplomacy. How this consensus emerged in a political arena in which consensus seldom, if ever, occurred, is a major theme of this study.

Few governments were as complicated as the Austro-Hungarian monarchy. Its complex political structure and organizational arrangements must necessarily receive extensive analysis. For the administrative structure helps to explain both the process of policy formation and much of its content. The very structure of the monarchy often dictated the range of options available to the policy-makers. Organizational and bureaucratic politics were interwoven into every aspect of the monarchy's life. To understand that structure and how it functioned constitutes the focus of the first six chapters in this book. The remaining four chapters then analyse the monarchy's decision-making as it confronted the challenges of the Balkan Wars and then the terrorist acts in Sarajevo.

Structure, personalities, foreign and domestic factors and periodic bouts of despair converged in the making of Habsburg foreign and strategic policy. As this study unfolds, the reader will traverse a sometimes unfamiliar road through an empire now long vanished, as it struggled with problems of nationalism and Russian assertiveness. These problems — that worried policy-makers in Vienna and Budapest from 1908 to 1914 — still trouble the leaders in Bonn, London and Washington. The legacy of the Habsburgs remains present in the lands of the former empire, seven decades after its demise. The function played by the Habsburg monarchy in helping Europe to contain Russia and to confront the Balkans remains. The Austro-Hungarian monarchy remains a conspicuous symbol of the past's continuing importance. In 'The Making of the Twentieth Century' the Austro-Hungarian government looms large: as legacy, as memory, as the initiator of the war of 1914. But why did Franz Joseph and his advisers opt for war in July 1914? This monograph will provide some answers to that central question in the origins of the First World War.

1 Austria–Hungary and the International System: Great Power or Doomed Anachronism?

The Austro-Hungarian monarchy collapsed in November 1918, a victim of German defeat and internal disintegration. That collapse, after four years of relentless war and untold privation, brought to an end a multinational government whose existence into the twentieth century amazed external observers and satisfied many of the more than fifty million people who lived within its boundaries. No single nationality dominated the government, though two controlled most of the political power. No single political structure unified the state, save a dynasty born of medieval ambitions and successful marriages. No consistent set of political or religious ideals united the people, only the omnipresent portrait of an emperor who had lived — so it seemed — forever. No single conception of *raison d'état* for the existence of the state animated either the governing elites or the populace. Yet many agreed with the Czech historian Francis Palacký's pronouncement in 1848 that 'truly, if the Austrian empire had not existed for ages, it would be necessary, in the interest of Europe, in the interest of mankind itself, to create it with all speed.' Coming close to a fundamental reason that kept the monarchy in place and that led to its decision to go to war in 1914, Palacký had asked his hearers to 'imagine if you will Austria divided into a number of republics and miniature republics. What a welcome basis for a Russian universal monarchy.'[1]

Despite these paradoxes and contradictions, so unfamiliar to the late-twentieth century observer, the Austro-Hungarian monarchy in 1910 constituted Europe's third largest state. With a population of more than fifty million people, divided among eleven nationalities, the borders ran from Switzerland in the west deep into present-day Russia in the east, from Cracow in Poland to Budua (Budva) on the Adriatic in present-day Yugoslavia. (See Map 1.) Bustling with intellectual and artistic activity, the monarchy enjoyed a robust economy and a steadily improving standard of living. In the years after 1900 crisis after crisis tested its political institutions, yet state

4

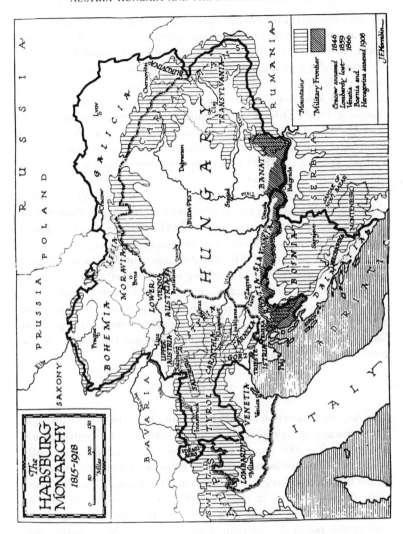

Map 1 The Habsburg Monarchy, 1815–1918

services continued to expand, the quality of education advanced and a measure of political pragmatism ultimately prevailed. In Count Alois Aehrenthal, the Habsburg foreign minister from 1906 to 1912, the monarchy had the most respected European foreign minister of the day. In 1908–09 Vienna had displayed assertive international activity in annexing Bosnia–Herzegovina and in resisting demands from the Triple Entente and Serbia for compromise or concession. The Habsburg monarchy had problems to be sure in 1912, but its future did not appear more uncertain than at earlier times in its history. Indeed, the Dual Monarchy appeared to have a vitality that would ensure its survival.

Two years later Vienna plunged Europe into war. What prompted those decisions by a group of senior leaders, many of whom had served for years in the same position? What led the Emperor Franz Joseph and his advisers to risk war to resolve the monarchy's foreign and domestic problems? Why did the leaders link those solutions to the fickle fortunes of war? In seeking to understand those decisions, an assessment of the monarchy's place in the European system and of its own internal viability is necessary. A survey of the unspoken assumptions that many of the Habsburg elite brought to the political life of the monarchy in 1912 and thereafter will help explicate the later decisions for war instead of peace.[2]

I

The Austro-Hungarian monarchy differed from the other European governments in complexity, political orientation, multinational character. Yet the monarchy continued to function, apparently conferred economic benefits upon its citizens, and offered protection in the treacherous jungle of international relations. But what did the individuals who lived in the monarchy and worked for its agencies think of the future? What were the agendas of the senior ministers and of the political leadership that operated in both Austria and Hungary? How did the political and military elite, that senior group of leaders who helped — along with the press and publicists — to make the state function, view the future? Answers to these questions and to these unspoken assumptions varied according to person, time and place. Nonetheless, a set of themes appeared frequently enough to create a kind of consensus that many of the elite would accept as worthy of their attention and their ambitions.[3]

Foremost among these was the future of the monarchy after Franz Joseph. In 1908 Franz Joseph had celebrated sixty years of rule; by 1912 at the age of eighty-two his health and his stamina were matters of public worry and private speculation. The emperor did not ignore the future. His nephew, Archduke Franz Ferdinand, had been exposed to political responsibilities since 1900, so that he had a broad knowledge of issues and political problems. Increasingly, he interfered in the military and diplomatic life of the state, not always happily, but with enough impact to remind contemporaries that one day he would be the ruler. What kind of a ruler? With what agenda? The answers were unclear, and that ambiguity alarmed and worried many.[4]

The Hungarian (Magyar) political leadership in particular looked more apprehensively at Franz Ferdinand and the future than did the other national groups. Budapest feared the heir-apparent would opt for a confrontation to diminish its position. Other ruling groups viewed Franz Ferdinand as a bellicose, mercurial individual, far too infatuated with the German kaiser. The danger, so contemporaries feared, stemmed from Franz Ferdinand's conception of the future: did he envisage a return to the feudal past which he seemed to embody? Or would he embrace the changing political environment? The question of what followed Franz Joseph loomed larger and larger.[5]

Closely linked to uncertainties about the monarchy under Franz Ferdinand was the future of the Austro-Hungarian compromise of 1867: the *Ausgleich*. Each decade its economic terms had to be renegotiated; each decade put the very constitutional fabric of the monarchy into question. In part by exhaustion, in part by threat of introducing universal suffrage into Hungary, Franz Joseph and his senior ministers had got the *Ausgleich* reaffirmed by Budapest in 1907. This settlement suggested almost a decade of relative constitutional stability. At the same time, given the confusing and often chaotic nature of Austrian political life, the monarchy had no effective Austrian ally as a counterweight in its negotiations with Budapest. This weakness worried the Austrian political elite, who correctly realized their relative disadvantage in confronting a generally unified Magyar group.[6]

A third issue, intimately linked to the first two, was the nationality question. The Hungarian elite preferred to continue their traditional political domination. If possible, the Magyars wanted to expand their control more effectively over Croatia and to resist concessions to other ethnic groups. With a parliamentary apparatus that allowed for differences of opinion and that remained effective within very narrow limits, the Magyars were the monarchy's 'hard-liners' on matters of nationality. Nationalism for Magyars was good, but not so for any others who lived within Magyar political jurisdiction. Moreover, Magyar ambitions from time to time included the incorporation of Bosnia–Herzegovina–Dalmatia into a greater Hungary. This prospect naturally alarmed the South Slavs and troubled Vienna.

The German–Austrian elite, challenged continually by the Czechs, found in political groups such as Karl Lueger's Christian Social party a vehicle for their interests. As the parliamentary stalemate persisted, with the Czech deputies generally united and the German ones ineffectual, parliamentary life in Vienna offered scant comfort about the monarchy's future. Intractable and dogmatic, the Czechs pressed every advantage; the Germans resisted skillfully, seeking to constrain the Czech influence in the bureaucratic apparatus in Bohemia. Frustration with this state of affairs made the use of emergency decrees tolerable. These conditions also increased cynicism about the future. Thanks in part to the loyalty of the Polish Club, successive Austrian prime ministers were able to muster the semblance of parliamentary majorities. Yet even here the Polish Club found its political position eroding as the Russians began to appeal effectively to the Ruthenians. Nor was the Club helped by growing demands for an independent Poland. A parliamentary life debilitated by nationality strife fascinated the Austrian political leaders, while offering the broader public comedy and topics for political conversation. As Frederic Morton has recently written of the Austrian parliament: 'It was less a legislature than a cacophony. But since it was a Viennese cacophony it shrilled and jangled with a certain flair.'[7]

In the south the most urgent problem was Serbia. In early 1912 Vienna could still hope that accommodation with Belgrade might be possible. Russian support for Serbia had clearly intensified, but appeared manageable. On the other hand, informed Habsburg observers worried about the future Serbia acting as a kind of Italian Piedmont, as an attractive alternative to the South Slavs living within the monarchy. In particular, such a Serbian approach might appeal to the Serbs, Bosnians and even Muslims living in Bosnia and Herzegovina. No one wanted those two provinces, however troublesome, to be snatched away by a new Piedmont or a revived Ottoman empire. Apprehension, verging on concern, characterized the informed public's views about the south.[8]

If the elite engaged in self-examination, the results were equally unsettling. A mixture of aristocratic privilege, careers helped by talent, and political leaders whose fortunes rose and fell as a function of opportunism, the ruling groups conceded that some effective centralized government was crucial for the monarchy's survival. Even the Magyars would recognize this, while they sought to expand their control of the central political organs. Some observers later on insisted that the bureaucratic elite increasingly lacked moral authority, as positions were less and less tied to performance or genuine distinction. More numerous because of recent expansions, the Habsburg bureaucrats progressively undermined the public's confidence in their efficiency and effectiveness. The ruling group, moreover, like the monarchy itself had to adjust to social changes that were rapidly challenging aristocratic and feudal values. These same changes were also diminishing the appeal of traditional liberalism. Buffeted by the growth of mass parties and unsure of its own agenda, liberalism verged easily into despair. The growth of the Christian Social party and talk of more draconian approaches to government suggest an elite losing confidence in itself, unable to adjust readily and uncertain about which direction offered the most protection and opportunities.[9]

Amid the changes, some verities remained. Few challenged the idea that the elite were destined to run the monarchy or to direct its foreign policy. Nor did many critics challenge the axiom that the German alliance constituted the bedrock of the monarchy's international position. The antics of German Kaiser William II might occasionally prompt sniggers, especially his tendency towards verbal overkill. Still, Berlin's friendship offered protection against a Russia which appeared increasingly assertive. Russian activity in the Balkans assured a repetition of the earlier struggles between St Petersburg and Vienna for influence and prestige. Still, the Habsburg elite could in 1912 remember the Russian defeat of 1905 and St Petersburg's acceptance of the annexation of Bosnia–Herzegovina in 1908. The ruling circles would, moreover, see in the Anglo-Russian accord of 1907 little more than an apparent colonial settlement. Mindful of the recent turmoil in French domestic politics, thoughtful Habsburg observers could still view the Franco-Russian alliance of 1894 as only a weak and belated retort to the Triple Alliance. The Russian problem worried the Habsburgs. But, like the question of Italian loyalty, the issue seemed so familiar that the leadership in early 1912 would acknowledge the problems while not becoming alarmed.[10]

The Habsburg decision-makers always viewed military power as the ultimate defence of the monarchy's interest. Consequently, the elite accorded senior generals and admirals deference and a measure of gratitude. Deference did not, however, extend to servitude, as often happened in Germany. Rather, the civilian leadership showed little disposition to be intimidated by the military or coerced by its demands for more men or more funds. Instead, fiscal prudence, amounting to penuriousness, remained a fact of life for the military. The political leaders appreciated their defenders but neither paid them well nor provided them with extensive budgetary resources.[11]

Another aspect of the elite's political world requires attention. Nearly every important political and diplomatic issue in the monarchy had dual faces: external (*Aussen*) and internal (*Innen*). In an unusual fashion, much of the content, style and operational approaches to policy issues were the product of the constant tension and interplay between domestic and foreign policy considerations. Four examples illustrate this interplay. Should Bucharest advocate concessions for fellow Rumanian nationals living in Hungary, a domestic problem for Budapest became a foreign policy one, a situation that could damage the secret Austro-Rumanian alliance. Russian espousal of Pan-Slavic activities *ipso facto* meant that Russia, a foreign power, was in effect meddling in Habsburg politics. And, vice versa, Habsburg attempts to repress Pan-Slav activity within the monarchy might impact upon Austro-Russian relations. Finally, after the annexation of Bosnia–Herzegovina in 1908, almost every facet of their administration impacted upon relations between Vienna and Belgrade. Thus the dichotomy of foreign versus domestic, of the primacy of foreign policy or the primacy of internal policy, simply does not encompass many of the basic questions that confronted Habsburg decision-makers. The Habsburg elite, accustomed to the interplay of domestic and foreign affairs, accepted this dialectic as a fact of life and proceeded. The problem for Vienna's leadership was often in convincing their allies and especially the Germans that a foreign policy issue could erode the domestic legitimacy of the government. So long as the tensions between the two dimensions did not see either domestic or foreign considerations entirely triumph, the greater the chances that peace would be preserved. The danger lay in seeking to resolve a domestic issue by a foreign policy adventure, since almost no one ever considered alleviating a foreign policy problem by domestic reform.[12]

II

The Austro-Hungarian monarchy differed fundamentally from the other governments of pre-1914 Europe. The genuinely joint government of Austria and Hungary was linked by a common monarchy and diplomatic and military forces. The multinational state functioned as the third largest government on the continent. A member of the Triple Alliance, a state whose recent economic development met or exceeded that of many other governments, a state that bridged the gap between the east and west, and an empire of eleven nationalities, Austria–Hungary appeared destined to survive despite its contradictions. Although torn by nationality issues, the monarchy enjoyed popular legitimacy. Anachronistic in its structure and surprisingly feudal and dynastic, Austria–Hungary had endured into the twentieth century as a high-ranking member of the international system. Because Austria–Hungary, like the Russian, German, and Turkish empires, disappeared after the First World War its dissolution is often described as inevitable. But evidence about the operations, the policies, the personalities of the Habsburg monarchy before the First World War allow another conclusion. Some external governments certainly wished to overturn the monarchy or partition its holdings. Others wanted a slice of territory here or there, yet many of these same governments feared the prospect of such collapse, worked carefully to avoid it and seldom left the Habsburg monarchy totally isolated.

In 1912 Austria–Hungary enjoyed great power status and represented a historic tradition of survival and dependability in Europe. Acting as a buffer state, the monarchy represented for the European governments a cushion against the Russians, the Balkan states and the Ottoman empire. This historic role had lost no appeal, indeed still contained validity and meaning. Only when the powers began to doubt this function and when the Habsburg leadership doubted its ability to execute the mission would the monarchy's future become less certain. The convergence of these facets would prove

catastrophic for the monarchy. A product of foreign policy requirements and sustained by them, yet always weakened by its internal
contradictions, the Habsburg monarchy remained a great power
through July 1914. Paradoxical, contradictory, illusory, and different, the Habsburg monarchy would finally decide that only war
could bring the necessary foreign policy success to ensure its
existence as a state. In 1914 external factors brought the Habsburg
decision-makers to war; internal factors would guarantee that the
war would destroy rather than rescue the monarchy.

2 The Domestic Context of Habsburg Foreign Policy

In 1866 the Prussians defeated Franz Joseph's forces at Sadowa. The competition between Berlin and Vienna for the domination of the German states had ended with Bismarck's victory. But there were other ramifications for Franz Joseph. Not only did he lose any chance of leadership in Germany, he also lost his effort of two decades to create an unitary Danubian state. In the wake of defeat, Franz Joseph could no longer resist Hungarian demands for political authority. The Habsburg monarch, negotiating for the dynasty with its hereditary Austrian holdings and in his capacity as king of Hungary, had no choice but to settle with the Magyar leadership. The resulting constitutional arrangements of the 1867 Compromise (*Ausgleich*) lasted until the monarchy's collapse in November 1918.[1]

I

The *Ausgleich* provided an organizational and political structure for the monarchy's domestic politics. But the arrangement inherently reflected the problems of nationality that so complicated domestic rule and foreign policy for Habsburg policy-makers. The *Ausgleich* thus reaffirmed the monarchy's overall responsibility for foreign and strategic policies, while sanctioning a special common status for these functions within the new Austro-Hungarian monarchy.[2]

The Compromise created overlapping political authorities; it thus had unifying as well as divisive elements. After 1867 Austria–Hungary consisted of two separate states, each with its own parliament and prime minister, and connected in a real union by a single monarch who was both Emperor of Austria and King of Hungary. A common army and navy, foreign policy and a customs unit with their bureaucracies held the two halves together. To complicate the military picture, both Austria and Hungary had military forces with separate national defence ministries. The

13

Austrian force was the *Landwehr*, the Hungarian the *Honvéd*. The *Ausgleich* also provided for two Delegations (one for Hungary and one for Austria) of sixty deputies each to vote on the common expenditures and hear addresses by the common ministers. But the Delegations never met jointly, even though they convened at the same time and in the same city. None of the ministers — whether common, Austrian or Hungarian — were responsible to any parliamentary body. Rather they were responsible only to the emperor/king. The Common Ministerial Council, consisting of the three common ministers and the two prime ministers, met frequently to coordinate affairs — primarily foreign policy and military and naval budgets. Normally the foreign minister conducted the meetings of the group. If the monarch attended, it became the Crown Council. After the Turks relinquished their administration of Bosnia and Herzegovina to Austria–Hungary in 1878, the Council also administered those imperial provinces. Vienna would formally annex them in 1908. Routine administrative responsibility for the two provinces rested with the common finance minister.[3]

These constitutional arrangements had a built-in element of instability, one that strongly influenced domestic politics on both sides of the River Leitha separating Austria and Hungary. Every ten years the Hungarians could renegotiate the terms of tax payments for common (chiefly military) purposes and the other commercial terms of the Compromise. Every decade Budapest pressed for extended privileges and lower taxes. After 1907 the Austrians paid 63.6 percent and the Magyars 36.4 percent of the common expenses. The *Ausgleich*, moreover, bound the Austrians to its terms, since the Magyars essentially could veto any proposed change.

By 1912 the *Ausgleich* institutions and the assumptions of forty-five years before were tattered, open to question and difficult to sustain with confidence. Among the critics the Archduke Franz Ferdinand, the heir-apparent, complained to intimates that the Compromise had unnecessarily enhanced Magyar power. Once he came to power, he boasted that things would change. Concurrently Habsburg loyalists, including many in the German–Austrian bureaucracy, blamed Budapest for obstructing the government in general and for failing to approve larger military expenditures in particular. Many Hungarians were, for their part, indifferent to the 1867 arrangements. Instead they preferred the road to independence that had been attempted in 1848. Although the National Party of Work, headed by István Tisza, returned to power in 1910 with a platform that adhered to the Compromise, it was understood that Magyar interests would be vigorously defended against any centralizing tendencies. For the Slavs, whether Czechs or South Slavs, a permanent dualistic structure did not offer much hope for the future. And indeed, some German–Austrians even talked of closer relations with the German *Reich* to the north. Of the various nationalities, only the Poles and especially the Polish landlords warmly embraced the *Ausgleich*. Of course, the Emperor Franz Joseph, now almost eighty-two years old, saw no reason to change. Indeed he would not allow his limited imagination even to contemplate an alteration of the settlement.[4]

In the spring of 1912, moreover, the governmental institutions of the monarchy were in fact functioning, if not in perfect fashion, nonetheless functioning more effectively than critics then or later have usually conceded. The story of the coming of the war of 1914 is in part a story of how this government came to convince itself that only force would resolve the problem of the South Slavs. Part of the reason for that belief would be a mounting sense that these institutions could not function in the future if the threat posed by Serbia to the foreign and domestic policies of the monarchy was allowed to go unchecked. The transformation of these beliefs and the problem of the operational effectiveness of the government thus form a major part of the coming of the war for Austria–Hungary.

Within the constitutional parameters of the Compromise, however fragile and imperfect, the responsibility for peace or war remained firmly monarchical. Franz Joseph retained the power to make the final decision for peace or war. His common ministers for foreign affairs, finance and war could, along with the two prime ministers, advise him on what to do. But the decision was his. On the other hand, he could not ignore the desires of the separate Austrian and Hungarian governments. Neither government could veto a declaration of war, but their assent was expected. Furthermore, the financial and manpower resources required for military forces depended upon the political support of the two cabinets.

Since 1907 Austria had had a House of Deputies, elected by universal male suffrage. Franz Joseph had accepted this measure of democracy to preserve his own position and to mute the nationality issues. But by 1910 he had begun to despair of this concession. His appointment of Karl Stürgkh as prime minister reflected this pessimism. An opponent of universal suffrage, Stürgkh remained in office until his murder in December 1916. Faced with continuous strife between the German and Czech factions, he resorted to Paragraph 14 of the Basic Law of Representation. This Austrian constitutional device permitted virtual emergency rule by the prime minister until the Reichsrat (Deputies and Lords) could retroactively ratify his decisions. Rule by Paragraph 14 became the easy way out for Stürgkh. Finally, in March 1914 he adjourned the parliamentary bodies altogether. Nevertheless, if in session, members of both houses of the Reichsrat asked questions about military matters, especially in the tense moments of December 1912.[5]

As Austrian prime minister, Stürgkh had, of course, an important bureaucratic role in strategic issues. He regularly participated in the Common Ministerial Council.[6] The Austrian finance minister, Wenzel Zaleski, the person responsible for finding money for the payment of the common programmes, would only attend the Council when revenue issues were discussed. Moreover, Stürgkh appointed the Austrian defence minister who managed a large bureaucracy and a budget that consumed a quarter of all Austrian state expenditures. For Stürgkh and his ministerial associates, defence and foreign policy issues generally had one of three dimensions: the annual military budget, the number of recruits, and policies for Bosnia and Herzegovina.[7]

Across the River Leitha in Hungary, a livelier situation persisted, livelier in part because of different, more animated personalities. The dominant Magyar politician was István Tisza. Premier from 1903 to 1905, Tisza had returned in 1910 to head the Party of Work (the reconstituted National Liberal Party) and lead it to electoral victory. After his win, he first became speaker of the Hungarian House of Deputies, allowing two of his party colleagues, Karl Khuen-Héderváry and Ladislaus von Lukács, to struggle as prime ministers with the unruly parliamentary situation in Budapest. When in the summer of 1913 Tisza resumed the prime ministership, his return heralded far more active Hungarian participation in foreign and defence matters.[8]

For Hungary, as for Austria, budgets, recruits and Bosnia–Herzegovina were the principal issues. But within Hungary the approach was always Magyar, not imperial. Almost every issue about common expenditures became one of bargaining for still further concessions to the Magyars. Contracts for ships or munitions often became points of extortion. Only in late 1912 would Budapest's resistance to larger military budgets change as Balkan developments prompted apprehension. Yet, even then, carefully defined limits existed, beyond which Budapest would not venture. The Hungarian finance minister, János Teleszky, like Zaleski, a frequent guest in many of the Common Ministerial Council discussions, had one familiar refrain — 'No' — to any request for new expenditures.[9]

Tisza added one twist to the pattern of Hungarian involvement. In 1913 he sent István Burián to Vienna to be his and the Hungarian government's representative to the imperial government. Burián knew Vienna well, having served as common finance minister from 1903 to 1912. He soon became a frequent participant in policy discussions at the Ballhausplatz and a reliable barometer of what Budapest would or would not do. Burián's presence complicated the decision-making process for Aehrenthal's successor, Foreign Minister Count Leopold Berchtold. But Burián also brought a moderating force that helped the Magyars take a somewhat wider view of the diplomatic and strategic issues confronting the Dual Monarchy after midsummer 1913.[10]

The Magyar challenges sometimes spilled over into the periodic meetings of the Delegations, a unique constitutional by-product of the *Ausgleich*.[11] Determined to resist the creation of any legislative body that could become a quasi-imperial parliament, the Magyar leadership helped to create two separate committees, called the Delegations, whose members were drawn from the respective parliamentary bodies of Austria and Hungary. Subcommittees of each Delegation dealt with specialized topics and prepared expert reports for each group. Each Delegation voted individually on the budget for common affairs, heard reports from the common ministers and peppered them with questions. Only within these forums were 'common' affairs regularly debated. Even here, the angle was depressingly of a nationality perspective. One such issue, as we shall see, involved Hungary's repression of Rumanians living in Transylvania and the foreign policy complications which this caused with Rumania. Other issues in the Delegations included, as one might expect, budget quotas, the size of the military and naval forces, and at the 1913 session, a general critique of Habsburg foreign policy.[12]

Because the Delegations had to approve the budgets for common expenditures, their annual sessions were the driving force for budget activity in both governments. The common ministries prepared budget requests. Negotiations between the two governments over the size and shape of the budget then took place in the Common Ministerial Council. Frequently this involved the intervention of the monarch, though he too was not always successful. In 1912 and 1913 the financial pressures of the Balkan Wars prompted intense negotiations, leading to larger defence expenditures and an increase in the size of the annual recruit contingent. In each instance the two governments negotiated the details before the Delegations met, then presented them with the proposed results. After suitable and heuristic verbal exercises, the respective delegate assemblies voted for their respective share of the 'common expenditures' and the Delegations adjourned until the next year.[13]

A comparative observation may be helpful. Despite their limited role, the Delegations were probably not much less effective than other parliamentary bodies of the time in forcing explicit, careful discussions of diplomatic and strategic policies. Whether in the House of Commons in London, the Chamber of Deputies in Paris or the Reichstag in Berlin, government ministers could evade, conceal and mislead with relative impunity. Only a major disaster would break the pattern of ministerial dogmatism and then only for brief moments. The Delegations matched their peer organizations.[14]

The *Ausgleich* had given constitutional stability. But the institutions of the Austro-Hungarian monarchical system, whether common or state, were complicated and complex. A common minister and a prime minister operated in several arenas simultaneously, often with concurrent negotiations underway among three sets of government officials. In this there was only one certainty: His Majesty, the Emperor/King Franz Joseph was in charge, as he had been, by 1912, for nearly sixty-four years. The monarch and the monarchy were the most crucial elements in the Compromise.

II

The Habsburg dynasty represented the monarchy's most unifying factor. Franz Joseph remained the physical tie uniting the disparate empire. In his person the monarchy had coherence, a *supra*-national dimension, a living tradition. Franz Joseph's longevity simply reinforced these impressions. Virtually every Austro-Hungarian citizen had seen him or had a relative who had. A kindly, grandfather figure whose benevolence protected the people, Franz Joseph symbolized continuity, dependability, stability. A survivor of his own family tragedies and dutiful to a fault, the emperor represented virtue that reinforced the people's loyalty to a larger, *supra*-national institution. Later political leaders, with more mass appeal techniques at their disposal, seldom came close to equalling Franz Joseph's skill at buttressing his image. For most of his subjects, Franz Joseph could legitimately assert the phrase attributed to Louis XIV: 'L'état, c'ést moi!'[15]

Franz Joseph, furthermore, embodied two of the most important common functions: defence and diplomacy. The *Ausgleich* explicitly entrusted them to the common monarchy and the common monarch. By recognizing these duties, the 1867 settlement acknowledged that the monarchy's chief function was — stated simply — to preserve itself. Dualism gave Austria and Hungary joint protection which neither state could achieve by itself. As the first soldier of the state, Franz Joseph, through the centralized military structure, declared war, made peace and appointed and dismissed military commanders. He controlled promotions, decorations and troop appointments. But he was dependent upon the two state governments for the size of the recruit contingent and for expenditures for the common army as well as the separate national defence forces.

The army remained Franz Joseph's first love. With every male liable to military service, the military forces became the great equalizing agent, the assimilating institution for education, state loyalty and military values. Led by men who rose to the top through ability, and unlike their Prussian counterparts for whom noble pedigree remained essential, the Habsburg military took eleven nationalities and tried to form cohesive military units. A few German words serving as the unifying language and the kaiser's portrait the unifying ideology, the military forces reached into the lives of every citizen. From Sigmund Freud to the son of the Bosnian peasant, citizens encountered the Habsburg military. These soldiers felt discipline, saw something of the monarchy and often left with a set of memories that enhanced the conception of the state. Like the dynasty, military service and the bureaucracy sent powerful, if often latent messages, to the populace about the monarchy and its place in the European system.[16]

In assessing the diplomatic and military situation, Franz Joseph had the Foreign Ministry and the War Ministry at his beck and call. (The composition, functions and attitudes of these subordinates will receive attention in the next chapter.) Willing to delegate consider-able authority to the responsible ministers, he in turn expected the ministers to keep him well informed. No major policy departure would take place without his knowledge and approval.

Two chancellory staffs, the military headed by Baron Arthur Bolfras and the civil by Baron Schiessl von Perstoff, bridged the gap between the court and the common ministries and between the court and the Austrian and Hungarian governments. These two organiza-tions sought to inform the monarch about political and diplomatic issues. These officials prepared much of his correspondence and alerted him to trouble spots. The chancellories, along with the household staff, provided the extended family for the lonely, aloof monarch whether he stayed at the Hofburg, at Schönbrunn on the edge of Vienna (increasingly his residence after 1912) or at Bad Ischl, his favourite hunting retreat near Salzburg. These officials worked for Franz Joseph, but few thought of themselves as the monarch's friends or doubted that he would dismiss them in a moment. Yet he liked familiar officials and he instituted few changes after 1912 among his close associates. No 'entourage', in the sense of the cliques that swirled around the German kaiser, William II, bothered Franz Joseph. By profession and by practice a monarch, Franz Joseph daily worked — from 5 a.m. onward — for twelve or more hours for the monarchy, his people, the dynasty. He gave unstintingly until December 1916 when he died in his eighty-sixth year.[17]

The question of the dynasty and thus of succession were im-portant domestic and international issues for Franz Joseph and for the monarchy. Having the characteristics of a survivor, he believed the house of Habsburg had a mission to fulfil. A series of family tragedies, including the violent deaths of his brother Maximilian, his son Rudolf, and his wife Elisabeth, left his hopes for the dynasty shaken but the duty intact. The conduct of that duty involved the question of succession and the role that his nephew, the Archduke Franz Ferdinand and heir-apparent, would play in the interval.

For the monarch and observers of the monarchy inside and outside the Habsburg realm, the prospect of Franz Ferdinand's succession fostered uncertainty and some trepidation. Each time the octogenarian's health waned, tremors about the monarchy's future began anew. Would the monarchy collapse without Franz Joseph there to hold it together? Would foreign powers seek to exploit the weakened Habsburg situation? Would Franz Ferdinand be prudent enough to keep the *Ausgleich* — at least initially — intact? Or, more pessimistically, could a dynastic state survive in an age of relentless nationalism within and without the monarchy? For the political, military and diplomatic elite of the monarchy and of Europe, the question, 'How is the emperor today?' was no rhetorical exercise.

No one, of course, pondered the questions more attentively than the *Thronfolger* himself, the Archduke Franz Ferdinand. A long and painful bout with tuberculosis delayed his designation as heir-apparent until 1898. Thereafter, Franz Ferdinand gradually expanded his involvement in the monarchy's activities. He participated in the annual army manoeuvres and read the military and naval correspondence. After his morganatic marriage to Countess Sophie Chotek, Franz Joseph allowed the couple to reside in the Belvedere Palace. Then in 1906 the emperor permitted the creation of an informal military chancellory for the archduke and gave it official status in 1908. This chancellory, Franz Ferdinand's own restless thoughts about the future of the monarchy and the emperor's tolerance of his nephew's intrusions into governmental matters gradually altered the decision-making process of the monarchy. Franz Ferdinand came to enjoy influence, even power, and to have a say if not a veto over the posts of war minister or chief of the General Staff. Moreover, on occasion he became involved in defence and foreign policy matters. By 1912, there was much truth in the observation of a senior Austrian official: 'We not only have two parliaments, we also have two emperors.'[18]

III

Everywhere the nationality issue, as we have already seen, pervasively influenced the monarchy. The central government in Vienna and the separate units in Austria and Hungary each year routinely transacted the familiar business of government: tariffs, taxes, educational expenditures, railway construction and operation, military and naval spending and social welfare programmes. But a set of larger domestic and international issues, broadly defined as nationalities and nationalism, often overshadowed these functional achievements. Eleven nationalities within a complex, virtually unique political structure would have presented sufficient problems. But the diversity of size, religion, political and historical tradition and whether or not the national groups were wholly in or only partly contained by the monarchy's geography indescribably complicated everything. Almost no generalization for one group held true for another; every concession for one had to be juggled against the other ten variables. Finally, and most importantly, nationality issues often transcended the borders. Thus a domestic nationality problem could be an international and diplomatic one.[19]

The Austrian and Hungarian governments dealt independently with the problems within their own borders. No common policy existed toward nationality issues other than the underlying assumptions that German–Austrians would dominate Austria and the Magyars would dominate Hungary. Only with regard to Bosnia and Herzegovina did the two governments occasionally seek to formulate a common policy. Otherwise Vienna and Budapest addressed the nationality problems within their own boundaries with scant regard for each other. (See Map 2.)

The population in the Austrian lands represented in the Reichsrat in Vienna totalled at least 28 million. Nine nationality groups had sizeable populations in Austria. The 1910 census indicated the following approximate composition: Germans, 35 percent; Czechs, 23 percent; Poles, 18 percent; Ruthenians, 13 percent; Slovenes, 4 percent; Italians, 3 percent; and a scattering of Magyars and gypsies.[20] The German–Austrians dominated because of their homogeneity in the crownlands of upper and lower Austria, Vorarlberg and Salzburg, because they controlled the bureaucratic and administrative structures and because they held important military posts. While some German–Austrians rallied to the approaches of Pan-German groups, Berlin did not encourage such appeals, and it was not a foreign policy issue. Far more serious was the effect of the Czech–German clash on the governance of Austria, since successive Austrian cabinets failed to find a compromise for Bohemia that would satisfy both groups.[21]

Always a potential problem, the Polish situation remained relatively quiet. The Polish group in the Reichsrat averaged about eighty of 516 deputies; they usually formed a dependable bloc of pro-government supporters. In return, the Poles expected protection

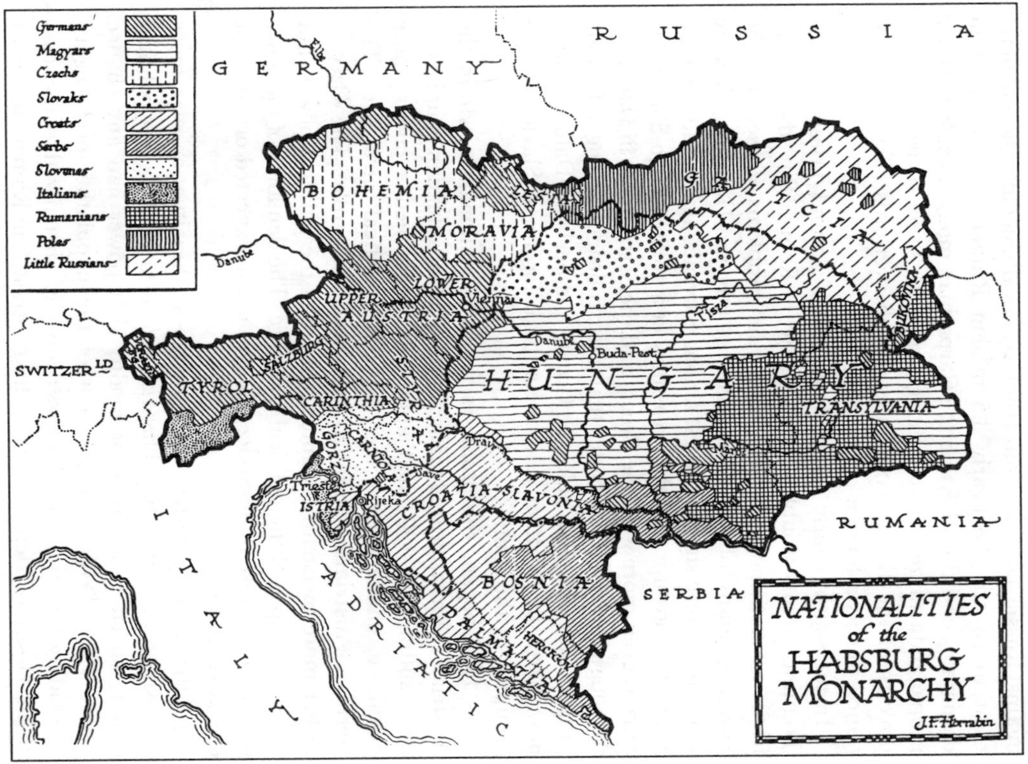

Map 2 Nationalities of the Habsburg Monarchy

against Russia, continuation of the German alliance and the unilateral right to govern the nearly 3.5 million Ruthenians who lived in desperate conditions beyond the Carpathian mountains. Pan-Slavic propaganda targeted the latter group, with some success. But the poverty of the Ruthenians under Polish overlords effectively contained this as a foreign policy issue.[22]

In the south, nearly one million Italians around Trieste and the Trentino areas troubled relations with Rome. But these were frictions, not more. So too were the problems caused by the Slovenes, many of whom remained stoutly pro-Habsburg. Yet by 1912 there were signs of unrest among Slovenes as Belgrade and the South Slav groups talked increasingly of a greater Yugo-Slav unity. Stirred even more were the Croats and the Serbs living in Dalmatia. Although they fared far better than their colleagues living in Croatia proper under Magyar rule, the Croats and Serbs in Dalmatia were now increasingly attentive to the appeals for a new Slavic political grouping in the south.[23]

As 1912 began, the problems posed by nationalism within the Austrian realm appeared manageable. The introduction of universal male suffrage in 1907 had apparently postponed a larger, more definitive challenge to the Austrian political structure. The German–Austrians continued their ascendant role. The Czechs, rather more insistently, wanted a share of the political power, but not the collapse of the political structure. The demands of the other nationalities were more noticeable, yet not unexpected or cause for excessive alarm.

In the areas governed from Budapest the situation was more explosive and intractable. The *Ausgleich* enshrined Magyar political power; no effort to dilute or modify that power had any chance before 1914. With 54.5 per cent of the population of Hungary (excluding Croatia), the Magyars controlled virtually all of the seats in the House of Deputies (405). By contrast, the Rumanians, with 16.1 percent of the population, had only five deputies. The sizeable Slovak and South Slav blocs suffered from similar political discrimination. In a way more urgent and far reaching than in Austria, any consideration of the nationality issue in Hungary was entwined with questions of political and economic power. The Magyars had constructed a political system that excluded any sharing of power. Successive Magyar politicians, whether for or against the *Ausgleich*, vied to show their adamancy against any change that benefited the minorities within the Hungarian half of the Habsburg dominions.[24]

For some, such as the Slovaks and Ruthenians, the Magyar stance could have prompted trouble with Russia. But the reality was otherwise. Despite their proximity to Russia, the Pan-Slavic appeals to the Ruthenians and Slovaks did not much worry Budapest.[25] Rather, the Magyar worries centred on the Rumanians, the Serbs and the Croats. Possibly the most dangerous by 1912 was the Rumanian problem and the 3 million Rumanians living in Transylvania. Not only were the 6.8 million Rumanians who lived in neighbouring Rumania hard to ignore, the Rumanian government's growing agitation on behalf of their fellow nationals made it a continuing diplomatic issue. Failure to resolve the Rumanian grievances might send Bucharest in the direction of St Petersburg; continued tensions could lead to still another defensive frontier for the Habsburg military to guard. Only the Serbian challenge had more ramifications upon Habsburg diplomatic and strategic policy than the Rumanian. Bucharest could not be brushed aside.[26]

The problems posed by the sizeable Serb and Croat populations living in the Vojvodina and in Croatia were a continuing agenda item for Budapest. The Magyars' tough stance towards the Serbs and Croats embittered them and fed directly into Serbia's talk about South Slav unity. The Magyars first made the problem worse, then thwarted policies to ameliorate some of the more dangerous international consequences. Each failure to co-opt the Croats made the task of governing more difficult. Each repressive step increased tension and sometimes provoked terrorist attacks upon government officials. South Slav propaganda found more and more supporters. The Hungarian policies provided a steady stream of recruits for the Yugo-Slav cause.[27]

Of the eleven nationalities, the German–Austrians and the Magyars were obviously dominant politically. Separately they controlled the political structure in the two halves of the monarchy. Yet by 1912, in Austria the Czechs in Bohemia had the German–Austrians on the defensive; in Galicia the Poles operated almost independently of the Vienna government. By contrast the Magyars, their political status enshrined by the *Ausgleich* of 1867, grew more powerful. Not only did the Magyars seek to maintain their privileges, Budapest ran roughshod over other nationalities under their jurisdiction. Serbs, Croats, Slovaks and Rumanians found little tolerance or understanding from their Magyar overlords. Thus the Magyars were at once both a nationality problem for the entire monarchy and the first cause of still more nationality problems by their own intolerance towards other groups.[28]

Yet behind the potpourri of nationalities there remained a strong, more unifying theme: coherence and cohesion within the monarchy. Scattered nationalists of any persuasion might talk of breaking up the monarchy. But before 1914 they were few, ineffective and without much credibility. However much national groups assailed the Habsburg government, none wanted the over-arching structure to disappear.

Rather, thoughtful people grappled with how to reform the monarchy. Parliamentarianism, the usual panacea of constitutional change in Europe, did not work well. Czechs and Germans soon managed to paralyse the Austrian parliament. Government by technocrats, emergency decrees, then political pay-offs basically kept the machinery functioning in Vienna. In Hungary (though minor suffrage concessions were made) ten million Magyars monopolized the political life of the eastern half of the monarchy. The Magyars had no intention of permitting genuine parliamentary government that would diminish their own power. Other reformers talked of trialism, letting the Slavs become a third ruling group along with the Magyars and Germans. This scheme enjoyed some currency, but always encountered a hostile reception in Budapest. Others talked of a federal scheme, possibly modelled on Switzerland or the United States. Here, political power would be vertically aligned among the nationality groups with the central government holding the disparate factions together. Other solutions proposed bureaucratic reform as the way to enhance the government, in turn muting nationality demands. Finally, some, like Archduke Franz Ferdinand, pondered more fundamental changes: the dismantling of Magyar power even at the risk of constitutional crisis and possible military confrontation.[29]

Equity, power, privilege, liberal values, ethnic domination and feudal remnants of the older monarchical order — all jumbled together to make the nationality issue the most fundamentally negative influence on the monarchy's future. Ironically, in fact paradoxically, the monarchy's very success in protecting, educating and facilitating economic development also ensured that the Habsburgs would be targeted by those who assailed it. Before 1914 none wanted to destroy the structure. Test it? Yes. Change it? Yes. But not vanquish it.

IV

Nationalist appeals from outside the monarchy, however, were far less restrained. Pan-Slavic rhetoric, whether aimed at the Ruthenians or Croats and Serbs living in the monarchy, had an unfriendly, disruptive tone. Whether Italian or Slavic, irredentism's emotional appeal from outside the monarchy stirred fellow nationals living inside the monarchy. Tantalizing, alluring themes of unity and a separate future characterized this nationalistic propaganda. The shrillness of the messages, especially the efforts of the Pan-Slavists in Russia, disturbed Habsburg policy-makers. After 1912, these entreaties gained strength and showed signs of growing acceptance, especially among South Slavs in the monarchy. In turn, officials in both Vienna and Budapest increasingly worried about the threats. But the governing elite could devise no approach that curbed, at least for very long, the seductive appeal of irredentism.[30]

Compounding the nationality issue still further were the problems spawned by the Habsburg acquisition of Bosnia–Herzegovina. The Congress of Berlin in 1878 had given Vienna administrative responsibility for the two provinces. Since Austria's defeat in 1859, Franz Joseph and the Habsburg military wanted the territory to protect the naval installations in Dalmatia. The great powers tacitly assumed that Austria–Hungary would eventually annex the territories. But thirty years passed before Franz Joseph and his advisers finally acted in 1908. The ensuing Bosnian crisis alienated Russia and the Anglo-French entente and left the Serbs and Croats in Dalmatia and Bosnia–Herzegovina newly aggrieved. Until the act of annexation the Serbs and Croats in the two provinces could contemplate possible union with Serbia. After 1908 the Habsburg monarchy replaced the Ottoman empire as their barrier.[31]

Serbia's humiliation in the crisis, moreover, led Serbian leaders to stir up nationalistic fervour in the two provinces, both openly and covertly. Thus the *Narodna Odbrana* (National Defence) began its propaganda efforts in the two areas; the Belgrade government invited Bosnian students to Serbia for education and indoctrination in the greater Yugo-Slav cause; and some Serbian military officers formed the Black Hand (*Crna ruka*), an organization pledged to use force to bring about a greater Serbia.[32]

The results came quickly. Nationalistic agitation mounted. Even the introduction of economic and political reforms in Bosnia and Herzegovina only blunted these attacks. For concessions came slowly, usually over Magyar opposition, and whetted the Bosnians' desire for more change. Moreover, by early 1912, General Oskar Potiorek, the Governor-General (*Landeschef*), found Austria and Hungary resistant to his pleas for economic development and for a military build-up to offset the dangers of a potential Serbian military threat.

Then, in late spring 1912, Serbia prompted the formation of the Balkan League aimed at Constantinople and Vienna. This step and the subsequent turmoil of 1912 kept the nationality issue alive in Bosnia and Herzegovina; then the Serbian military victories in late 1912 made Belgrade appear still more attractive. The removal of the two provinces from the Dual Monarchy became an avowed goal of many Serbo-Croatian intellectuals and political leaders. The Austro-Hungarian monarchy soon saw itself engaged in a campaign to protect its share of the spoils of the Ottoman empire.

Contemporaries lamented this failure to blunt the external nationalist agitation among those within the monarchy. Part of the blame was assigned to the machinations of foreign governments: Rome, St Petersburg, Belgrade and later Bucharest. The critics also faulted the dynasty for its failure to grapple with dynastic survival in an age of mounting democratic practice and expectation. The Emperor Franz Joseph, on the throne since 1848, showed no disposition to alter his practice of reliance upon the German–Austrians and the Magyars and upon a sizeable cadre of officials who (ostensibly above nationality) administered the monarchy. The Habsburg tactic of divide and rule, so rehearsed as to become automatic, appeared adequate. Failure to appoint ministers who would challenge this 'stumble ahead' approach prompted public criticism.

Nevertheless, Franz Joseph and his heir-apparent remained unaltered in their determination to limit, to contain and to divert the disruptive energies that assailed the political structure. There were no efforts to create a new structure. Even Franz Ferdinand, who talked contemptuously of his uncle's failure to grapple with the constitutional challenges, showed little inclination to think more creatively about the problem. Willing to blame the Magyars for most of the monarchy's afflictions, Franz Ferdinand could not embrace the path to a parliamentary monarchy or to more defined constitutional practice. To have expected more creativity, or even solutions, may have been unfair to the Habsburgs. Their leadership reflected conservative, monarchical, cautious values. To do more meant to risk. To seek was to run the chance of loss. Thus the Habsburgs, having already lost much, deliberately avoided losing still more. The erosion of that attitude of caution by July 1914 constitutes a major interpretive theme of this book.[33]

V

Nationalism and its many ramifications influenced every aspect of the Habsburg monarchy. But the monarchy's economy also touched upon every institution in the realm, while shaping military expenditures and the functioning of the Austro-Hungarian governments. Recent research permits new observations about the economic life of the Danubian state.[34]

Put succinctly, from 1900 to 1912 both halves of the monarchy shared a slow but sustained period of economic growth. Both remained predominantly agrarian, the Hungarian sector far more so. But Magyar farming was inefficient and suffered from a distortion of land ownership. In fact, the monarchy imported foodstuffs in part because of Hungarian inefficiencies. On the other hand, there were signs of progressive modernization and industrial development in Hungary. The gross national product jumped approximately 42 percent from 1900 to 1913 and the industrial work force doubled. Moreover, industrial production increased by 5.1 percent annually. In Austria, meanwhile, industrial productivity jumped 50 percent in the decade after 1900, while steel and textile production doubled. Railway expansion continued, joint stock companies proliferated and Austrian banking assets sharply increased.

Like all governments, Vienna and Budapest always remained concerned about state finances. In the decade after 1900 state expenditures climbed sharply. Conventional explanations have focused upon international factors for these increases but domestic reasons, including railway expenditures and social programmes, actually explain much of the spurt of state obligations. Austrian expenditures doubled from 1900 to 1910; a similar pattern developed in Hungary. Bond sales, foreign borrowing, tariffs, lottery tickets and indirect taxes constituted the main sources of state revenue. When the Balkan Crisis began in late 1912, neither government increased taxes to meet the surge of common expenditures. Instead, each wanted to borrow on foreign markets and to refinance older obligations. Despite an almost total lack of access to the Triple Entente capital markets, Habsburg credit remained good. As in earlier crises, the creditor, whether at home or abroad, rather than the taxman, offered the initial answer to the Habsburg need for state finances.[35]

Substantial weaknesses existed, of course, in this pattern of economic activity and state finance. The importation of agricultural goods weakened the economy. So too did the rise in government debt, a function of the state's takeover of the rail systems in both halves of the monarchy. The absence of a substantial consumer market also restrained the economic pace. Finally, possibly most alarming to the bankers, the economists and government finance officials was the balance of trade figures that saw the monarchy with substantial imbalances in the hundreds of millions of crowns.[36] This upward trend since 1910 suggested a state living beyond its means. The culprit was the surge of the economy itself, not military expenses. With the onset of the Balkan Wars and the staggering expenses that came with them, this economic imbalance sharply worsened. The entire economy dramatically turned sour throughout the empire. Nonetheless, when 1912 began, Franz Joseph's realm enjoyed a relative economic boom; the country was prosperous.

VI

The Habsburg leadership could not ignore public opinion, however diffuse, contradictory or difficult to discern. Public opinion remained a parameter that defined the limits of what Habsburg policy-makers could and would not do. To be sure, as we saw in Chapter 1, the attitudes of the elite played a crucial role in shaping the views of the policy-makers themselves; the transformation of their opinions from moderate optimism to mounting despair is a major theme of this study. But these officials had always to be concerned with what the 'public' would tolerate.[37]

Nationality issues as reflected in parliamentary debates could not be ignored. Nor could officials dismiss the hardships imposed by conscription, reservists serving on active military duty and increased financial burdens upon the monarchy's population. These considerations defined the political options. Although Franz Joseph and his ministers were largely removed from the public, they and their bureaucratic subordinates could not be insensitive to these issues. Nor did the quasi-parliamentary bodies (when in session), such as the Delegations and the Austrian and Hungarian parliaments, allow these issues to lie dormant. Often the politicians directed their comments at narrow financial issues or the prudence of more military expenditures. In the crisis of December 1912, for example, the parliamentary members were vocal, sarcastic, even bitter in attacking government policy. In late 1913 and again in early 1914, Foreign Minister Leopold Berchtold faced hostile questions reflecting public frustrations over the monarchy's foreign policy. The parliamentary members, though a limited sample of the broader population, provided a gauge of opinion. Unlike its Russian counterpart, the Austro-Hungarian monarchy had legislative forums that allowed public concerns to be addressed about foreign and strategic policy, even if only for rhetorical effect.[38]

Newspapers in both halves of the monarchy also provided a barometer of public opinion, though limited to the educated elements to be sure. Not surprisingly, no newspaper dominated the monarchy, as did *The Times* in Great Britain or *Le Temps* in France. In Austria, the *Neue Freie Presse*, which enjoyed a wide circulation, promoted a cautious foreign policy. *Fremdenblatt*, always especially close to the Foreign Ministry, had Franz Joseph as its most notable reader. Franz Ferdinand had close ties with the *Reichspost*. In Hungary, *Pester Lloyd* reflected István Tisza's views, which surprisingly were often those of the *Neue Freie Presse*. The *Az Est* frequently embarrassed the Magyar regimes on domestic issues, but seldom commented on foreign policy matters. For the most part, the Hungarian press covered domestic issues with only occasional comments about foreign policy.[39]

A survey of public opinion organs in early 1912 reveals few sharply defined limits upon Habsburg policy-makers. The economy was prosperous. Franz Joseph appeared healthy; the heir-apparent was accepted as a public figure; the army and navy were anxious — as always — for more funds; and the different nationalities were

clamouring at a familiar level, though possibly a shade higher in
Croatia and the south generally. The dangers of monarchical
succession, of a confrontation with Russia, or the sudden disappear-
ance of the Turkish presence in the Balkans — these possibilities
seemed remote, improbable.

Rather, the political processes remained preoccupied with traditional issues: the clash over budget requests and relations between
the Austrian and Hungarian governments. The friction between
Vienna and Budapest over every facet of public policy, but especially
military expenditures and the administration of Bosnia–
Herzegovina, were key items. These tasks represented the fundamental feature of the monarchy's unusual constitutional structure:
the 1867 *Ausgleich* and the creation of a Dual Monarchy. That
settlement created the most decisive features of the domestic context
for the conduct of Habsburg foreign policy.

VII

The foreign policy functions of the Habsburg monarchy buttressed
each of the unifying forces — dynasty, military bureaucracy,
economy — in their impact upon the overall life of the state. A state
born of foreign wars and conflict, the monarchy had repeatedly, if
not always successfully, played a role in the emergence of a
European state system. If Austria–Hungary's existence contradicted the era of the nation states so also did Switzerland, whose
origin and survival rested upon foreign policy. The Danubian
monarchy provided a protective umbrella under which eleven
nationalities could live, argue and struggle with each other, and yet
feel secure that their futures would be protected against external
challenge. In fulfilling that responsibility the Habsburgs gained
their *raison d'être*, gave currency to the importance of international
politics in the life of the monarchy and conferred legitimacy upon
political arrangements that — on their face — were anachronistic.
So long as the national groups felt protected, the monarchy reaffirmed
its position.

At the start of 1912 the Habsburg monarchy had a modest aura of
confidence about its future. The competition between Schönbrunn
and Belvedere was irritating but not crippling. The economy
continued its decade plus record of improvement. Public opinion

still rallied towards the monarch and the monarchy, whether in parliamentary forums or the press. While the monarchy's elite could worry about the future, few believed the Dual Monarchy doomed to collapse. The *Ausgleich* accord, unique and cumbersome, represented an acceptable and accepted constitutional format for the conduct of the monarchy's business. While internal political issues in both Austria and Hungary were disruptive, few believed the power of the state was seriously threatened. On the other hand, the nationality issue remained potentially explosive. If within acceptable limits at the start of 1912 and not much different from earlier, nationalism with its domestic and international ramifications remained volatile and threatening. And nowhere were there greater explosive possibilities than in Bosnia and Herzegovina, the monarchy's two imperial provinces. But as 1912 began, even in Sarajevo, calm and order dominated.

Thus, 1912 opened for the Habsburgs with a measure of confidence for the future. But for one person, Count Aehrenthal, Habsburg foreign minister since 1906, the year brought grave news. He was losing his struggle with leukemia. In early 1912 he told Franz Joseph that he must resign. This news foreshadowed a change of personnel and possibly of the direction of Habsburg foreign policy. Within months, developments in the Balkans would prompt even greater changes in the agenda of Habsburg foreign policy. The continuing interaction of domestic political considerations and foreign policy demands would surface anew — and dangerously so. For the Habsburg monarchy, the first months of 1912 were truly the last months of peace.

3 Dynasty, Generals, Diplomats: the Instruments of Habsburg Foreign Policy

The state, regardless of its political structure, exists in part to protect its citizens and their property, to defend their interests abroad and to pursue a foreign policy that achieves these goals. Diplomatic service, military and naval forces, economic and propaganda activities all facilitate the state's execution of its responsibilities.[1] The Austro-Hungarian state constituted a special case, for foreign policy provided the essential *raison d'être* of the Dual Monarchy. This foreign policy function had impelled two increasingly quasi-independent states to share a common monarch, a common army and navy and a common foreign policy after 1867. Beyond the monarchy's sheer survival, it existed to fulfil a set of familiar foreign policy functions in central and southern Europe. If it achieved those tasks, the multinational, dynastic enterprise might endure despite its anomalous status during an age of nationalism. Failure to fulfil those tasks would almost certainly ensure the monarchy's decline, if not demise.[2]

In the performance of these foreign policy functions, the Habsburg state depended upon the monarchy and monarch, the military forces, the diplomatic establishment and the support they received from banking and economic interests. These institutions performed the 'common' functions of diplomacy and defence for the Habsburg government. Although not immune from the internal pressures of nationality considerations nor the conflicting visions of the monarchy's future, these common instruments represented a considerable force for monarchical unity and had more quality and effectiveness than is usually conceded. Their units represented the internal dimension of the monarchy's standing as a great power.[3]

I

The Emperor/King Franz Joseph knowingly represented another epoch of monarchical leaders. But the aura conferred by his survival

34

while most of his peers, including Queen Victoria, showed their mortality could not be ignored. Festivals celebrated his personal longevity and lengthy rule. The jubilee year of 1908 honoured Franz Joseph's sixtieth year of rule as emperor; 1910 marked his eightieth birthday. The celebrations further accentuated an awareness that Franz Joseph still dominated his government. On matters of defence and foreign policy he was the ruler. Since 1866 his foreign policy had been cautious, yet with occasional moments of assertiveness over Bosnia–Herzegovina in 1878 and again in 1908. The monarch had become a fixture whose personal future became increasingly inseparable from the future of the monarchy as a whole.[4]

Franz Joseph contributed to this image by never shirking his foreign policy responsibilities. A diligent reader of foreign ministry dispatches, no matter what the season or where his residence, he carefully followed the implementation of his policies.[5] Not surprisingly, he personally assumed a key role in diplomatic relations with the other monarchs. The German Kaiser William II was a frequent visitor in Vienna, often stopping twice a year, as he travelled to and from the Mediterranean. King Edward VII visited Bad Ischl. The lesser Balkan monarchs were frequent guests as well, especially King Carol of Rumania, his secret ally. But no Italian monarch came, since Franz Joseph, ever the devout Catholic, rejected a visit to Rome for fear of offending the Pope. Nor did any French head of state come, though the French ambassador was warmly received. In addition to official visits, the monarch penned a steady stream of notes to fellow rulers, congratulating them on their birthdays, wishing them well on their children's marriages and expressing shared sorrows at the time of deaths. Franz Joseph had become the patriarch of the monarchical system.

As commander of the Habsburg military and naval forces, the emperor always placed his responsibilities for the security of the state first. Promotions, budgets, troop assignments and military plans were a staple of his bureaucratic life. On foreign policy issues he dealt in general principles and within parameters, on military matters he dealt with precise personnel assignments and mundane affairs. In Franz Conrad von Hötzendorf as chief of the General Staff after 1906, Franz Joseph had a subordinate who repeatedly demanded the modernization of the military forces. Regrettably, the emperor soon found Conrad clashing with others in the government: War Minister Franz von Schönaich over budgets, Foreign Minister

Aehrenthal over Italy and subsequently Foreign Minister Berchtold over a fight with Serbia. Franz Joseph became a pivotal figure in keeping the army chief restrained.[6]

With the Habsburg navy the ruler's problems were far less consequential. He did not quarrel with a naval build-up that consumed almost 15 per cent of the defence budget. He regularly received Admiral Rudolf Montecuccoli, head of the naval section within the War Ministry. After 1902, however, Franz Joseph never visited a naval installation. In fact, he never wore an admiral's uniform in public, yet he sported constantly a variety of military dress. The navy represented a strategic inconvenience, or rather, a great power prestige symbol with possible strategic uses. The army, on the other hand, represented the bedrock of Habsburg security: the first line of defence against Russia, the Balkan states, or even Italy, and, if necessary, internal rebellion.[7]

Franz Ferdinand shared his uncle's fascination with military matters, though his devotion to the navy was far greater. At the same time, the heir-apparent gradually emerged as another participant in the foreign policy process. Although a visitor to Russia in 1891, the archduke's active involvement in foreign policy did not begin until his designation as heir-apparent in 1898. As the emperor became more feeble, Franz Ferdinand became the surrogate Habsburg visitor abroad. The *Thronfolger* particularly relished his contacts with William II. The German ruler treated Sophie, the Princess (later Duchess) of Hohenburg, with genuine kindness (a treatment not accorded in Vienna because of her less worthy aristocratic status). In turn, Franz Ferdinand played host to the German emperor, visited him and his army's manoeuvres, exchanged letters and shared ambitions and plans with him. If the archduke never fell entirely under the charm of the mercurial German ruler, he nonetheless viewed the Austro-German connection as the pivot point of Habsburg diplomacy.[8]

But Franz Ferdinand did not limit his approach just to Berlin. He managed three visits to London, including one in November 1913 with Sophie when they stayed at Windsor Castle. The archduke hoped for better relations with Britain after his accession, a fact that George V's gracious reception of Sophie doubtless reinforced.[9]

Franz Ferdinand carefully distinguished between the greater and lesser monarchs. He was open to King Carol, not least because he was an ally. But he regarded the other Balkan rulers as nuisances.

At one point, the old kaiser essentially had to command his nephew to meet King Ferdinand of Bulgaria. King Peter of Serbia and King Nikita of Montenegro did not even get that courtesy. Nor would the archduke receive their ministers when they visited Vienna.

Franz Ferdinand's contacts among the European royalty had few disadvantages for the monarchy. After all, he was the heir-apparent. Furthermore, the German alliance was an imperative working relationship that had to survive Franz Joseph's death. The archduke also offered a way for both Berlin and Vienna to convey information. The royal 'network' provided communications channels and alternate ways to calibrate governmental positions. Ironically, although Franz Ferdinand desired better ties with Russia, he never visited St Petersburg after his 1891 trip. The Russian perception of him as head of an anti-Russian 'war party' thus easily flourished, with serious policy consequences for the diplomacy of both governments.[10]

The archduke's diplomatic participation went further. He actively dealt with the foreign ministers and sought to influence the conduct of Habsburg foreign policy. Franz Ferdinand warmly approved Alois Lexa von Aehrenthal's appointment as Habsburg foreign minister in 1906. He believed Aehrenthal's long experience in St Petersburg might revive a Russian connection. But this did not happen. The Anglo-Russian entente and the question of Bosnia and Berlin's own reservations blocked any improvement of relations between St Petersburg and Vienna. This disappointed the archduke, whose relations with the foreign minister progressively deteriorated.

When Foreign Minister Leopold Berchtold took office in February 1912, the situation changed. The new minister corresponded with Franz Ferdinand, allowed the heir-apparent some intrusion into personnel matters and consulted him on the broader issues of peace and war. Berchtold also could not forget Franz Ferdinand's personal relationship with William II. And, throughout the Balkan crises of 1912–13, Franz Ferdinand would find in Berchtold's peaceful, cautious stance a far more congenial pose than that of his military protégé, General Conrad von Hötzendorf. When in June 1914 Berchtold and his wife, Nandine, visited Franz Ferdinand and Sophie at their beloved Konopischt, the friendship between the two men was apparent. The Sarajevo assassination only days later profoundly altered Berchtold's approach to the South Slav issue and the use of force.[11]

Franz Ferdinand's third area of activity centred upon his responsibilities for the army and navy. While Franz Joseph never precisely
defined these duties, he had allowed them to expand and in 1913
named the archduke the general inspector of the armed forces. This
delegation allowed the *Thronfolger* to participate in virtually all
aspects of military and naval policy. Already in 1906 Franz Ferdinand had participated in the appointment of Conrad as chief of the
General Staff and Schönaich as war minister. Thereafter Franz
Ferdinand effectively controlled one of the two senior military
positions. Further, the emperor's toleration of Franz Ferdinand's
military chancellory and his working relationship with Conrad
made an impact upon the Austro-Hungarian defence community.
The archduke's strong support for larger military expenditures,
better weapons and a bigger army pleased the Habsburg military.
Franz Ferdinand exploited every opportunity to buttress this identi-
fication with the army. Unlike his uncle, the nephew found time to
become the virtual patron of the Habsburg navy. Dressed in an
admiral's uniform, he frequently attended ship launchings and
naval exercises.

By 1912 Franz Ferdinand had an established place in the Habsburg
defence establishment. He had strong, occasionally decisive influence,
as in the selection of either the chief of staff or war minister. This
increasingly important military status strengthened his already potent
position as heir-apparent. As the next ruler, he could not be ignored. If
Franz Joseph were an institution in the foreign relations of the
monarchy, his nephew worked hard to create a special institutional
role for the *Thronfolger* — always ready and available.

Thus by 1912 two senior members of the House of Habsburg
shaped and helped to direct Austro-Hungarian foreign policy. The
diplomatic and military bureaucracies would translate Habsburg
wishes into policy and action. These common activities represented,
along with the dynasty, important elements of unity in the far-flung
monarchy. They also represented the routine, everyday manifestations of state sovereignty and power.[12]

II

The Ballhausplatz, the home of the foreign minister and the Foreign
Ministry, lay adjacent to the Hofburg palace, the in-town residence

of Franz Joseph. When the emperor resided at the Hofburg, the foreign minister could walk to the monarch's office within five minutes. After 1912, as His Majesty came to prefer Schönbrunn, the trip took longer, and the visits were less frequent. But whatever the physical arrangements, few doubted that the Habsburg foreign minister, who also served as the Minister of the Imperial and Royal House, was the senior government official. He was the custodian during peacetime of the monarchy's common affairs. To assist him in that task, the minister had a foreign ministry staff and a foreign service. These groups were the product of long years of evolution into an effective, *supra*-national institution that served the regime's interests first and national groups second.[13]

At the age of forty-nine, Count Leopold Berchtold succeeded Aehrenthal on 17 February 1912. In the Foreign Ministry he had a bureaucratic apparatus with about 230 officials and employees; abroad there were about 150 diplomats. These officials, many educated in the Theresianum ('an institution founded by Maria Theresa as a centre for patriotic imperial officialdom') and later in the Consular Academy, had — like Berchtold — received their effective training on the job.[14]

A typical career for a successful Habsburg diplomat included an assignment in one of the major European capitals, then a tour in Vienna, followed by another foreign assignment in a medium-level post, often in the Balkans. Returning to Vienna, some of the promising diplomats stayed in the Ministry and others got a senior posting at one of the major embassies — St Petersburg, Berlin, London, Paris or Rome. Eventually, after thirty years service, a diplomat might become an ambassador or minister or win a senior post in the Foreign Ministry.

The atmosphere within the Habsburg foreign service was distinctly international and aristocratic. Only 3 per cent of the seventy-two senior diplomats posted outside Austria–Hungary had no noble title. At the Ballhausplatz a prince, ten counts, twenty-four barons, and thirty-two with simple noble predicates controlled the bulk of the senior positions. Aristocrats, whether Austrian or Hungarian, held the top diplomatic posts abroad and usually represented decades of familial service to the Habsburg dynasty.[15]

Within this context the Magyars fared increasingly well. From 1870 to 1906 the percentage of Magyar diplomats increased from 13.1 to 30.2. In 1912, Hungarians held the embassies in Berlin,

Rome, Paris, Constantinople, Belgrade, Dresden and Tokyo, and key positions in Vienna. But the record strongly suggests that these men remained *supra*-national Habsburg loyalists, not Magyar patriots. Rather, the Magyar influence came from the *Ausgleich* accord that said the Hungarian prime minister had to be consulted on foreign policy issues. And this prerogative was reinforced by the use of Magyar emissaries to the government in Vienna, such as Tisza's appointment of István Burián to that post in mid-1913. The Magyar influence was constitutional, not incidental.[16]

Within the Ballhausplatz the fundamental organizational structure had changed little since the days of Count Metternich. The chief differences were the size of the staff, its professionalization and the enormous increase in paper. A small personal staff, headed by a *chef de cabinet*, assisted the foreign minister. After April 1912, thirty-four year old Count Alexander (Alek) Hoyos held the post under Berchtold. Of the senior officials, the five section heads were the most important. The first served as the permanent under-secretary and the representative of the foreign minister during his absence. In addition the first section chief was responsible for the routine operations of the Ministry. The second chief, to whom the political departments reported, was the crucial post for substantive diplomatic policies. All of the political departments, organized along geographical lines, reported to him. Of these, the first, which handled Russia, the Balkans and Turkish affairs, was the most important. In addition, the Ministry had seventeen administrative units, ranging from protocol issues to cyphers to consular affairs. While their chiefs played no role in policy formulation, the administrative support units played an unstated, unheralded role in the actual implementation of Habsburg foreign policy.[17]

Abroad, the senior ambassadors and ministers were the visible manifestations of Habsburg foreign policy. The most senior among them was Count Ladislaus Szögyény-Marich, appointed ambassador to Berlin in 1892 and still serving at this post in 1914. A reliable reporter, Szögyény retained Franz Joseph's and William's confidence. The ambassador embraced the Dual Alliance but with Austria–Hungary as a full partner, not a dependent one. In Paris, the able Count Nikolaus Szécsen de Temerin reported on French affairs, while in Constantinople Marquis Johann Pallavicini excelled in understanding the complexities of Turkish politics. Kajetan Mérey von Kapos-Mére was decidedly less effective in Rome; his jealousy of Berchtold increasingly marred his performance. In London, Count Albert Mensdorff-Pouilly-Dietrichstein failed, despite personal ties to the British royal family, to convince Sir Edward Grey, the British foreign secretary, that Austria–Hungary could pursue a policy independent of Berlin. The embassy in St Petersburg was, of course, the major trouble spot. Successive Habsburg foreign ministers — Aehrenthal and Berchtold — had held the post without necessarily becoming more adept as foreign ministers in handling Russian affairs. In 1912, Count Duglas Thurn und Valsássina held the position. His ineptitude during the Balkan Wars led to his replacement by Friedrich Szápáry in late 1913. Unfortunately, personal problems kept Szápáry from St Petersburg during much of early 1914.

In the Balkan capitals the representation ranged from adequate to poor, with Baron Wladimir Giesl von Gieslingen, first in Montenegro and then in Belgrade, a significant figure. The presence of the one-time confidant of Franz Ferdinand, Ottokar Czernin, in Bucharest in late 1913 and early 1914 also reflected the importance attached by Vienna to Rumania's continued loyalty to the Triple Alliance.

Two final comments about the Habsburg diplomats are required. To a very large extent, the diplomats were representatives and reporters, not shapers of policy. Occasionally the men initiated a step, but for the most part the direction came from Vienna. Given the monarchy's defensive, status quo stance, this is not surprising. But this approach also led to the neglect of some opportunities, especially in Rome and Sofia, and subjected Habsburg diplomats in the various capitals to intensive Franco-Russian efforts to erode their individual credibility.[18]

But this defensive posture did not mean that the diplomats could not observe. Ambassadors, ministers and lesser officials reported on all aspects of life in their assigned countries. Usually the reports focused on diplomatic and political events. Most representatives did not flinch from sending reports that might disturb Vienna. In times of stress the consular officials in the Balkans and in Russia provided timely intelligence on mobilization orders, grain and horse purchases and the general tenor of the countryside. What reports often lacked, however, was detailed analyses of economic issues. Aside from tariff problems, these questions simply did not get much scrutiny. This weakness reflected the general failure within the Habsburg leadership to recognize until too late the potential of economic tools for political purposes. In the meantime, the diplomats observed, reported and executed their instructions from Vienna. Those instructions came, of course, from the foreign minister.

III

Once Franz Joseph established the general guidelines, the foreign ministers were responsible for the overall direction of Habsburg foreign policy. The minister's first duty was to protect the dynastic interests of the House of Habsburg; his second was to manage the monarchy's relations with other governments. Without *de jure* status, the foreign minister became the *de facto* equivalent to a chancellor. He set the agenda for the Common Ministerial Council, attempted to resolve policy and budget differences between the Austrian and Hungarian governments and became a 'broker' in pushing both Vienna and Budapest to agreement. These functions made the foreign minister, necessarily, a domestic political figure. They also entangled him, albeit reluctantly, in domestic squabbles, particularly over budget matters. The Habsburg foreign minister was thus at once a foreign minister like Sir Edward Grey and a quasi-chancellor. The task was not an easy one.[19]

Alois Lexa von Aehrenthal had become foreign minister in 1906, succeeding the Polish Count Agenor Goluchowski. A member of a prominent Bohemian family, Aehrenthal had entered the foreign service in the 1870s. In 1878 he went to St Petersburg, would return there in 1894 and again in 1899. Count Gustav Kálnoky, while serving as foreign minister, had been Aehrenthal's early patron and he also fared well with Goluchowski, becoming minister to Bucharest in 1895 and ambassador to Russia in 1899. His selection in 1906 as foreign minister represented a part of the overall upheaval in the monarchy's common affairs when a new foreign minister, a new war minister and a new chief of the General Staff all took office.[20]

Aehrenthal had a keen interest in Austrian and Hungarian domestic politics. Indeed, he probably understood the monarchy's complicated structure better than his predecessors or his successors. Perhaps as a result he concluded that the Danubian state needed a more assertive foreign policy, one less tolerant of Berlin's blissful assumptions. He hoped that a restored sense of destiny for the monarchy would assure German-Austrian and Magyar support for the dynasty. The foreign minister would combat the disintegrating influence of nationalism by reviving the monarchy's foreign fortunes. In pursuing this objective Aehrenthal was, moreover, prepared to challenge the Russians whom he knew so well.[21]

Aehrenthal wanted to buttress the monarchy's position in the Balkans and bring about the long delayed annexation of Bosnia–Herzegovina. These steps would, he believed, bolster self-confidence at home. He achieved some of these goals. Under his leadership Austria–Hungary initiated a more assertive Balkan policy and annexed the two provinces. Such policies had consequences, however. His actions alarmed the British, humiliated the Russians and embittered still further the Serbians. A policy of activism in the Balkans might have worked had the Russia that Aehrenthal had known still been fascinated with the Far East. But Russia's debacle in the Russo-Japanese war prompted a new Russian focus on the Balkans. Furthermore, Aehrenthal also failed to win more domestic support for the dynasty, despite his foreign policy gains. Foreign policy success could not overcome the deeper nationalistic fissures of the Habsburg regime.

Count Leopold Berchtold, as ambassador to Russia until 1911 and retirement to his Moravian estates, actively participated in most of Aehrenthal's foreign policy. Summoned by Franz Joseph to succeed the dying Aehrenthal, Berchtold reluctantly accepted the post. At forty-nine, he was Europe's youngest foreign minister. In nineteen years he had gone from the Moravian administration to chief of the monarchy's foreign policy establishment. Berchtold embodied the old diplomacy; his and his wife's land holdings made him at once both an Austrian noble and a Hungarian magnate.

Until recently portrayed as a dilettante, more interested in racing and art than diplomacy, Berchtold deserves a better press. He accepted office with few ambitions. Nonetheless he recognized the essentially defensive position of the monarchy and the vulnerability left by Aehrenthal's assertive efforts in the Balkans. What Berchtold and his colleagues failed to appreciate in early 1912 was the new assertiveness in St Petersburg's foreign policy, first seen in late 1911 with renewed pressures on the Ottoman empire. Nor did he and his associates fully apprehend the full ramification of Italy's attack upon the Ottoman empire in Tripoli (Libya) in September 1911. Vienna failed to perceive how that attack weakened the Ottoman position in Macedonia and the Balkans. Berchtold's lack of experience in the

Balkans may have contributed to this failure. In any event, neither Aehrenthal nor Berchtold underestimated the monarchy's need to integrate its foreign policy with its domestic problems and to wage a defensive, holding operation in the process. Furthermore, Berchtold, more than Aehrenthal, understood that diplomacy without military power could lead to ineffective diplomacy and to failure in the international arena. On this point he and the Habsburg military and naval leadership essentially agreed.[22]

IV

The Imperial and Royal (k.u.k.) War Ministry, headed by one of the three common ministers, represented the second strongest unifying element in the monarchy: the army and the navy. The ministry, the General Staff, three operational armies (Austro-Hungarian, Austrian and Hungarian) and the common navy tied the monarchy together. The defence forces provided visual symbols throughout the country of the power of the dynasty and the state. The military would, moreover, help to shape the progressively militant content of Habsburg diplomacy after 1912. The military's position in the Habsburg decision process is of fundamental importance in understanding Vienna's steady slide to war.[23]

Located until 1913 on the Am Hof not far from the Ballhausplatz, the War Ministry was a modest bureaucracy.[24] The entire Ministry constituted approximately 1,350 officers and staff. These men had the major tasks of securing and training manpower for the services, providing funds for the operation and development of the army and navy and overseeing the expenditure of those funds.[25]

Core issues of the *Ausgleich* accord centred upon manpower and financial matters. Thus the War Ministry and the war ministers were assured of difficulties with the Magyars. Repeated efforts to increase the annual intake of recruits fell victim to Hungarian efforts to extort concessions that would make Magyar the language of command or allow more autonomy for the separate *Honvéd* force. From 1889 to 1912 the annual contingent for the monarchy remained fixed at 136,000 men. By 1912 the actual breakdown of forces saw 103,100 serving in the common army, 20,000 in the Austrian defence force and 12,500 in the Hungarian defence force. Royal threats, constitutional crises, even foreign threats did not move Budapest's leadership to accept the War Ministry's requests for more men. Not until 1912 and Tisza's growing realization of the monarchy's exposed strategy *vis-à-vis* Russia would Budapest accede to some troop increase over a four-year period.[26]

A central task of the War Ministry was to coordinate the efforts of its own bureaucrats with those in the General Staff and the Naval Command, and those in two separate Austrian and Hungarian defence ministries. The separate Austrian and Hungarian defence ministries had their own staffs, though closely linked with the central one in Vienna. The two chief problems confronting the separate ministries concerned logistics and supply and the scheduling of training exercises. By contrast, a single naval command meant that construction issues and contracts were resolved in Vienna, while the base at Pola handled operational and command issues. Successive war ministers had to confront chiefs of staff, general staff officers and admirals, all demanding more money and more men for the army and navy. Invariably, not enough men or funds were available to satisfy the operational commanders. Inevitably, tensions between the administrative units developed. During peacetime the war minister remained the senior military figure, met with the other common ministers and addressed the Delegations. In war, however, the war minister occupied a secondary position, in effect the quartermaster general: in war the chief of the General Staff and his staff became the dominant partner. The potential reversal of these roles, common throughout most such command arrangements, created friction between the War Ministry and the General Staff and its leadership. Seldom, however, did this reach the point of a constitutional confrontation.[27]

The War Ministry's agenda necessitated constant contact with Franz Joseph and after 1898 with the *Thronfolger*. War ministers met with the emperor and the heir-apparent on a regular basis. But much of their normal contact came through the two military chancellories. General Arthur Bolfras, the (in 1912) seventy-four year old head of the kaiser's apparatus, brought conservative caution to his task, along with distinct favourites among the younger generals. By contrast, a colonel (first Alexander Brosch von Aarenau, then Karl Bardolff) headed Franz Ferdinand's military chancellory. Though more vulnerable because of their rank, these officers worked hard to provide the archduke with detailed information about Ministry proposals. On more than one occasion, they worked for or against proposals within the Kriegsministerium, especially on the size of the budget and funding for naval construction.[28]

Each year, preparation of the annual military budget occupied much of the Ministry's attention. The process began with queries to the General Staff and the army and naval commanders about their needs. Then negotiations began with the two governments over their willingness to provide the funds. Further discussions with the military and naval leadership and finally a meeting of the Common Ministerial Council concluded the process. In these sessions the Austrian government generally proved more supportive than the Hungarian, which was nearly always unwilling to increase the funding. Usually Budapest prevailed in setting the budget figures. Once the Council and Franz Joseph accepted the number, a detailed budget was prepared for the Delegations, who could discuss it but were also obliged to approve it.[29]

At the start of 1912 General Moritz von Auffenberg served as war minister, having come to power as a protégé of the heir-apparent in the autumn of 1911. Although Auffenberg never enjoyed Franz Joseph's confidence, he achieved two things during 1912 that none of his immediate predecessors had managed: an increase in the size of the common army and a substantial jump in military spending.

Auffenberg had replaced Franz von Schönaich as war minister in September 1911. Already inclined to criticize the monarchy's military readiness, the war minister quickly discovered that conditions were worse than he had anticipated. Almost immediately he campaigned to increase the military budget and renewed the efforts to build a larger army. When refused funds for artillery purchases, Auffenberg ordered the *matériel* anyway. Chastised for this unilateral action, Auffenberg chose to moderate his tactics but not his goals.[30]

In the spring of 1912 he continued to press for military reform and the budget to implement it. A major break came when István Tisza decided to back a manpower increase. In return, the Magyar leader demanded that the service period be reduced from three to two years. In June Tisza used questionable parliamentary tactics to force the measure through the Hungarian House of Deputies. Later that month the Austrian Lower House also passed the measure.

The military reform measure called for the recruits in the common army to increase from 103,000 in 1912 to 159,000 in 1914. The total standing army would climb from 405,120 to 494,120 — a substantial 22 percent increase. Although a belated catch-up effort for the

Danubian monarchy, Franz Joseph, Franz Ferdinand and the senior military leadership jubilantly welcomed this measure. The outbreak of the First Balkan War a few months later made these increases seem providential.[31]

But more men without increased military spending, Auffenberg steadfastly argued, would do the monarchy little good. He wanted to add to the annual budget of 350 million crowns a special appropriation of 250 million, distributed over a six-year period. On this issue the war minister found the Magyar leadership implacable. The economic situation, Budapest insisted, would not permit such a budget commitment. Instead, in July 1912 the Common Ministerial Council actually reduced Auffenberg's annual budget for the army and navy in spite of the passage only weeks earlier of the higher personnel authorization. He and other generals implored Franz Joseph and Franz Ferdinand to help reverse the Magyar position; all were unsuccessful in getting Budapest to yield.

Then in September 1912, with the Balkan and Turkish armies on the verge of mobilization and war, the Delegations convened to approve (months behind schedule) the 1912 budget. Even as the foreign situation deteriorated, Auffenberg could win no support for increased military spending. But the actual mobilization of the Balkan armies in early October, coupled with Russia's military exercises, altered attitudes. On 9 October the two governments agreed to a 250 million crown military package, the first instalment of which would be 41.6 million in 1912–13. This belated step did not lead to further generosity. Neither government would give Auffenberg a 'blank cheque' for military spending and the second instalment of the new appropriation was actually deferred until 1914. The war minister had more money; he also had to move cautiously if he wanted still more. On the eve of the Balkan fighting, the Habsburg forces had gained legislative support for more men and money (and ultimately *matériel*); within weeks the need for these increases became abundantly clear.[32]

V

The General Staff and its chief had the task of linking the operational and mobilization planning of the three separate armies. In developing its war plans and in making its operational decisions, the

General Staff provided the networking for the three armies and served as their integrating mechanism. A product of the defeat at Sadowa in 1866, the General Staff had over four decades evolved into a separate entity, reporting directly to the monarch and with its chief having a status independent of the war minister and often more important than the war minister. Charged with drafting the war plans and with conducting the training functions for the army, the General Staff in 1912 had 280 officers assigned to it.[33]

Within the General Staff the operations and intelligence bureaux were the most crucial for strategic planning. Staffed by senior officers, these two bureaux were coordinated through the chief of the General Staff and his deputy. At the start of the Balkan Wars in 1912, the intelligence section had twenty-eight officers; by 1914, forty-two.[34] If its espionage coups were limited, the intelligence bureau did provide systematic appraisals of foreign armies, reasonably accurate force assessments and a fledgling code operation. Inadequate resources and the emperor's restrictions on the use of military attachés for spying functions limited the bureau's operational capabilities. Well informed about Russian troop strength and Serbian military politics, the intelligence bureau would, paradoxically, misinterpret both topics in the critical days of July 1914. Of the celebrated scandal involving Colonel Alfred Redl's homosexual liaisons and treason, little needs to be said. His revelations, though numerous, had minimal impact upon Russian plans against Austria–Hungary, though were possibly of some influence on Serbian arrangements. More surprising, the treason did not lead Vienna to change its own plans after the treachery was discovered.[35]

The views and strategic conceptions of the chief of the General Staff thoroughly shaped the drafting of war plans, possibly more so in the Habsburg forces than in any other European military establishment. No army was so dominated by its chief as were the Danubian forces by General Franz Conrad von Hötzendorf. From the moment he succeeded the ageing Friedrich Beck as chief in November 1906, Conrad worked to expand his powers, to press for increases in military manpower and budgets and to prepare Austria–Hungary for the war he believed would come. Continuously, acerbically, tenaciously, he argued for more military funds from War Minister Schönaich. A tough bureaucratic infighter, Conrad overstepped the bounds in late 1911 by demanding an attack on Italy while it was fighting in North Africa against the Turks. Franz

Joseph relieved him in November 1911 at Foreign Minister Aehrenthal's insistence. Only a year later, however, Franz Ferdinand successfully pressed the emperor to restore Conrad, since the archduke did not believe that Conrad's replacement, General Blasius Schemua, had the experience to handle the Balkan crisis. From December 1912 until March 1917, Conrad remained chief of staff, an overall tenure longer than any of his counterparts in the European armies and possibly none with more disastrous consequences for his own government.[36]

Conrad was also a more interesting personality than any of his counterparts. The only son of an ageing Napoleonic veteran, Conrad had spent nearly his entire life in uniform. A brief stint in Bosnia in 1878–79 constituted his closest brush with combat (he visited the front only three times during the First World War). He won early fame as a young officer writing about infantry tactics. Trained as a general staff officer, the future chief hated parades and believed field exercises were the only way to train troops. As an instructor at the War School he impressed a series of younger officers, who later became a reservoir for his future staff appointments. To this devoted group of admirers he preached the value of the offensive, the army as the instrument of salvation for the monarchy and the inevitability of struggle. He stressed the need for defensive imperialism to protect the monarchy. Thus he backed the annexation of Bosnia–Herzegovina, pressed for a showdown with Serbia, advocated a preemptive attack on Italy and wanted to annex Albania. Only in this aggressive fashion, he argued, could the monarchy overcome its inherent inner weaknesses.[37]

Behind his strident postures and zealous physical activity lurked another Conrad, one who needed and sought feminine flattery. Several women provided this companionship: his mother who lived with him until her death in 1915; his wife (the mother of four sons) who died in 1905; and Gina von Reininghaus, married, mother of six children and twenty-eight years younger than Conrad. He first encountered Gina at a party in Trieste in 1900, but then not again until at another party in Vienna in 1907. For the general, it was a case of immediate love, a love he wished to consummate but which Gina refused in 1907. His passion remained undiminished. He wrote thousands of letters filled with sensuous endearment, some so passionate that they were not sent. After Gina's husband returned to a former love, Conrad, Gina and Hermann von Reininghaus appeared *à trois*. Allegedly, Franz Joseph knew of the situation which grew increasingly more public. For Conrad, a hero's welcome following a military victory might offer the possibility of marrying Gina. This prospect may, as his letters suggest, have propelled Conrad forward in his constant advocacy of military action. Finally, in 1915, after his mother's death, he got his heart's desire. Franz Joseph agreed to let Gina be adopted by a protestant Hungarian general, have her marriage annulled and then allowed to marry Conrad. To the scandal of many, Gina then travelled to Conrad's army headquarters at Teschen where he exclaimed on her arrival: 'Now you are mine!' Conrad had got his war and his wife; his war plans and the monarchy's strategic position did not allow him to have victory as well.[38]

As chief of the General Staff, Conrad faced an unenviable challenge. Three potential enemies — Russia, Serbia and Italy — had to be considered. If Rumania ever left the alliance, there would be a fourth exposed flank. Russia loomed the most dangerous of the possible foes and Conrad's war plans concentrated upon the Russian threat. Furthermore, his military arrangements with the Germans centred upon Berlin deterring the Russians and if deterrence failed, then Germany's defeat of Russia. Conrad acknowledged St Petersburg as a danger, yet he occasionally treated this threat (even after the Balkan Wars) with a degree of carelessness that remains inexplicable. Still, he designed his operational war plans as a defence against Russia, for not even Conrad thought Austria–Hungary could do more. Only Germany, he believed, could deliver the knockout punch.[39]

After 1906 Conrad had gradually developed the new war plans. With Plan I (Italy) and B (Balkans), Conrad believed he could win a decisive victory. Both plans called for an Austro-Hungarian offensive against these lesser powers while providing a minimum defensive force against Russia. Plan R (Russia) dealt with Russian intervention after Vienna had attacked Serbia. In Plan R, Conrad believed he could still shift his offensive forces northward to meet the Russians. In this way, Conrad hoped to overcome his biggest strategic risk: a move against Serbia followed by a Russian attack once he had deployed his troops in the south. To that end, Conrad's plans had two defensive deployments, one in the Balkans and one along the Russian border. A third set of divisions, Echelon B, represented the decisive commitment. If the Echelon went south,

Plan I or B went into effect; if it went north, Plan R and total mobilization would take place. As a further safeguard against the Russian threat, Conrad also had a German commitment for offensive action in the east in the hope of deterring Russian intervention.

In late 1911 Conrad believed Plan B or Plan R offered the monarchy a chance of victory. He was confident that he and his associates had anticipated many of the details of a successful war. Because of Conrad's position, his plans and his personality, the general had a pivotal role in any decision about going to war. Franz Joseph and the other ministers must turn to him if they decided for war. Conrad's assessments and his plans would thus prove decisive. After 1906 he recognized the Russian danger and the trap of getting involved prematurely against Serbia. In 1914 he nevertheless fell into this trap. Other commanders erred in the summer of 1914, but none so grievously in spite of ample evidence advising caution as did General Conrad von Hötzendorf.

VI

Admiral Count Rudolf Montecuccoli, the naval counterpart to Conrad, was just as active prior to and during 1912. Modern observers generally smile at the Habsburg navy, but this reaction overlooks the size of the Habsburg naval forces, its impact on the budget process and its place in the formation of Habsburg strategic policies. In January 1914, for example, Austria–Hungary had more dreadnought tonnage at sea than Italy, its naval rival, and devoted at least 20 percent of its overall defence spending to naval forces. Indeed, the amounts assigned to naval construction (to Conrad's dismay) had steadily increased, in part because the new dreadnought construction offered the monarchy the possibility of parity with its Italian neighbour. The navy benefitted, moreover, from pressures from the big industrialists for naval contracts, from the example of the German naval build-up and from the continuing expansion of Habsburg maritime trade.[40]

Admiral Rudolf Montecuccoli headed the naval section within the War Ministry and served as commander of the naval forces from 1904 to early 1913. Despite the divided command responsibilities between Vienna and Pola, Montecuccoli played a major part in the development of Habsburg defence policy. He could attend the

Common Ministerial Council and represent the navy before the Delegations (the war minister, not Conrad, did this for the army). The admiral relentlessly pursued funds for the navy. In 1909–10 Montecuccoli even exceeded the bounds of established constitutional practice. Acting on his own authority (with possibly a wink from the Hofburg), he permitted civilian contractors to initiate construction on two dreadnoughts without formal authorization from the common ministers or the Delegations. He wanted the ships but also hoped the contracts would allow the construction firms to keep their workers. His actions prompted, however, a major crisis with the Hungarian government. Eventually, the impasse was defused when Montecuccoli agreed to build another dreadnought at the Hungarian shipyard in Fiume.[41]

Montecuccoli did not rest upon this triumph. Like Conrad, he pushed repeatedly during 1911 and 1912 for additional funds for construction. Indeed, even in October 1912 as the First Balkan War began, Montecuccoli still found Budapest unwilling to authorize more funds for still more dreadnought construction. The only concessions granted in October 1912 were authority and additional resources to complete the earlier programme more quickly. Frustrated and unable to obtain Franz Ferdinand's ambitious naval goals, Montecuccoli decided to accept retirement at the age of seventy in February 1913. He was immediately replaced by Admiral Anton Haus.[42]

The son of a farmer, Haus had entered the navy at eighteen and steadily worked his way to the top, becoming a rear-admiral in 1905 and a vice-admiral in 1912. With little hesitation, Haus quickly resumed Montecuccoli's demands for a second dreadnought squadron. At first his pleas were no more successful than his predecessor's. Then, with the completion of the first squadron nearing a reality and thus threatening to leave the shipyards without work, the two governments in the autumn of 1913 sanctioned a 1914–19 programme of 427 million crowns for four new dreadnoughts.[43]

In the effort to gain these funds, Admiral Haus, as had Montecuccoli, defined and defended the navy's role in the monarchy's overall strategic situation. Each argued that great power status required capital ships. At the same time, the dreadnoughts made Austria–Hungary a worthy ally to Italy and Germany who were themselves constructing such units. Furthermore, a sizeable force would ensure that Italy (the most probable enemy) remained a loyal ally or at least neutral. Of these justifications, the Italian problem was the most cogent, though often unstated. The naval build-up served to check Italy, protect the Dalmatian coast from possible Italian attacks should the two powers come to blows and provided Vienna with additional diplomatic leverage in the Balkans. On the other hand, Austria–Hungary in early 1913 also sought to expand its naval arrangements with Italy and Germany in case the Triple Alliance were an effective partnership in the Mediterranean. The prospects of alliance help, rather than a possibly hostile Italy, were the public stances used to justify the construction of the new dreadnoughts.[44]

The navy, like the army, had several contingency plans, but the admirals were notably vague about what followed mobilization. Beyond the obvious defensive measures in the Adriatic and along the monarchy's coasts, the fleet would 'await developments', — meaning Italian action. The plans in addition called for active coastal defences and an attack upon the Montenegrin batteries on Mount Lovčen in order to protect the inland harbour at Cattaro (Kotor). Whether the dreadnoughts would sail from Pola into the Adriatic depended upon the monarchy's enemies.[45]

Paradoxically, one part of the navy had no ambiguity about its role. The monitor flotilla on the Danube, six with supplemental motorboats, would from the start be used against Serbia. The ugly, flat-bottomed vessels would patrol the Danube and be ready for nearly instant action against Serbia. But for the moment, the public's eyes focused on the dreadnoughts, the governments bickered over their cost and the politicians counted the jobs the navy created both at the ports and with their suppliers. Almost as important, the ships represented also another visible symbol of Habsburg power. The admirals, like the generals, were leading participants in the foreign policy process.[46]

VII

The Habsburg monarchy's economic strength also influenced its foreign policy. In 1912 the monarchy had substantial investments in Rumania, Bulgaria and Serbia. It also attempted to foster economic development in Bosnia–Herzegovina as a possible way to reduce the attractiveness of Pan-Slav appeals. Furthermore, Vienna reacted aggressively to protect its substantial investments in the railways located in Macedonia and seized by Serbia during the Balkan Wars. But Vienna's financial activity in support of its diplomacy was modest and belated. For example, Berchtold only ordered subordinates to draft an economic package to entice Serbia from Russia *after* the Balkan conflicts began in 1912. By then the Habsburg offers were too little, too late.

There are several explanations for Vienna's failure to use economic leverage effectively in its foreign policy. First, the monarchy's banks simply did not have much excess capital. Though progressively stronger in the period of economic boom which began in 1900, the monarchy's own development left little for investment abroad. Indeed, the monarchy continued to receive significant infusions of foreign investment, principally German, to meet its own capital needs. With the French money markets closed because of the Franco-Russian alliance, and those in Britain not always available, the monarchy's ability to find capital was limited. While the percentage of external capital dropped proportionately after 1900, its presence served as a painful reminder of the monarchy's need for help.[47]

Also, Vienna found its German ally increasingly a competitor for influence in the Balkans. The German efforts, principally directed at Rumania and Greece, were more coherent than the erratic Habsburg endeavours. The German aggressiveness compounded Vienna's diminishing economic position in the Balkans.[48]

A third factor, especially after 1912, was Vienna's own pressing need for funds. The costs of the quasi-mobilization during the Balkan crisis not only dampened the monarchy's economic prosperity; it meant that capital was needed merely to make the government function. As a result, Vienna could not expand its early economic position in the Balkan capitals or use economic leverage to buttress its foreign policy objectives. More and more, German and French investors (the latter often at Russia's behest) filled the vacuum. In the scramble for influence and prestige in the Balkans, Vienna and Budapest relied less and less on economic measures and more and more on militant diplomacy and militant instruments. This shift of emphasis did not help to ensure the preservation of peace.[49]

VIII

The dynasty, the ministers, the diplomats and the generals were each participants in the Habsburg policy process. Each player had a special sphere of responsibility, each worked under Franz Joseph's overall direction and each represented a part of the monarchy's response to its foreign policy obligations. Tying these various actors together in the Habsburg policy apparatus depended in the final instance, as we have seen, on the emperor/king. But Franz Joseph also utilized the Common Ministerial Council for this purpose as well. By 1912 the Council had become the crucial forum for decisions affecting the development, coordination and execution of Habsburg strategic policy. Linking the two governments and the common ministers together, the Council consisted of the three common ministers and the two prime ministers. The naval head could attend the Council when naval issues were discussed and Conrad also gained the right to appear if strategic issues were being considered. In addition, the finance ministers of the two governments were often present.[50]

The Common Ministerial Council represented a pragmatic response to the constitutional arrangements created by the *Ausgleich*. Determined to create no imperial or *Reich* institution for the joint state beyond the monarchy and the defence forces, the Magyars had eschewed any idea of a common cabinet or common parliament. Every institution that represented common interests had to be carefully circumscribed to prevent any usurpation of Hungarian rights. Thus the Common Ministerial Council was just that, not a free-standing institution but an arrangement for the conduct of the common affairs of the monarchy and the two national governments. The limits of the Council's jurisdiction were more carefully defined than its powers. Above all, the Council could not intrude into the domestic affairs of the two governments. Those remained the sole province of Budapest and Vienna. Commitments made in the Council would be translated into action by the separate ministers at home if necessary or by the common ministers as appropriate. In each instance, the definitions were finite and precise.

Nevertheless, the Common Ministerial Council addressed significant topics. Meeting, for example, thirty-nine times from 1910 to July 31, 1914 (an average of every six weeks), the ministers debated Bosnia–Herzegovina, military reform, naval construction, army requests and general budget questions. In each instance, the topics were common and reflected the *Ausgleich* commitment to great power status. More importantly, the Council repeatedly discussed issues of war and peace during the crises of the Balkan Wars and, of course, after Sarajevo. The discussions were throughout frank, revealing and sometimes bitter. The Council met to define and to resolve, not merely to ratify. Summoned by the foreign minister who acted as convener and record keeper, the participants did not hesitate to invoke national considerations as each bargained for position. Budget discussions were especially lively, since commitments there defined the common budget for the Delegations and a major share of the national budgets as well.

Since the *Ausgleich* gave the Magyar prime minister a voice in foreign-policy decisions (replicated less explicitly for the Austrian one as well), major foreign-policy decisions were discussed in advance with each government. Thus Aehrenthal disclosed his intention to annex Bosnia–Herzegovina two months before acting. Later, Berchtold would present his plans for action against Montenegro in May 1913 as he did his thoughts in July 1914 about action against Serbia. Yet the requirement for consultation could be loosely interpreted. A foreign minister such as Berchtold could take action that came dangerously close to committing the monarchy to a policy of conflict. Neither the foreign minister nor the military chiefs felt compelled to define for the Common Ministerial Council the operational details of their plans. The Council forum existed to coordinate and facilitate. It did not act as an operational centre once a policy had been decided. That remained the sole responsibility of the monarch. Once the Council accepted the outlines of a policy, its detailed implementation fell to the respective ministries or governments.

IX

The eve of the Balkan crisis of 1912 found the Habsburg monarchy in a period of ambivalent confidence. An ageing emperor stirred doubts about the future, as did the judgement and temperament of his heir-apparent. A new foreign minister, relatively inexperienced and untested, had replaced a veteran who had major diplomatic successes to his credit. Indeed, the alliance and entente structures had survived the Second Moroccan Crisis in the summer of 1911, when German manoeuvres for a Moroccan port threatened an Anglo-French-German military and naval confrontation. Ironically, as Paris and Berlin moved to resolve their differences, Rome decided to exploit the situation by attacking Turkish-held Tripoli (Libya) in late September 1911, thus reopening the question of Turkey's survival. A Habsburg army, meanwhile, remained inadequate to meet its strategic assignments, not having been altered in size since 1889. The Austro-Hungarian navy had a dreadnought squadron under construction but few other impressive assets. While the domestic economy appeared sound, the idea of an assertive Habsburg economic policy in the Balkans played no role in the foreign policy agenda. On almost every issue the strengths, but more critically the weaknesses, of the *Ausgleich* were evident. Common goals, agreed programmes and a discernible future seldom found expression at the same time. Above all, the Balkans and the nationality issues there could not be ignored. The annexation of Bosnia–Herzegovina in 1908 had solved some issues while creating new ones. A vulnerable Ottoman empire endangered not only itself but the unstable situation that had prevailed in the Balkans since 1908. These concerns were real and urgent, a powerful and dangerous legacy of Aehrenthal's earlier success.

4   Aehrenthal's Legacy: Bosnian Colonial Success and the Italo-Turkish War

Accounts of nineteenth-century European imperialism usually omit Austria–Hungary. Yet at the Congress of Berlin in 1878 Vienna gained administrative responsibility for the Turkish provinces of Bosnia and Herzegovina. The Dual Monarchy thus participated in the liquidation of the Ottoman empire from the start. Cyprus, Egypt, Tunisia, Morocco and eventually Tripoli (Libya) would thereafter also be lost to Constantinople. Vienna set the pattern that other states would imitate in the scramble for lands in the Mediterranean. Local unrest, fears of political instability, strategic concerns, a collective 'official mind' pressing for action and fears that another government might seize the opportunity first: all spurred Habsburg action as later they would London, Paris and Rome. The problems encountered in administering Bosnia and Herzegovina after 1878 would come to set much of the subsequent strategic and economic agenda for the Dual Monarchy.[1]

With the occupation of the two provinces the Danubian monarchy formally acknowledged that the Balkans had replaced Germany as Austria–Hungary's principal sphere of concern. The monarchy had thus resumed its earlier mission of serving as a bridge to the east. With this step Franz Joseph, his foreign minister Count Julius Andrássy and their advisers put into sharper focus two issues which the German question had often obscured: Russia's potential hostility over the future of the Balkan peninsula and the fate of the South Slavs already living in the Habsburg realms. Although Bosnian issues were often crucial for the monarchy's future, political leaders had to operate within the framework of the joint state. By design the *Ausgleich* deliberately avoided any appearance of a commonality or imperial concern that would strengthen the overall monarchy instead of its two constituent states. Thus the administration of Bosnia–Herzegovina raised issues the *Ausgleich* had not anticipated. Yet not until 1908 and the Bosnian crisis would the full ramifications of the 1878 decision be unmistakably clear.

Aehrenthal's decision in 1908 to annex formally the provinces revived the Balkan tension. It would soon be exacerbated by the Second Moroccan Crisis and Italy's invasion of Tripoli. The Congress of Berlin, the development of the Triple Alliance and the events at Sarajevo in 1914, though separated by decades, are inextricably linked together.

I

After 1871 Austria–Hungary's most fundamental foreign policy problems centred upon its relationship with St Petersburg. The progressive collapse of Ottoman power realigned the interests of the two powers. As Serbia, Rumania and Bulgaria emerged as independent states, Vienna and St Petersburg strove to win influence over the new governments. For Vienna, a strong presence in the Balkans constituted a continuation of its historic mission as a bridge between west and east, Christians and Turks, civilization and barbarism. Willing to share that role with Russia under defined conditions, Vienna could never accept that Pan-Slavism gave St Petersburg any legitimate right to endanger Habsburg interests by supporting the South Slavs. Yet it was precisely Pan-Slavism's relentless claim to universality and to the kinship of all Slavs, wherever in the Habsburg monarchy and in the Balkans, that challenged the Habsburg monarchy's very existence. Nonetheless, for three decades after 1878, the two governments masked their potential confrontation through cooperation, abstinence and spheres of influence. And, on occasion, St Petersburg sought to muffle the Pan-Slav appeals. But when the Russians turned back to Europe and the Balkans following the czar's retreat before the Japanese in 1905, tensions between Vienna and St Petersburg increased. The 1908 crisis over Bosnia simply magnified the antagonisms while also making accommodation with each other more difficult. Both states were determined to play in the same Balkan sandbox, so to speak, both thus increased the stakes of their competition.

As this rivalry intensified, so did the value of Vienna's alliance with Berlin. Signed in 1879, this alliance had ensured both Berlin and Vienna that neither would find itself isolated against Russia. Yet for much of the Dual Alliance's existence, it was a passive relationship, without specific military or naval dimensions, reflecting

more an attitude of cooperation than a latent defensive arrangement. Neither Germany nor Austria–Hungary originally considered
their actions rigidly bound by the accord. Then Germany pursued a
more aggressive *Weltpolitik*, an Anglo-French understanding
emerged and Russia decided after 1905 to focus its attention upon
Europe. As the Triple Entente of Britain, France and Russia
gradually took shape, Vienna's alliance ties with Berlin became
increasingly important.[2]

The Austro-Italian alliance, which with the Dual Alliance constituted the Triple Alliance, also became potentially more important
for Vienna. Always divided by Italian irredentism's claim to the
Italian part of the Tirol and Trieste and by Vienna's ties with the
Vatican, the relationship between Rome and Vienna fluctuated
dramatically. The two governments usually saw more benefits from
talking to each other — often through the medium of German
diplomats in the context of the Triple Alliance — than in being
openly hostile. Both looked upon the Balkans as a natural field
for their expansion, though Italy paid more attention to Albania
and Montenegro than to the upper Adriatic coast. As long as
French ambitions in the Mediterranean defused the Austro-Italian
rivalry and German capital continued to flow into Italy, the alliance
had positive benefits for both Austria and Italy. But Italian
nationalism, the defeats of 1859, and the memories of Italian
cupidity, all helped to shape the way Franz Joseph and some of his
subordinates, especially Conrad, viewed Italy. Nationalism Italian-
style could be damaging, even disastrous to the Habsburgs. Franz
Joseph never forgot this lesson of history after the first two decades
of his rule.[3]

After the defeats in Italy and Germany in the 1850s and 1860s,
the Balkans had, not surprisingly, become the renewed focus of
Habsburg diplomatic activity. In earlier centuries Vienna had
defended the west against the Turks, then assisted in the gradual
erosion of Ottoman power in the Balkans. Now, as the Turkish
power receded, Austria–Hungary hoped to move into the vacuum
— if not as ruler, at least as the dominant political and cultural
power. With Turkey still strong enough in the Balkans to threaten
the independence of Bulgaria, Rumania and Serbia, Constantinople
became a virtual silent partner with Vienna in keeping the Balkan
states from becoming too assertive. Until a palace coup in 1903,

Vienna manipulated the Serbian royal family. After 1903 Serbia awakened images of a new Italy for the Habsburg policy-makers: difficult, expansive, intemperate. Furthermore, Serbia had in Russia a major patron. The growing fusion of interests between Belgrade and St Petersburg would constitute the most dynamic change in the international system for Habsburg diplomats. Subsequent efforts to create Albania and to thwart Serbian access to the Adriatic sprang from Vienna's perception of a Serbian threat supported by the czar. This apprehension came to dominate Habsburg decision-making, and especially in the summer of 1914.[4]

Buffeted by the growing Serbo-Russian collaboration and the evolving effectiveness of the Triple Entente, Austria–Hungary after 1907 operated in a European international system subtly, progressively in the process of a change. Berlin's aggressive *Weltpolitik* swept Austria–Hungary along, not as a participant but as perceived accomplice. With no alternative to German friendship and with St Petersburg less congenial, Vienna found its alliance ties with Berlin becoming ever closer. As Berlin challenged the Triple Entente, the other Triple Alliance powers — albeit with fits and starts — found themselves pulled along. For Austria–Hungary the surge of Russian activity in Europe meant a direct, rather than a peripheral challenge. The Anglo-French and the Anglo-Russian ententes of 1904 and 1907 freed those powers from colonial disputes. The net benefit, not least from Britain's viewpoint, was the ability of France and a reviving Russia to provide counterweights against Berlin. In this arrangement, Austria–Hungary had much to lose and very little to gain.[5]

The Habsburg monarchy, largely held together because of foreign policy considerations, thus confronted a changing international scene. Adroit defensive diplomacy constituted one of the monarchy's tools for survival. After 1912 that tool would, however, be viewed as increasingly less effective. Military force, not negotiation, soon preoccupied the policy-makers as a possible option. In July 1914 the Habsburg decision-makers opted for war; that decision would doom the monarchy. In one sense, therefore, Vienna's road to war sprang from its own disillusioned perspective of the European diplomatic scene. Those disappointments were, however, amply reinforced by internal political considerations, and, most of all, from its problems in Bosnia–Herzegovina.[6]

II

In 1871 Julius Andrássy, until then the Hungarian prime minister, became the Habsburg foreign minister. His early preferences were to preserve the Ottoman empire and especially the Turkish position in the Balkans. After the outbreak of rebellion in Herzegovina and then Bosnia in 1875, Andrássy eventually agreed with St Petersburg on a limited partition of the Balkans. The Hungarian statesman had no wish to add more Slavs to the Danubian monarchy; he feared endless complications with Russia and recognized that seizing Bosnia–Herzegovina might be followed by a dangerous partitioning of Macedonia. Yet Andrássy could not risk allowing the two provinces to go to Serbia or Russia. Thus, demonstrating his conservative realism, he accepted the concept of partition by negotiating the Reichstadt agreement of July 1876 with Russia.[7]

Meanwhile, the Emperor Franz Joseph and his military advisers pondered the deteriorating Ottoman position. For decades unrest in Bosnia had plagued the Habsburg military, prompting apprehension about their borders and the strategic protection of the Dalmatian coast line. Serbian and Montenegrin leadership in the unrest among the Christian subjects could not be ignored either. Serbian speeches about uniting Bosnia and Herzegovina with Belgrade at some future point were not comforting. Indeed, preventing the very possibility of a Serbian grab of the two provinces had long preoccupied the Habsburg military. As early as 1856, Field Marshall Count Josef Wenzel Radetzky had actually proposed the incorporation of the two provinces. In the early 1870s, with the German issue settled, Archduke Albrecht and Friedrich Beck renewed the pressure to take the adjacent lands. Franz Joseph demonstrated his interest with his extended visit to Dalmatia in the spring of 1875 when he met Prince Nikita (later King) of Montenegro and received deputations from Bosnia–Herzegovina pleading for protection against the Ottoman rule. For the emperor, military concerns meshed easily with concerns about his prestige: acquiring territory instead of losing it had a definite appeal.[8]

The Congress of Berlin allowed Andrássy to collect his share of the Reichstadt accord. Bosnia and Herzegovina were entrusted to Habsburg rule for administrative purposes; the other great powers believed this arrangement would lead to eventual annexation. Franz Joseph and the military were jubilant. The public reception, however, throughout the monarchy was less enthusiastic. The Hungarians as well as the German-Austrians disliked the prospect of still more South Slavs. Nor were the Bosnians happy with the turn of events. Habsburg forces encountered tough resistance when they occupied the lands in the summer of 1878. The military mobilized 250,000 men and were soon engaged in a campaign that lasted until early autumn, with 5,198 casualties. But through the occupation Austria–Hungary became a colonial power. The emperor and the military achieved strategic protection over Dalmatia and the monarchy's southern flank. The new questions were now how to administer, defend and develop the new colonial acquisitions.

After some hesitation, the two governments in 1880 assigned Bosnia and Herzegovina to the common finance minister for administrative purposes. So long as the Ottoman empire retained titular sovereignty, the emperor/king remained the source of all authority and law. The common finance minister answered only to Franz Joseph and in practice offered only modest and sometimes misleading information to the Delegations or other authorities.[9]

The common finance ministers, first Benjamin Kállay (1882–1903) and then István Burián (1903–12) quickly became more powerful than the military authorities in the two areas. In Sarajevo a *Landeschef* (a military officer) and a civilian bureaucrat (the Civil Adlatus) oversaw the day-to-day administrative operations of the two provinces and reported in detail to the common finance minister. As would be true for the other imperial powers, the Habsburg colonial bureaucracy rapidly expanded. The Ottoman rulers had used 180 agents; in contrast, the Habsburgs paid at least 7,300 by 1897 and 9,500 by 1908.

These officials worked within a narrow set of parameters. The 1880 imperial rescript for Bosnia–Herzegovina decreed that Austria–Hungary would extract the costs of operating the provinces from the revenues of the provinces *per se*. Budapest wanted no common funds (that is, no Hungarian funds) to go to Sarajevo. This policy remained intact until 1914 and as a result of it many of the efforts to improve the lives of the populace and to dim the allure of Serbia to the South Slavs were destined to fail. Kállay and Burián managed to get some common funds for railway construction, while strategic and military purposes consumed other common resources. All other capital improvements had to come from the capital-poor agriculture economy (at least 85 percent of the total). These same policy considerations governed all other aspects of the colonial administration. Vienna and Budapest denied any initiative that might help the other if the provinces were ever partitioned between the two governments. Despite these restrictions, the common finance ministers were able to govern and achieve modest economic and social progress.[10]

Several areas reveal the magnitude of change in Bosnia–Herzegovina in the thirty years after the Congress of Berlin. First, the population increased significantly, from approximately one million in 1878 to 1,898,055 in 1910. Improved medical and sanitation facilities contributed to this growth. Second, the number of students in schools went from 22,748 in 1894–5 to 41,130 in 1909–10 and illiteracy was reduced (though it still remained very high). Yet only a handful of gymnasiums and a few confessional schools existed in the two provinces. For higher education, dozens of Bosnian students were still forced to go to Austria–Hungary or to Belgrade.[11]

Industrial development in the area gained some impetus under the Habsburgs. Metallurgy and forestry advanced and to a lesser extent so did mining and textiles. Facing a lack of capital that hampered industrialization, Kállay attacked the problem by forming state enterprises and offering investment concessions to those who would put their capital into the colonies. For example, a Bavarian entrepreneur, with a forestry concession near Doberlin and Jajce, built 375.3 kilometres of railway to transport his products and employed 3,000 workers. When he wished to retire in 1913, the government bought this profitable enterprise. Kállay also encouraged the formation of banks, usually with Austrian or Hungarian capital, but these institutions did not promote industrialization. Rather, they concentrated on merchant and agricultural loans. Finally, the ministers improved the tax-collection system, raised the levies and skillfully administered tobacco and salt monopolies. This provided some investment capital and the funds necessary to operate the government in the provinces. In fact, the consolidated budgets for Bosnia and Herzegovina after 1882 nearly always balanced or came closer than either the Austrian or the Hungarian efforts. Given their constraints, Kállay and Burián turned in creditable performances.[12]

In the crucial area of land reform and agricultural production, however, an exploitive mentality continued to prevail. The inhabitants of the provinces fell into three major religious groupings:

Orthodox Christian 42 percent, Muslim 38 percent and Catholic 18 percent. These groupings profoundly influenced the approach to land reform. In 1878, approximately two-thirds of the population, often Orthodox Christians, had a *kmet* (serf) relationship (a form of tenant farmer with restrictions on movement) with Muslim landlords. In contrast, nearly 80 percent of all Muslims were free men. Any land reform would help the larger Orthodox Christian group. But this group, often Serb and using the Cyrillic alphabet, aroused Austro-Hungarian suspicions because of possible South Slav sympathies. Thus Vienna and Budapest were prepared to ally with the Muslims (despite religious differences) because the landlords were perceived to be more loyal to the Habsburg system.[13]

Rather than make any systematic effort to correct this socioeconomic imbalance caused by Muslim law restricting land holding to Muslims, the Habsburgs pampered the Muslim landlords in an effort to buttress Habsburg authority. The monarchy eventually allowed the *kmets* to purchase the lands they cultivated. But these changes were slow and cumbersome. Only after 1900 would the Habsburgs belatedly encourage more effective efforts to rectify the landholding patterns and thus neutralize South Slav criticism. By then the opportunity to gain Orthodox gratitude had passed and the Bosnian Muslims responded by organizing against the Habsburgs as well. Land reform in the two colonies, as in Hungary, was stymied.

Elsewhere, the railway system improved, yet the military requirements for this network were never met. In 1880 the railways covered approximately 290 kilometres, including lines built to assist the occupation. By 1908 the track reached nearly 1,500 kilometres. Military expenditures account for some of the increase, but Kállay also tried to modernize transport capabilities. Still problems persisted. Much of the track was small gauge, necessitating transshipment of goods and people at the borders. Some track did not connect with other lines, which hindered efficient movement. Poor construction required constant repairs and caused delays. The Budapest government nullified efforts to construct a trans-Bosnian railway that would connect an Adriatic port and greatly improve commerce and troop movements. Instead, the Magyars wanted to direct the lines exclusively through Budapest and thus put them under Magyar control. For years, disputes between the Austrian and Hungarian governments prevented the emergence of a major building programme that would have rationalized the systems. The Magyars held firm on every point even in the face of military pleas. Finally, in February 1913 a more comprehensive plan emerged. But construction had not begun when the fighting started in 1914. An underdeveloped railway system denied the Habsburg military a truly effective geographical barrier in Bosnia and Herzegovina against Serbia.[14]

The Habsburg presence in the two provinces was a constant reminder of the colonial status of the area. So also was the Habsburg military presence in the Sanjak of Novi Pazar, still under active Turkish administration but with the Habsburg troops there as an added barrier. Except for the fighting that accompanied the organized occupation and some resistance when conscription was introduced in Bosnia and Herzegovina in 1882, the provinces were quiet and remarkably peaceful. Bosnian recruits made excellent soldiers and provided a pool of some trained manpower. New fortifications were completed along the border areas, though much more remained to be done. Headquartered at Sarajevo, the XV Corps constituted the monarchy's first line of defence against Serbia and Montenegro. In each instance, the primary role of Habsburg forces was defence. Paradoxically, the occupation of the two provinces did not produce a major realignment of the monarchy's war plans. Not until Conrad's arrival in 1906 would there be a more systematic appraisal of the monarchy's military vulnerabilities in Bosnia–Herzegovina, a situation now rendered far more dangerous by the accession of the Karadjordjević dynasty to the throne in Belgrade and hence a more defiant Serbia.[15]

III

Aehrenthal's arrival at the Ballhausplatz brought no immediate alteration in Habsburg foreign policy nor of Habsburg policy toward Bosnia and Herzegovina. Anxious to re-establish the monarchy's diplomatic position and to assert its independence of Berlin, the new minister at first continued the existing Austro-Russian entente in the Balkans. He sought to buttress that cooperation and force changes in Turkish rule in Macedonia, hoping to forestall a return to a policy of partition. Aehrenthal planned for an assertive Habsburg foreign policy, but not before he had laid the ground work for it.

Events and his own colleagues did not allow Aehrenthal the luxury of proceeding cautiously for too long. The conclusion of the Anglo-Russian accord in 1907, while focused on a series of extra-European issues, heralded still another change in the diplomatic alignment on the Continent. While the *entente cordiale* was not yet the Triple Entente, the London–St Petersburg connection jolted the international system at a time when the Anglo-German naval rivalry was growing more intense. The success of Russian Foreign Minister Alexander Izvolsky in offsetting the worst effects of the Japanese defeat provided a challenge that the Habsburg minister could not ignore.[16]

Vienna's relations with Serbia had, meanwhile, continued to deteriorate. The first issues centred upon trade questions. Serbia's efforts to escape Habsburg hegemony on trade questions led to the so-called Pig War, in which Hungary closed its borders to pork imports. This step in 1906 exacerbated Habsburg–Serb relations without resolving any basic issues. Clearly, the Habsburg policy of economic intimidation through border closings had not worked. Serbia's new self-confidence also challenged one of the primary assumptions governing the administration of Bosnia–Herzegovina: that Serbian agitation could be kept in check and the colonies left to develop independently. Equally disturbing, turmoil among the Macedonian Christians flared again. There were new demands for Turkish reform; the Serbian, Bulgarian and Montenegrin govern-ments at the same time accelerated their own involvement with these insurgent Christian groups.[17]

While Aehrenthal pondered these developments, he had also to deal with the impetuous demands of Conrad von Hötzendorf, the new chief of the General Staff. While the general blustered about attacking Italy in 1907, his attention soon shifted to the Balkans later that year. What he saw disturbed him. He began to press Aehrenthal for a two-pronged policy: annexation of Bosnia–Herzegovina and the partition of Serbia. During late 1907 and early 1908 Conrad repeatedly urged these views on Aehrenthal, whether in person, by letter or via memoranda and in his audiences with Emperor/King Franz Joseph. Suddenly, the senior military leadership wanted to change the legal status of the two provinces and to resolve relations with Serbia, even at the risk of war. To make all of this more tolerable, Conrad suggested giving the European powers the assurance that Austria–Hungary did not want more Balkan territory and that Turkey could completely reoccupy the Sanjak of Novi Pazar.[18]

Conrad's insistent pressures and the rapidly shifting international situation meshed with Aehrenthal's own desire to revive the monarchy's prestige. Their efforts resulted in the Bosnian crisis of 1908–09 in which the foreign minister successfully annexed the two provinces, destroyed a decade or more of Austro-Russian cooperation and brought Austria and Serbia to the brink of military confrontation. To understand the evolution of Habsburg foreign and strategic policy after 1912, four interlocking themes from the 1908–09 crisis require analysis: how the Austro-Russian relationship collapsed, the method by which the Triple Alliance operated during the crisis, the extent of Habsburg military preparations and the continuing impact of the *Ausgleich* upon the style and substance of Habsburg decision-making.[19]

Initially, an Austro-Russian deal over the Balkans and the Straits at Constantinople seemed entirely possible. By midsummer 1908, both Aehrenthal and Izvolsky believed they could reach a *quid pro quo* agreement. The areas for compromise included Balkan railway construction, the annexation of Bosnia–Herzegovina and changes in the legal status of the Straits at Constantinople. On 27 August 1908 the Habsburg foreign minister, after making a few important changes, accepted the Russian offer of 2 July to discuss a settlement on these points.[20]

The two men agreed to meet at Buchlau, the Moravian estate of Berchtold (then Habsburg ambassador to Russia) on 16 September while Izvolsky toured the western capitals. This timing suited Aehrenthal beautifully, for he had become increasingly alarmed over the potential impact of the recent Young Turk revolution upon the constitutional status of Bosnia–Herzegovina. Izvolsky was also pleased, for the timing gave him the opportunity to raise the Straits questions in each of the European capitals.

The conversations were vigorous and productive. The major lines of an agreement were in place and the Austro-Russian entente apparently reinvigorated. Bosnia–Herzegovina would be annexed, the Sanjak evacuated, Bulgaria would receive *de jure* independence from Turkey and Vienna would strongly support a change in the Straits. On one detail — the timing of the annexation — much discussion later followed. But at the time neither Izvolsky nor Aehrenthal questioned that the latter would announce the step before the Delegations met in early October. The Russian statesman accepted this concession, apparently confident that the czar would support any agreement that settled the Straits issue. But Izvolsky failed to appreciate adequately the fact that he was sanctioning the annexation of the two provinces without any compensation for Serbia. When Aehrenthal and Izvolsky parted from Berchtold's estate, the Vienna–St Petersburg connection looked intact. Within weeks it was in shambles.

As Aehrenthal negotiated with St Petersburg, he also carefully and discretely sounded his Italian and German counterparts, both of whom were on summer vacation. He met Italian Foreign Minister Tommaso Tittoni on 4 September at Salzburg and German Foreign Secretary Wilhelm Schoen the next day at Berchtesgaden. In these sessions, Aehrenthal hinted broadly at possible changes in the status of Bosnia–Herzegovina but offered no details. He had alerted his allies without permitting them to intrude. These sessions reaffirmed the pattern of German support and Italian acquiesence to Habsburg action. Vienna did not test the waters with the other European states.

Aehrenthal worked meanwhile to secure the approval of his associates in the Habsburg government. Worried about the pace of the Young Turk revolt, Franz Joseph readily agreed to annexation. Significantly, the *Thronfolger* was not informed. Aehrenthal feared Franz Ferdinand might prematurely tell Kaiser William II about Vienna's intentions. Conrad, as expected, backed the action and still hoped that he might have a showdown with Serbia. War Minister Schönaich and Common Finance Minister Burián assented. But the Austrian and Hungarian prime ministers expressed major reservations over the intended annexation in a Common Ministerial Council meeting on 19 August. The Austrian leader, Max Wladimir Beck, questioned whether the foreign minister had prepared the international scene for this action and the Hungarian leader, Alexander Wekerle, objected on constitutional grounds. Their resistance forced the foreign minister to delay any further steps and necessitated a second Council meeting in Budapest on 10 September. This time the two prime ministers gave their support. The constitutional process prescribed by the 1867 accord had been carefully followed, causing some confusion but not essentially altering Aehrenthal's programme. Given this approval and then his subsequent success with Izvolsky, the foreign minister wrote to

Franz Joseph on 17 September that only details remained to be settled.[21]

By late September Aehrenthal probably congratulated himself on having beautifully manipulated both the international and the domestic contexts. His haste to complete the annexation before the Delegations met in Budapest on 8 October and Izvolsky's gross misreading of the situation in St Petersburg, however, set the stage for a major diplomatic crisis. The premature announcement of the impending annexation (on 4 October instead of 7 October) provoked sharp reactions from the emergent Triple Entente, from Italy, privately from Germany and resoundingly from Serbia and Turkey. Aehrenthal's desire to present the Delegations with a *fait accompli* rather than wait until their adjournment, represented a major tactical misjudgement. Whether he could have avoided a significant crisis, given Izvolsky's haphazard assessment of his own position, is very doubtful. But Aehrenthal's timing ensured that the Austro-Russian entente had no chance of survival.

The ensuing Bosnian crisis lasted until the very last day of March 1909. During the dispute Aehrenthal managed to offend, temporarily, almost all of the powers. Nevertheless, the foreign minister never wavered: he would not agree to an international conference except to ratify the results; make any concessions to Serbia beyond the withdrawal from the Sanjak; or offer payment to the Turks for annexing Bosnia–Herzegovina. He did finally, through a series of artifices, agree to financial compensation to Constantinople and he permitted Montenegro a minor treaty change which allowed it to defend itself better against Austria–Hungary. Moreover, he offered to sign a new trade treaty with Belgrade and talked of the possibility of a Danube to the Adriatic railway line to benefit Serbia. Yet Aehrenthal would entertain no thought of territorial compensation to Belgrade. Nor would he agree to establish an Italian university in Trieste as a sop to Rome. The French, after an initial outburst against Vienna, turned to other things. By contrast, Sir Edward Grey (the British foreign secretary) and the British played a continuing role, especially in March 1909 when Fairfax Cartwright, their ambassador to Austria–Hungary, helped the Austrian leaders find a way to allow St Petersburg to extricate itself from the crisis. Berlin's barely concealed ultimatum to Russia in March 1909, along with London's help, quickly brought the crisis to an end.[22]

Vienna's troubles with Serbia were more difficult and dangerous.

Serbia had immediately ordered military measures, launched vitriolic press attacks on the Danubian monarchy and encouraged the
formation of the *Narodna Odbrana* as a political pressure group.
While the Serbian military received little overt encouragement from
their Russian counterparts, their own hubris made the situation
explosive, especially since their actions challenged a truculent
Conrad. With each belligerent Serbian step, Conrad renewed his
demands for military action.[23]

Throughout the crisis Foreign Minister Aehrenthal, Franz Joseph
and Archduke Franz Ferdinand restrained the Habsburg military.
Indeed, the foreign minister managed to keep the policy process
dominated by political and diplomatic considerations, not military
ones. At the start of the crisis Conrad had been allowed to mobilize
some extra units. But the political authorities blocked his pleas for
more measures until the crisis culminated in March. At that time
many, even Aehrenthal, thought war was likely. Hence the government allowed the General Staff to begin mobilizing extra men. Since
Serbia still refused to capitulate, on 27 March the Common
Ministerial Council authorized Conrad to move to partial mobilization in the Plan B scenario. Before these measures could be
implemented, however, Belgrade, left without Russian support,
capitulated. No longer deemed necessary, the partial military
measures were halted. Probably the March measures urged by
Conrad had made no impression in Belgrade. Rather, staunch
German support for its Austrian partner made St Petersburg relent
and force Belgrade to yield. Yet Conrad and the diplomats could
also believe that militant behaviour had reinforced the Habsburg
position. That lesson would not be forgotten. Nor would the
governments forget the costs — 180 million crowns or almost half of
a year's regular army budget. Assertive diplomacy did not come
cheaply.[24]

Two further by-products of the crisis influenced future strategic
planning. First, with Aehrenthal's consent, Conrad contacted General
Helmut von Moltke, chief of the German General Staff, about
coordinating war plans. From these discussions, which continued
until 1914, came enhanced military cooperation and a definite
German willingness to be drawn into a possible Balkan conflict.
Second, Conrad left the crisis angry with Aehrenthal for not having
demanded war with Serbia and thus completing the plan for
partition. The general would repeatedly bewail the monarchy's

failure to destroy the Serbian threat when it knew that Russia would not intervene. Hereafter Conrad would return, endlessly, to cite the Habsburg lack of resolve in 1909 as a major policy defeat and to chastise Aehrenthal, then Berchtold and even Franz Joseph for this failure. His refrain may have mesmerized him in 1914, when he was oblivious to the fact that Russia would intervene if necessary.[25]

The Bosnian crisis left a mixed legacy for Aehrenthal. Austria–Hungary had demonstrated its resolve to act independently of Berlin. But the Habsburg minister also wrecked the Austro-Hungarian détente with St Petersburg and helped to strengthen the Anglo-Russian connection. Within the Triple Alliance he had shown Bülow and Schoen that he could be resolute, even deceitful. Their successors, Theobald von Bethmann Hollweg and Alfred von Kiderlen-Wächter, respectively, took less charitable views of Aehrenthal's self-assertiveness. Like Bismarck after 1870, Aehrenthal's actions in 1908 made his subsequent protestations — that the monarchy was now 'saturated' — suspect. Rome remained antagonized, willing to flirt anew with members of the Triple Entente and to seek a more independent role in the Balkans. The Turks lost only prestige. Yet the Turkish inability to respond made them a very tempting target later for Italy and Russia through the Balkan League.

In the south the Serbian problem had increased, not diminished. Instead of exorcising the Serbian issue, annexation of the two provinces inflamed Serbian passions. Although Austria–Hungary and Serbia would sign a trade treaty in July 1910, relations between the two neighbours grew steadily worse. Bosnia–Herzegovina now became the focus of Serbian intrigue, *Narodna Odbrana* activity and the rallying cry for South Slavs. The colonies, though now in a kind of 'commonwealth' status, were in fact more susceptible than ever to South Slav agitation. Furthermore, Conrad soon realized that the decision to abandon the Sanjak left a tempting target for both Serbia and Montenegro to seize. Although originally advocated by Conrad, he roundly criticized Aehrenthal for this strategic *faux pas*. The South Slav neighbours could now be physically linked, allowing new opportunities to harass the Dual Monarchy. Aehrenthal's diplomatic gesture to the Turks had strategic liabilities.[26]

Within the Habsburg monarchy the diplomatic success did not arrest the downward swirl of Austrian or Hungarian domestic politics. Friction between the two governments over the annexation inflamed differences. And there were other consequences, still less pleasant, when the public learned in the Friedjung trial later in 1909 of the government's use of forged documents to discredit Slav politicians. During the Bosnian crisis Aehrenthal had asked his friend, the Austrian historian Heinrich Friedjung, to examine documents from Belgrade and then write a press column assailing the South Slav political figures for disloyalty. Friedjung complied with the request, only to learn that the documents had been forged. These revelations of political intimidation focused on Aehrenthal and the Ballhausplatz; they helped neither the minister's reputation nor the amelioration of Slavic discontent. Domestic political rancor, long entrenched on nationality issues, could not be diverted by international diplomatic success, even for the German and Magyar ruling groups. Furthermore, with the colonial possessions now formally a part of the monarchy, though neither Austrian nor Hungarian, their status caused even more bickering between Vienna and Budapest. Every attempt at an initiative in Bosnia won the immediate and intense scrutiny of Vienna and Budapest, as Minister Burián repeatedly discovered.[27]

Within Bosnia and Herzegovina, Common Finance Minister Burián tried hard to create a new political and administrative system. In 1910 Franz Joseph sanctioned the creation of a Landtag in Sarajevo with a carefully designed curial system that gave the Catholics and Muslims the upper hand politically over the Orthodox Serbs. A rudimentary parliamentary life jolted along in a highly politicized atmosphere. Efforts for land reform intensified; the drive for a comprehensive railway network found new impetus; and demands for improving social and educational issues were renewed.[28]

Burián's agent on the scene in Sarajevo after 1911 was General Oskar Potiorek. With Potiorek's arrival, the Bosnian administration gained a man of great energy, intellect and ego. Nor did Potiorek hesitate to use the change of common finance ministers in February 1912 (the Pole Leon von Biliński replaced Burián) to gain a redefinition of the powers of the *Landeschef* and thereby reduce the power of the civilian authorities in the two provinces. Henceforth, Potiorek became the point of contact with the Common Finance Ministry in Vienna. While this gave the new administration a more militant tone, Potiorek usually sought to make the Landtag function, while pushing relentlessly for the new railway system and cultivating ties with the political and factional leaders. With the onset of the

Balkan fighting in 1912, Potiorek's attention centred on strategic issues. Yet even then he worried about the political life and wanted to assure the populace that the Landtag could function. He still thought, as had Kállay, that economic success and commercial development in Bosnia–Herzegovina might reduce the appeal of Serbia's South Slav propaganda. But, like Conrad, Potiorek also came to believe that crushing Serbia would be easier than waiting for economic prosperity to dilute the appeal of a Greater Serbia. Soon the military option would come to be seen as the only option.[29]

IV

After the culmination of the Bosnian crises in March 1909, normalcy gradually returned to the international system. Domestic politics dominated the news in many European capitals. The German–Austrian alliance found new leadership in Berlin as Bethmann Hollweg and Kiderlen took over in mid-1909. Although Aehrenthal's policy had shown independence of the German ally, the dénouement of the crisis with Berlin's ultimatum to St Petersburg laid bare the dependent nature of Austria–Hungary's security policy. Austria's relations with the French and British resumed their earlier distant posture, with French money markets still closed to Vienna, and Britain casting Vienna into the role of Berlin's lackey. With the Ottoman empire the situation eased; the Turks seemed willing to accept the declaration that Vienna supported their position in Macedonia and wanted no further Balkan territory. Ambassador Johann Pallavicini repeatedly assured the Turkish leadership that Vienna once again defended the status quo on the Balkan peninsula and elsewhere.[30]

Less successful were Aehrenthal's efforts to mend relations with St Petersburg. Izvolsky lasted another year as foreign minister before being sent to Paris as the Russian ambassador; Serge Sazonov now became the Russian foreign minister. Humiliation in the Balkans goaded the Russian military to work harder to repair the damage inflicted by the Japanese in 1905. Diplomatically, Russia drew closer to London and Paris, though the Triple Entente remained looser and less dependable than either St Petersburg or Paris desired. Nevertheless, the assertive Russian policy in the Balkans, initiated by Izvolsky, continued. The assignment in 1909 of the Austrophobe

Nicholas Hartwig as Russian minister to Belgrade adumbrated further trouble. Still, Aehrenthal sought to repair relations with the Russians after 1909; before Berchtold's departure from St Petersburg in early 1911 a certain calmness had returned. But the era of active cooperation in the Balkans had long since vanished.[31]

Austro-Serbian relations, by comparison, proceeded to deteriorate. The *Narodna Odbrana* continued its propaganda attacks and its political activity among the monarchy's South Slavs. In 1911 a group of ardent nationalists and army officers went a step further by forming the *Ujedinjenje ili Smrt* (Unification or Death) and popularly known as the Black Hand. The activities of these two groups nullified the pledges made by the Serbian government in 1909 to desist from interfering in Habsburg affairs. The question for many Serbian nationalists was not whether to interfere but how and to what effect. Still, Vienna wanted to mend affairs with Belgrade. In 1910 Aehrenthal signed a new trade treaty with Belgrade and suggested that a railway to the Adriatic might be considered. But nothing happened. Mutual suspicion and recrimination even blocked the visit of Serbian King Peter to Vienna. The Slavic appeals, coupled with terrorist attacks against Habsburg officials, inflamed the situation still further. The frequent talk of Serbia as the new Piedmont, in direct allusion to Piedmont's success in unifying Italy, horrified leaders in Vienna and Budapest. The annexation of Bosnia–Herzegovina had settled little. Serbia had become more, not less, dangerous to the Dual Monarchy.[32]

Vienna's strained relations with Rome after the 1909 crisis eventually improved. The Italian political leadership resented Aehrenthal's cavalier attitude toward them, a fact amply reflected in the press and parliamentary debates. Gradually, emotions cooled. At the same time Rome sought to protect its future position in the Balkans, since the Italians fully expected a further contraction of Turkish power. The most significant step came when Czar Nicholas II visited Racconigi in late 1909. At the conclusion of these discussions, a treaty was signed which guaranteed that Russia and Italy would consult with each other about any territorial adjustments in the Balkans. Furthermore, the Russians approved any future Italian move against Tripoli. Aehrenthal, however, saw little danger from this accord. While Rome and Vienna fretted over Albania and Crete, and while Conrad still fulminated about the need for a pre-emptive attack against Italy, Austro-Italian relations as of 1911 had returned to their usual ambiguous, suspicious state, or what one observer later described as 'allied enemies'.[33]

V

The first months of 1911 witnessed increasing tensions in the Mediterranean. In late 1910 the Young Turks had installed a new functionary in Tripoli. Almost immediately he began to curb the rights of some of the Italians operating there, and this prompted concerns in Rome. In Morocco, unrest at Fez prompted a French decision to resolve its position. In Macedonia, strife between and among the Christian population and the Turkish authorities continued. The Italian government followed each development with interest, and no minister more carefully than Antonio di San Giuliano who had returned from Paris in March 1910 to direct Italian foreign policy. An avowed colonialist, San Giuliano operated in a political environment in which nationalism and an Italian sense of 'great power' pride intermingled and surged — often out of control. Careful and cautious in his first months in office, he soon suffered attacks from the nationalists because of his inaction in Tripoli where the Turks were obviously challenging the Italian position. The Italian public already believed Tripoli to be a legitimate part of Italy's colonial and imperial destiny. In fact, since the renewal of the Triple Alliance in 1887, successive Italian diplomats had systematically collected assurances from the other powers that Tripoli would fall into Italian hands at some point. During 1911 the public wanted to know when Tripoli would become Italian. The diplomatic preparations had been achieved; the next decision would come when Rome felt it safe to act.[34]

As the French moved to consolidate their position in Fez and assume a protectorate status over Morocco in 1911, the public clamour for Italian action increased. San Giuliano and his prime minister, Giovanni Giolitti, confronted public and parliamentary demands for military action against the Turks. A summer of patriotic celebrations on the fiftieth anniversary of Italian unification helped fuel the issue of Italian greatness. But Giolitti and San Giuliano hesitated. Then came the German *démarche* at Agadir on 1 July and the start of the Second Moroccan Crisis. These steps embroiled the Triple Entente with Germany and conveniently shifted attention away from Italy. As the Franco-German crisis continued through July and August 1911, San Giuliano and Giolitti found themselves with a seductive opportunity to seize Tripoli that they could not resist.[35]

At the same time, the Italian leadership acted to protect its alliance relationship. Rome notified Berlin and Vienna of its desire for an early renewal of the Triple Alliance although the alliance did not expire until 1914. This overture suggested that the Italians wanted to be loyal, at least for now. In addition, the Italians wanted to forestall any Austrian move to insert a new interpretation requiring territorial compensation in case Italy seized Tripoli. Both Berlin and Vienna indicated an understanding of Italy's frustration over Tripoli but advised caution before taking any decisive step. Then in mid-September San Giuliano and Giolitti impetuously decided to act. The reasons for this haste and for their failure to consult with the Italian military and naval commanders still remain unclear. In any event the Italian leadership wanted to exploit the favourable international moment: to seize Tripoli in a short (four week) 'coup' operation with glorious success and few risks. Thus, on 26 September Italy delivered an ultimatum to the Turkish government. Three days later Rome declared war. As anticipated, by 11 October the city of Tripoli was in Italian control.

But the Turks and their Libyan troops quickly regrouped and the frustration for Italy began. The fighting grew in intensity. Soon the Italians were forced to put more troops into the field until, by the end of the campaign, they had 100,000 men under arms. On 5 November, with Tripoli and not much else under Italian control, Rome announced that Libya had been annexed. This step, which left the Turks no diplomatic escape, ensured that the war would continue. Eventually, the fighting spread beyond Libya to the Dodecanese Islands and at one point to Constantinople itself. Not until October 1912 and the conclusion of the Treaty of Lausanne would Italy achieve its victory. Italian military prowess had once again been found wanting: but Libya had finally become Italian.[36]

As the Italian debacle in Libya had unfolded, Aehrenthal and Vienna continually reassured the Ottoman leadership of the Habsburg desire to let the status quo prevail in the Balkans. When acting Russian Foreign Minister Nicholas Charykov offered in October 1911 to support the Turks against Italy in return for Russian privileges in the Straits, Austria–Hungary and the other powers winced. A united European front scuttled the 'Charykov kite', but not before giving Vienna a fright.

Blunting Russian activities in the Balkan capitals proved more difficult for Vienna. Already by early 1912 initial Russian efforts to form a Balkan League were underway. The league, under considerable Russian influence, was directed against Turkey and indirectly Austria–Hungary. Aehrenthal's belated efforts to shore up the Turkish position could not offset the Italian attacks or the Russian machinations in the Balkans. The long-established symbiotic relationship between Constantinople and Vienna continued in early 1912 as the shifting international system made each a loser.[37]

Aehrenthal had more success within the monarchy as he retained complete control over Habsburg foreign policy. In the months after the Bosnian crisis the minister had defended his policy adroitly and forcefully. Clearly, he was the dominant personality in the Habsburg policy process. To be sure, his relations with the Archduke Franz Ferdinand had cooled, not least because of Aehrenthal's careful efforts to appease the Magyar political leadership over the military budget and the unauthorized dreadnought construction. But the minister's biggest challenge came from his constant antagonist — Franz Conrad von Hötzendorf. The general continually pressed the foreign minister with his advice, while always professing not to interfere in the making of diplomatic policy. Disappointed that Aehrenthal had not brutalized the Serbs, the chief of the General Staff lectured the foreign minister on the Serbian danger, the need for more funds and men for the army and the advantages of a reckoning with the unreliable Italian ally. In 1911, when new tensions flared in Albania, Conrad urged Aehrenthal to prepare for a showdown with Turkey over Albania. On one occasion he predicted that the Italians would attack in 1912 — a Cassandra-like pronouncement that Aehrenthal referred to Ambassador Mérey in Rome for evaluation. The ambassador rightly concluded that no one could make such an assertion. Deciding when a country would be ready to fight, Mérey wrote, would only be made when the moment came. But such common sense did not deter Conrad. The general harassed Aehrenthal and War Minister Schönaich relentlessly to prepare for an Italian attack and on the need for larger military budgets.[38]

In the summer of 1911 the clashes between Conrad and Aehrenthal reached new highs. The general accused Ambassador Mérey of overlooking incidents of Italian espionage against the Danubian monarchy. Aehrenthal defended his ambassador and demanded an apology. Even General Bolfras, head of the emperor's military chancellory, tried to mediate, only to have Conrad retort that he would cut off his arm before writing a contrite note. Then came the Italian attack on Tripoli. Conrad immediately proposed that the Habsburgs attack their Italian ally. This time Aehrenthal struck back. Preparing a long memorandum of indictment against Conrad on 22 October 1911, the foreign minister sought Franz Joseph's resolution of who controlled Habsburg foreign policy. On 15 November the emperor pointedly told Conrad that the monarchy's policy was a policy of peace; there would be no attack on Italy. Then on 30 November the emperor abruptly relieved Conrad of his duties as chief of the General Staff, to the delight of Aehrenthal, the Italians and possibly even of Conrad's sometime patron, Franz Ferdinand. Blasius Schemua became the new army commander and Conrad assumed the post of army inspector. The general's only satisfaction from his exit came from the fact that Schönaich was also out, replaced by Auffenberg who almost immediately began to clash with Aehrenthal over the poor condition of the Habsburg military forces.[39]

Aehrenthal's successful defence of his diplomatic prerogatives reflected his personal standing with Franz Joseph and the monarch's commitment to peace. Although anxious for a strong military force and the ability to defend his dynastic holdings, the ageing emperor also recognized that the monarchy could not attack Italy or Serbia in a deliberate, pre-emptive fashion. Conrad's aggressive defensive imperialism had a certain grim logic. But the schemes also carried catastrophic risks which Conrad chose not to recognize. Aehrenthal assessed the monarchy's vulnerabilities more accurately; so did Franz Ferdinand who realized the dangers to his accession if war came. And, Berchtold, Aehrenthal's successor, likewise assessed the risks that a military confrontation would have for Austria–Hungary. But unlike Aehrenthal, Berchtold would have no Bosnian annexation victory to offset the bombast of Conrad. More importantly, after Sarajevo, there would be no Franz Ferdinand to shore up Franz Joseph's commitment to peace.

But as 1911 ended and Aehrenthal's leukemia grew more acute, the foreign minister could take satisfaction that he and the

Ballhausplatz controlled the machinery for making diplomatic and strategic policy. That pattern of civilian control may have been the most important legacy Aehrenthal left to Leopold Berchtold on the eve of the Balkan fighting.[40]

VI

Two Moroccan crises, the annexation of Bosnia–Herzegovina and the Libyan war marked the re-emergence of the eastern question in the twentieth century. The colonial scrambles in the Far East and Africa of the late nineteenth century had now moved dangerously closer home. Aehrenthal had secured, in a legal fashion, the Habsburg gains of 1878 with his annexation manoeuvre. Acting for defensive strategic reasons and with the domestic ramifications of the South Slav issue in mind, he attempted to buttress the monarchy, not to weaken it. He failed. The monarchy was unable to exploit the opportunities in Bosnia–Herzegovina, partly because Hungary permitted no genuine economic development there. Equally important, the act of annexation antagonized the Slavs living in the two provinces, while infuriating the Serbs in Serbia still more. Instead of a weaker foe, Serbia had become even more dangerous. The foreign minister was also unsuccessful with a more powerful enemy: Russia. The Austro-Russian entente vanished, replaced by a policy of Russian patronage of Belgrade and Cetinje.

Yet Aehrenthal deserves praise as well. He reversed the trend in Berlin of treating Vienna as the 'brilliant second'. Although Berlin still dominated the power relationship, the Wilhelmstrasse had to follow a more considered assessment of Habsburg foreign policy. Vienna developed a greater sense of independence that persisted into the Berchtold years. Moreover, the consolidation of the Triple Entente did not owe its momentum solely to the Bosnian crisis. The Second Moroccan Crisis helped and so did the military conversations among the three entente powers. With the Italians, Aehrenthal's legacy was less apparent at his death than by the end of 1912. Vienna's patience with Rome as the war with Turkey dragged on prompted a new Italian appreciation of the values of the alliance. When the Balkan fighting started in the autumn of 1912, this attitude greatly benefited Berchtold. Finally, Franz Joseph had in Aehrenthal a minister who, despite his occasional impetuosity and duplicity, served him well. At least he made the government function. The foreign minister had helped the common ministries cooperate at a time when the domestic consensus in Hungary and in Austria grew ever more brittle and fragile.[41]

Aehrenthal's death in February 1912 marked a transition for Habsburg *and* European diplomacy. The Second Moroccan Crisis rattled Britain, France, Germany and Russia. Each state reacted with a new round of military and naval expenditures. Each state felt as if it were on the defensive. The clashes during the summer of 1911 had a poisonous effect on the international system. With the Italians still bogged down in their fighting as 1911 became 1912, a new and dangerous dimension to the eastern question emerged. As Berchtold settled in as foreign minister at the Ballhausplatz, the alliances with Berlin and Rome appeared more valuable than ever for Austria–Hungary. In the Triple Alliance, Vienna found protection and room to manoeuvre if the Balkan question flared anew.

5 The Monarchy's Allies: Aggressive Berlin, Dubious Rome, Uncertain Bucharest

In 1867 Count Julius Andrássy, as a leading Magyar, negotiated the *Ausgleich*. Twelve years later, as foreign minister of Austria–Hungary, Andrássy signed a secret, five-year alliance with Otto von Bismarck. Together the *Ausgleich* and Dual Alliance defined the parameters of Habsburg domestic and foreign policies from 1879 until the monarchy's collapse in November 1918. The impact of the Compromise on the conduct of Habsburg foreign and strategic policies has already been examined. An analysis of the monarchy's place in the international system is now necessary, focusing in this chapter upon the Triple Alliance and in the next the Triple Entente and Vienna's probable enemies.

By 1912 mounting friction between the alliance/entente systems, especially after the Bosnian crisis of 1908–09, shaped much of the international agenda for Franz Joseph and his advisers. The clash of alliances was no longer potential but actual. Furthermore, the linkages between the members of the systems were becoming progressively more important, giving each issue, each crisis, a European rather than a regional dimension. Just as Italy's aggressive attack on Tripoli in September 1911 disturbed the alliance groupings, so also did the Anglo-German naval race, the fate of Macedonia and the nationalistic outbursts in France and Germany after the Second Moroccan Crisis. The alliance structures were crucial for Vienna's diplomacy — defining its erstwhile friends and identifying its most likely enemies if war should ever come.[1]

I

The Austro-German alliance of 1879 constituted a radical departure in the practice of European diplomacy. A five-year, secret agreement, the alliance was negotiated not in preparation for a war nor for the conduct of an existing war but as a peacetime arrangement. Bismarck's earlier diplomacy had exploited only transient arrangements. Now he and Andrássy made a more lasting agreement to protect their countries against Russia.

Bismarck did not, however, intend to isolate St Petersburg. Consistent with his policy of thwarting any French attempt to recoup its Napoleonic dominance, the German chancellor sought to entangle Russia in a closer relationship as well. This he did, first with the *Dreikaiserbund* of 1881 (renewed in 1884) and later by his secret, bilateral Reinsurance Treaty with Russia in 1887. The latter treaty, with its semi-hostile tone toward the Habsburgs, kept Bismarck in contact with Russia. Only when William II impetuously abandoned the treaty in 1890 would Russia be left alone and thus susceptible to French overtures. Gradually the full impact of the alliance with Austria–Hungary became apparent, as Europe drifted toward two alliances rather than a concert system.[2]

Andrássy and his successors, meanwhile, always viewed the German alliance differently than Berlin. For Vienna, the agreement formed the major component in its effort to contain Russia and to protect the Habsburg monarchy from Pan-Slavic threats. From 1879 to 1918 the containment of Russia remained the dominant thrust of the Dual Alliance for Vienna. This need also led Vienna to conclude the Italian alliance in 1882, hoping thereby to protect the monarchy's southern flank. And the Russian danger led to the secret alliance with King Carol of Rumania in 1883. But Vienna in the 1880s, like Bismarck, did not desire to confront Russia directly. To be sure, the prolonged crisis over Bulgaria in the middle of that decade ruffled the situation. Nevertheless, during the 1890s and into the 1900s St Petersburg and Vienna worked together to keep Balkan problems under wraps. Helped by a compliant Serbian king and Russia's involvement in the Far East, Austro-Russian frictions would be handled diplomatically. In fact, by 1900 a period of entente characterized the relationships between the two eastern powers. Not until the start of the Bosnian crisis in late 1908 would this pattern of co-existence erode and the alliance systems clash directly.[3]

From the start the Dual Alliance had a Balkan dimension despite Bismarck's aversion to eastern affairs. The alliance protected the Danubian monarchy against Russia when and if the two states clashed over the Balkans. Bismarck's diplomatic skills kept this possibility masked, as did the Habsburg ability to deal directly with the Russians. In a crucial sense, the alliance provided the bulwark missing from Vienna's diplomacy since the failures of the Crimean era. Bismarck appreciated the Balkan connection; so did his successors. But the problem of the Balkans and a possible Austro-Russian confrontation required constant efforts at either containment or deferral. After 1908–09 neither of these conditions would be present. Very quickly the Germans found the Austro-Russian clashes in the Balkans embroiling them further than they wished.[4]

After 1908 the clashes between the diplomatic groupings began to alter the nature and the operation of the Austro-German alliance. Those changes constituted a central feature of Habsburg diplomacy until the 1914 July crisis. This evaluation reflected and was influenced by the general breakdown of European diplomacy after 1900. The emergence of the Triple Alliance and Triple Entente systems, the Anglo-German naval race and an aggressive Serbia shifted the European diplomatic agenda and its risks. Alliance/entente competition assumed a new character and a higher level of danger.[5]

II

The Austro-German alliance represented the central feature of the Habsburg diplomatic system after 1908. The alliance's operational components and its perceptual impact upon Habsburg policy-makers are crucial to an understanding of the evolution of the Dual Monarchy's foreign policy. Prussia and Austria had battled throughout much of the nineteenth century for the control of Germany. Franz Joseph's military defeat at Sadowa — quickly and decisively — had been followed by Bismarck's gracious peace terms. If Franz Joseph never entirely overcame his bitterness at this humiliation, he nevertheless recognized after 1870 that Austria and the new Germany must work together.[6]

To mend and advance this relationship the role of the monarchs remained pivotal. The ties between William II and the Austrian emperor/king were correct, frequent and ostentatious. Franz Joseph would, until 1900, pay visits to Berlin and the German manoeuvres; William II visited Vienna once or twice a year. State visits, stops by William II on his way to and from the Mediterranean, and his presence at Habsburg military manoeuvres buttressed the connection. During these visits, exchanges between the two, in so far as they can be reconstructed, dealt with Russia, domestic political issues and their common love of hunting. If the German kaiser found Franz Joseph obsessed with the Balkans, William still expected the Danubian ruler to be cautious and hesitant. The Austrian monarch regarded his younger colleague (by twenty-nine years) as mercurial, unpredictable and excessively devoted to the German naval build-up. Nevertheless, Franz Joseph appreciated William II's attention. At the same time, the German monarch would worry, as did his advisers, about the older man's health and the future of the Habsburg monarchy after the ageing monarch died.[7]

A second set of royal ties emerged after 1900: the friendship between Franz Ferdinand and William II. Visitors to each other's private estates and the army manoeuvres, the two exchanged private correspondence. Opinionated and feudalistic, both men longed for an earlier world in which their subjects recognized monarchical power as divine. Franz Ferdinand and William II reveled in the symbols and substance of power. Naval forces were their toys; the military embodied autocratic, obedient power. Yet for all of their bombast, each man remained cautious, almost a man of peace. Unfortunately, their bellicose rhetoric constituted the public and diplomatic perception and hence the harsh assessments by foreign governments of each of them. William genuinely grieved over the murders at Sarajevo. His decision to back Austria–Hungary in resolving the Serbian problem came in part from a sense of personal loss.[8]

A second level of contact came from the ambassadors who carried out the routine relations between Berlin and Vienna. In Berlin since 1892, Habsburg Ambassador Ladislaus Szögyény-Marich had established warm personal ties with the German kaiser and possessed the confidence of Franz Joseph. In Vienna, by contrast, the Germans in 1912 had an energetic man who often showed poor judgement: Heinrich von Tschirschky. After a year as head of the German foreign office (1906–07), Tschirschky had moved to Vienna with William II's blessing. That backing remained crucial to his stay in Vienna, since the Habsburg policy-makers found him arrogant, tiresome and condescending. More often than not, Aehrenthal and then Berchtold used Szögyény and not Tschirschky for communications with Berlin. When this avenue failed, the Ballhausplatz and the Wilhelmstrasse communicated through special agents rather than through Tschirschky.[9]

The ties between the foreign ministers themselves, although not so important in personal terms, affected policy matters. Aehrenthal had infrequent contacts with Bülow and Bethmann Hollweg. Berchtold visited Berlin in April 1912 to meet Bethmann Hollweg and Kiderlen, but no great personal attachments emerged. Berchtold had even greater reservations about Gottlieb von Jagow who in 1913 replaced Kiderlen after the latter's unexpected death. Still, the ministers knew each other. In the limited world of senior officialdom, these personal contacts allowed each to calibrate the other and perhaps engage in speculation about their decision processes. A surprising contact was István Tisza who first met William II in the March of 1914. Like many others, the German kaiser was immediately impressed by Tisza's vigour, knowledge and insights. William II later implored Franz Ferdinand to think more generously about the Magyar leader.[10]

This welter of personal and diplomatic contacts formed the structure and much of the content of the Austro-German alliance. After the Bosnian crisis subsided, Austro-German relations resumed a more placid course. Vienna grew nervous over the Potsdam interview in late 1910 between William II and Nicholas II, but the Germans reassured them that the alliance remained secure. During the spring and summer of 1911 Vienna watched with concern, even dismay, at the clash between Germany and the *entente cordiale* over Morocco. St Petersburg's decision to steer clear of the crisis helped the Habsburg position enormously. Focusing chiefly in 1911 upon Habsburg domestic political problems, where Berlin to its credit did not interfere, Vienna found solace in the secure German alliance. At the same time, however, Vienna could fret over the ramifications of Germany's attachment to *Weltpolitik* and to a naval policy that alienated Britain from the Danubian monarchy. With the end of the Moroccan crisis and Berlin's new emphasis on strengthening the German army, Vienna could at least be comforted that the continent (and not the world) had re-entered Berlin's policy horizons.[11]

Although allies, the two states had several areas of substantial disagreement. Berlin's generous stance toward Rome consistently annoyed Vienna. Rome's dependence upon the alliance in its war with Turkey helped to diminish some of the Austro-Hungarian concerns. Germany's aggressive economic penetration into the Balkans proved more troublesome. The Habsburg's 'Pig War' with Serbia provided opportunities for Germany; Berlin progressively expanded its economic influence in the other Balkan states as well.

These German moves were not easily resisted, partly because Vienna lacked capital to invest. Frictions over the economic rivalry reinforced Vienna's fears about Berlin's reliability against Serbia. While Berlin's true intentions had not been in doubt in the 1908–09 crisis, they would surface repeatedly during the Balkan Wars. Alliance politics would become a major worry for Vienna as 1912 turned to 1913. Cautiously, both capitals assessed the other's intentions and wanted assurances before they made a policy decision. If there was not a clearly coordinated policy, there were at least efforts to ensure a degree of alliance unity. [12]

The alliance also brought confidential military arrangements between the Habsburgs and the Hohenzollerns. Staff talks had occurred in the 1880s and 1890s, but these had broken down during General von Schlieffen's term as chief of the German General Staff. Berlin's substantially reworked war plans were never communicated to Vienna. Until January 1909 this situation persisted, then Conrad initiated talks with Schlieffen's successor, General von Moltke. [13]

With the passage of two decades, all previous planning was obsolete. Historians have often argued that in 1909 Moltke's arrangements with Conrad endorsed a Habsburg offensive in the Balkans. This is only partially true. Many have overlooked that Conrad implicitly and explicitly also endorsed the Schlieffen–Moltke plan which would attack France first rather than Russia, even though Russia had been the original *raison d'être* of the Dual Alliance. In the 1880s the elder Moltke had talked of an attack against Russia and a defensive stance toward France. Vienna warmly endorsed this concept. But Schlieffen, especially after the conclusion of the Franco-Russian alliance in 1894, shifted the emphasis westward. Eventually, in 1905 Berlin adopted a new war plan that called for a massive attack on France, a defensive stance in the east and the violation of Belgian neutrality. Without being consulted and in a dependent status, Austria–Hungary found the very military basis of the alliance fundamentally altered. In that sense, Berlin, like Conrad, had converted the defensive alliance into a more aggressive and dangerous political relationship. [14]

Conrad resumed the military conversations in 1909 with Franz Joseph's and Aehrenthal's approval. Thereafter, letters, meetings at the annual manoeuvres, attaché exchanges, and some consultation during the Balkan crises would constitute the fabric of the military and later naval conversations. During these exchanges, broad strategic conceptions were discussed, but seldom the operational details required for effective cooperation. For example, the two army staffs never really exchanged precise information about each other's war plans. Nor did they trade extensive data about their forces. While the staffs shared information about Russian mobilization plans, especially in late 1913 and early 1914, they revealed little about their plans to meet the increasing threat. Notably, Berlin and Vienna never touched on the question of command coordination once the fighting started, although that question was clearly essential for any success in a war.[15]

Moltke and Conrad, moreover, recognized the nature of their strategic dilemmas — the two-front war — but could not overcome the problem. Dismissing the Italians as a threat to Austria–Hungary, Moltke still had to concede that the Habsburgs faced Russian and Serbian threats just as he faced Russian and French threats. Moltke needed Vienna to distract Russia while Germany won the decisive victory in the west, then dealt with Russia. Conrad depended upon Berlin to intimidate Russia and, if that failed, to contain Russia. A Russian attack against Germany might spoil the Schlieffen–Moltke campaign; it would not defeat Germany. But a Russian attack against Austria–Hungary might undo the Habsburg system.

What emerged from the Austro-German staff conversations after 1909 over these asymmetrical strategic problems has a paradoxical, almost contradictory dimension. Conrad pledged to launch a Habsburg offensive from Galicia against Russian forces in Poland; Moltke committed forces to the east that would give Conrad time to shift troops northward if they were already engaged against Serbia. Each general counted upon the other, despite the absence of any written commitments. In the summer of 1914 Moltke failed to keep his promises, with disastrous results for Conrad and the Danubian monarchy. The military conversations were the most practical, dangerous expressions of alliance planning.[16]

But equally important to the alliance were the mental images, the 'unspoken assumptions', in both capitals about the Austro-German relationship. In Berlin the political elite viewed the future prospects of the Danubian monarchy with alarm. Franz Ferdinand appeared a capable enough successor to the institution that was Franz Joseph, but could the Habsburg nephew deal with the Magyars and the Slav problem? William II had high hopes but few illusions. Not surprisingly, the German kaiser found Tisza and the other Magyar statesmen more determined and ruthless, more attractive to the Germans despite the archduke's dislike of them. Yet to Berlin's credit, it expended very little effort to encourage German-Austrians to look toward a Pan-German solution. On the other hand, confident assertions about Germany's destiny contrasted sharply with the weaknesses of the Habsburg monarchy despite its economic successes since 1900.[17]

By 1912 Berlin could not, however, ignore strategic realities. Bethmann Hollweg, Kiderlen and William II might fret about Austria–Hungary, but Berlin could not dispense with the alliance. The ramifications of Germany's *Weltpolitik* had consolidated the Triple Entente and profoundly altered continental alignments. Better relations with Russia might reduce the importance of the Vienna connection, but even a détente could not render the Habsburgs unnecessary. Berlin had transformed the defensive alliance against Russia into a necessary part of its strategic posture. Austrian reliability against Russia was an axiom of German policy-makers, but only Russia or the Balkans — a fact more clearly appreciated after the Second Moroccan Crisis — would force Conrad and his forces into battle. Vienna was the secondary partner in the thirty-year-old alliance, yet its policy-makers had carefully defined the limits of what they would support. By 1912 Berlin and Vienna had become virtual hostages to their own alliance relationship.[18]

In Vienna, meanwhile, however much the political elites might resent German boasts and talk of *Mitteleuropa*, few could deny the power of their neighbours or the fact of German economic success. Germany remained the monarchy's major trading partner, a steady source of funds and a military deterrent against Russia. Certainly, Vienna and Budapest desired greater German understanding of the South Slav problem and a less provocative *Weltpolitik*. The Habsburg leaders, obsessed with their *Balkanpolitik*, wanted German understanding of the Habsburg dilemma. For Franz Ferdinand the need went further. The heir-apparent would require strong German support if he sought to make any constitutional changes in the 1867 Compromise. For the archduke the German alliance, even if occasionally demeaning, might be the difference between successful domestic change and stalemate or defeat. The Austro-German alliance had become a virtual quasi-constitutional basis for Habsburg diplomacy; it might also provide the support necessary to overturn or modify the *Ausgleich* as well.

Despite the convergence of interests between Vienna and Berlin, significant differences persisted between them. None threatened the essential relationship. On the other hand the Austro-German relationships with their Italian and Rumanian allies would be the source of frequent misunderstanding and tension between Berlin and Vienna. These frictions weakened the Triple Alliance.

III

Italy joined the Dual Alliance in May 1882. Drawn into the alliance by Bismarck's diplomatic efforts to isolate France, the Italians found in the alliance a certain measure of security against the French after they moved into Tunisia the year before. For Austria–Hungary, the Triple Alliance offered the prospect that its southern neighbour might dampen its irredentist talk about the Trentino and Trieste and let the Habsburgs focus on the Russians. Renewed and expanded to cover the Balkans in 1887, the Triple Alliance would be renewed in 1891, 1902 and again in 1912.[19]

The alliance never had the unity and strength that its appearance suggested. A number of paradoxes negated its value. Far more than either Austria–Hungary or Germany, the Italians, in part because of geography and history and their weakness as the 'Least of the Great Powers', were more fickle and ambivalent about their alliance obligations. Never anxious to antagonize the British, the Italians blew hot and cold toward France. In the 1890s tensions mounted with France but Théophile Delcassé's arrival as French foreign minister in 1898 soon lowered anxieties and led to several deals. By its secret agreements of 1900 and 1902 with Paris, Rome effectively nullified its obligations to Berlin and to Vienna.

Nevertheless Rome remained in the Triple Alliance. The reasons for this dubious loyalty centred upon the positive financial advantages that Germany provided to Rome and because neither France nor Britain were willing to encourage the Italians to defect altogether. Furthermore, participation in the alliance offered Italy the chance to influence Austro-Hungarian policy in the Balkans. Membership in the rival alliance/entente grouping would have made that effort far more difficult. In addition, the Triple Alliance offered Italy the promise of help should France seek to thwart a Libyan move, a consideration that had real meaning in the Italo-Turkish War of

1911–12. Italy's duplicitous behaviour must not be condemned too severely. Richard Bosworth correctly insists that Italy's place in the Triple Alliance must be assessed in pre-1914 terms and with adequate recognition of Conrad's bellicose talk.[20]

Whereas personal ties helped cement the Austro-German alliance, this element did not develop in the case of Austro-Italian relations. The Italian King Umberto visited the Danubian monarchy in December 1881, before the alliance was signed. But Franz Joseph, a faithful defender of the Vatican in its political and religious struggles with the secular Italian government, never returned the visit. He would do nothing to offend the papacy. Franz Ferdinand did not help with the Italian relationship either, though he had inherited possessions in Italy. Nor did Victor Emmanuel III, king after his father's assassination in 1900, make things easier. His marriage to the statuesque Elena, daughter of King Nikita of Montenegro, gave him both a personal and a state reason for active involvement in the Balkans. Such prospects did not engender cordiality with Austria–Hungary. On the other hand, William II's ability to move in his peripatetic way between the two governments and to meet with their leadership offset some of the stiffness in the dynastic relations.[21]

Devoid of personal ties at the top level, the Austro-Italian alliance depended on personal contacts between the ministers and ambassadors. During the Aehrenthal and Berchtold eras at the Ballhausplatz, these ties could be described as reasonably satisfactory. Both men met their Italian counterparts, and Berchtold saw San Giuliano several times after February 1912. Indeed, when Berchtold visited Pisa in mid-1912 he got a rousing welcome. Total candour may not have always prevailed at these meetings, yet each minister developed an appreciation of the other's position. In this effort the Italian ambassador in Vienna, Giuseppe, the Duke of Avarna, helped considerably, largely because of his pro-Austrian views. The Habsburgs were served less well in Rome. Kajetan Mérey von Kapos-Mére, ambitious, opinionated and lazy, never meshed well with his Italian hosts.[22]

A further complication in Austro-Italian relations existed in the person of the Habsburg representative to the Vatican, Prince Johann Schönburg-Hartenstein, appointed in 1911 to succeed Nikolaus Szécsen. Schönburg's presence meant that Vienna always had two ambassadors in Rome, a fact that created confusion for the Italian government and little favour. Schönburg's relationships with the

Vatican were careful and circumspect, centring chiefly upon the possible reform of curial representation. Moreover, both Vienna and other governments preferred some resolution of the friction between the papacy and the Italian government. In fact, in the spring of 1914 this issue reached the agenda, only to be overtaken by the war, the death of Pius X and the election of his successor, Benedict XV.[23]

The content of the Austro-Italian relationship reflected the varying fortunes of the alliance. Economically, the Danubian monarchy maintained a favourable trade balance with Italy that grew modestly. But little Austrian capital flowed southward to reinforce any sense of economic interaction. Politically, after a war scare in late 1904, relations gradually improved. Italian irredentism, though not absent altogether, grew less strident. Some matters, such as the creation of an Italian law faculty at the University of Innsbruck and the treatment of Italians employed by the municipal government of Trieste irritated relations. But such issues did not threaten the existence of the alliance.[24]

Unlike the military cooperation between Berlin and Vienna, the Habsburg military contacts with their southern neighbour were more erratic. After some staff talks in the 1890s, little contact followed. The tensions of 1904 and persistent fears about the 'allied enemy' complicated military planning between the ostensible allies. Conrad's appointment in 1906 as chief of the General Staff only exacerbated matters. He consistently advocated a pre-emptive strike against Italy and conspicuously revamped Habsburg war plans against Italy (Plan I). Conrad also demanded more funds for border fortifications along the Italian frontier. With Conrad's views well known and frequently expressed, the Italian military could only plan accordingly. Rome greeted his dismissal in late 1911, after demanding a Habsburg attack on an Italy at war in Libya, with relief. When Conrad returned to power in December 1912, the Balkan imbroglio would prompt a shift in his views about the value of Italian help.[25]

Conrad's rhetoric left no doubts about Habsburg military policy. But naval issues also stimulated anxieties in both countries, even if in a *sotto voce* fashion. Italy justified naval construction in terms of the Anglo-French threat, especially after 1904. Austria–Hungary talked of needing dreadnoughts for usually unspecified strategic purposes and for carrying out equally unspecified alliance obligations. More realistically, both countries knew the Habsburgs built dreadnoughts to match the Italians and to defend against Italian units, not French or British. But the tenor of competition was far less than the Anglo-German race, and the lack of funds retarded the pace. Naval cooperation existed on paper, but the expectation was often of 'allied conflict'.[26]

Diplomatically, the years after 1908 were less erratic. Rome buttressed its Balkan position with Russia, signing the Racconigi Agreement in 1909. Yet the Italians had accepted the annexation of Bosnia–Herzegovina without pressing any claim for compensation under Article VII of the alliance. Thus, when the war with Turkey began in September 1911, Rome found a measure of sympathy in Vienna for its action so long as the war did not spill into the Aegean or weaken Ottoman rule in Macedonia. Even when these eventualities did occur in 1912, Vienna carefully refused to panic or be too difficult. Berchtold found that the more the two governments co-operated, the less dependent each was on a Berlin that viewed Libya and the Balkans from a quite different perspective.

Thus Austro-Italian cooperation would in fact continue during the Balkan Wars as both governments sought to protect their mutual interests in the Balkans. In the process they also sought to prevent the other from gaining the upper hand. As the earlier pattern of informal imperialism practised in the Balkans by both parties was threatened in late 1912, the two governments had a common identity of 'jeopardized interests' prompting cooperation and coordination. The future of Albania, which both governments viewed as potentially in their 'sphere of influence', was the most sensitive concern for them.

Even though these Balkan developments thrust the two states together, another dimension could not be ignored: Victor Emmanuel's personal ties with his father-in-law, King Nikita of Montenegro, and the extent of Montenegrin ambition. Nikita's active role in the Balkan League and his insistence later on retaining Scutari challenged the European Concert, Austro-Hungarian diplomacy and the alliance ties with Italy.[27]

The third partner of the Triple Alliance closely followed the Austro-Italian interaction. Germany consistently took a generous position toward Italy's flirtation with the Triple Entente. Berlin, confident of its own position with Italy, could afford to be forgiving. But when Berlin insisted that Vienna be equally understanding, friction often ensued. Repeatedly, Vienna objected that Berlin did not appreciate the problem of Italian perfidy, of Italy's willingness to oppose Habsburg policy in the Balkans and of Rome's tolerance of agitation in the Trentino. But Bülow and then Bethmann Hollweg, Kiderlen and then Jagow, brushed these complaints aside and insisted on keeping Italy in the Triple Alliance. If the alliance had little proven capacity to navigate the rough waters of actual military conflict, its value as part of the overall diplomatic structure remained. The Habsburg statesmen, Aehrenthal, Berchtold, and occasionally Franz Ferdinand, recognized this value and tolerated Italian fickleness as a given fact.

From Vienna's perspective, the Italians occupied the uncomfortable position of peacetime ally and a potential wartime enemy. Military and naval preparations against their ally continued, as did Conrad's occasional demands for a war. But these considerations were submerged in larger diplomatic necessities. As the Balkan scene unfolded in 1912, Rome and Vienna largely shared common interests: Albania, the power shifts in the Balkans, the future of Montenegro. In these circumstances, the alliance ties proved helpful in achieving modest coordination and what contemporary analysts would call 'confidence-building' measures. So too would the efforts to enhance the military and naval planning of the Triple Alliance that resumed in December 1912. Despite internal strains, the Triple Alliance probably had more cohesion in 1912 and thereafter than at any point in its history. Vienna did not have an effective military ally on its southwestern border. But the Danubian monarchy had contained a potential threat whose presence in the Triple Entente would have been disastrous. Denial as well as gain constitute diplomatic achievement; in the case of Italy, the Triple Alliance achieved this for both Berlin and Vienna.

IV

In October 1883 King Carol of Rumania signed an alliance with Austria–Hungary that the Germans also joined. Five years later, Italy would align itself with the secret accord. Periodically renewed and for a final time in February 1913, the secret alliance with the Rumanian king remained just that. Known only to a few senior Bucharest officials during its first three decades, the obligation of the Hohenzollern King Carol (king since 1881 and prince from 1866) remained concealed from the public. If the precise terms of the Triple Alliance remained unknown but suspected by the other governments, the Triple Alliance's actual existence did not. In contrast, Rumania cultivated friendly relations with Austria–Hungary and Germany, but the treaty obligations among the three states which were deliberately aimed at Russia remained unknown. This remarkable secret thoroughly complicated Vienna's relations with Carol and with the Rumanian government. Since Carol alone held the alliance together, his continued support and loyalty were crucial. A crafty, industrious ruler, the Rumanian monarch adjusted his support for the agreement after carefully assessing the ups and downs of Rumanian politics. When his senior Rumanian advisers who did know of the treaty wavered, so did he. When they were confident, so was he.[28]

Germany's ties with Rumania were always strong. Despite considerable French success in expanding its economic position in Bucharest, the Disconto-Gesellschaft and the Deutsche Bank remained important to Rumania's financial and economic life. While Berlin really did not need Rumanian military assistance, Germany could not ignore the possible diversion of Russian troops that a Rumanian ally would cause. Furthermore, William II always gave the Hohenzollern ties great weight and confidently asserted that family connections would ensure King Carol's reliability. This conviction, which Vienna never shared, stood in the face of much evidence to the contrary.[29]

If the German presence in Bucharest was strong, the Italian was virtually non-existent. But Rumanian assertions of historical linkages with the Roman empire guaranteed a level of friendliness. So too did the language. Nor could either government ignore their shared interests: both wanted to contain and moderate any Habsburg activity in the Balkans. Otherwise, their mutual interests were few.

By contrast, the Habsburg relationship with Rumania was complex, continuous and always susceptible to rapid alteration. First, and most importantly, the presence of three million Rumanians in Transylvania under Magyar rule meant that domestic and foreign policies overlapped. The secret alliance with King Carol did not remove the geographic and demographic realities of Transylvania. While the issue did not erupt from 1900–12, the possibility loomed. Second, both Austria–Hungary and Rumania worried about Russia.

The Congress of Berlin cost Rumania the possibility of Bessarabia; future clashes with Russia might cost more. So long as King Carol and the Rumanians fretted more about the Russians than their compatriots in Transylvania, the alliance would remain intact. The secret links formed a non-Slavic barrier to block Russian access to the Balkans.[30]

Adding further complexity to the Rumanian relationship were Bucharest's tenuous relations with Bulgaria. A certain wariness had characterized Bucharest's attitude toward Sofia since their emergence from Ottoman rule. Russia's intervention in Sofia accentuated Rumanian fears while prompting apprehension in Vienna. Bulgaria, moreover, had land in Silistria which Rumania openly coveted. On the other hand, Vienna considered Bulgaria a potential counter-weight to Serbia even if King Ferdinand was openly despised. Already in the 1908 Bosnian crisis, Ferdinand had overthrown his remaining obligations to Turkey, a move that most incorrectly thought Aehrenthal had sanctioned in advance. When the Balkan Wars began, Bulgaria's relations with Rumania would become an increasingly difficult juggling act for Vienna to sustain.[31]

If Transylvania and Bulgaria complicated Austro-Rumanian contacts, these should not obscure the strategic benefits that might come from the alliance. Occasionally the two armies exchanged military information and talked of future operations against Russia. At the very least, Conrad required a neutral Rumania that would divert some Russian forces. When that expectation became increasingly unlikely after 1913, Conrad faced a major strategic challenge: Rumania presented a fourth hostile front.[32]

Frequent visits among the royal families also helped to keep the alliance plausible. Franz Ferdinand, considered a friend by the Rumanians in Hungary, enjoyed a warm reception when he and Sophie went to Bucharest in 1909. King Carol often visited Vienna. His long reign, like Franz Joseph's, made him a survivor among European rulers. These state visits also permitted contacts between senior Rumanian ministers, who knew of the secret alliance, and Habsburg officials. Nevertheless, however well disposed King Carol or the Rumanian party leaders might be toward Aehrenthal and Berchtold, they could not overcome the problem of Transylvania.[33]

After 1900 the Rumanian problem in Austria–Hungary loomed larger and larger. The formation of the Rumanian National Party in Transylvania and the intensification of Budapest's Magyarization efforts under Prime Minister Dezsö Bánffy exacerbated the situation. Yet some still believed the situation could be saved. Franz Ferdinand, busy with reform schemes that would give the Rumanians more power once he became monarch, established contacts with a leading Rumanian political leader, Alexander Vaida. This show of favour encouraged the Rumanians who pinned their hopes for relief upon the anti-Magyar heir-apparent. Other Rumanian leaders argued that a combination of royal pressure and their own demands on Budapest might change things.[34]

In 1910 István Tisza, whose National Party of Work had swept the election, expressed the desire to resolve the Transylvanian issue. His willingness to discuss the problem and to think of ameliorating some of the worst features of Magyarization initially offered some hope. But such expectations quickly faded when Tisza remained intransigent on two fundamental issues: the sharing of political power and a measure of autonomy for Transylvania. Confronted with a situation in which three million Rumanians had only five deputies in Budapest (compared to ten million Magyars having at least 390 Magyar deputies), Tisza's apparent willingness to talk had no productive outcome.[35]

As 1912 began, the Rumanians in Transylvania were a time bomb within the alliance. Failure to resolve domestic discrimination endangered Habsburg foreign policies. This integral connection made the Rumanian problem far more than a minor distraction for the monarchy's leadership. Unless resolved, Rumania's reliability was questionable. A flare-up of nationalism in the Balkans and a new wave of Rumanian self-confidence would create problems with Budapest, weaken the alliance and compound the South Slav threat. Bucharest's progressive defection from the Austrian alliance constituted one of the troubling possibilities confronting Habsburg policymakers when the Balkan upheaval started in October 1912.

V

Alliance politics, an analytical term in vogue since the late 1960s, describes the interaction among and between alliance and entente partners. What emerges from such an analysis, as this chapter has shown, is a chronicle of nearly continuous bargaining, of frequent shifts of perspective by the governments and of constant questioning about loyalties. As the first peacetime alliance, the Triple Alliance created patterns of behaviour that would be repeated with the Franco-Russian alliance and then the Triple Entente. Yet to argue that these patterns were readily apparent would be an exaggeration. Rather they were the gradual by-product, though the pace of alliance politics spurted dramatically after 1900. With the formation of the Triple Entente and Sir Edward Grey's commitment to an active balance of power policy for Britain, the systems became more important to each of their members.[36]

As the alliance and ententes became more crucial, so also did the issues of coordination and cooperation. If diplomatic coordination was still sporadic and inconsistent, the attempts to work together were still more systematic than the traditional norms before 1879. Flowing naturally but erratically from the need to cooperate and plan were the military and financial aspects of the alliance and entente relationships. Only gradually did the Triple Alliance partners come to regularize their discussions and their exchanges of information. Even after 1909, the military in Vienna and Berlin remained discrete and circumspect in their dealings with each other. In the case of Vienna and Rome after 1912, a détente among the allied generals virtually constituted a new era even if planning between the Austrian and Italian staffs still left much to be desired. In any event, the Austrian leadership assumed that the linkages between diplomacy and strategic policy were in place. The reality was different.

Less tangible than military plans but equally important were the unspoken assumptions and presumptions that came to dominate the Triple Alliance. Austria–Hungary and Germany eventually expected each other's help against a Slavic enemy whose ambition they never doubted. This assumption became an article of faith. Yet just enough fissures weakened the alliance to make Vienna worry about Berlin concluding a separate arrangement with St Petersburg at Vienna's expense. This would utterly expose the Habsburgs. The mere possibility meant that the Danubian monarchy would never forget its dependence nor stray too far from Germany. But the Russian threat also meant that Germany needed Austria–Hungary. Even if one did not subscribe to the theory of a massive Russian build-up scheduled to be complete in 1917, the generals and statesmen could not discount accelerations in Russian armaments and a return of Russian interests to eastern Europe and the Balkans.

Berlin noted Russia's willingness to support one or more Balkan clients against Germany's ally — the Habsburgs. Thus as the alliance became a protective mechanism, the dependence limited one's options. Only slowly did Vienna and Berlin come to perceive this during the Balkan crises of 1912–13, each drawing dangerous conclusions from its experiences.

For Italy the Triple Alliance linked them with great power politics. This suited Italian ambitions if not Italian resources. The connection offered Rome both a means of sometimes influencing Habsburg policy and a device to extort concessions if necessary. In turn, the arrangement allowed Vienna to focus upon the Balkans and Russia and worry less about irredentist ambitions.

But in the case of Rumania, the alliances did not offer Vienna or Berlin much solace. The problem of Transylvania struck at the heart of the problem of Austria–Hungary: how to reconcile national groups to some form of *supra*-national government? For a generation the Ottoman presence and the Russian threat had made the Habsburgs appear to King Carol and his closest advisers like potential protectors. If Ottoman power ebbed, if Russia proved malleable and if the Magyars offered only minor concessions in Transylvania, the Rumanians were not likely to be loyal to an alliance of whose existence the public at large had no knowledge.

Until 1912 only a few of these features of alliance politics had come together in a single diplomatic crisis, whether Morocco, Bosnia or the Italian war in Libya. But the creation of the Balkan League and the apparent unity of the Triple Entente posed dangers not encountered in the previous three decades of alliance politics. Austria–Hungary would not benefit from these new circumstances.

6 The Monarchy's Enemies: Serbia, Montenegro and the Triple Entente

Intelligence, often called the 'missing dimension' of diplomatic history, played a crucial part in shaping Habsburg perceptions about the monarchy's future. Like other European states, the Danubian government had in the first decade of the twentieth century gradually developed a more systematic approach to the collection, assessment and use of intelligence data. No other government had as many potential enemies: Italy, the 'allied enemy' has been discussed, while the more openly hostile neighbours included Serbia, Montenegro and Russia backed by France and Britain. Further, the problem of the Slavs within the monarchy provided each of the possible neighbouring enemies with an ability to confuse and disturb the domestic peace of the Habsburg state. As with so many other features of Austro-Hungarian life, intelligence operations were a fusion of external and domestic considerations. Because of the monarchy's vulnerable strategic situation, intelligence operations and intelligence data facilitate an understanding of the Habsburg decision-making process. The threat assessments drawn from these intelligence activities also permit insights into the Habsburg 'official mind' as it grappled with international and domestic problems confronting Vienna in the era of the Balkan Wars.[1]

I

The Ballhausplatz collected the bulk of diplomatic intelligence. The ambassadors and ministers abroad reported frequently. Assignments in the major capitals of St Petersburg, Paris and London were prestigious and important. If a ministerial assignment to Cetinje was not coveted, nevertheless this post was critical, given Nikita's antics. And the diplomats assigned to Belgrade often played crucial roles in shaping bureaucratic attitudes in Vienna. In 1912 Stephan von Ugron zu Abránfalva, a former consular official who had served in Russia and as minister to Bucharest, held the Belgrade ministry. A competent consular reporter, Ugron had few illusions about Austro-Serbian relations. After a series of frustrating experiences, he occasionally counselled confrontation rather than accommodation with Belgrade. This stance apparently shaped the views of many in Vienna.[2]

The ambassadors and ministers depended upon consular officials for local, regional information. Whether situated in Serbia or Russia, their location often enabled them to spot actions that indicated military measures or unusual strategic developments—such as large purchases of material, whether grain or horses. Similar information often came from Habsburg officials stationed along the joint borders with Russia, Serbia and Montenegro. Reports of military deserters, word of unexpected military activities, even political information, were gleaned from the daily contacts and forwarded to Vienna or Budapest. Such information, when coupled with police data on 'alleged' subversive activity, offered policy-makers a barometer of relations with their neighbours.[3]

The General Staff agency charged with assessing the data and collecting its own was the Evidenz Bureau. Reorganized and expanded by Conrad, the Evidenz Bureau had two dozen officers assigned to it plus the military attachés serving abroad. After 1909, Colonel August von Urbanski, one of Conrad's protégés, headed the operation. The bureau had sections that dealt with intelligence collection, assessment and counter-espionage activity. Geographical areas, such as Russia, were assigned to a particular officer, as well as specialized topics such as fortresses or artillery. In addition, Andreas Figl headed an innovative code-breaking section, one of the few bright spots in Habsburg intelligence operations.[4]

The military attachés used open sources and visits to manoeuvres to provide extremely valuable information to Conrad and the Evidenz Bureau. Franz Joseph forbade spying by his attachés; nevertheless they provided quite useful information. In particular, Major Otto Gellinek in Belgrade and Captain Gustav Hubka in Cetinje sent reports that closely tracked developments in both capitals. Gellinek was particularly adept at following the ins and outs of Serbian party politics and especially Serbian military politics. Both had excellent contacts and their information gave analysts much to assess.[5]

The Evidenz Bureau also had agents in the field. With passports still an infrequent requirement, these men, controlled by Major Max Ronge, travelled easily across national borders, seeking information on railway construction, mobilization plans and troop morale. Apparently, some of the agents were well placed, for they gathered some high-level data on the Serbian military. The post-1918 destruction of the intelligence records, however, makes an evaluation of the overall effort difficult. But Ronge's memoirs suggest few spectacular successes for Habsburg spies; rather a series of minor achievements.[6]

Conrad had one other set of intelligence contacts: the German General Staff with its intelligence and counter-espionage capabilities. The Evidenz Bureau maintained reasonably close ties with its German counterpart. The agencies exchanged information about Russian war plans and shared some technological data about weapons and railway systems. Also, the two groups attempted to protect themselves against Russian espionage. Recent studies suggest that the German counter-espionage effort enjoyed notable successes, the Habsburgs less so, partly because of the celebrated Redl case.

Because of its sensational impact, the Redl case deserves additional comments. Alfred Redl had served as Urbanski's chief of counter intelligence until April 1911, before becoming chief of staff of the Eighth Army Corps in Prague. His homosexual liaisons made him the target of Russian blackmail; he routinely supplied information to St Petersburg. The level and importance of that information remains in debate, though Serbian deployments in 1914 were apparently influenced by information conveyed from St Petersburg. With help from the German authorities, the Habsburgs discovered Redl's treason in May 1913, whereupon he was allowed to commit suicide. This episode has, however, often obscured the achievements of Conrad's intelligence apparatus and of the wealth of information available to Vienna.[7]

Once gathered, the intelligence went to Conrad and his most senior associates. They then used it to assess the current situation, to assist in the review of Habsburg war plans and to validate (or invalidate) their evaluation of foreign military forces. Occasionally, and jealously, Conrad shared some of the information with the civilian leadership, just as they shared some important telegrams and reports with him. But, like other European states of the day, no agency or group assessed the information collectively or ensured that the broader evaluation had any significant circulation in a crisis. Instead, policy-makers had bits and pieces of information that might reinforce their predilection for a certain course of action. Sometimes the intelligence data was valid, sometimes plainly wrong. Conrad, for example, possessed detailed information about enemy force structures and about possible places of deployment. But information that he alone (and without debate) assessed through his offensive ideology led him to exaggerate or minimize the importance of intelligence as it fitted his own preconceptions. Conrad seldom had to explain his analysis or submit to a counter-factual set of arguments. He had the intelligence; he drafted the war plans; he made the mistakes.[8]

The problem in Vienna was not inadequate information. Rather, the problem centred upon the assessment of the danger and the unilateral, compartmental approach that Franz Joseph's style particularly encouraged. To these structural problems must be added the nature of the *Ausgleich* government in which so many domestic issues were foreign issues and vice versa. Detached analysis was rare indeed; even the *supra*-national Ballhausplatz could not entirely remove itself from this web. Yet the dynasty, diplomatic and military leaders had to worry about the foreign threat to the monarchy. Their assessment of the strategic situation at the start of 1912 offers a convenient survey — state by state — of the monarchy's foreign situation on the eve of the Balkan conflagration.

II

By 1912 Serbia constituted the most persistent threat to Austria–Hungary. After 1903, Habsburg policy toward Belgrade gradually moved from *control* to *constraint* and finally to *combat*. From the 1870s to 1903, Vienna had managed to control Serbian politics by subverting through bribes and other inducements the Obrenović kings — first Milan and then the hapless Alexander. Finally, a group of military officers led by a young lieutenant, Dragutin Dimitrijević (nicknamed 'Apis') plotted to kill King Alexander and his wife, Queen Draga, a woman of dubious moral character. The extraordinarily brutal assassinations, on the night of 10–11 June 1903, ended the Obrenović dynasty and brought Peter Karadjordjević to power.[9]

The new king, the former son-in-law of King Nikita of Montenegro, quickly consolidated his power. In this he had the assistance of Nikola Pašić and the Radical Party, who gained the respect of the people and edged the country carefully but steadily away from its earlier chaos. But Pašić, Peter and the Serbian military also formulated a more confrontational agenda: talk of a greater Serbia, independence from Vienna and closer ties with St Petersburg.

The only Balkan state completely landlocked, Serbia wanted to expand its access to markets beyond Austria–Hungary. A route to the sea, preferably to the Adriatic and under Serbian control, became a longterm priority for the Serbian government. In the meantime, however, Belgrade in June 1905 negotiated a trade arrangement with neighbouring Bulgaria that established a customs union. With the publication of the treaty in late 1905, an angry Vienna, pushed along by Budapest, embarked on the ill-fated 'Pig War' in which Austria–Hungary essentially banned Serbian pork products. Having lost the ability to control Serbia, Vienna now sought to constrain it.[10]

The Dual Monarchy's trade relations with Serbia soon came to an impasse. But the impasse did nothing to constrain Belgrade. Austro-Hungary's exports to Serbia fell precipitously, yet the Germans quickly filled the shortfall at the expense of their allies. Moreover, French capital soon established itself in Belgrade. This episode strengthened the Russophiles in Belgrade at a time when Russia was slowly beginning to turn its attention back to the Balkans. The Pig War damaged Habsburg prestige, while doing little to thwart Serbia.

The emergent Russo-Serbian connection was strengthened in 1908 with Vienna's decision to annex Bosnia–Herzegovina. Aehrenthal's decision shocked Belgrade. Overlooking Izvolsky's willingness to sacrifice Serbian interests, Belgrade's leadership turned to St Petersburg for support and fulminated against Vienna's actions. Tensions built until Russia's abrupt decision to abandon the Belgrade regime in March 1909. This ended the crisis, but its ramifications were consequential. Thereafter, chances for longterm improvements in Austro-Serbian relations virtually disappeared. Furthermore, despite Russia's lack of support during the crisis, Serbia clearly linked itself with St Petersburg. Nicholas Hartwig's arrival as Russian minister to Belgrade in the autumn of 1909 buttressed this inclination. Virulently anti-Habsburg and a Pan-Slav envoy of considerable skill and energy, Hartwig worked diligently to push the

Belgrade regime into a more active policy against Turkish rule in Macedonia, as well as a more assertive policy against Vienna.

Hartwig's declamations found fertile soil in Serbia and with many South Slavs within the Habsburg monarchy. Despite Belgrade's commitment in the 1909 treaty to limit the *Narodna Odbrana* to cultural activities, it grew quickly to 220 branches in Serbia and soon spilled over into Bosnia. The *Narodna Odbrana*'s stress on Serbian values and a greater Serbia had a disruptive appeal in Bosnia. And the network provided the cover for other anti-Habsburg groups as well, a fact which Vienna quickly recognized. Vienna tracked the *Narodna Odbrana* with concern and anxiety.[11]

Other, more fragmented Pan-Slav terrorist activity also emerged. For example, Bogdan Žerajič, already implicated in another plot against Franz Joseph, tried on 15 June 1910 to assassinate the Governor General of Bosnia–Herzegovina. Thereafter, assassination attempts against Habsburg officials, both in Bosnia and in Croatia, increased dramatically.[12]

The aggressive moves by the Serbians provided momentum for the South Slav movement within the monarchy. Vienna's efforts to discredit the political leadership of the South Slav group simply backfired. At one point, in an attempt to intimidate the Croatian politicians, some were arrested and accused of alleged ties with Serbia. At the subsequent Agram (Zagreb) trials, many of the accused were convicted on evidence that could only be described as 'suspect'. Compounding this debacle was the subsequent Friedjung affair. In March 1909 Professor Heinrich Friedjung asserted in the *Neue Freie Presse* that leading South Slav politicians, including members of the Austrian Lower House, had almost treasonous connections with Serbia. More provocatively, he claimed to have documents that proved their treason. The trial demolished Friedjung's claims, when it was shown that the documents produced by the Habsburg ministry in Belgrade were forgeries. This Habsburg fiasco, instead of damaging Belgrade, conferred still greater credibility on the Yugoslav movement.[13]

A more ominous development for Vienna was the creation of the Black Hand in May 1911. Angered by Pašić's parliamentary tactics, a group of extreme Serbian nationalists and army officers formed the secret society, the *Ujedinjenje ili Smrt*. These conspirators were committed to a violent solution to the Macedonian and South Slav problems. The ultra-secret society soon infiltrated the *Narodna*

Odbrana, supported terrorist groups operating in Macedonia and launched the newspaper *Piedmont*. The Black Hand never precisely defined its aspirations by opting for Yugoslavia or for greater Serbia. Nevertheless, the Black Hand's Central Committee soon found in Apis a dynamic and energetic leader. Apparently, Vienna over-looked Apis's role, even though it knew of the group by late 1911. An ambiguous relationship emerged between the Black Hand and the Serbian government, although the Serbian foreign minister Milovan Milovanovič exploited the organization in South Serbia in 1912–13. Certainly the senior leadership of the Serbian government knew of the society and of Apis's role in it. But at the end of 1911, the group was just one of several that had begun to grow and to plot. Later events would distinguish the Black Hand from other such groups. [14]

The aggressive Hartwig, meanwhile, worked in the autumn of 1911 to exploit the Turkish exposure in Macedonia caused by the Italian attack on Tripoli. In this Hartwig first had to reconcile relations between Sofia and Belgrade, a task not rendered easier because of each's conflicting ambitions in Macedonia. Yet without Bulgarian consent, a Serbian move in Macedonia was foreclosed. Furthermore, Hartwig recognized that a Sofia aligned with Belgrade could not be later used by Austria–Hungary against Serbia. Hart-wig's labours to mend the relationships succeeded. On 13 March 1912 Serbian and Bulgarian statesmen concluded a secret treaty aimed at the Ottoman Empire and Austria–Hungary. A resolution of the Macedonian issue now seemed possible; it might also prepare the Slavs for a subsequent move against Austria–Hungary. [15]

For some weeks Vienna was unaware of the secret treaty. But the Habsburg government in early 1912 possessed few illusions about Serbia's overall ambitions. Foreign Minister Berchtold wanted correct relations with Belgrade but doubted that an acceptable South Slav solution could be found. Nor was he comfortable with Russian motives. On the other hand, political figures pressed for a détente with Belgrade. Arguing that such an overture might help to resolve the South Slav issue, this group travelled frequently to Belgrade and had contacts with Serbian politicians. Although willing to discuss an overture to Belgrade, few among the ministerial elite wanted to provide the monarchy's South Slav leadership with still another justification for turning to Belgrade should the détente effort fail. [16]

The fears of the Ballhausplatz about Serbia were matched by those of Conrad and his successor, General Schemua. For the military planners, Serbia presented a series of interlocking problems: the defence of the monarchy's southern borders and domestic order; the Serbo-Russian relationship; a possible Serbian-Montenegrin union and thus Serbian access to the Adriatic; the future of Albania and Serbian ambitions for Macedonian territory. In assessing these threats, the Habsburg generals consistently forecast a capable Ottoman defence against Serbia in Albania and Macedonia. What worried the Habsburg generals was the Serbo-Russian connection. The greatest strategic danger, Conrad constantly argued, would come if Russia intervened after Vienna was already at war with Serbia. If only Austria–Hungary had attacked in 1909, Conrad repeatedly complained, when Russia would not have been able to intervene.

Unfortunately, for the Habsburgs, Serbia's stunning military success in late 1912 did not alter Vienna's assessment of the Serbian army. Conrad never doubted that the Danubian monarchy could crush Serbia if Russia stayed out. His strategic Plan B always called for an offensive launched from Bosnia–Herzegovina that quickly annihilated the Serbian forces. Against an estimated ten or eleven Serbian divisions, Conrad and Schemua planned to deploy twenty Habsburg divisions. If Russia did not interfere, the planners believed these troops would be more than adequate to ensure victory. As protection against possible Russian intervention in Galicia, Conrad planned to deploy a defence force of twenty-eight divisions along the monarchy's northern frontiers.

While Conrad worried about Russia, his mounting preoccupation, especially as the events of 1912 unfolded, was the Balkans. Here the annihilation of Serbia remained his abiding passion. He gave scant attention to any other plan, including the rapid seizure of Belgrade which lay just across from Habsburg territory. Instead, Conrad focused his energies entirely upon an offensive attack launched eastward through the rugged terrain along the Bosnia–Herzegovina frontier. His confidence in the offensive wished away the problems that mountains and valleys posed for mobility. He wanted to partition Serbia or put it into a Bavarian-like status *vis-à-vis* Vienna and Budapest. Sceptical of Serbian military forces and disturbed by the South Slav menace, Conrad would attack it 'root and branch'. But Conrad depended upon Germany to deter Russia for his

southern operation to work. Here was Austria–Hungary's fundamental strategic dependence and its strategic dilemma. For Germany
wanted Austria–Hungary to attack Russia, not Serbia. This paradox Conrad, Austria–Hungary and Germany could never escape.[17]

When the Balkan fighting began in October 1912, Schemua and
Conrad (from his post as army inspector) believed that the Turkish
forces would hold their own. Those assumptions soon proved
erroneous. The Serbian successes quickly demonstrated that
Belgrade posed a substantial military threat to the Habsburg
monarchy. Each Serbian victory in 1912 and 1913 reinforced the
perception of the South Slav threat to the Dual Monarchy. The
Habsburg policy of constraining Serbia seemed increasingly inadequate; Vienna's decision-makers moved ever closer to combat as an
option.

III

Montenegro, in contrast to Serbia, posed no fundamental challenge
to the Austro-Hungarian monarchy. Indeed, the parody of the
Montenegrin monarchy in Franz Lehar's 1905 operetta, 'The Merry
Widow', had elements of truth. The tiny, mountainous kingdom of
250,000 had a population less than the Habsburg city of Prague.
Cetinje, the capital with slightly more than 5000-plus inhabitants,
had few notable buildings and even fewer distractions. An economic
backwater, poor even by Balkan standards, Montenegro did, however, possess a coveted Adriatic coastline with navigable ports at
Antivari (Bar) and Ulcinj. But Montenegro's biggest assets, as well
as the cause of much of its poverty, were its geographical location
and its wily, rambunctious old monarch, King Nikita, ruler of the
diminutive country since 1860 and king since 1910.[18]

Craftily and skillfully, Nikita had expanded Montenegro's territory in the 1878 Berlin settlement and then during the Bosnian crisis
of 1908. He envisioned, moreover, an enlarged Montenegro as the
centre of a new Slavic state. At the same time, he exploited his
progeny; his daughters married very well. Two became wives of
Russian archdukes, another had married King Peter of Serbia, and
most importantly, one was the queen of Italy. These international
connections, Nikita's willingness to accept foreign funds and his
mercurial stances made him a more important figure in Balkan

politics than the realm deserved. Because the regime was so personal, Nikita could reverse loyalties without the least concern for consistency. Before 1912 Vienna could classify Nikita as 'neutral'; after 1912 his dependency upon Russia moved him more firmly into the 'potential enemy' category.

The chief threats posed to the Habsburg monarchy by Montenegro were not military. The kingdom had an army of at most four divisions of approximately 50,000, without reserves or a financial base to support a war effort. Geography, however, posed one threat to Habsburg naval forces: Montenegro's possession of Mount Lovčen overlooking the Cattaro harbour. Artillery on Lovčen could dominate the inland harbour and indeed could threaten the Adriatic coastline. While a possibility, one that preoccupied generations of Habsburg military planners, in reality Montenegro was not capable of blunting Habsburg naval power.

But Montenegro did pose a significant political and diplomatic threat to Austria–Hungary, a threat that easily could become strategic. Thus Habsburg policy-makers preferred the status quo, fearful that Montenegro might try to alter the role carefully defined for it by the great powers when the country emerged from the Ottoman rule. For the Habsburgs four issues were of utmost import- ance: the possibility of a Serb-Montenegrin union that would give Serbia access to the Adriatic and economic independence; Monte- negrin ambitions for Albanian territory; the family relationship with Italy that Vienna always considered troublesome; and the exagger- ated perception of the Russian presence in the small country.

At the start of 1912, a Montenegrin union with Serbia looked very unlikely. Since 1909 Nikita had repeatedly suspected Serbia of assisting his domestic opponents, including those involved in the abortive Kolasin conspiracy. Charges and countercharges abounded. Furthermore, the conflicting ambitions of the two states over any partition of Macedonian territory also drove them apart. Because of these tensions, Serbia excluded Montenegro from the negotiations creating the Balkan League in the spring of 1912. Not until late that summer would the other powers decide to include the fickle Nikita.

Montenegrin ambitions for sizeable chunks of Albanian territory in the event of a collapse of Turkish power represented a more serious threat. Repeatedly, Nikita tried to exploit the chaos in the Albanian Christian communities for his benefit. Ostensible

Turkish control checked Nikita's aspirations. If Turkish rule ended, the Albanian question would surface and conflict with Vienna would be deemed highly probable.[19]

Nikita's relations with the other ambitious Adriatic power — Italy — frequently disturbed the elite in Vienna. Italian economic activity in the country, but especially at the port of Antivari, generated concern. Nikita's occasional suggestions that he would exploit his status as father-in-law of the Italian monarch to the detriment of Austro-Hungarian interests proved even more vexing. In particular, Vienna feared an Italian-Montenegrin arrangement that allowed the Italian navy to use Antivari in time of war. While the fear was not realized before 1914, the prospect remained troubling. Yet both Rome and Cetinje realized that any such agreement would have a volatile impact upon Austro-Montenegrin-Italian relations. Montenegro's Italian connection required Vienna's attention.

Surprisingly, Vienna did not fret much about improved Russian-Montenegrin relations. To be sure, the Russians had treaty obligations for continuing financial assistance to Nikita. Russian threats to curtail this aid could occasionally alter Nikita's position, but that did not make him reliable. His capriciousness often affected St Petersburg's willingness to offer him more funds, a fact he discovered in early 1912 when he visited the Russian capital. On that occasion, the Russians bluntly dampened his plans for involvement in Albania. And St Petersburg generally sought to restrain the tempestuous monarch, not encourage him to adventure.[20]

For Conrad and the Habsburgs, Montenegro's defeat would negate the Lovčen batteries and offer some strategic advantages against Serbia. In 1908 Conrad had allocated five Habsburg divisions (68,000 men) for an attack on Montenegrin forces estimated at 50,000. Subsequently, in Plan B Conrad had Habsburg forces remain on the defensive *vis-à-vis* Montenegro, while the main offensive was directed at Serbia. Montenegro posed no major military threat, and Plan B reflected that reality. Nevertheless, Montenegrin forces were capable of tying down Habsburg troops in Bosnia–Herzegovina and along the Cattaro inlet. Furthermore, if aligned with Serbia, these troops might threaten Habsburg interests and especially in Albania. For the strategic planners in Vienna, the defeat of Montenegro would gain little, but neglecting to deal with Nikita could be costly indeed.[21]

On the eve of the Balkan Wars, however, relations between Cetinje and Vienna appeared pleasant, almost cordial. In October 1911 the Austrians had arranged a 3.5 million crown loan for Nikita. Franz Joseph, who had warmly endorsed Nikita's self-elevation to king in 1910, conferred a colonelcy of an Austrian infantry regiment on his fellow monarch in mid-1912 when Nikita visited Vienna. In Cetinje, moreover, the Habsburg minister, Wladimir Giesl, enjoyed relatively easy access to the colourful ruler who occasionally proposed grandiose territorial swaps, all to no avail.[22]

Consequently, at the start of Berchtold's tenure as foreign minister, Montenegro was a potential threat rather than a definite problem like Serbia. But Nikita was too unpredictable, his financial needs too constant and his vanity and ego too monumental to allow policy-makers to rely either on his word or his longterm adherence to any course of action. His instability enhanced the possibilities for mischief, as Britain and the great powers discovered in early 1913 when the Scutari crisis erupted. King Nikita, the swashbuckling Balkan ruler, proved that threats and personality could play havoc with international politics. He is the forerunner of imitators in the late twentieth century.

IV

The Balkans and Italy formed a set of enemies for Austria–Hungary; the Triple Entente, however, contained more formidable opponents. Russia alone would have constituted the Danubian monarchy's most serious strategic and diplomatic preoccupation. But the rapid consolidation of the Triple Entente after 1907 dramatically altered the situation for Berlin and Vienna. The Second Moroccan Crisis in 1911 reinforced these changes as it convinced policy-makers in London and Paris that they needed closer relations, and stirred the French to pursue a more assertive diplomacy. Vienna and Berlin belatedly grasped this danger. As the cohesion of the Triple Entente increased, so did the dangers for Austria–Hungary and for the peace of Europe. Still, moments of détente and opportunities for cooperation occurred in 1912.[23]

One 'lost opportunity' for Vienna was its failure to develop closer relations with Great Britain. The two capitals had often cooperated on the Eastern question and no natural points of friction existed between the two states. London, moreover, had played a positive role in resolving the Bosnian crisis in March 1909. British officials developed considerable respect for Aehrenthal, as some believed the foreign minister might lead Austria–Hungary away from Berlin and thus weaken the Triple Alliance. Even with Berchtold, who had served in London, some thought opportunities were present for Anglo-Austrian relations to become more cordial. Personal ties pointed in the same direction. Count Alexander Mensdorff, the Habsburg ambassador since 1904, was Edward VII's cousin. The popular British monarch twice visited Franz Joseph at Bad Ischl. Later, Mensdorff's friendship with George V allowed the Austrian easy access to aristocratic circles in Britain. At Edward VII's funeral in 1910 Archduke Franz Ferdinand represented his uncle. The heir-apparent also visited George V at Windsor. And in Vienna, Fairfax Cartwright, the British ambassador from 1908–12, assiduously worked to improve Britain's relations with Austria–Hungary. Yet surprisingly none of these ties had much effect; certainly none altered the dominant convictions in Whitehall that Austria–Hungary was almost an appendage of the German empire.[24]

Complex reasons explain the gradual deterioration of Anglo-Austrian relations. Certainly, one factor was the mounting disaffection of the British intelligentsia against the seemingly antiquated Danubian monarchy. R. W. Seton-Watson's writings about Habsburg misrule of the nationalities sowed doubt among the British on whether the multinational state could or even should survive. Henry Wickham Steed, stationed in Vienna as the reporter for *The Times* of London, buttressed this opinion with his stories. His pen, while occasionally sympathetic, chronicled the foibles of Habsburg rule and suggested that the monarchy might not endure. The impact of the Anglo-German naval race and the willingness of the British public and the Foreign Office to lump Austria–Hungary willy-nilly into the 'enemy camp' further undermined any positive elements. So also did pressures in Vienna and Budapest for a larger Habsburg navy. Often posed in terms of making the Habsburg monarchy more alliance-worthy, the new naval programme naturally reinforced British strategic fears.[25]

The growing importance of the Anglo-Russian relationship after 1907 probably had the greatest influence in frustrating any improvement of Anglo-Habsburg relations. The British Foreign Office would permit nothing to intrude upon this new level of understanding with the czar. Any visible improvement of London's relations with Vienna would require some British equivocation in the Balkans and Eastern Europe. British statesmen could argue that any concessions to Vienna might jeopardize the connection with St Petersburg, threaten the Triple Entente and in turn expose India and Persia to renewed Russian pressure. Or the Foreign Office could pose an equally disastrous scenario: an offended Russia might link itself with Germany. Finally, any British movement toward détente with Austria–Hungary that troubled the Russians would doubly upset Paris. Under no circumstances would Grey permit any action that damaged his policy of the *entente cordiale*. He wanted to contain Germany and was unwilling to take chances. In early 1912 Anglo-Austrian relations, therefore, were technically correct, but Vienna had almost no access to British capital and British policy-makers viewed Vienna as a dependency of Berlin. Still, during 1912, Grey remained more flexible than his hard-line, anti-German subordinates. And, during the First Balkan War, the two governments worked together to contain the crisis.[26]

In terms of Habsburg military planning the British represented a paradox. The British army had no consequence for Conrad. The British navy was a different matter altogether. In early 1912 British and French ships dominated the Mediterranean, despite the building efforts of both Austria–Hungary and Italy. On the other hand, the Austro-Italian construction programme insured that London and Paris had to reckon with Vienna's naval potential. Furthermore, the intensification of the Anglo-German naval race in 1912 necessarily heightened the importance of the Habsburg naval forces. The new round of German naval construction and new manning schemes threatened British naval effectiveness in the North Sea. To offset these developments Winston Churchill, as First Lord of the Admiralty, and the British admirals decided to withdraw the British battleship squadron (six older ships) from Malta to Gibraltar. Four British battle cruisers would be left at Malta. This redeployment meant that the Austro-Italian forces, especially after each completed construction on their dreadnoughts in 1912, would approach parity with the combined Anglo-French forces in the Mediterranean. Thus the existence of the Habsburg naval forces offered London and Vienna both a possible subject for negotiations but also for tension. With the arrival in the Mediterranean of the German cruisers *Goeben* and *Breslau* during the Balkan Crisis, the balance of naval forces became an urgent matter for British leaders. But negotiations between London and Vienna never occurred, nor indeed were even seriously considered.[27]

Although plausible possibilities for improved Anglo-Austrian relations existed, the practical results were nil. The British hesitated to coax Vienna away from Berlin. With little to offer London except a curb on Habsburg naval forces, Berchtold had no leverage with Grey. Anglo-Austrian relations had become a dependent variable, placed at the mercy of Anglo-German and Anglo-Russian relations. On the eve of the Balkan fighting, Berchtold and his colleagues could at best hope that Grey would give the Habsburg monarchy a respectful hearing.

With the French leadership Vienna expected much less. Already confronted with aggressive French economic diplomacy in south-eastern Europe, especially in Belgrade and Bucharest, the Habsburg statesmen found the Paris money markets also closed. The French closed-door policy, a feature of the Franco-Russian alliance, neces-sarily pushed the Habsburg financiers into German and American markets. Rather than isolate the Germans, the French and British financial strategy drove Vienna closer to Berlin. Except for the economic considerations and the naval problems in the Mediter-ranean, the Habsburgs and the French had few areas of contact. Diplomatic ties between the Third Republic and the venerable monarchy were proper but no more. On the other hand, two personnel changes in 1911 and 1912 require that even that statement be qualified. Indeed, had Vienna known the full impact of the changes under way in Paris after the Second Moroccan Crisis, it would have been thoroughly alarmed. For the appointments of General Joseph Joffre as chief of the French General Staff in the summer of 1911 and then Raymond Poincaré as French premier in early 1912 heralded a new closeness in Franco-Russian relations.[28]

The French were important to Austria–Hungary primarily because of their alliance with Russia. The new French leadership in particu-lar injected three elements into the relationship: capital, military improvements and confidence. French capital, a notable feature of Russian public finance since the late nineteenth century, became even more important after 1911. Anxious to accelerate the construc-tion of the Russian rail system in the west to expedite Russian mobilization, the French government contributed an additional 500 million francs annually to Russia from 1911–14. This infusion of funds had an impact upon the political relationship and upon strategic planning. These loans in turn also made possible a progressive revamping of the Franco-Russian military relationship. At first the changes were barely noticeable. In late 1911 Joffre began shifting French planning away from a defensive–offensive strategy to an all-out offensive scheme. A prerequisite for the new plan to work was an early Russian attack on Germany if war came. Joffre repeatedly pressured the Russians for definite assistance. These pressures intensified in subsequent Franco-Russian staff talks, with Joffre in 1913 securing a Russian pledge to attack eastern Prussia by the fifteenth day after the outbreak of war. The Franco-Russian alliance had acquired a new, more effective military component that would endanger the Habsburg monarchy in a European war.[29]

The third feature of the Franco-Russian relationship after Agadir was France's own growing self-confidence. Poincaré's premiership (and subsequently his presidency) brought a new, more assertive tone to French foreign policy. The successful conclusion of the Second Moroccan Crisis stimulated a surge of French nationalism. Poincaré buttressed this feeling while zealously working to tighten the Russian alliance. As a part of his effort, Poincaré travelled to St Petersburg in mid-1912. Later he sent Théophile Delcassé, the architect of the Anglo-French entente, to Russia as ambassador. Poincaré, moreover, authorized the start of Franco-Russian naval conversations and sought to consolidate the Triple Entente as a political and strategic unit. The Russians in turn responded to Poincaré's efforts, as a new, more confident and aggressive mood also appeared in St Petersburg. The Franco-Russian alliance had become a unity that Vienna could not ignore, a fact that progressively became clearer as the events of 1912–13 unfolded.[30]

V

On the eve of the Balkan fighting, Russia remained Vienna's most dangerous, implacable foe. Yet the Habsburg leadership — both civilian and diplomatic — continued to harbour some hope that ties with St Petersburg might be improved. While Franz Joseph apparently had doubts about the improvement of Habsburg–Romanov relations, Franz Ferdinand believed it possible. In fact, the archduke toyed with the idea of an overture to St Petersburg as the necessary first step to renewing an alignment like the Three Emperors

League. In February 1912, when Berchtold took office, he also expressed his hope that ties with Russia would improve. The former ambassador to Russia (1906–11) had no desire to relive the tensions of the Bosnian Crisis. Instead, he explored with his associates how to engage in an exchange of ideas with St Petersburg. Ambassador Count Duglas Thurn, Berchtold's successor, supported a policy that called for understanding and even détente.

But Berchtold and the Ballhausplatz did not translate these vague ideas into any systematic policy initiatives toward St Petersburg in early 1912. The pressures of the Italo-Turkish war partly account for this failure, while the suspicions about a Balkan League under Russian sponsorship dampened Habsburg enthusiasm. Nevertheless, until mid-1912 the perceptions of the Ballhausplatz toward Russia were open, even flexible. The outbreak of the First Balkan War would dramatically alter these Habsburg attitudes.[31]

Three areas of Russian activity persistently caused trouble for Vienna: St Petersburg's Pan-Slavic machinations, its diplomacy with the Balkan states and Russia's rapidly changing strategic position. Of these issues, the Pan-Slavic agitation was the most predictable but least coherent. St Petersburg never entirely abandoned its Pan-Slavic activities, though the degree of official sanction varied from year to year. In Galicia, Russian propagandists agitated against Habsburg rule and boasted of the common interests between the Ruthenians in both countries. In Bohemia, the Czech leaders often expressed gratitude for St Petersburg's understanding of their plight in the Habsburg monarchy. Nor were the Russians inactive in Bukovina.[32]

Pan-Slavism was less threatening to the Dual Monarchy than Russia's moral and tangible support of South Slav activities inside the Habsburg monarchy. For the Russians did encourage Serbian propaganda for a greater Serbia or a Yugoslav state that could only come at Habsburg expense. Minister Hartwig remained unchecked in his exuberant backing of the South Slav cause. Few Habsburg statesmen held the Russians responsible for the growth of Slavic feeling in the Habsburg domain, yet none doubted that Russian support exacerbated the problem. In a mirror-image effect, Habsburg policy-makers occasionally allowed their troubles with nationality issues to influence their assessments of Russian strength, reasoning that the Romanovs would also be hurt by nationality pressures should war come. Curiously, however, and indicative of its own sense of vulnerability, Vienna did not reciprocate by stirring up nationality groups within the Russian monarchy.

Russian diplomatic activities in the Balkans were a constant concern to Vienna. In the autumn of 1911 Sazonov and N. V. Charykov had shown renewed interest in the Ottoman empire, pressing Constantinople, as it fought Italy, for concessions at the Straits. The *démarche* came to nothing. More successful were Russia's covert efforts to encourage a Serbo-Bulgarian reconciliation. With Hartwig's active assistance, the two governments in March 1912 negotiated a treaty that constituted the first stage of the Balkan League. Designed to link Sofia and Belgrade together in a move against Turkey on the Macedonian question, the agreement arranged for the partition of Macedonia rather than for its continued autonomy. Two months later, in May, again with Russian encouragement, the two governments agreed upon a military convention that transformed the so-called 'defensive' accord into a clearly 'offensive' one. Poincaré, who learned of the accords when he visited St Petersburg in August, justifiably called them 'a convention of War'.

While Serbia and Bulgaria worked, again with Russian sanction to include Greece in the new Balkan alignment, St Petersburg counselled King Nikita against any further unilateral adventures in Albania or in Macedonia. Later that summer, Belgrade moved to include the Montenegrin ruler in the alliance accord. That move, given Nikita's pattern of erratic behaviour, came only weeks before the start of Balkan hostilities. Once the war began and the magnitude of Russia's role in prompting the Balkan League became apparent, Austro-Russian relations were irrevocably damaged.[33]

The only Balkan state not subject in 1912 to the Russian diplomatic effort was Rumania. Thus the Rumanian connection remained intact for Vienna and Berlin, a fact that offered them some strategic solace. If Vienna wanted to risk conflict in the Balkans, Berlin and Vienna could hope to use Rumania against Bulgaria or Serbia. Should Russia decide to 'work' the Bucharest angle, however, the Habsburg position in the Balkans would be still further threatened.

The Habsburg military followed each turn and twist of Russian diplomacy in early 1912. While unaware of the shift in French strategy, the Habsburg military leadership quickly grasped the importance of St Petersburg's efforts to accelerate its mobilization process. In January 1909 Conrad and Moltke had envisioned that Russia would have fifty-one and a half divisions available in the west by the twentieth day of mobilization, with twenty-four units aimed at Austria–Hungary. The number of available Russian divisions gradually increased. By 1912 Conrad expected that his forces alone would confront a total of fifty divisions within six weeks. To meet this danger he and his associates expected to have forty infantry divisions (and some calvary divisions) along the Russian frontier by the twentieth day of mobilization. Given these assessments, the Austro-Hungarian military leadership in 1912 still believed it could resist Russia. But no one thought the odds for victory were better than even. Conrad and Schemua, moreover, always warned that the Habsburg position was deteriorating. Each year, as the Russians rebuilt their military machine, they were able to take advantage of their superior numbers and their geographic advantages, all to the discomfort of Austria–Hungary.[34]

Yet despite the cautionary note sounded by the military leadership in Vienna, the Habsburg leadership in the years after 1910 remained surprisingly nonchalant about the Russian threat. To be sure, Conrad wanted a commitment from Moltke — for a strong German deployment in the east that would deter the Russians. Moreover, Conrad appreciated the dangers that Russia posed to Vienna and especially the perils of a two-front war with Russia and Serbia simultaneously. But there remained, for all of these concerns, a puzzling tendency by Vienna and Berlin to belittle the quality of Russian forces and their probable effect in a European war. Such attitudes before the Balkan Wars are possibly understandable; after the Russian military measures of 1912–13, such perceptions are indefensible. Conrad's arrogant belief that Austria–Hungary had stood Russia down in 1909 may have been a factor in this. While Conrad knew that Russia had improved its forces since then, the indicators about Russian troop morale, weapons and discipline were less clear-cut. Furthermore, information coming from Berlin suggested that Russian military strength should not be overrated. These German evaluations reinforced misleading Habsburg perceptions rather than prompting further investigation.[35]

Conrad's fanatical faith in the offensive and his belief in a short war also worked to diminish his fears about Russia. These two mindsets, shared elsewhere by European military staffs, were nonetheless even more crucial for Habsburg strategy. Determined to save the monarchy from its rotting conditions by initiating military actions against Serbia or, if the czar intervened, Russia and then

Serbia, Conrad believed a well-executed offensive ensured the decisive advantage. Because of the offensive strategy, the war would also be brief. This circular logic prevented any realistic assessment of the counter-factual possibilities. Because an outcome had to be, it would be. For Conrad to believe Russia could be defeated, he had to assess the Russian forces as being relatively ineffective. For if he assessed them more accurately, then he could not have the military confrontation he so desperately wanted. In 1912 Schemua and then Conrad still believed that the Habsburg monarchy could win against Russia; those perceptions would not change by July 1914. At that point Russia was also confident that it could win. If war is a test of strength or a verification of power, then these perceptions played their part in the Austro-Hungarian descent into the abyss.[36]

VI

On the eve of the First Balkan War, the Austro-Hungarian monarchy had the protection of a Triple Alliance about to be renewed for another five years. Rumania's fidelity to the alliance grouping appeared assured. Peace talks to end the Italo-Turkish war were underway. The intelligence agencies and the General Staffs in Berlin and Vienna were in frequent contact; conversations between the allied staffs for naval and military cooperation were about to start. In Vienna, Berchtold had survived the first six months in office and had succeeded during the summer in resolving a series of domestic issues over the budget. Thanks to István Tisza's assistance, the two governments had agreed to raise the intake of military recruits for the first time since 1889. In both halves of the monarchy a vibrant economy continued to show signs of growth. Franz Joseph appeared active and well, while Franz Ferdinand carefully nurtured his expanding relationship with Foreign Minister Berchtold. Although domestic politics on both sides of the River Leitha remained acrimonious, the future, if not bright, looked acceptable for the Danubian state.[37]

Offsetting this assessment, however, were some disturbing pieces of intelligence. Rumours about a new Balkan League were alarming. Renewed clashes between Christian subjects in Macedonia and the Turkish authorities foreshadowed possible trouble for Vienna. Nor was the presence of Poincaré in St Petersburg in August entirely reassuring. And Sazonov's presence in Britain a month later reinforced growing concern within the Triple Alliance about the enhanced cohesion of the Triple Entente. The rival grouping appeared stronger politically than ever before. Equally alarming, the Balkan League's existence offered the potential for great mischief in the south. A coordinated Balkan attack upon the Ottoman empire would reopen the Macedonian question and bring war to the European continent for the first time in more than three decades. Yet how could the Balkan states resist the temptation to resolve the Macedonian issue with a Turkish government already under attack by the Italians? The fears that first haunted Aehrenthal and then Berchtold — that the Italian war would spill over into the Balkans — received confirmation as the August days of 1912 gave way to those of September. Then on 8 October Montenegro declared war on Turkey; Serbia, Greece, and Bulgaria rapidly followed King Nikita's lead. For the next six years Europe was the scene of horrendous military hostilities as the First Balkan War gave way to the Second and then to the Third in July 1914.

7 Militant Diplomacy: the Habsburgs and the First Balkan War, August 1912–May 1913

During the summer of 1912 the Balkan League states — Serbia, Bulgaria and Greece — furtively worked to prepare for a clash with the Turks. In August the Montenegrins and the Turks had an armed clash along the Albanian border. Tensions mounted, so much so that Austria–Hungary, Russia and even France grew alarmed. In mid-September Montenegro joined the Balkan League. An attack on Turkey appeared imminent, prompting Constantinople to mobilize troops in Thrace on 22 September. Eight days later the Balkan League mobilized. Then on 8 October Montenegro declared war on the Ottoman empire. On 18 October all the other League members declared war. The First Balkan War had begun.[1]

The military struggles came almost immediately. The Montenegrins moved against the Kossovo *vilayet* and toward Scutari. But the major battles involved the Bulgarians and the Serbians who won decisive victories on 22–23 October at Kirk–Kilisse and Kumanovo. Other victories quickly followed, with the Serbian forces capturing Monastir (Bitolj) and Bulgarian troops advancing to the Chatalja fortification on the way to Constantinople. The Greeks, meanwhile, encountered little opposition and in early November King Constantine led his troops into Salonika. The possible fall of the Turkish capital — Constantinople — was no longer hypothetical. To the surprise of all the European powers and to the utter consternation of the Habsburg military leadership the Turks had been routed in a few short weeks. (See Map 3.)

During November the great powers desperately worked to end the fighting. At the same time Austro-Russian and Austro-Serbian tensions increased. By early December the warring factions consented to a Balkan cease-fire. All of the states agreed to participate in two international conferences scheduled to begin in London in mid-December. The major goal would be to arrange a peace settlement. Thus by the end of 1912, fundamental changes in Balkan geography

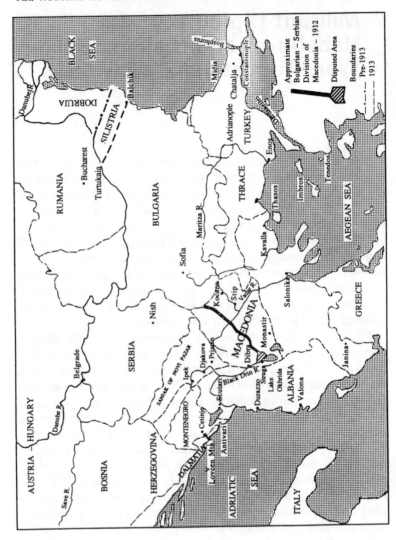

Map 3
The Balkan Wars,
1912–13

had occurred: when peace was restored, the old status quo in the Balkans would have finally disappeared.

But the peace negotiations, after a promising start, suddenly collapsed in early January. The victors could not agree among themselves on the division of the spoils; Montenegro determined to seize Scutari, Serbia to grab Albanian territory. Tension between St Petersburg, Belgrade and Vienna reached new heights. Not until mid-March would a final resolution of the first Balkan crisis begin. Russia curbed its support of Serbia; in turn, Belgrade moved away from supporting Montenegro's capture of Scutari. The Bulgarians, their army suffering from the ravages of disease, welcomed the prospect of peace.

But the Montenegrins remained determined to get Scutari. During April the great powers tried to coerce Montenegro to abandon Scutari. Nikita balked. Even a European naval demonstration along the skimpy Montenegrin coastline failed to budge him. Finally, in early May, bribes and the threat of Austrian mobilization prompted Nikita to abandon the Scutari he had recently captured. On 30 May the belligerent states signed the London peace accords, formally ending the First Balkan War. The terms can be quickly summarized: Turkey lost all of its territory in the Balkans west of a line from Enos to Midia; Crete went to the allies; the fate of the other Turkish islands in the Aegean was to be settled by the great powers; and Albania's future and its borders would be resolved by the great powers. Almost immediately the victorious allies began to squabble over the spoils; the second conflict began less than a month later.

I

In August 1912 the impending threat of a Balkan war jolted Foreign Minister Berchtold. Desperately he sought to forestall a war. He got, however, no effective help from the other European powers. Soon a diplomatic and military crisis confronted him that threatened fundamental Habsburg security interests. During the First Balkan War Berchtold's and Habsburg policy evolved through five overlapping stages: the diplomatic reaction at the onset of fighting, the response of the Habsburg military toward Serbia in November and December, a series of Austro-Russian confrontations in late 1912 and early 1913, the problem of Albanian borders and the war–peace crisis with Montenegro in May 1913.[2]

As Berchtold and his advisers pondered the rapidly deteriorating situation in mid-September 1912, they had three major options: a carefully articulated and executed policy of 'wait and see'; the option of modest military intervention to convince the Balkan governments of Vienna's willingness to act; and a policy of wider military intervention, using a war to resolve other issues with Serbia. Of these options, only the first and second received much attention or support. Moreover, Berchtold, the Habsburgs (Franz Joseph and Franz Ferdinand) and the political structure in Austria and Hungary provided little support for even modest intervention. Only Generals Schemua and Potiorek pressed for a wider effort and only on the assumption that Russia would not intervene. When the Russians ordered their trial mobilization in the Warsaw district in late September, that action cast serious doubt on the generals' precondition.[3]

Equally discouraging, Berlin showed no enthusiasm for any Habsburg activism in the Balkans. With Italy still engaged in its war with Turkey, Vienna thus had scant support for its second option: modest intervention in the Balkans. Without the alliance, Berchtold and the Ballhausplatz were forced to pursue the option of watchful diplomacy — a choice that matched their analysis of the situation. Furthermore, the Habsburg elite were confident that if war came, it would replicate the sluggish path of the Italo-Turkish fighting. Vienna believed that any military confrontation between the Balkan states and the Ottoman empire would still allow the Habsburgs enough time for intervention — if necessary — in the fighting.[4]

Berchtold did not, however, leave the Habsburg position to chance. With a singular purpose and skill of execution not usually attributed to him, Berchtold deftly prepared the Habsburg position of 'wait and see'. If intervention did not appear feasible, this did not translate into inactivity for Vienna. Quite to the contrary, the Ballhausplatz worked hard to define the monarchy's essential interests in any Balkan upheaval and to resolve how to protect them.

Quickly, two major points emerged from the bureaucratic analysis in Vienna: Albania, if freed from Turkish rule, must be an independent state rather than being joined with Serbia, Montenegro or Greece, and Serbia should not have direct access to the Adriatic. In adopting these two positions, Berchtold continued Aehrenthal's policy of containing Serbia and Montenegro, while appearing to champion the national claims of the Albanians to their own government. Containment of Serbia remained the mainstay of the monarchy's Balkan policy. A Serbia denied free access to the sea would still be a dependent Serbia; Albanian independence would help assure Vienna's policy.[5]

With these objectives defined, Vienna worked during early October to prepare the international terrain for their acceptance. First Vienna wanted to ensure closer ties with Berlin and Rome. These efforts achieved some immediate success. Even more important, Berchtold exploited the status of the Sanjak of Novi Pazar to manoeuvre Russia into a diplomatic concession without Sazonov realizing the nature of his defeat. Habsburg troops had occupied the Sanjak from 1878 to 1908. This territorial appendage, extending from Herzegovina southward, separated Montenegro from Serbia. It remained in Turkish possession after Aehrenthal foolishly withdrew Habsburg's troops in 1908 to signify his goodwill to the Turks. Thereafter the territory remained as a political vacuum, beckoning Cetinje and Belgrade to intervene or the Habsburgs to return to the Sanjak. This latter possibility, though not a feature of Habsburg military planning, offered Berchtold a trump card with which he could transform any Balkan crisis into a major international confrontation. A Habsburg military move into the Sanjak would constitute intervention in the Balkan crisis, a step which the other powers — most of all Russia — could not accept without a bitter diplomatic defeat.

Berchtold exploited the Sanjak issue skillfully. When St Petersburg asked Vienna on 1 October what would happen if Serbia moved its troops into the Sanjak, the Habsburg foreign minister refused to respond. Berchtold used the same tactic on 5 October when Russian Ambassador Giers pushed for a statement; again, the foreign minister refused to commit himself to a policy of localization. Not until Sazonov formally pledged Russia to a policy of no territorial changes in the Balkans on 8 October would Berchtold even discuss the Sanjak question. Thereafter Berchtold cautioned Serbia and Montenegro to avoid the Sanjak: if their troops entered it, they would have to evacuate it later under the terms of the *status quo ante* policy.[6]

Berchtold had succeeded in getting a Russian commitment to allow no territorial changes in Macedonia. In the process, Vienna had forced Sazonov to commit Russia (and France indirectly) to a policy that protected both the Balkan states if Turkey won and Austria if the Balkan states won. If territorial changes were imminent, Europe was committed to intervene. Then Vienna could insist on its minimum demands: an independent Albania and no Serbian access to the Adriatic. Berchtold's ploy of linking the Sanjak issue with the localization of the war had worked. By early October, before the Balkan fighting began, he possessed a European commitment that appeared to protect the Habsburgs' irreducible interests.[7]

While the Ballhausplatz achieved these remarkable diplomatic safeguards, the Habsburg military aggressively demanded quasi-mobilization measures. But the generals stood alone. Franz Joseph, Franz Ferdinand and the civilian leaders wanted no steps taken that appeared to commit them to a military course of action. Vienna waited for the Balkan War to begin, confident that diplomacy would protect its essential interests and of the Turks' ability to defeat the Balkan states.

II

From late September to early December Generals Schemua and Potiorek — with Conrad cheering them on from the sidelines — pressed for military measures. Indeed, during a four-week period Potiorek urged various mobilization options thirteen separate times. The Governor-General repeatedly asked for more troops in Bosnia–Herzegovina to deter Serbia, to prevent local unrest and to influence any subsequent peace negotiations. Just as often, Kaiser Franz Joseph, supported by War Minister Auffenberg, resisted the importuning from the military. While the venerable monarch assented to some precautionary measures, he also delayed their implementation. Until late October the Habsburg military was limited to increased border controls, precautions against agitation among the nationalities and the early dispatch of fresh recruits to their units. In the north no counter-measures were taken despite sizeable increases in Russian troop strength along the Galician frontier. To be sure, many were concerned about the Russian moves but few panicked; for the moment the only Habsburg response was heightened intelligence activity.[8]

Then came the unpleasant surprises of late October: Turkish defeat after Turkish defeat. Everywhere the forces of the Balkan League won until they threatened the Turkish capital. The collapse of the Turkish counterweight against Serbia and Montenegro radically changed Austria-Hungary's strategic situation. More dangerous still, the Montenegrins advanced toward Scutari and Serbian troops advanced on Durazzo (Durres), finally reaching the Albanian port on 11 November. Suddenly, dramatically, two central tenets of Habsburg diplomacy — an independent Albania and no Serbian access to the sea — were jeopardized. The Habsburg policy-makers now had to reconsider their reliance upon a policy of containment and diplomacy. From those examinations a more militant diplomacy would slowly emerge. No longer could Vienna rely on diplomacy. The time had come for some military measures.[9]

On 28 October the Common Ministerial Council discussed at length the deteriorating Balkan situation. At the conclusion the Council agreed to ask Franz Joseph to increase the troop strength in Bosnia–Herzegovina by nearly 50 percent. Schemua and Potiorek accepted these steps as the opening wedge to a policy of confrontation in the south. This was not, however, the way the political leadership of the monarchy publicly portrayed these measures. On 29 October Prime Minister Stürgkh reassured the Austrian House of Deputies that the Danubian state wanted a policy of peace and that no troop increases had taken place, a statement that was only technically correct. On the other hand, the Austrian leader hinted that the monarchy would only pursue a policy of peace if it did not endanger Habsburg interests. Yet more and more those interests appeared in danger.[10]

By early November three separate but connected threads defined Habsburg policy: limited military preparations in the south; a restatement of its fundamental demands about Albania and Serbian access to the sea and an effort for a separate accommodation with the Serbs. The last option produced no results. Despite direct appeals to Prime Minister Pašić and offers of an economic consortium, the Serbian leadership adamantly insisted on direct access to the sea. The impasse turned ugly, with rumours (later proven false) that Serbian troops had emasculated Oskar Prochaska, the Austrian consul in Prizren who could not be contacted. Finally, the presence of Serbian troops in Durazzo and San Giovanni de Medua on the Adriatic deepened Vienna's apprehensions.[11]

The Habsburg–Montenegrin relationship was scarcely better. King Nikita brushed off efforts for a détente. Following his usual method of self-aggrandizement, the king demanded that Scutari, despite its Albanian ethnic character, become Montenegrin. He insisted that this demand was not negotiable: Montenegro would capture and keep Scutari, come what may.[12]

Vienna's relations with Belgrade and Cetinje by mid-November had obviously worsened; so too, as one would expect, had Vienna's ties with St Petersburg. Sazonov, seeking to escape his earlier impetuous commitments to Vienna, now openly backed Serbia's demands for a port on the Adriatic and offered little support for the Habsburg concept of an independent Albania. St Petersburg pressed to see if it could isolate Vienna; its deployment of Russian military forces buttressed this effort. Russian troop strength along the Galician border increased until it reached nearly 220,000 men. Austro-Russian relations were approaching a crisis point, one that threatened to make localization of the Balkan conflict impossible.

Fortunately for Vienna, as the dangers mounted, its ties with Berlin, Bucharest and Rome improved. None of its allies could be comfortable with the tenor of events, though none encouraged a Habsburg military response. Yet the Habsburg decision in mid-November, just as the Delegations were adjourning in Budapest, to implement military measures in Galicia and Bosnia–Herzegovina surprised no one. Indeed, Archduke Franz Ferdinand and General Schemua travelled to Berlin to explain the gravity of the situation. The former's conversion to a policy of action injected a new dimension into the policy discussions, one which War Minister Auffenberg could not resist using. On 21 November he ordered an increase in troop strength in Galicia by 50 percent; two days later he ordered more reserve troops to the colours in the southern provinces. In addition, the fleet was instructed to prepare for mobilization and the Danube flotilla of small monitor ships actually mobilized. These actions convinced the German military attaché, Count Kageneck, that Austria–Hungary had resolved to go to war. But the Habsburg leadership had not, by late November, reached that conclusion. A major policy clash between militant diplomacy and a purely military option was, however, at hand. In December the Habsburg monarchy came to a major war–peace crisis.[13]

III

Surprisingly, a series of Habsburg diplomatic successes matched the pressures for a Habsburg military response. The interaction between the two processes helps explain how Berchtold managed to retain control of the policy apparatus. By late November the Balkan armies made fewer advances; in fact the Bulgarians fell victim to Turkish forces at Chatalja. Armistice negotiations began with an agreement on 3 December for a cease-fire. Peace talks were set to begin in London on 16 December. The great powers, moreover, agreed that their ambassadors stationed in London would represent their Balkan interests in the discussions. For the first time since September, the momentum toward a wider European war had ceased.[14]

Other diplomatic developments also eased Vienna's position. After a bout of diplomatic skirmishing, St Petersburg on 26 November abandoned Belgrade on the port issue and became more flexible on Albania. Furthermore, Sir Edward Grey, as convener of the London Conference, accepted the concept of an independent Albania in order to gain Austria's participation in the negotiations. Once again, Berchtold had obtained recognition for his minimum demands. The Habsburg minister soon added another achievement: the renewal of the Triple Alliance on 5 December for another five years and Bucharest's agreement to join in any war with Russia. Thus, when Habsburg decision-makers faced a series of war–peace decisions on 11 December and 23 December, Berchtold had a series of significant diplomatic victories to his credit. Those diplomatic gains helped him as he confronted the military leadership and Archduke Franz Ferdinand during December.[15]

Paradoxically, the prospect of a Balkan armistice triggered a crisis for the Habsburg leadership. With Serbian forces no longer engaged against Turkish troops, the Serbian units could, so the Habsburg generals argued, be deployed at their mobilized strength against the Danubian monarchy. This 'worst case' analysis suggested that Serbia might actually attack Austria–Hungary. Using these arguments in early December, the military leadership converted Archduke Franz Ferdinand to their point of view. Thus, in the first week of December, Generals Schemua, Potiorek and Auffenberg, joined by the heir-apparent and even the emperor's military chancellory, advocated further troop increases in Bosnia–Herzegovina. Finally, on 5 December Franz Joseph and Berchtold agreed to activate 27,000 more troops, but without formally declaring mobilization in the south. Once in place, these troops would almost be ready to fight Serbia.[16]

The sense of a major crisis for Vienna was heightened by two other events: Conrad returned as chief of the General Staff on 7 December, at Franz Ferdinand's insistence, and the hawkish General Alexander Krobatin replaced War Minister Auffenberg on 9 December. In these personnel shifts, Berchtold had acquired two crafty bureaucratic foes. In particular, Conrad, whose seemingly tireless energy never let an adversary have much peace, represented a formidable new antagonist. Furthermore, Berchtold's possible rift with Franz Ferdinand, with whom he had previously had good relations, posed a new and unwelcome political danger for Berchtold. To be at odds with the heir-apparent would not help the foreign minister. However assessed, in early December Foreign Minister Berchtold's diplomacy found itself — despite its recent successes — facing a strong challenge from the archduke and the military.[17]

With his position thus weakened, Berchtold decided to force a showdown in the presence of Franz Joseph. It came — without Conrad and Krobatin present — on December 11 at Schönbrunn when the emperor received the heir-apparent, Biliński, Stürgkh, Zaleski (the Austrian finance minister), General Friedrich Georgi (the Austrian defence minister) and Berchtold. Earlier in the morning the *Thronfolger* had seen the foreign minister at Belvedere. In their discussion the archduke had pressed for a military confrontation with Serbia and argued that Russia would tolerate such a step. Berchtold had turned aside this advice. His central point of resistance was his well-founded belief that Berlin would never agree to a unilateral move by Vienna.[18]

At Schönbrunn Franz Ferdinand again advocated settling accounts with Serbia and Montenegro. Nothing would be gained by waiting, he argued. Over the next hour Franz Joseph heard his civilian ministers resist any policy of 'military adventure'. In particular, Berchtold opposed the idea, citing the lack of German agreement and stressing his recent diplomatic successes on the eve of the London Conference. Stürgkh, mindful of the unrest already caused among the Austrian population by the military measures, urged more diplomacy. Zaleski, not surprisingly, stressed the economic burden of the military measures already taken: 190,000,000 crowns for the army (or half a year's ordinary budget) and a naval bill of at least 83,000,000 crowns. Indeed, Zaleski wondered if the military were simply exploiting the situation to get more funds.

After listening to the give and take, Franz Joseph, 'unusually serious, composed and determined', emphatically sided with Berchtold. For the one person in the monarchy who alone could tilt the balance for peace or war, the future course remained that of peace, not war. In doing so the emperor/king supported his foreign minister against his generals and his nephew. The military would persist in their demands for action. But the archduke almost immediately backed away from a belligerent policy and returned instead to his own more cautious, peaceful stance of September and October. Hereafter, the two Habsburgs would stand together, until one fell and left the other alone against the generals.[19]

Berchtold's success on 11 December did not, however, end military demands for still further mobilization measures. On 23 December Conrad and Krobatin, with Biliński's support, confronted Berchtold; the trio pressed the foreign minister to permit new military measures in the south. War, the generals insisted, offered the only solution to the South Slav problem. In the meantime they wanted still another 48,000 men stationed in Bosnia–Herzegovina. Biliński, as the civilian minister responsible for the two 'colonial provinces', advocated instituting emergency rule there to check any civilian unrest. The Habsburg foreign minister refused. Why, he countered, were the measures needed? What had changed? The generals had no answers to these questions. Berchtold agreed to raise the matter once again with Franz Joseph. At their session, on 27 December, the monarch again agreed with his foreign minister. With this decision, the emperor ensured that the danger of a war in the south had passed. The first war–peace crisis for Vienna in the era of the Balkan Wars had ended. Peace had been preserved, at least for the moment.[20]

When the Common Ministerial Council convened on 3 January 1913, for the first time since mid-November, the mood was peaceful, not confrontational. Already the earlier military measures carried staggering financial costs. Hungarian Finance Minister Teleszky predicted economic ruin if the expenses continued at this rate.

Certainly neither Vienna nor Budapest would agree to a fourth round of troop increases unless they had no other choice.[21]

Meanwhile, the measures already authorized would continue until a Balkan peace was signed. This meant that Austria–Hungary had added at least 86,000 troops to those on active duty in the north, 86,000 in the south and 50,000 at other locations. An additional 6,500 naval personnel were also on active duty, the Danube flotilla mobilized and naval forces in the Adriatic at virtual mobilization readiness. Thus, despite Berchtold's success, the monarchy remained poised for possible military action. Yet ironically and dangerously, if war came in early 1913, the real danger lay in the north, with Russia, not in the south: this prospect none of the European statesmen found reassuring.[22]

IV

The Austro-Russian tension had begun in late September 1912 with Russia's announcement of an exercise called 'trial mobilization' in the Warsaw military district. Days later St Petersburg declared that third-year troops, normally scheduled for release, would stay on active duty. Within weeks Russia had increased its troop strength by 270,000 men (more than half the size of the Habsburg army), apparently to deter Vienna from any intervention in the Balkan imbroglio. But, as already discussed, the Habsburg decision-makers did not respond militarily to these Russian moves. Through October and the first days of November the Austro-Hungarian General Staff and its German counterpart assessed the Russian actions and their impact on the military balance.[23]

Then, with the collapse of Turkish power and the continuing Russian presence, Vienna responded in mid-November with troop increases along the Galician border. Franz Joseph, pressured by Franz Ferdinand and Generals Schemua, Conrad and Auffenberg, agreed to these measures. Slowly, during the rest of November and early December, these troop increases took place, causing a veritable panic among a civilian population in Galicia fearful that war would not be far away.

Vienna's counter-measures understandably also disturbed the Russian generals. On 21 November the Russian commanders in the western districts urged the czar to activate more troops and talked of a showdown with the Habsburgs. Only the intervention of civilian leaders, Prime Minister Vladimir Kokovtsov and Foreign Minister Sazonov, on 23 November thwarted the Russian military ambitions. Furthermore, Sazonov, almost certainly influenced by Vienna's willingness to escalate the crisis, immediately moved to moderate Russian support for Serbia. No longer could Belgrade count on St Petersburg's backing for an Adriatic port. Berchtold's militant diplomacy appeared to have brought results in St Petersburg.[24]

In early December Vienna's attention shifted abruptly back to the problem of Bosnia–Herzegovina and Serbia. When Franz Joseph and Berchtold had their showdown with the archduke at Schönbrunn on 11 December, Russia was scarcely mentioned. But Conrad's return to power altered the nature of the debate almost immediately. The general wasted no time in addressing the alleged Russian danger. Directly and disdainfully, he dismissed the Russian threat and argued for an attack on Serbia and Montenegro before the opportunity passed. His presence changed both the substance and urgency of the policy discussions in Vienna: his presence also stirred fears in St Petersburg and in Berlin that the Austro-Russian crisis might grow nasty.

During January 1913 tensions mounted dramatically between St Petersburg and Vienna. No group was more alarmed than the leadership in Berlin. Each report from St Petersburg and Vienna gave the German leaders new cause for concern. In this charged atmosphere Berchtold secretly sent Count Szápáry, one of his most senior advisers, to Berlin in mid-January to explore German thinking. What Szápáry heard was unpleasant: neither William nor Chancellor Bethmann Hollweg had any desire for a showdown with the Russians over a Balkan issue. The Habsburg's chief ally had no intention of clashing with Russia, Szápáry reported when he returned to Vienna.[25]

The foreign minister received similar cautious advice from some of his subordinates. Arguing that the Russian moderates clustered around Kokovtsov and Sazonov should be encouraged, Ambassador Thurn, Julius Szilassy (a senior Habsburg diplomat and just returned from Russia) and others advocated concessions to Belgrade. Such steps, they contended, would furnish the Russian political leadership with incentives for reducing the border tensions with Austria–Hungary. Archduke Franz Ferdinand also backed this approach; the heir-apparent now wanted the crisis to ease quickly. A further incentive for reducing tension came from the Austrian and Hungarian politicians who resented the huge military expenditures. Given these considerations, Berchtold resolved to make an overture to St Petersburg.[26]

Prince Hohenlohe's secret trip to St Petersburg in early February became the vehicle for moderating Austro-Russian tensions. A personal friend of Czar Nicholas II, the prince had been carefully instructed by the Ballhausplatz. His mission achieved its purpose. It reassured the Russian statesmen that the diplomats and not Conrad still controlled the Habsburg government. The trip also focused attention on the single issue of troop reductions. Hohenlohe's chilling prediction that war might come within six to eight weeks if nothing were done added urgency to a resolution of the tension.[27]

Despite the danger, however, another month passed before any actual troop reductions took place along the Austro-Russian border. During the month, Berchtold negotiated with Russia over who got what in the Balkans and dealt with German pressures for a settlement. Though bedridden with flu, the foreign minister jousted with the Russians over a series of Albanian towns claimed by Serbia. On 18 February Berchtold yielded on Dibra. But he refused the Russian demand for Djakova until he got Russian and European assurances that Scutari would under *all* conditions remain Albanian. At the same time the Germans were leaving no doubt about their position. Vienna got repeated advice from Berlin to come to terms with St Petersburg. General von Moltke, for example, told Gottlieb von Jagow, the new German foreign secretary (Kiderlen had died suddenly in December), that he must 'prevent Austrian foolishness, no agreeable and easy task'. Chancellor Bethmann Hollweg had Moltke urge Conrad to reach an agreement with St Petersburg. These German declarations buttressed and doubtless influenced the views of Franz Joseph and Franz Ferdinand, who brushed aside Conrad's talk of a showdown.[28]

Foreign Minister Berchtold, who personally did not want war with Russia, successfully manoeuvred to ease the Russian tension and secure a European mandate on Scutari. By mid-March both Russia and the European Concert declared that Scutari would be a part of the new Albania. In turn Berchtold conceded Djakova to Serbia. Paralleling this effort was the mutual reduction of Austro-Russian troop strength along the Galician frontier. On 11 March the two governments announced substantial troop cuts — the Russians released 370,000 men and the Habsburgs 40,000. These reductions immediately eased the Austro-Russian crisis, even if Vienna re-remained intensely suspicious of the St Petersburg–Belgrade relationship. As word of the reductions circulated among the governments, the German emperor wrote to Franz Ferdinand in almost rhapsodic tones: 'You have won undying gains, for you have redeemed Europe from the spell which oppressed it. Millions of thankful hearts will think of you in their prayers. I believe also that Tsar Nicholas will be happy that he can send his reservists home. Everyone will breathe easier when that is done'.[29]

By mid-March the worst moments of the Austro-Russian crisis were over. Disputes continued during the next few weeks, but none matched those from November 1912 to March 1913. These months of confrontation left permanent legacies and altered perceptions. The Russians believed that a strong show of force had intimidated Vienna. Conrad believed that Russia had given way because of the Austro-Hungarian counter-measures. These two divergent conclusions would have disastrous consequences in the summer of 1914, as each power put these 'lessons' into practice. Moreover, Conrad continued to believe that Russia might — in certain circumstances — tolerate a limited Habsburg attack on Serbia and Montenegro. This view would also resurface during the July 1914 crisis. For the moment, however, the two eastern powers had achieved a *modus vivendi*. Troops were headed home, with tensions easing.[30]

V

In the Balkans, the fighting continued and the Scutari problem remained explosive. Despite the European decision about Scutari, in the first weeks of March Serbia and Montenegro were unwilling to abandon their siege of Scutari. Meanwhile, the Balkan struggle against the Turks continued, with the Bulgarians attacking Adrianople and on 26 March capturing it. Previously resistant to peace talks, the Ottoman leaders were finally ready to negotiate. But Scutari's fate remained unresolved.

As Scutari remained surrounded and as the moral suasion of the European Concert remained ineffective, Conrad pressed for Habsburg military intervention. Berchtold's bargains with the Russians and the European Concert looked, from the general's perspective, to be one-sided. Instead of diplomacy, he wanted a substantial military confrontation. Dismissing any show of force or a naval blockade as inadequate, Conrad demanded the implementation of Plan B. But Berchtold, backed by Franz Joseph, Franz Ferdinand and Berlin, resisted the call for widespread military action. The most the foreign minister would accept was a Habsburg naval demonstration against Montenegro. On 20 March three battleships, two cruisers and a torpedo flotilla were in place. To Conrad's dismay, his naval subordinates rather than his army ones managed to escalate the pressure on Montenegro.[31]

This unilateral naval demonstration had several intended audiences: St Petersburg, Belgrade and Cetinje. The Russians with their troops returning homeward were unhappy. Sazonov complained of Vienna's handling of Cetinje and of the Habsburg display of naval power. At one point the Russian foreign minister exclaimed that he could not understand how Vienna 'could not be conscious of the monstrous danger which this isolated act involved for the European peace'. In Belgrade and Cetinje the Habsburg actions prompted no change in policy. Indeed, the two governments intensified their military pressure on the besieged town of Scutari, confident that its fall was imminent.[32]

Rather than undertake any further unilateral coercion, Berchtold now opted for an international show of force against Nikita. This step, which especially pleased Sir Edward Grey, offended Conrad. Nevertheless, by 30 March British and Italian ships joined those of Austria–Hungary in a naval demonstration off the tiny Montenegrin coast. A day later St Petersburg also accepted the principle of international coercion to end the siege at Scutari.[33]

By 5 April five ships from the European Concert, excluding a Russian vessel, steamed off the tiny Montenegrin coast. The British commander of the ships, Admiral Sir Cecil Burney, demanded that Montenegro end the siege. Nikita spurned the request. But the Serbians, thanks to pressure from St Petersburg, were more malleable. On 11 April Prime Minister Pašić announced the withdrawal of Serbian troops. Suddenly and to Conrad's surprise, the general had lost one potential foe. The remaining enemy remained defiant, however; nothing appeared capable of shaking Nikita's determination to take and keep Scutari.[34]

From Vienna's point of view, the situation was simpler yet still unacceptable: Serbia had withdrawn and Russian involvement in the situation seemed less likely. But the problem of Montenegro and Scutari remained. If military action were necessary, its focus would be limited to Montenegro and probably not have European complications. Moreover, the European Concert, if not yet able to coerce King Nikita, was committed to the principle that Scutari belonged to a future Albanian government. Habsburg diplomacy had succeeded in internationalizing an issue of fundamental importance to the monarchy. A Habsburg success on Scutari was merely damage-control; a Habsburg failure on Scutari, while of little consequence to Berlin or London, would further damage the monarchy's already severely battered prestige. A Montenegrin retreat from Scutari would constitute success for Vienna's militant diplomacy. But a diplomatic failure on Scutari would make containing the Habsburg military, who wanted confrontation with the South Slavs regardless, far more difficult.

The generals nearly got their wish. During April Montenegro continued to defy the European powers. The international squadron failed to impress Nikita. Viennese policy-makers considered a series of escalatory steps: a tight blockade of the Montenegrin coast, a Habsburg troop landing, a substantial bribe to the rapacious Montenegrin ruler, even closing the Bosnia–Herzegovina border to land traffic. Berchtold continued to resist Conrad's still more bellicose demands, determined for the moment to stay with a 'European approach'.[35]

Then on the night of 22–23 April, Essad Pasha, the Turkish commander at Scutari, surrendered the town to the Montenegrins. The final crisis of the First Balkan War was at hand. Europe, and more particularly, Austria–Hungary, faced the challenge of forcing Nikita to disgorge his territorial gain. In Vienna, tempers flared, perspectives changed. Once more the Habsburgs considered unilateral action, as in the naval deployment of late March.

In these renewed discussions about military actions, a fundamental question emerged: what would Russia and the two entente powers do? Based on their assessments and biased by prejudices, the Habsburg military assumed that Russia would not interfere in any action directed solely at Montenegro. The Habsburg diplomats also concluded that the French and British, though unhappy at the prospect of a unilateral Habsburg move, would accept it. Given the line-up of the monarchy's possible enemies, the crucial variables were the probable reaction of Vienna's two allies. Rome presented the usual confused response but no indication that it would stop a unilateral move. Most importantly, by 28 April, German Foreign Minister Jagow would accept a Habsburg action solely directed at Montenegro. In fact, he cabled London on 2 May that Berlin would back such a Habsburg decision. Thus Vienna moved ever closer to a decision about the use of force against Cetinje. The plan now under consideration — Plan M — envisaged the deployment of 50,000 Habsburg troops against the smaller Montenegrin force. While Conrad still hoped for a larger war with Serbia and would risk Russian intervention, he was prepared to accept whatever fighting he could get. Franz Joseph and Franz Ferdinand, hitherto cautious and peaceful, now resolved to end Montenegro's defiance. From Sarajevo General Potiorek pressed for action to keep the two provinces under control. Closer to home, in Vienna and Budapest, popular enthusiasm endorsed a clash with the tiny neighbouring kingdom.[36]

In this atmosphere of tension and crisis, the Common Ministerial Council met at the Ballhausplatz on 2 May. Unlike the celebrated *Kriegsrat* in Berlin in December 1912, the Council was considering an actual problem and was taking active steps toward a military confrontation. Those May discussions and actions had, moreover, much in common with those taken fourteen months later. When the ministers gathered, Nikita had again on 30 April thumbed his nose at the European powers. That gesture had prompted Franz Joseph to sanction emergency rule in Bosnia–Herzegovina, effective from 1 May, and to approve funds for purchasing horses for the 15th and 16th Corps. Now Stürgkh, Biliński, Lukács (the Hungarian prime minister), Teleszky, Zaleski, Krobatin and Berchtold — as the Common Ministerial Council — met to discuss what further steps to take against Cetinje.[37]

From the moment the meeting began, Berchtold left no doubt of his exasperation with Nikita. He quickly chronicled the disastrous consequences of a Scutari that remained Montenegrin. This would cripple Albania and offer Serbia a possible outlet on the sea. For the first and only time during the era of the Balkan Wars, Berchtold argued for military instead of diplomatic action, even at the risk of a wider war. The other civilian ministers strongly supported Berchtold. Stürgkh, normally the most hesitant of men, now wanted action, as did Zaleski. Displaying his zeal, Common Finance Minister Biliński demanded more than a showdown with Montenegro; he wanted to attack the Serbian army even if it involved war with Russia. Following a victorious war over Serbia–Montenegro, Biliński proposed adding the new territories to the monarchy's holdings.[38]

Biliński's sweeping demands found little favour with Berchtold and none with the Magyar leaders. Realizing the financial requirements for such a showdown, Teleszky argued that Plan B would bankrupt the monarchy, a view Biliński rejected. Krobatin, as the senior military figure present, could hardly have been more bellicose than his civilian colleagues. But, unlike Conrad, Krobatin moderated his demands for action. He requested the call-up of the remaining reserves in Bosnia–Herzegovina, followed by a forty-eight-hour ultimatum to Cetinje and then action. At the end of the two-hour meeting, the ministers agreed to Krobatin's programme and allocated 12.9 million crowns for additional horse purchases. For the first time, the monarchy had opted for a military showdown.

This belligerent decision reflected the Habsburg policy-makers' acute frustration as they assessed the sagging prestige of the monarchy. The Balkan fighting, the Scutari issue and the crisis with St Petersburg had left a group of fearful, worried leaders. The tensions caused by a quasi-state of mobilization in the south had in turn militarized civilian attitudes. These leaders were ready for war in 1913, a dress rehearsal for a far more inflamed situation in July 1914.

Three further observations about the Council meeting are necessary. First, Conrad's absence meant that the decision-makers could not question him on the details of Plan M or probably understand that merely ordering the measures might prompt Montenegro to yield. Second, the discussions failed to speculate upon Berlin's reaction, yet devoted careful attention to St Petersburg's views. In the 1914 discussions the emphasis would be exactly and more dangerously reversed. Finally, in 1913 Berchtold held the pivotal position at each step of the way. Now he favoured action, but he carefully pointed to the risks of an unacceptable wider war. Fully aware that Conrad wanted a major confrontation, a prospect that neither the Habsburg family nor Berlin favoured, Berchtold sought to keep the military option under tight restrictions. Still, his militant diplomacy did not exclude the threat of mobilization as a tool — albeit an expensive one — and this card he agreed to play in May 1913.[39]

On 3 May Potiorek proclaimed emergency rule in Bosnia–Herzegovina. Within two days the troops and the provinces were at the status of war readiness. Horse purchases had begun as signs from St Petersburg indicated that the Russians disliked Vienna's unilateral action. Suddenly, Montenegro capitulated. On 3 May the Montenegrin Crown Prince Danilo asked Vienna to delay the ultimatum. Berchtold accepted this request despite pressures from Conrad to reject it. Franz Joseph supported his foreign minister in this cautious approach when they met on 4 May. News from Cetinje that same day indicated that Nikita would abandon Scutari and that Serbian troops would leave San Giovanni de Medua and Durazzo. On 14 May an international detachment reached Scutari and started the arduous process of creating the Albanian government.

In Bosnia–Herzegovina horse purchases were immediately halted, emergency regulations rescinded and the extra troops sent home. Although 60,000 additional Habsburg reserves remained on active duty, tensions had eased precipitously. The European powers were especially grateful for an end to the crisis. An appreciative Franz Joseph bestowed a new decoration on his foreign minister and displayed his rarest form of approval: he shook Berchtold's hand when they met at Schönbrunn on 8 May. The Archduke Franz Ferdinand was equally appreciative. The two Habsburgs welcomed the preservation of peace. The Austro-Hungarian generals, for their part, sulked.[40]

VI

The conclusion of the peace negotiations in London on 30 May 1913 brought the First Balkan War to a close. For more than nine months Habsburg and Balkan statesmen had dealt with the problems of a limited war and the possibility of a still wider war. Soon the victorious Balkan states, discontent with their share of the spoils, would again be at war. Vienna too was dissatisfied. Peace had been preserved, the Habsburg monarchy's minimal demands on Albania upheld, Serbian access to the sea prevented and Scutari destined to be a part of Albania. But offsetting these defensive gains was the grim realization for Habsburg leaders that Serbia had doubled its population and its territory. Turkey no longer served as a counterweight in the Balkans; only Bulgaria and Rumania remained as possible allies to check Serbian expansion. The Habsburg policy of containing Serbia had failed to keep Serbia from enlarging its boundaries. The momentum in the Balkans had clearly shifted to Belgrade and the South Slavs, even if Vienna was still the greater power.

The Russian role in the diplomacy of the war also sobered the Triple Alliance. Willing to keep troops on duty and to play aggressive *Realpolitik*, St Petersburg had threatened Vienna, had acted as Serbia's broker and had shown a willingness to intervene militarily. The Austro-Russian military tension in Galicia had revealed a new danger for Austria–Hungary, ironically one that the policy-makers recognized more clearly in 1912 and 1913 than they would in 1914. On the other hand, Britain and France had generally played a moderating role that sympathized with Habsburg aims, especially in resolving the Scutari issue.

Within the Triple Alliance the political situation was hardly reassuring. While the alliance had been renewed in December, 1912, Rumania had demanded compensation from Bulgaria for Bucharest's neutrality during the conflict. Vienna had pressed Sofia, in the process damaging Vienna's relations with the Bulgarian leaders. Ties with Italy improved somewhat after the end of May. More enigmatic was the alliance with Berlin. For months, the German policy-makers had alternated between moments of support and declarations of extreme caution. The Germany ally had flinched from the commitment while always proclaiming loyalty. The fundamental question remained, as it had in the autumn of 1912: did Berlin grasp the dangers posed to Austria–Hungary by the South Slav issue? Would Germany allow Vienna to resolve the problem even at the risk of war with Russia? Berchtold, in spite of months of grappling with these questions, still had no clear answer as the crisis ended. But the German acquiesence to the ultimatum to Montenegro suggested a cautious 'yes'.

Within the Habsburg government the months of tension had militarized attitudes and prompted despair at the economic impact of the prolonged military measures. The tensions had also left the military more dissatisfied and less willing to accept any measure short of war in the future. In the power struggle within the government, the trio of Franz Joseph, Franz Ferdinand and Berchtold remained the obstacles to war. Yet even this group in early May 1913 demonstrated that under certain circumstances they would accept the prospect of an armed clash. What most, if not all, of the Habsburg leaders could accept was the efficacy of militant diplomacy and military measures as a legitimate aspect of diplomacy. Hence the monarchy's elite was becoming subtly more committed to a policy of force. Only Montenegro's decision to yield in May 1913 had prevented a military conflict. A future crisis, especially with a different government, might end otherwise. But in 1913 peace had prevailed. The Balkan fighting was over. Or so it seemed.

8 Diplomatic Options Reconsidered: the Second Balkan War and After, June–December 1913

Berchtold's successful coercion of Montenegro in early May 1913 constituted his greatest diplomatic success. The creation of Albania, the denial of Serbian access to the sea and the effective use of military threats for foreign policy purposes — all characterized his efforts from September 1912 to May 1913. Although they were rearguard, holding actions, he nevertheless achieved his goals. But within a few weeks the Second Balkan War challenged his policy assumptions and left the Austro-Hungarian monarchy and its leadership dangerously short of confidence. Whereas the First Balkan War troubled the monarchy, the Second sealed its fate.

Berchtold's and the monarchy's troubles extended beyond the Balkans. Abroad, Berlin's inconsistent policy stances often hampered Habsburg diplomacy. At home, in both Austria and Hungary the populace resented the recent tension and economic troubles. The new Magyar premier, István Tisza, challenged the Ballhausplatz as the primary locus for the formation of Habsburg policy. From June to December 1913 Berchtold and his associates also confronted the Second Balkan War, negotiations for the Peace of Bucharest that ended the brief war, and then a new crisis with Serbia over the Albanian border. Simultaneously, the Habsburg leadership — more divided than ever and now uncertain about the reliability of its Triple Alliance partners — groped for a policy to protect Vienna's fundamental interests. By December 1913 the Dual Monarchy found little cause for rejoicing.[1]

I

The Ballhausplatz's success on the Albanian question helped paradoxically to foment the Second Balkan War. Belgrade, angry at losing part of its promised territorial gains in Albania, demanded a realignment of the remaining shares. But Sofia had already reluctantly conceded Silistria to Rumania as payment for Bucharest's neutrality during the First War. Thus Bulgaria would offer Serbia no further territorial adjustments. Even as the fighting from the First War ended, Belgrade made a secret agreement with Athens for a possible clash with Bulgaria. To complicate Bulgaria's position, Serbian diplomats also wooed King Carol and the Rumanians. Before the ink on the London Peace Accords had scarcely begun to dry, the prospect of more fighting loomed.[2]

For Vienna any squabble between Serbia and Bulgaria might be beneficial since it would wreck the Balkan League. Such a showdown from the Habsburg perspective required that Bulgaria triumph. This meant, however, that Rumania had to remain neutral. A Bulgaria fighting Serbia or Greece might win; a Bulgaria facing three Balkan opponents would surely lose. Given this unhappy situation, Vienna tried to convince Bucharest that Sofia would reward Rumania with still more territory. In Sofia, meanwhile, Habsburg diplomats pressed the Bulgarians to offer an adequate concession to Bucharest and thus limit its potential enemies.[3]

For once the Romanovs and the Habsburgs wanted a similar alignment in the Balkans, but for different reasons. Anxious to keep the Balkan League intact, the Russians pressed for Bulgarian accommodation toward Rumania without exerting, however, similar pressure on Belgrade. Still, the Russian foreign minister genuinely persisted during June in an effort to avert another war. The Russians, like the Habsburgs, failed partly because the Bulgarian statesmen believed that St Petersburg could deter Rumanian participation in any war. Furthermore, Sazonov's offer to mediate between Sofia and Belgrade appeared to have possibilities. But Sazonov failed.[4]

Despite close German ties with King Carol, Berlin made little effort to preserve the peace. Since Berlin was unwilling to acknowledge that Serbia posed a fundamental threat to Austria–Hungary, the Germans saw no reason to prevent another Balkan war. Rather than coaching King Carol to be more reasonable, the Germans encouraged him to squeeze Sofia a little harder. As a further complication, William II encouraged his brother-in-law, King Constantine of Greece, to expand his domain at Bulgaria's expense. Prior to this, Berlin had usually followed Austria–Hungary's lead in Balkan affairs. Suddenly the Germans emerged at every sensitive step for the Habsburgs and urged policies directly counter to those of Berchtold and Vienna.[5]

Amid this confusion Sofia unwisely decided to strike. On 29–30 June, King Ferdinand of Bulgaria ordered his troops to attack Greek and Serbian positions. As a result the Balkan League collapsed. Bulgaria's military pretensions suffered a similar fate. In debacle after debacle, the Serbians, Greeks and the Rumanians — who joined the fray almost gleefully — routed the Bulgarians. Even the Turks resumed fighting and by 22 July had regained Adrianople at the expense of Sofia. An armistice and peace settlement seemed imperative for the Bulgarians lest they be more thoroughly defeated and lose still more of the gains made in the First Balkan War.[6]

Vienna watched these developments with undisguised apprehension. Habsburg policy-makers realized that renewed fighting would entangle Rumania and damage the security of the Danubian monarchy. Yet Austria–Hungary, who still retained 60,000 reservists on active duty in Bosnia–Herzegovina, did not intervene militarily or even threaten to do so in July 1913. Why? A partial explanation stems from Vienna's misreading of the probable course of the combat itself. Once again, the Habsburg military believed the fighting would be prosaic, indecisive and open to later intervention by other parties. Bulgaria's military forces were, Vienna's analysts believed, better than the Turks. The unexpected total defeat and total collapse of Bulgarian forces in three short weeks robbed the policy-makers in Vienna of their anticipated options for manoeuvre.

Domestic and national considerations also combined to weigh heavily against active Habsburg intervention after diplomacy failed to deter the war. When the First Balkan War ended and the crisis eased, public opinion that had been controlled and restrained became more pointed. In both the Austrian and Hungarian parliaments, speakers criticized Berchtold's conduct of Habsburg policy. The economic drain of the prolonged mobilization of troops coupled with the panic produced in Galicia and Bosnia–Herzegovina troubled the deputies. Continuing to keep nearly 60,000 reservists on active duty also fuelled anxiety in the Dual Monarchy. Their presence with the regular units, which Berchtold and Conrad argued gave credence to Habsburg warnings, drew much comment and indeed criticism from both Franz Joseph and Franz Ferdinand.

The Habsburg military leadership, which could have been expected to demand intervention in the new war, was also muted in its demands. Put on the defensive by the Redl scandal, the Habsburg generals were busy during much of June trying to salvage their reputations. Lurid tales of spying, homosexuality and corruption circulated; Redl's forced suicide seemed particularly inappropriate. The Magyar press attacked the military leadership so vigorously that War Minister Krobatin had to ask the Hungarian government for help against the journalists. The public mood over the reserve issue and the Redl affair did not suggest public support for an assertive, exploitive foreign policy that sought to crush rather than contain Serbia.[7]

Thus throughout July, Conrad and Krobatin were curiously inept and inconsistent in pressing for military action. The generals believed the Bulgarians would be competent fighters, at least until the Rumanians entered the struggle. Conrad, who was away from Vienna in late June and early July, only saw Berchtold twice during the early stages of the fighting. On both occasions he urged a 'wait and see' stance. Krobatin spent his time worrying about the reservists and their morale. Anxious to end the erosion of military discipline rather than intrude in the Balkan fighting, Krobatin urged the reduction, not the increase, of Habsburg troop strength.[8]

Conrad's failure to press for action probably had another reason as well. It reflected his battered political position. The Archduke Franz Ferdinand held no illusions about his one-time protégé. On 4 July 1913 he warned Berchtold that Conrad might 'seek' his entire salvation in a war which would be a misfortune for the monarchy. In short, Berchtold did not confront — as he had from December 1912 to May 1913 — calls from the Habsburg military leadership for intervention in the renewed Balkan bloodletting.[9]

Berchtold, not surprisingly, had no pressure from the Habsburgs for action. The archduke, writing frequently from Holland where he was on vacation throughout July, fretted about any diplomatic move toward Bulgaria and urged Berchtold to keep close to Berlin. The Emperor/King Franz Joseph equally disliked the prospect of a clash. Surveying developments from his beloved hunting estate at Bad Ischl, Franz Joseph saw no reason to help King Ferdinand, whom he had always distrusted and disliked. In short, no one among the senior Habsburg leadership advocated military intervention.[10]

Finally, two entirely new participants in the policy process — Hungarian Prime Minister István Tisza and his representative in Vienna, Count István Burián — supported a non-interventionist policy. Tisza, son of Kálmán Tisza, was a devout, unyielding Magyar Calvinist, who had strongly influenced Hungarian political life since the turn of the century. Prime Minister from 1903–05, Tisza had regained power in 1910 with the stunning election of his reconstituted Party of Work. An intriguer within the Hungarian House of Deputies until he became Speaker of the House in the summer of 1912, Tisza had pushed through the military bill and ruthlessly excluded recalcitrant opponents from the parliamentary buildings in Budapest. Not given to modesty, Tisza was both respected and feared. Franz Joseph regarded him as the most formidable figure since Prince Felix Schwarzenberg; Franz Ferdinand thought of him as the 'most dangerous man in the Monarchy' and made no effort to seek a détente with him.[11]

On 10 July 1913 Tisza once again became Hungarian prime minister, replacing Lukács. Almost immediately the Magyar's personality, views and ambitions intruded upon the making of strategic policy. Tisza travelled to Vienna and demanded briefings from the common ministers. To represent his interests, he asked Count Burián, a Magyar statesman of great Viennese experience (he had been common finance minister from 1903 to 1912) to be his representative in Vienna. Burián soon became a frequent visitor to the Ballhausplatz and would tutor his compatriot in the nuances of international politics. From the start Tisza made clear his intention to participate in the policy process, both procedurally and substantively. Franz Ferdinand and others saw the prime minister as a force for a pro-Bulgarian policy since it deflected the troublesome Rumanian question. During July 1913 Tisza and Burián thus buttressed the waiting policy that Berchtold had followed once the fighting began. Even if the Hungarian presence did not immediately assume policy overtones, it certainly took on a personal aspect as the press soon talked of Tisza replacing Berchtold. Furthermore, active Hungarian involvement meant that Berchtold would have to overcome a new set of arguments if he wished to maintain his paramount role over the foreign policy apparatus.[12]

Berchtold's alliance partners offered little help against the Magyar challenge. In early July Berchtold got no effective German support in persuading the Rumanians not to intervene. Even the threat of possible unilateral Habsburg military intervention failed to change the German position. Rather, Berlin espoused Rumanian ambitions, alarmed the Italians with talk of Habsburg action and did nothing to calm the situation. The threat posed to Austria–Hungary by Serbia remained unappreciated and minimized by Chancellor Bethmann Hollweg and Foreign Secretary Jagow.

The Italians were more excited about the Balkan unrest, but for different reasons. Anxious less Austria–Hungary take unilateral action, Rome cautioned Vienna against any hasty decision. The terms of the alliance, San Giuliano noted, required consultation with Italy, a stipulation that Berchtold had resisted. Even if within the Dual Monarchy all of the policy-makers had favoured helping Bulgaria, the Habsburg foreign minister could not ignore the fact that his two chief European allies opposed Habsburg intervention. The possibility of any Habsburg military move during the Second Balkan War was thus foreclosed.[13]

Surprisingly, during the brief war, Vienna's diplomatic contacts with St Petersburg were virtually non-existent. Only as the Bulgarians collapsed were there some exchanges. By then, however, neither capital considered active intervention. Instead, both Sazonov and Berchtold waited for the armistice and the peace process to begin so they could protect their respective interests. But this time both men were profoundly disappointed.

II

The Second Balkan War caused the Balkan League to collapse; the Peace of Bucharest of August 1913 that ended the conflict damaged Austro-German relations. The peace process also reinforced Vienna's despair about the future. As the fighting ended and the peace talks began, Berchtold sought to rescue something from the debris. Anxious to keep the Rumanians in the Triple Alliance, he nevertheless explored the possibility of an agreement with Bulgaria. By supporting Bulgaria's hopes to retain Kavalla against the Greeks, Berchtold offended Berlin by his apparent anti-Greek stance. And of course the Rumanians were even less enthusiastic about an Austro-Bulgarian rapprochement. In any event, on 10 August the Balkan powers concluded the Peace of Bucharest that dashed Berchtold's hopes for a salvage operation in the Balkans. In the treaty, Rumania got Silistria above a line running from Turkukaia to Balchik on the Black Sea; Serbia got the Vadar valley between Kočana and Štip; Greece got Crete, Kavalla and a Macedonian border on a line running to Monastir. In a separate Turco-Bulgarian treaty,

Constantinople regained Adrianople and Kirk-Kilisse, thus regaining substantial lands at Sofia's expense. (See Map 3.)

Unlike the London negotiations of three months earlier, the great powers were excluded from these settlements. Still, Vienna and St Petersburg thought they could impose their viewpoints. But the German kaiser halted that idea with his effusive congratulatory telegram to King Carol giving a German stamp of approval to the Peace of Bucharest. This preemptory step thwarted any possibility that the great powers could insist on modifications of the peace settlement. With Berlin's move negating any possibility of boundary revisions, the Peace of Bucharest had only disagreeable consequences for Vienna.[14]

Prompted by defeat and prodded by Tisza, the Habsburg leadership began to assess the damage caused by the Second Balkan War. The diplomacy of the war had badly strained the Austro-German relationship. An exasperated Foreign Minister Berchtold caustically told German Ambassador Tschirschky that Austria–Hungary might just as well belong 'to the other grouping' for all the good Berlin had been. Serbia had become for Vienna the equivalent to the British Royal Navy for Germany. Yet Berlin stubbornly refused to recognize this perspective. Instead, Jagow and his colleagues preferred to compete with Vienna for leadership in the Balkans. What was fundamental to Vienna was but part of a larger mosaic of German *Weltpolitik*. The German government accepted neither Vienna's assessment of Serbia nor the ally's clamour that something be done about the Balkan threat.

Vienna's disagreements with Berlin also influenced its approach to Bulgaria. The defeated Sofia government could not check the ambitions of the victorious Serbs. A Bulgaria linked with the Triple Alliance might, however, help redress the Balkan balance of power. This assessment, advocated by Tisza and half-heartedly accepted by Berchtold, found little favour in Berlin. Any move to incorporate Sofia into the alliance, German policy-makers warned, risked alienating the Rumanians even further. The Wilhelmstrasse would not accept this risk in the late summer of 1913 or thereafter. These differences would continue to divide the two allies to July 1914. Vienna, desperate to find aid against growing Serbian strengths, increasingly found Bucharest and the Rumanian politicians undependable. Rumania's gradual defection from the Triple Alliance would thus become a major concern for Vienna, as we shall see, as one of the longer-term results of the Second Balkan War.[15]

Each of the consequences of the Second Balkan War — an enlarged Serbia and Austro-German disagreements over Bulgaria and Rumania — was predictable. What was unexpected, and far less public, was Tisza's surprising advocacy of a new departure in Habsburg foreign policy. His memoranda, written on 11 and 25 August, urged Berchtold and Franz Joseph to consider cooperating with Russia in support of Bulgaria's continuing struggle with the Turks. Even a two-year accord with St Petersburg, Tisza argued, would allow the Habsburg monarchy to strengthen its defensive posture. Tisza's radical proposals, unusual in style and still more so in content, represented a major bureaucratic challenge to the beleaguered foreign minister.

But Berchtold met the challenge head-on. He insisted that the public would not understand any policy that suddenly appeared pro-Russian and not anti-Serbian. Nor would Tisza's proposals, Berchtold could have added, have found favour in Berlin — a point that Tisza's own naïveté about foreign policy had overlooked. The Magyar was a proponent of better relations with Bulgaria; Berlin scorned Sofia. Still, Berchtold had to deal with Tisza's proposals, including his demand for a Crown Council with Franz Joseph present to review Habsburg foreign policy. Each proposal Berchtold managed to deflect. But the halcyon days of Budapest only worrying about the cost and not the content of Habsburg diplomacy were clearly over. Berchtold now confronted two major protagonists in the Habsburg policy process: Conrad and Tisza.[16]

September 1913 saw the European ministers and their families, as customary, on vacation. Meanwhile, a harassed Berchtold lingered in Vienna to prepare for the forthcoming meeting of the Delegations. Franz Joseph remained in Bad Ischl. Meanwhile the army manoeuvres were taking place in Bohemia, where Franz Ferdinand and Conrad had another confrontation. Indeed, the general, furious at Franz Ferdinand's criticisms of him, abruptly left the manoeuvres and hurried to be comforted by his beloved Gina. Eventually the two men would reach a new understanding, but the longer-term, more corrosive effects of the Redl affair continued within the senior military leadership. The spat between the heir-apparent and Conrad prompted embarrassing press commentary and did little to reassure Berlin of stability in Vienna.[17]

As September continued, the Habsburg policy-makers began to have a more serious set of concerns. Reports reached Vienna that Serbia had not only failed to evacuate Albanian territory, but had in fact expanded into new Albanian areas. Earlier warnings from the great powers had produced no tangible Serbian withdrawals. Instead, the Serbians hinted of certain border changes at 'strategic points'. Then in late September Serbian troops resumed fighting with Albanian guerrillas and occupied still more territory. To complicate the Balkan situation, St Petersburg did nothing to restrain Belgrade. A warning from Vienna to Serbia on 1 October brought only an evasive Serbian response. Berchtold's year-long policy of an independent, viable Albania now appeared challenged, not by tiny Montenegro at Scutari but by a more expansive, troublesome Serbia.[18]

Vienna continued to hope that Serbia would concede to international pressure. Premier Pašić's decision to visit Vienna in early October suggested the possibility of better relations. Hints of Pašić's troubles with the Serbian military, the need to address the fate of the Oriental Railroad Company (now in Serbian hands) and a possible trade agreement all suggested that the radical leader might be amenable to serious negotiations with Vienna despite differences over the Albanian border problems.

Pašić's official visit of 3 October did not, however, go well. The Austrian statesman got no Serbian commitment to respect the Albanian boundaries. Instead, Pašić merely repeated his earlier vague assurances that all would be well. At a lunch for Pašić, attended by nearly all of the *dramatis personae* of 1914 — Stürgkh, Tisza, Biliński, Forgách, Macchio and Berchtold among others — no one raised the Albanian issue. When someone mentioned the possibility of improved economic ties, the discussion did not get very far either. With only one exception, Pašić dealt in generalities. He did hint at conciliation by Serbia and a willingness to let the Serbs and Croats living within Austria–Hungary go their own way. Although offering the possibility of better Austro-Serbian relations, this episode in 'summit diplomacy' produced little.[19]

The failure of Pašić's visit is less surprising when placed in the context of the other events of 3 October. A Common Ministerial Council meeting, the first since mid-May, met concurrently with the Serbian visit. In the discussions the ministers, led by Tisza as a new participant, left no doubt of a tougher, more resolute line toward

Belgrade. Serbia must evacuate Albanian territory or military measures might be considered. Conrad, whose presence at the meeting was novel, went further still by renewing his talk of an *Anschluss* (annexation) of Serbia. This proposal meant of course more Slavs in the monarchy. None among the civilian ministers favoured Conrad's suggestion. Yet, ominously, all of the participants at the meeting had shifted in favour of a military solution if diplomacy failed. Berchtold did not resist this momentum and indeed appeared to share this attitude. Thus the militarization of Habsburg attitudes went a step further.[20]

Having stated their views and leaving the implementation of policy to Foreign Minister Berchtold, the ministers departed and waited to see what Belgrade would do. During this interlude the Ballhausplatz tried to alert Berlin and Rome to its concerns. Both allies agreed to increase pressure upon Belgrade to comply with the border arrangements. At the same time, Berchtold briefed the emperor and heir-apparent. Franz Ferdinand pointedly warned that Conrad could not be trusted and accused Tisza of 'war lust'. Berchtold made no effort to refute these archducal assertions. Instead he simply bypassed the heir-apparent in the next two weeks, because he found Franz Joseph far more favourable to talk of a showdown with Serbia. At Schönbrunn Berchtold had all the backing he required.[21]

The first days of October passed. Serbia did not withdraw its troops from Albania. Rather, new intelligence data indicated further Serbian intransigence. Whatever hopes Berchtold may have taken from his talk with Pašić soon dissipated. The foreign minister, moreover, found himself barraged by Conrad and Tisza with demands for action. On 9 October Tisza wrote to Berchtold that the border issue would show whether Austria–Hungary was a 'viable power' or had fallen into a 'laughable decadence'. Conrad, as usual, argued for mobilization and war, rather than any half-measures.[22]

As the pressure mounted upon Berchtold, he secretly convened a 'rump' session of the Common Ministerial Council on 13 October. This session found the ministers more divided than earlier. Tisza and Biliński wanted to humiliate Serbia but not partition it. Stürgkh would replace the Serbian dynasty; Burián would seize Serbian territory and hold it as a ransom. Only Conrad remained consistent: a war to resolve the Serbian issue. At the end of their discussions the ministers agreed on three courses of action: to issue a warning to

Belgrade to be followed by an ultimatum; to inform Berlin and Rome of the possible Habsburg action if Serbia did not yield and to dispatch four soldiers in civilian clothes to observe whether the Serbs actually abandoned the disputed territory. The Habsburg monarchy would press the Serbs to evacuate the territory. If the Serbs still refused to evacuate the disputed territory, the ministers and Franz Joseph had agreed to resort to force.[23]

When Belgrade failed to comply with the warning, the third war–peace crisis for Vienna was at hand. Serbia's defiant response to the warning exhausted Habsburg patience. Berchtold informed Berlin and Rome that 'categorical action' was necessary. When he asked the allies for their moral support, both agreed. Without further consultation with Berlin, Berchtold dispatched the ultimatum to Belgrade on 17 October. Unlike December 1912 and May 1913, Vienna presented the Germans and the Italians with a *fait accompli*. Berlin only got a copy of the ultimatum simultaneously with its transmission to Belgrade. The German leadership, however, chose to offer solid encouragement for action. William was at his bellicose worst.[24]

When the Serbian government received the ultimatum on 18 October, the wording left no doubt of Vienna's intentions. If Serbia did not evacuate Albanian territory within eight days, the Austro-Hungarian government would have 'recourse to proper means to assure the realization of its demands.' This *démarche* enjoyed broad press support in Austria and in Hungary; the governing elites also responded favourably. The common view among the citizens was that enough was enough from Belgrade.[25]

Within a day or two, Pašić suggested that Serbia would meet the deadline. Pressure from St Petersburg may have helped him reach a decision. A new French loan for Serbia, negotiated by Sazonov, cushioned the blow of the Serbian retreat. On 20 October Pašić announced the Serbian troops would be out by 26 October; his troops met that deadline. Serbia's compliance bitterly disappointed Conrad, relieved Berchtold and made many in Vienna and Budapest happy that the monarchy had achieved a foreign policy triumph. Berchtold had managed to retain his position as director of the policy machinery against the importunings of Conrad and Tisza.[26]

Several days after the crisis, the German Kaiser William II visited Vienna on a private hunting trip. Effusive in his praise of the Habsburg success, he spoke dogmatically about Germany's backing of its

Danubian ally. Although he also talked confusedly about possible Austro-Serbian cooperation, his mere presence in Vienna affirmed that the Austro-German alliance had more coherence than during its mid-summer doldrums. Major differences over Rumania, Bulgaria and economic issues in the Balkans remained; but at least the publicized leadership of the two powers appeared on good terms.[27]

The resolution of the crisis did not entirely assure the Italians. Vienna's unilateral action was disturbing. It followed an unfortunate Habsburg decision to oust Italians from local government jobs in Trieste, a mistake that had sparked new irredentist demands. Vienna's *démarche* at Belgrade also awakened San Giuliano's fears about possible Habsburg action in Albania. Although relieved to have the Serbians out of the newly created state, Rome nevertheless realized (sooner than Vienna) that competition with its ally for the 'indirect' political control of Albania was about to begin.[28]

On the broader European canvas, the Habsburg success was greeted with concern but acceptance. London and Paris disliked the unilateral action, yet they were delighted to see the Albanian border problem concluded. Russian Foreign Minister Sazonov, already buffeted by the summer's disasters, disliked the coercion of Serbia, but could not defend Pašić's flouting of the European position on the border. Relations between St Petersburg and Vienna were not cordial, but the October crisis caused little added damage. With the Albanian issues settled, the possibilities for improved Austro-Russian relations did not appear excluded.[29]

Vienna's triumph did, however, severely damage the opportunity for improved Austro-Serbian ties. Pašić did not enjoy the diplomatic humiliation; the Serbian military found new causes for hostility. The bitterness of the military and their numbers in the *Crna ruka* (the Black Hand) mounted. The bitterness was so public that Habsburg observers in Belgrade noticed it. One Habsburg diplomat despairingly wrote in late fall, '*Sooner or later a war with Serbia and perhaps other Balkan states must come.*'[30]

This new militant perspective, increasingly prevalent among the civilian as well as military leaders within the Danubian monarchy, was the most fateful consequence of the third war–peace crisis. Berchtold put it most cogently when he wrote to a sceptical Franz Ferdinand on 21 October: 'This action [the ultimatum] has had the beneficial effect of clearing the air, so that Europe now recognizes that we, even without tutelage, can act independently if our interests are threatened and that our allies will stand closely behind us.' In other circumstances, this conviction could prompt a repeat of these dangerous 'lessons' with less peaceful results.[31]

The success of the Habsburg ultimatum of October 1913 had at least two other consequences. One was procedural with substantive impact. Since returning in December 1912 as chief of the General Staff, Conrad had often been excluded from the final, most intimate decision-making. Now, despite the military's embarrassment over the Redl affair, the general was physically present at the decisive junctures. Unmerciful in his demands for action and scornful of any temporizing measures, such as seizing the Serbian town of Šabac as a territorial hostage, Conrad was a consistent hawk. He represented, along with Generals Potiorek and Krobatin, the 'war party' which journalists believed existed in Vienna. This party did not, however, include Franz Ferdinand whose own views continued to be cautious and irenic. Conrad's access to Franz Joseph, his compulsive letter writing and his dogmatic approach to interpersonal relations made him a dangerous advocate of a showdown with Serbia.

The second consequence may have been — because of its perceptual dimensions — still more crucial to the monarchy's future. Diplomacy no longer appeared adequate to meet the most fundamental threat to the monarchy's survival: the South Slav issue. By making every facet of the Albanian problem a test case, Berchtold managed to confront Serbia, Montenegro *and* Austria–Hungary with situations that demanded success for the latter. By converting issues into prestige matters on which compromise was impossible, the minister necessarily had to escalate his pressures if the other party balked. Prestige politics, that most dangerous and self-fulfilling of all diplomatic pursuits, had replaced interest politics. To make prestige politics an interest is an easy mistake for foreign ministers and diplomats. To keep them distinct and to keep one's own prestige and credibility intact is harder still. By late 1913 this confusion had become more pronounced in Berchtold's conduct, while his colleagues suffered similar bewilderment as well. A dangerous consensus was emerging, thanks in part to Habsburg diplomacy, Serbo-Russian irresponsibility and the European ethos that viewed war and force as necessary elements of the international system. The conviction that Serbia would only understand force emerged as a 'lesson of history' to the senior decision-makers in Austria–

Hungary. Aehrenthal's failure in 1909 to defeat Serbia militarily was increasingly regarded, as Conrad the critic had often asserted, as misguided and wrong. In contrast, forceful, aggressive diplomacy brought its rewards. That was the experience that the third war–peace crisis riveted into the consciences and memories of the policy-makers. The era of half-measures or half-mobilized armies backing diplomatic demands was over. Once the barrier to mobilization was crossed, Austria–Hungary would plunge to war.

III

The emotive tensions of the October crisis were soon followed by longer-term Habsburg assessments of the damage of the Balkan Wars. Only two areas will be explored here: the economic consequences of the monarchy's year-long military preparations and efforts in late 1913 to resuscitate the Rumanian relationship with the Triple Alliance. These two issues reveal, moreover, the dynamic, incessant fusion of external and domestic factors in the conduct of Habsburg foreign policy. As these aspects meshed or clashed, they restricted the policy options available for the benefit of the monarchy as a whole, as opposed to benefitting either Hungary or Austria.

The annual meeting of the Delegations always highlighted the interaction of the external and domestic perspectives; the November 1913 session in Vienna was no exception. Meeting for the first time since the initial weeks of the First Balkan War in November 1912, the delegates sharply questioned the three common ministers about the conduct of Habsburg policy. Berchtold faced especially severe interrogation. With the Hungarian deputies, only Tisza's intervention in the debate spared Berchtold's nerves and honour. The Austrian Delegation also treated Berchtold roughly, while adding an ideological angle as well. The attacks targeted the monarchy's vacillation during the Second Balkan War and the paucity of its triumph in Albania. All of the ministers were targets. Berchtold's confident, some thought blasé, stance drew the deputies's anger. Tisza found his recent efforts to improve relations with Bucharest the subject of vituperative criticism from his fellow Magyars. In addition to these attacks, ideological complaints were added. The socialists assailed the military and the Slavs complained that Berchtold's policy guaranteed that Serbia would never be friendly.

Frustrated over the Balkan Wars and the costs of the monarchy's strategic policy, the delegates from both halves of the country could explore their misgivings about the ministerial performance.[32]

Behind these attacks were the uncomfortable economic facts confronting the Delegations. The two Houses had to approve a budget that included provisions for additional troop increases, the authorization for more capital ships in 1915 and, most damaging of all, an allocation of almost 390 million crowns to cover the extra defence costs of 1912–13. The magnitude of these latter costs, virtually equal to the 1912 budget for the common army, was not lost upon the delegates. A constant refrain throughout the debate was: what had all these expenditures actually purchased? Had the military achieved anything? War Minister Krobatin defended his actions, arguing that he had enhanced the efficiency of the army and the military in general. The Magyar deputies accepted these assurances. The larger socialist contingent in the Austrian Delegation was more critical. Yet both Houses eventually approved the budget and left to the respective state governments the task of covering the costs.

The monarchy's economic indicators reinforced the political concerns. However assessed, the current economic data offered little solace to the policy-makers. Commentators have often asserted incorrectly that the monarchy was failing economically before 1912. In fact, its economic reversal dates from the Balkan Wars. Until September 1912 the Habsburg political elite and their banking, industrial and agrarian friends could point to more than a decade of steady economic growth. The monarchy's annual growth rate possibly topped 3.5 per cent during the decade before 1912, with gains in industrial production ranging from 4 to 5 per cent and the production of steel goods up 15 per cent in 1912 alone. The importance of foreign capital had diminished, government expenditures — though growing — were under control and agricultural production increased annually. Against this pattern of prosperity, a poor domestic consumer market and an unfavourable balance of trade were also part of the reality. But ample reason existed for self-congratulation in the economic sphere.[33]

Then came the sudden surge of government spending in late 1912, the disruption of Balkan trading patterns and waning confidence about the monarchy's future. Vaulted from the comfortable and reassuring position of economic growth, the elite became apprehensive and alarmed. Bankruptcies soared, rumours of war devastated the Galician banks and required governmental intervention, and trade with the Balkan peninsula suffered. Steel production sagged for the first time since 1902. Even textile sales were down. Stock prices fell in September–October 1912 like 'leaves in autumn woods' so wrote one commentator, and did not regain their strength. One of the largest firms, the Alpine Mining and Ironworks stock lost, for example, 20 per cent of its value. Bank shares declined an average of 8 per cent, despite heightened interest rates and profits.[34]

The government, moreover, had to fund the sudden surge of military spending. Each of the governments evaded tax increases as it opted for new bond issues rather than raise revenues. The governments sold new bonds to meet the Balkan expenses or rolled over earlier obligations. It is estimated that two-thirds of the bond debt accumulated from 1908 to 1913 came in the years 1912–13. Searching for foreign funds to service the debt became a significant task for the monarchy's three finance ministers and their bankers. The United States, Germany and in the spring of 1914 Great Britain provided some of the funds at rates slightly higher than the prevailing ones. The ease with which the debt issues were sold did not disguise from the senior Habsburg elite the real financial problems for the monarchy. The psychological impact of the economic downturn upon the policy elite cannot be accurately gauged. Nonetheless, the finance ministers and bankers grew progressively more uncomfortable with the situation. Some even said that a war would not be much more disruptive than a renewed Balkan crisis in which the army was mobilized for political effect.[35]

The holdings of the Oriental Railway Company (O.R.C.) chart the rise in apprehension. Initially, an international company operating in Macedonia on a concession from Turkey that was to last until 1958, the Balkan Wars totally altered the O.R.C.'s operating environment. The company had substantial holdings in the now-partitioned Macedonia, with lines from Salonika to Mitrovica, Alexandroúpolis and Monastir (Bitolj). Serbia now possessed most of the track while Greece and Bulgaria had far smaller holdings. The questions became: who owned the track, who would pay for the damage to the rail equipment caused by the war and would rail construction in the Balkan peninsula continue? To complicate matters, the Austro-Hungarian government, in a desire to protect its Balkan political interests, had in the spring of 1913 bought a controlling interest (51 percent) in the O.R.C. Thus, in addition to the already extensive litany of problems between Serbia and Austria–Hungary was added the O.R.C. What had begun as a political investment for the Habsburgs soon acquired more tangled dimensions.[36]

Yet Berchtold viewed the railway issue as offering Austria–Hungary a possible back door into the European financial community. He could, for instance, link concessions on the Adriatic port issue with a satisfactory resolution of the O.R.C. questions. He made this effort but to no particular success. He also sought to use an international approach that extricated Vienna from the ownership question, while placating Serbian sensibilities and conceivably opening the Parisian money market to the Habsburg monarchy. To this end he and others tried to convince the Pašić government to accept a new international operating company that would assume the ownership and debts of the O.R.C. In turn the European financial groups, especially the French, would fund the take-over — a fact that might also ease Vienna's financial dependence on Berlin. The Serbian leaders swayed to and fro, finally opting in April 1914 to scuttle any international approach. To Berchtold's dismay, Pašić and his colleagues demanded sole ownership of the O.R.C. lines inside Serbia. This decision left Vienna with no option but to begin negotiations for the sale of the lines and to seek compensation for the war damages. These negotiations were still underway on 30 June and 1 July 1914 — after Sarajevo — until Vienna recalled its envoys. When the talks broke off, the major obstacle to a settlement was the price: 42 or 46 million crowns. Whether and how the Serbian government could pay any final price remained, even as the negotiations proceeded, unclear.[37]

The fate of the O.R.C., with its incompleteness and ambiguity, symbolized the economic impact of the Balkan Wars upon the Austro-Hungarian monarchy. The wars disturbed given situations, interrupted prosperity, revealed new vulnerabilities and shook confidences. The ramifications were practical: a loss of investor confidence, the need for new government funds and the prospect of lost investments such as the O.R.C. In the O.R.C. issue, moreover, still another grievance was added to the growing list with Belgrade. The failure to internationalize the rail line hurt Habsburg government investments, kept the Paris money market closed to the monarchy and appeared as still another Habsburg setback in the

Balkans. By focusing attention upon Serbia, the railway issue provided — in a different but crucial sphere — still another reason to resolve the Serbian problem. But before that move could come, and many in the monarchy now accepted this as inevitable, the relationship with Rumania required mending. That task began in the autumn of 1913. Its eventual failure in the spring and early summer of 1914 forms a part of the explanation for Vienna's mounting sense of isolation and strategic vulnerability during the July crisis.

IV

In the autumn of 1913 Foreign Minister Berchtold sent Ottokar Czernin, a Bohemian confidant of Archduke Franz Ferdinand and rumoured to be his future foreign minister, on a make-or-break mission to Bucharest. In making the appointment Berchtold had obtained not only Franz Joseph's and Franz Ferdinand's consent but Tisza's as well. Tisza agreed to the mission on the explicit condition that Czernin did not intrude into Hungarian politics, a promise soon violated and one which necessarily doomed the mission in advance. Czernin's mission was a surprising, bold move that failed. Czernin was the wrong man at the wrong time at the wrong place. An articulate aristocratic opportunist, he became easily frustrated. Viewed by many as anti-Magyar and as too close to the archduke, he was from the start — and despite Tisza's approval — suspect in Budapest as one who would sacrifice Magyar interests to the Rumanians.[37]

By the time Czernin arrived in Bucharest in late November 1913, the Rumanian alliance had already become increasingly problematic. A secret arrangement with King Carol, ostensibly known to only three senior Rumanian politicians, the alliance ties with Berlin and Vienna had been sorely tested during the Balkan Wars. Neither Vienna's alleged encouragement of Bulgaria in June 1913 nor Berchtold's graceless reaction to King Carol's personal success in staging the Peace of Bucharest had helped. More disturbing, Rumania's brief burst of military glory in July 1913 stirred Rumanian nationalists, so much so that King Carol had to respect their views. Furthermore, the Rumanian political leadership now turned its attention to the three million Rumanians living under Magyar rule. Forced Magyarization, harrassment and virtually no political representation in Budapest made the Rumanians in Transylvania easy targets for appeals from Bucharest. To his credit, Tisza had already recognized this danger. On three earlier occasions he had sought accommodation with the Rumanian National Party. He pledged more political power to the Rumanians if their party agreed to integrate into Hungarian life. This Faustian offer the Rumanians rejected. The nationality issues made Transylvania the obstacle to an effective Rumanian alliance with Austria–Hungary.[38]

Within this nearly impossible context Czernin sought to operate. Indeed, his instructions reflected the failure of the Ballhausplatz to accept hard political realities. Czernin was instructed to assure Carol and the Rumanian leadership of both Habsburg friendship and loyalty. He was to proclaim the virtues afforded Rumanians living inside the Habsburg monarchy and to ask Bucharest to refrain from close relations with Belgrade. The Habsburgs had given nothing in return, yet they wanted King Carol to publish the secret alliance and thereby pledge Rumania publicly to the Triple Alliance. At no point did Czernin's instructions show an awareness that Magyar flexibility was necessary or that the Triple Entente and French money were at work in the Rumanian capital. Czernin's mission was not to negotiate. He was armed only with illusions, wishes and hopes, but nothing to give them tangible meaning. The new envoy quickly discovered this.[39]

Czernin's impatience also made him move too rapidly. He soon found every planned avenue blocked or thwarted. Carol accepted the assurances of Franz Joseph's goodwill and would acknowledge the dangers posed by Serbia. But the king would not publish the terms of the alliance. More ominously, each conversation with the king or the senior ministers quickly turned to Transylvania and its Rumanian inhabitants. Austria–Hungary, Czernin cabled on 5 December, might treat Transylvania as an internal issue; the Rumanians did not. Only concessions by Budapest would make possible a long-term commitment by Rumania to the Triple Alliance. Otherwise, Rumanian nationalism would soon match that of Serbia, thereby creating still another external threat to the Dual Monarchy. The solution to strengthening the Triple Alliance and resolving differences with Rumania, Czernin believed, rested with Budapest, not Vienna or Bucharest.[40]

Berchtold and his associates found these reports in early December distasteful. The foreign minister urged the envoy to keep trying.

After all, Tisza had said he would negotiate. The Germans had promised assistance and possibly this might help.[41]

Berchtold, Franz Joseph, Franz Ferdinand and even Tisza tried to bolster Czernin's spirits when he returned to Vienna at Christmas time. On 27 December, on his way back to Bucharest, Berchtold, Czernin and Tisza lunched at the Hotel Sacher. In this setting, Tisza assured Czernin that he would seek an *Ausgleich* with the Rumanians in Hungary. Franz Joseph expressed a similar hope later that day at Schönbrunn.

Writing from the Rumanian capital three days later, Czernin had renewed spirits and believed that Hungarian concessions might just manage to rescue the alliance. As 1913 gave way to 1914, chances for salvaging the relationship with Bucharest from the wreckage of a year of steady Balkan fighting appeared a possibility. Berchtold should have known better, but he could hope. Instead, the foreign minister should have heeded his New Year's Eve dream of death and destruction. Later he would interpret his turning and tossing as a premonition of the subsequent horrors of 1914.[42]

V

As 1913 ended, the two senior Habsburgs, the foreign ministry and its senior leadership reviewed the previous twelve months. In December 1912 the danger of a war with Russia was a possibility, the German alliance was in disarray, Conrad's insistent pleas for a war with Serbia just barely quashed and the Scutari issue flammable. In 1913 one Balkan War had ended only to be followed by another. In both, the Habsburg position took a further beating. The monarchy's economy had suffered and the political circles were increasingly bitter and resentful. No one could be confident about the future, especially given the prospect of transition from Franz Joseph to Franz Ferdinand. The possibility of a Rumanian defection and trouble with Italy over Albania were also disturbing. And the recent acrimony between Berlin and St Petersburg over the status of General Liman von Sanders in Constantinople had troubling aspects.

Yet Serbia had yielded to a Habsburg ultimatum in October. The monarchy's population apparently favoured a tougher stance. Thanks to the 1912 legislation, the Habsburg military were finally getting more men and more *materiél*. The Habsburg leadership, with the exception of Franz Ferdinand, had itself been unified, moreover, in the October war–peace crisis. Only the heir-apparent had argued that militancy did not constitute a policy. Except for Franz Ferdinand, no one challenged this 'group think' approach to the monarchy's Balkan problems. Without Franz Ferdinand the momentum of 'group think' would render the chances for peace very unlikely. But a trip to Sarajevo, though already on the archduke's summer calendar, was months away. In the meantime, Czernin might rescue the Rumanian alliance, Albania might stop being a point of contention with Italy and Austro-Russian relations might yet improve. The monarchy's Balkan policy, although shaken, had not been shattered. Conrad as always argued that the only option was a military confrontation; Berchtold could only hope that the general was wrong.

9 Austria–Hungary and the Last Months Before Sarajevo: January–June 1914

The diplomatic and strategic history of states can and does have a personal side that is often ignored or pushed aside in the explication of policy decisions. A vignette from June 1914 illustrates this graphically.

Nandine Berchtold, a friend since childhood of Sophie Hohenberg, and her husband Leopold arrived at Franz Ferdinand's estate at Konopischt for a day visit on Sunday, 14 June 1914. The two couples breakfasted, dined, toured the gardens and looked at the archduke's art collection which Berchtold, also a collector, found interesting. Finally at the end of the day, the Berchtolds returned to the train station and travelled back to Vienna. Less than two weeks later the royal couple would travel to Bosnia–Herzegovina for the army manoeuvres; the four never saw each other again.

Berchtold's visit at Konopischt has been overshadowed in historical accounts by that of William II who left the day before. The William–Franz Ferdinand visit, so celebrated in the literature on the origins of the war as a sinister gathering, was in fact quite prosaic and humdrum. More consequential was the foreign minister's visit, since his perceptions and his reactions to the meeting would have a decided impact upon Berchtold's decisions after Sarajevo. Thus Berchtold's discussions with the *Thronfolger* and the follow-up steps that he took upon returning to Vienna merit analysis. Together these events provide a format for reviewing Austria–Hungary's foreign and strategic policies in the last months before 28 June 1914.[1]

I

In their discussions Franz Ferdinand summarized for Berchtold his conversations with the German ruler. Inevitably the talk had revolved around some of the monarchy's most immediate issues: the

Rumanian question and Tisza's possible role in alleviating the problem, Italian duplicity over Albania and the question of an overture to Bulgaria. At no point, however, had the archduke and the German kaiser discussed any military action against Serbia. Indeed, Serbia had not loomed large in their discussion. After evaluating William's visit, the archduke and the foreign minister touched upon larger, more strategic questions, such as Russia's behaviour and the need to isolate Serbia. For his part Franz Ferdinand continued to hope for a détente with St Petersburg, a view the foreign minister no longer accepted. But the two men agreed on the need to take immediate steps to isolate Serbia and thus thwart the revival of any Balkan League against Austria–Hungary. The time had come for a new policy initiative, one that Berlin and Tisza would support and that would seek anew to contain neighbouring Serbia. On this note, without any specific references to Franz Ferdinand's future trip to the two colonial provinces, the two men parted. Berchtold left convinced the time had come for a new, decisive diplomatic overture to restore a sense of direction to Habsburg foreign policy. Drift and reaction would no longer suffice; a clean, decisive approach was required.[2]

Berchtold wasted no time in implementing this resolve. Immediately upon his return to Vienna he asked Franz von Matscheko, a senior section chief, to draft a memorandum for his use with Berlin in proposing a new, more dramatic *Balkanpolitik*. Working quickly, the senior official met with Berchtold and Forgách, the senior political official, for guidance and then completed the first draft on 24 June. Since this memorandum was greatly altered after Sarajevo, the pre-28 June version offers a framework for analysing the condition of the monarchy's foreign policy as it had evolved during the previous six months. The document also provides valuable insights into this last effort to use a diplomatic approach to restore the Danubian monarchy's foreign policy leadership. After Sarajevo the document would be redrafted and used to justify force, not diplomacy, as a foreign policy option.[3]

From the start Berchtold and his associates recognized that their proposed policy memorandum had four distinct audiences: Franz Joseph, Franz Ferdinand, Tisza and the Germans. Without co-operation from each, no new initiative would be successful: without their support, the circularity and ineffectiveness of the monarchy's policies would continue. To win over these audiences, Matscheko carefully defined the options, reviewed the pros and cons and then left the reader with the conviction that the time for action had come. At no point did he paper over the situation. Indeed, the memorandum had a strident shrillness that could only alarm and stir any reader worried about the longterm survival of the Habsburgs.

Vienna's recent foreign policy successes were few: the creation of Albania, the possible Greek alignment with the Triple Alliance and a Bulgaria that no longer looked to St Petersburg and might now consider joining with Berlin and Vienna. More than offsetting these favourable trends were the apparent defection of Rumania from the Triple Alliance, the possibility of a Serbian-Montenegrin union that would give Belgrade access to the sea, new evidence of Franco-Russian aggressiveness and fear that a new Balkan League might emerge against the Dual Monarchy. Put tersely, Matscheko believed the intrusion of Russia and France in the Straits and in the Balkans was of a decidedly 'offensive nature'. What led to this conclusion and to this alarm? A brief survey of events in each of these areas helps put Matscheko's conclusions into perspective.

The creation of an Albania that denied Serbia access to the sea had been Berchtold's major triumph of the Balkan Wars. Yet by June 1914 that success suddenly appeared threatened from two sides: first, the inability of the prince of Wied to establish himself as the ruler of the newly created principality; and second, the obvious intention of the Italian government to carve for itself a position of influence and power in the strife-torn country. The prince, who had finally arrived at his new home on 7 February, found no royal reception. Instead, chaos reigned and behind much of it was Essad Pasha, the former Turkish commander at Scutari who now was in the pay of the Italians. The challenge posed by Essad Pasha grew so serious that the prince of Wied had to flee for protection to an Italian ship anchored in the harbour at Durazzo. Even the other great powers became alarmed and talked of a possible naval demonstration in support of the new prince. The creation of the Albanian government had been the chief Habsburg success of recent months. Now even that appeared endangered.[4]

What especially troubled the policy-makers in Vienna was Italy's role in fostering the unrest. Report after report reached Vienna that the Italian consul in Durazzo, Carlo Aliotti, had given money to Essad, had sought to turn the populace against the inept prince and had manipulated the Italian press to celebrate his own action. When Berchtold met with San Giuliano in Abazzia on 14 April, the

Habsburg foreign minister repeatedly pressed his Italian counter-part to seek a coordinated approach to Albania. Berchtold especially hoped that Aliotti's actions could be curbed. The Italian foreign minister promised to do better. Yet San Giuliano also conceded to Berlin in early June that Aliotti had so much domestic support in Italy that he could not in fact be recalled without endangering the viability of the Italian government. For their part the Austrians allowed newspapers on 27 June to advertise for 'mercenaries' to go to Albania to help the prince. Clearly the two allies were raising the stakes for each other over the future of Albania. By the end of June their friction had grown to such a point that Berlin would warn Vienna to 'cool' things. No issue, Serbia included, so preoccupied Vienna in the months before Sarajevo as did the Albanian question and the alleged Italian disloyalty there. Matscheko may have assessed Albania a plus for Vienna, but it was a tenuous asset.[5]

The Ballhausplatz could be happier about improved relations with Athens. But good ties with Greece and the memorandum's mention of this were designed to win favour in Berlin. Greece offered few perceived policy advantages to the Danubian monarchy. The Habsburg ambassador in Athens, Julius Szilassy (now with his own post after months of grousing in Vienna), expressed his hopes for stronger ties. Certainly, restraining Greece from membership in any Balkan League would lessen the threat to Habsburg fortunes. In blocking such a threat Berlin's assistance might be crucial. On the other hand, Greek claims for territory in Epirus along the Albanian border added tension to the already complicated Albanian problem. Each Greek claim, despite the efforts of the international commis-sion to resolve all these matters, led to delays and frustrations. Each Greek claim both fuelled Serbian appetites and allowed the Italians more opportunities to intrude.

In addition, the Vienna–Sofia connection worked for and against improved relations with Greece. A Greece hostile to Bulgarian involvement with the Triple Alliance would make an already difficult policy choice even more unpalatable to Berlin or to Franz Joseph and Franz Ferdinand, the principal opponents of such an overture. Better ties with Athens would help in this matter. Cordial relations with the Greek government were chiefly negligible assets; on the other hand, poor relations, including Greek participation in a new Balkan League, would be a distinct liability.[6]

Bulgaria constituted a third possible asset in Matscheko's analysis.

Even before the end of the First Balkan War, Berchtold had gingerly attempted to forge a closer working relationship with Sofia. In June 1913 Berchtold had played a dangerous game that could be interpreted as encouraging Bulgaria to attack Serbia. The disasters of the Second War left Sofia less alliance-worthy, yet nonetheless a government whose possible assistance was desirable. Thus during the remainder of 1913 the Habsburg policy-makers debated whether to press for closer ties with Bulgaria; the Hungarians were especially insistent on this point. A disastrous meeting between King Ferdinand and senior Habsburg officials in early November, however, did not help. The assignment of Ottokar Czernin as the new minister to Bucharest in the late autumn reinforced the desire to stay with Rumania rather than opt for Bulgaria. In doing so, Berchtold won German plaudits and kept the pressure on the Magyars to make concessions in Transylvania. Equally important, Rumania as an ally or as a neutral offered significant strategic assets to Conrad and the military planners.[7]

The Matscheko memorandum nevertheless made abundantly clear that Bucharest had not grown friendlier toward Vienna. Thus throughout the first months of 1914 the policy-makers in Vienna considered and reconsidered the Bulgarian ploy. Two issues were troublesome: Sofia had agreed to better relations with Bucharest and that meant accepting the hated Peace of Bucharest which had signalled Bulgaria's defeat. This step would be difficult for any Bulgarian politician. On the other hand, Sofia badly needed foreign capital. If Vienna could provide such a loan, that would do wonders for Austrian foreign policy. But Vienna had no surplus capital, only Berlin. Yet Berlin still scorned Sofia in favour of Bucharest, poohpoohed fears of a new Balkan League and generally minimized the dangers of the Balkan situation.[8]

The more Czernin's mission appeared in jeopardy, the more attractive Bulgaria became to Vienna. In early March 1914, Tisza pressured Berchtold to move toward Sofia as a way to frustrate a new Balkan League. The Magyar leader even talked of a Greek–Rumanian–Bulgarian alignment that would encircle and isolate Serbia. Tisza made these points directly to William II when he visited Vienna on 23 March. The German emperor, who had not met the Magyar prime minister before, found him an articulate, forceful and attractive personality. Tisza did not spare his rhetoric with the German ruler. Arguing that King Carol was lost to the alliance, a position which Franz Joseph and Berchtold were also close to believing, Tisza urged that Berlin pressure Bucharest into accepting some Magyar concessions. Tisza did not stop there. He wanted German backing for a Bulgarian overture. William II evaded the request, while dutifully reporting it to his governmental officials in Berlin.[9]

The Ballhausplatz did not relent in its efforts toward Sofia. Repeatedly during April and May Berchtold, Tisza and the others pressed the Germans to agree to a Bulgarian overture and to provide money for an agreement. With a loan, the Bulgarians could pay off their sizeable debts from the Balkan Wars and proceed to new economic development projects. Still Berlin hesitated. Moreover, on 8 May Chancellor Bethmann Hollweg warned Jagow about Austria–Hungary's increasingly aggressive stance on the Bulgarian question. He wanted a 'frank exchange' of views and talked of vetoing Vienna's initiative on this matter. Still Berchtold pressed harder, instructing Ambassador Szögyény in early June to put the case more insistently to the Wilhelmstrasse. In his appeals, the Austrian ambassador could point to Bulgarian hints of better ties with Bucharest. Nevertheless, Berlin resisted, in part because German bankers, rightly sceptical of Bulgarian fiscal policy, wanted the Bulgarian tobacco concession as collateral for their loan.[10]

The Bulgaria–Rumania trade-off had not changed when Matscheko wrote his analysis of Habsburg foreign policy. Insisting that Russia might force Serbia to offer Bulgaria a part of Macedonia in an effort to keep the Bulgarians away from the Triple Alliance, the Austrian official stressed Bulgaria's vulnerability. Throughout Matscheko's explication ran the assumption that if a strong policy initiative toward Bucharest failed, then Bulgaria was the only option left for the Triple Alliance. Thus, to keep the Bulgarian option open was crucial, in part to keep the Bulgarians away from the increasingly aggressive government in St Petersburg. A Bulgaria allied with the Triple Alliance would be extremely helpful. And, if Turkey could be added as well, the Triple Alliance would be even more formidable. Hence Sofia, even if considered unreliable, could not be dismissed.[11]

On 12 July the German Discount Bank, operating for a German–Austrian consortium, loaned 450 million Reichsmarks to Bulgaria. These funds would help to remit Bulgaria's debt and allow new financial ventures. In return, Bulgaria remained neutral in 1914.

Later Sofia would take the plunge, on the side of the Central Powers, with military results reminiscent of its performance in the Second Balkan War. Nonetheless, in June 1914 the Bulgarian question was a major issue for Habsburg statesmen.[12]

II

Albania, Greece, Bulgaria: these constituted possible advantages for Austria–Hungary as the senior Habsburg statesmen assessed the monarchy's international position. The negatives were far more threatening. Of these the Rumanian question had the most urgency, the Serbian the most emotion, the Russian the most danger and the alliance–entente competition the most complications. Above all, relations with Rumania had the intensity of a flickering, dying love affair, about to collapse despite desperate efforts by one suitor to revive it. Berchtold, Forgách and Matscheko had only to consider recent developments and become profoundly depressed.

Minister Czernin had returned to Bucharest after spending Christmas 1913 at home. The Bohemian noble still hoped for a diplomatic success leading to improved relations with Rumania. After all, Tisza had promised to make concessions to the Rumanian National Party by increasing the number of deputies in the Hungarian parliament. The Archduke Franz Ferdinand continued to press for a Rumanian rather than a Bulgarian orientation. Czernin still enjoyed Berchtold's support if not his confidence. Yet early in 1914 Czernin saw his hopes dashed, in part because Tisza demanded that Bucharest assure its support for Austria–Hungary in return for any concessions. No Rumanian politician could accept this, since it would effectively curb Rumanian agitation in Transylvania. By the end of January the negotiations with the Rumanian National Party had collapsed.[13] The repercussions from Czernin's own maladroit pronouncement to a Magyar newspaper, *Az Est* , compounded the issue. In the interview Czernin had declared that Rumanians living in Transylvania did not have adequate political rights. This statement, later labelled by Czernin as an act of 'stupidity', exposed Tisza to vicious parliamentary attacks. A chastened Czernin offered to resign; Tisza and Berchtold asked him to remain. But the damage was done. The Rumanian politicians could not yield to Tisza; Tisza, now under attack from his fellow Magyars, could not make concessions to ease Rumanian concerns even if he had wanted to do so. The domestic politics of both countries were thoroughly entangled with their foreign policies.[14]

During March, April and May Berchtold and his associates scrambled to find a way to restart the Rumanian negotiations. Both Berlin and Archduke Franz Ferdinand pressured the Ballhausplatz not to give up on King Carol and still hoped for an opening. The situation did not improve. Anti-Habsburg demonstrations occurred in Bucharest, Tisza remained under vitriolic attack in Budapest and Czernin continued to lose credibility. When the minister advocated that Vienna threaten King Carol with the publication of the secret alliance, Berchtold demurred. He refused, at this point, to embrace an 'all or nothing' strategy. By the end of June, however, he began to reconsider that stance. For his part, Czernin now saw enemies everywhere, blamed the Hoyos-Forgách clique at the Ballhausplatz for his troubles and assailed Rumanian Prime Minister Bratianu and Rumanian politicians in general.[15]

In spite of these setbacks, Berchtold persisted. In early April he asked Czernin to see whether King Carol would make a purely foreign policy accord: Austria–Hungary would guarantee the Peace of Bucharest and thus protect Rumania from Bulgaria if Carol would agree to the publication of the secret alliance. This gambit also came to nothing. By early May Berchtold was uncomfortable with the situation, for Franz Joseph was seriously ill and the Bulgarian option was still in abeyance. Furthermore, the criticism of Berchtold in the Delegations in May merely highlighted the urgency of the Rumanian question.[16]

In late May worries about Rumania's role in the alliance turned to apprehension mixed with fear. St Petersburg announced that Nicholas and Alexandra would visit Constanza, Rumania on 14 June. The Russian move rattled all of the Habsburg assumptions, as the Matscheko memorandum makes clear. No longer could Vienna and Budapest and Berlin ignore Rumania's drift away from the alliance. The Russians and the French were now actively seeking to incorporate Bucharest into their orbit. The Russian royal visit was but one more step in the process of courtship. Profusions of Russian-Rumanian goodwill flowed on both sides; Vienna could worry again about a new Balkan League. In fact, had Vienna known that King Carol had assured his Russian guest that Bucharest would under no circumstances enter a war on Austria–Hungary's side, their fears would have increased still more. Some ominous signs were evident publicly. Russian Foreign Minister Sazonov conspicuously crossed into Transylvania to show support for the Rumanians who lived under Magyar rule. Czernin's warning about Russia seeking to achieve a 'step by step encirclement of the monarchy' had new meaning.[17]

As Matscheko had drafted his analysis, in almost every paragraph he reflected upon the Rumanian problem and its relationship to Russian activism. The secret alliance with King Carol, in place since 1883, now appeared destroyed. However much Berlin might wish otherwise, the king and the Rumanian politicians could not think of helping the Triple Alliance. After August 1913 the revival of Rumanian nationalism rendered relationships between Budapest and Bucharest almost impossible; demographic factors constituted *Realpolitik*. Only a Rumania frightened by Russia would seek help from Vienna. A Rumania befriended by St Petersburg would no longer need Vienna or Berlin. Berchtold and his colleagues had cause for despair; the Habsburg military planners found a reason to fret and complain anew.

III

The Rumanian question by itself constituted a crisis situation; the Rumanian problem juxtaposed with Serbia's recent gains and Russian aggressiveness threatened the very future of the venerable Danubian regime. Yet in Matscheko's assessment the problem of Serbia received almost *sotto voce* treatment, as if the reader did not have to be reminded of Belgrade's importance to Vienna. Surprisingly, if one did a quantitative analysis of Habsburg diplomatic correspondence in the first six months of 1914, Albania and Rumania would dominate over Serbia. Yet no statesman in Vienna or Budapest had any illusions; Serbia coupled with Russia posed a decisive and growing danger.

At moments, however, Vienna and Belgrade sought normality. The negotiations for the future of the O.R.C. indicated that fact. To be sure, nothing came of the Habsburg effort to internationalize the rail line and thus maintain some economic leverage with Belgrade. Instead, the two governments negotiated for a sale, the price still unresolved when the events at Sarajevo intervened. On a quite different front the two states exchanged a half-dozen prisoners held on various espionage charges. Their release at the end of May followed months of bureaucratic jockeying and showed that the two governments could cooperate on a specific issue. Furthermore, the activist tenor of anti-Habsburg propaganda, emanating from Belgrade, eased a bit in early 1914. Even inside Bosnia–Herzegovina the debates in the Landtag were productive, some economic projects offered promise and the long-delayed Bosnian railway construction was on the verge of initiation.[18]

At another level, however, the signs were less friendly. Increasingly, politicians in Belgrade and Cetinje talked of a fusion of the two kingdoms. Berchtold and his associates cringed each time the topic surfaced. Unifying Serbia with Montenegro would give Serbia access to the sea, extend the common frontier controlled by Belgrade and confer upon the Lovčen heights a still greater strategic significance for Habsburg naval planners. Because such a move fundamentally challenged Vienna's success of the previous year, any union between the two governments was guaranteed to prompt adamant Habsburg opposition. Although some Montenegrin politicians wanted to sell out to Belgrade, the scheming Nikita hesitated. In this arena Berchtold sought and expected Italian help, especially since King Victor Emmanuel had a familial stake in the outcome of any fusion. Vienna's position was unambiguous: Russian sponsorship of a Montenegrin-Serbian union was a 'trip wire' that might provoke a sudden international crisis. While this Habsburg stance alarmed Berlin, the position was never abandoned. Matscheko's memorandum recognized it in the context of the Serbian threat. On this issue, as on Serbian access to the sea in November 1912 and Montenegro's desire for Scutari in May 1913, Vienna would throw down the gauntlet. However much Berlin might seek to diminish the threat of the fusion of Montenegro and Serbia, Vienna never agreed. Serbia and Montenegro as allies was troublesome; a Serbia–Montenegro united under the Karadjordjevićs and with Russia as its protector was unacceptable.[19]

Serbo-Russian relations were the most threatening foreign combination for any Austro-Hungarian statesman. Memories of the 1908 crisis, the creation of the Balkan League, the Serbian successes of the Balkan Wars — each presented another dimension of the minuet between and among the three powers. The military coup of 1903 had ousted the Habsburgs from their control of the Belgrade government. Since then Vienna had witnessed the steady emergence of Russian influence in the neighbouring kingdom. By 1914 the activism of Russian Minister Hartwig was a matter of growing concern. The minister's frequent references to Austria–Hungary as the 'next sick man of Europe', his evident patronage of Pan-Slavic groups and his ubiquitous presence in Serbian politics could not be disregarded. Events of May and the first two weeks of June 1914 served to emphasize Hartwig's influence as Pašić and Interior Minister Protić struggled to retain power against the Serbian military. In their efforts, Hartwig's and Russian support was crucial for their success.[20]

Vienna had carefully followed Pašić's struggle with the Serbian military. The officer party, using The Piedmont as their journal, had sought to wrest control of the newly conquered territories from the civilian authorities. To thwart this, Protić had attempted to discredit the military by disclosing widespread corruption among the officer corps. The effort backfired. By mid-May, reports reached Vienna of a possible military coup and of the Black Hand being solidly aligned against Pašić. These machinations, carefully monitored by Habsburg intelligence, received new credence when Pašić submitted his resignation. Only Russian pressure upon King Peter brought Pašić back, along with a pledge to call new elections. Rescued by Hartwig from the military, Pašić would in June 1914 not easily be able to curb the powerful Colonel Apis, leader of the Black Hand. Thus, in a strange, contorted way, Serbian domestic politics, mixed with Russia's support of Pašić, helped to create the situation in which the assassination plot — even though suspected — could not be thwarted by Pašić and Protić. Although rightly concerned about the St Petersburg–Belgrade relationship, Vienna had even more to fear than it realized and than Matscheko's analysis spelled out. The suspicions were present, the details incomplete.[21]

In the June reassessment of Habsburg foreign policy the most striking feature, though almost unnoticed by historians, is its fixation on Russia's more active, assertive foreign policy. Throughout the memorandum, alongside the evaluation of the Rumanian problem, runs a deeper, more disturbing theme of Russia's willingness to challenge Austria–Hungary at every turn. Russia became the ever-probing, ever-aggressive adversary. Only the superior Austro-German military forces had kept the peace thus far. Now with the Rumanians defecting and the Balkan power alignments in upheaval, Berlin and Vienna, so the analysis argued, were slowly being pushed to the defensive. What gave the Russian presence more effectiveness was French money, which could easily recreate a new Balkan League. At the very least the Franco-Russian allies might neutralize both Bulgaria and Turkey, leaving Vienna with no alternative counterweights against Serbia. Above all else, if Rumania went into the Russian camp, the strategic position of the Danubian monarchy would be thoroughly compromised. These fears, which Matscheko carefully delineated, were the product of the Ballhausplatz's new threat assessment of Russia. Vienna no longer thought that Russia would agree to a policy of détente; it was now convinced that St Petersburg would press every advantage. Vienna wanted the Germans to realize just how dangerous the Russian threat had become and possibly appreciate that some action now, rather than later, might be preferable.[22]

Several recent episodes stirred Vienna's alarm. The confrontation of the Balkan Wars left strong impressions on both the Austrian and German General Staffs. So also did the Russian steps to accelerate their mobilization and the continuing progress of the Russian re-armament efforts, in which 1917 was often seen as the date for completion. Still more worrisome were reports of another Russian 'trial mobilization' scheduled for the summer of 1914. Just such a 'trial mobilization', both Vienna and Berlin well remembered, had been the mode for keeping hundreds of thousands of extra Russian troops on duty at the outbreak of the Balkan Wars. Finally, the military press in all three countries jabbed at each other throughout the spring. When the Russian paper, *Nowoje Wremje*, published a piece on 'The Partition of Austria–Hungary', Vienna understandably regarded the action as hostile. The Austrian military press reported that Russia's own ethnic problems were considerable and that the Habsburgs would survive even if the Romanovs did not. Given such rhetoric, Conrad could genuinely worry about the ability of the Triple Alliance, especially if Rumania defected, to offset the surging Franco-Russian strength.[23]

The diplomatic arena was not much more promising. A glimpse of hope for productive discussions came occasionally. The dispatch of new ambassadors to each capital, Szápáry to St Petersburg and Nicholas Shekebo to Vienna, offered an opportunity for new discussions. Szápáry's own instructions expressed a desire for better relations. When the new ambassador met Prime Minister Goremykin and Foreign Minister Sazonov, he received a cordial welcome;

Nicholas II reciprocated as well. What was needed, Szápáry correctly observed, was something precise to negotiate about rather than the ambiguous issues of Pan-Slavic agitation. Unfortunately no such issue existed. And to complicate matters, personal problems forced Szápáry to leave St Petersburg almost as soon as he had arrived. When he returned later in the spring, the possible 'opportune' moment had slipped away.[24]

Political as well as military factors made negotiation difficult. The Russo-German clash over the status of General Liman von Sanders in Constantinople had appeared to signal a new Russian aggressiveness. Hartwig's belligerent language against Austria–Hungary likewise reflected a policy of adventure. So too did reports that Russia wanted to encourage a new Balkan League whose chief catalyst would have to be the partition of Austria–Hungary. Equally unsettling was new evidence of still closer Serbo-Russian ties. Pašić visited St Petersburg in early 1914; the Russians agreed to a large arms sale at cost for Belgrade. There were even hints of a marriage alignment between the two royal courts. St Petersburg's suspected involvement in a possible Serbo-Montenegrin union also frightened Berchtold. And Russia's evident determination to intrude into the monarchy's domestic affairs by stirring Pan-Slavic feeling in Galicia and Bukovina could not be ignored. Meanwhile, Austria–Hungary believed that its abstention from stirring the Polish pot should have been reciprocated. Instead the Russians encouraged the agitation. The clamour of Pan-Slavic demands thus further restricted the few productive areas for negotiation. If Sazonov or Nicholas wanted better relations, they extended few olive branches to Vienna. St Petersburg did not make détente easy.[25]

Still, given Vienna's battered position, Franz Ferdinand's disposition for better Russian relations and the changing military balance, the puzzle is why Berchtold did not press harder. Tisza did not discourage such a step, nor did Berlin. In fact, both might have favoured an amelioration of the situation. Interestingly, Conrad did not intrude on the matter either. Rather, the negative influence, the issues that deterred Vienna from rapprochement with St Petersburg, flowed from Pan-Slavic activity. In Russia, the nationalistic considerations had long since melded with strategic factors in the case of Serbia. To control Belgrade would be difficult under any circumstances; by 1914 the client had indeed become the manipulator and initiator.

While Matscheko focused upon Russia, he ignored Great Britain and its military and naval relationship with Austria–Hungary and the Triple Alliance. The Continental thrust of his argument remains undiluted by any consideration of the naval race or other West European issues. In that sense, the memorandum mirrored the shift in German strategic thinking that had occurred since the Second Moroccan Crisis. Matscheko's concentration on the Continent and the Russian threat placed Habsburg fears within a Berlin–Vienna context.[26]

Possibly more surprising, the status of the Triple Alliance itself did not receive explicit attention. This omission reflected the nature of the document: a piece arguing for action. Had Matscheko dealt with the alliance, the prose would have been circumspect and careful. The alliance had not prospered noticeably in the first half of 1914. The principal problems were twofold: Rumania and Italian activities in Albania. The continuation of the subtle Austro-Italian struggle for influence in Albania threatened to erupt at any moment into a more hostile situation. Yet the impact of the Albanian issue upon Austro-Italian relations was not conspicuously mentioned in Matscheko's analysis. In a document designed to convince Berlin of the need for new diplomatic initiatives, Vienna had no wish to emphasize alliance weakness. Nevertheless, relations with Rome had deteriorated since their cooperation during the Balkan Wars. Although the two military staffs continued to talk, political differences drove the two alliance partners further apart. Not only the Albanian problem, but the resurgence of Italian irredentism about Trieste and Trentino complicated matters.

In September 1913 the Trieste city government decided to discharge all non-Habsburg citizens from municipal positions. The step had sparked instant Italian recrimination. Demands for the fulfilment of the *Risorgimento* echoed in the Italian parliament and the Italian press. The shallow roots of domestic political support for the alliance with Vienna soon withered in Italy. Once again Berlin found itself trying to mediate and to placate its two partners.[27]

Austro-Italian relations were also troubled by diplomatic reports of an Italo-German accord to carve up a part of Asia Minor if the Turkish government collapsed. In mid-summer 1913 Berchtold discovered that his two allies had agreed upon spheres of influence for themselves if the Ottoman empire totally collapsed. Since Berlin had earlier rebuffed Berchtold's overtures on this matter, the foreign minister almost felt betrayed. After failing to win any possible concessions directly from the Turks, Vienna in October demanded that Berlin reconsider its position. Szilassy, sent to Berlin to pressure the Wilhelmstrasse, returned in early November with a German agreement to let the Habsburgs have Alanya if partition occurred. Vienna could also seek a railway concession from Akseki. These 'meagre' results, as Szilassy called them, assuaged Habsburg feelings. But the entire episode did not bolster Vienna's confidence in either ally's political judgement or loyalty.[28]

Except for Berchtold's meetings with Italian Foreign Minister San Giuliano, which were useful, and military staff conversations, no other personal political ties between the Habsburg and Italian rulers existed. Franz Ferdinand would not visit Italy; Franz Joseph was too old to go; and the Austrians did not invite their Italian counterparts. The absence of a personal relationship worried Berlin. In the spring of 1914 Jagow explored with Tschirschky the idea of inviting Franz Ferdinand to attend the German manoeuvres, where Jagow would arrange a meeting between the archduke and General Pollio, chief of the Italian General Staff. Worried about the viability of the alliance and cognizant of Conrad's well-known anti-Italian outbursts, the Germans sought to patch up the alliance.[29]

Of the German relationship *per se* Vienna had little overt reason for complaint in the spring of 1914. William II had visited Vienna and Franz Joseph, had seen Franz Ferdinand twice during the spring and remained ebullient and irresponsible. On the other hand, the German political leadership worried whether the Habsburg succession issue would provoke a crisis. In particular, Jagow feared the impact of Franz Ferdinand's opposition to Tisza, the man who ran Hungary and whose cooperation the new emperor/king would need if he were to keep the multinational state together. At another level, Berchtold could rightly fret about Berlin's persistent failure to appreciate the threat posed by Serbia. Paradoxically, the growing assertiveness of the Russians helped to make the point in Berlin. In late June, the senior Habsburg leadership sought to exploit heightened German anxiety over Russian aggressiveness. From Vienna's viewpoint, if the German leadership would only accept that Rumania was irrevocably lost, then the Bulgarian option offered a possible means to realign the Balkan power balance. With the German bankers becoming more agreeable to a Bulgarian loan, the Ballhausplatz could believe that even the Germans might consider a major shift in their diplomatic policy. Certainly the press coverage of William's visit to Konopischt and the frank exchange of views between the two senior figures suggested that the Austro-German alliance was strong and dependable.

Two final questions about Austro-German relations deserve attention: how did the Vienna policy-makers view their relationship with Berlin and how did those perceptions possibly shape their reaction to the events at Sarajevo? None of the evidence suggests that Vienna thought of itself as Germany's Ireland. The Habsburg statesmen envisioned themselves as a great power. The Habsburg monarchy was not a satellite or a client state. On some issues the Dual Monarchy pursued a dependent policy, on others an independent policy, and occasionally the two governments even clashed.

Yet the leaders in Vienna and Budapest also knew that Berlin worried about the future of the monarchy. The commentators in Germany talked about the possible collapse of Austria–Hungary after Franz Joseph's death. In this milieu the Habsburg desire to be assertive and independent did have an impact. Rather than believing that Austria–Hungary could lose German support, the Habsburgs feared the consequences of not taking advantage of Berlin's backing. In 1914 the perception that counted most was not how Berlin viewed Vienna or how Vienna perceived that Berlin viewed Vienna, but rather how Vienna conceived of itself as a great power. To uphold that status the policy-makers in the Dual Monarchy believed that they needed to demonstrate their strength to the Serbians — and to the Russians. A great power had to act like a great power, to show that it had the capacity to determine its own future.[30]

From this myriad of considerations Matscheko's final recommendations were unambiguous. The monarchy must pursue an aggressive diplomatic policy, backed by Germany, that forced Rumania to commit itself publicly to the alliance. If Bucharest refused, then Berlin and Vienna would turn to Bulgaria, seek an alliance with Turkey and move to isolate both Rumania and Serbia. Above all, the Austro-German alliance would thwart Russia's bold moves and preserve its position all the way to the Straits. The diplomatic policies of the Central Powers, when the war actually came, were already forecast by Matscheko's assessment. What he could not know was how soon his analysis would be translated into action.

IV

The Habsburg ability to demonstrate its power rested ultimately upon its military and naval strategies and the capacity to implement those plans. But the monarchy's military and naval performance were intimately connected with German strategic plans, while always hoping for assistance from Rome. Conrad's military plans dramatically revealed the inner connection between alliance planning and the individual war plans of a state. The Austro-Hungarian strategy reflected one of the longer-term structural impacts of alliances and ententes upon international relations. These arrangements confined, facilitated and often determined the military programmes of the member governments. With cooperation and assistance came confinement and dependence, as well as support for great power status. Given the Habsburg monarchy's exposed frontiers and its own awkward domestic political structure, the alliance relationship became ever more crucial.

In the months before Sarajevo the military staffs of the three allies continued to meet routinely and to refine their preparations for a possible military conflict. Among the topics were how to repatriate those nationals living abroad if a war came (Adolf Hitler would be a case in point) and who would care for families left behind if the nationals returned home to fight. At a different level, the staffs also wrestled with the possibility of Italian military help on the western front. General Pollio continued to express hopes for such assistance even as the Italian political environment suggested otherwise. The possible arrival of Italian troops to fight France did not fundamentally impact upon the Austro-German plans, but the prospect did keep alive the possibility of alliance cohesion. But the central issue for the Austrians was to delineate every aspect of Austro-German plans in the east. Air surveillance of Russian troop moves, the timing of a possible Austro-Hungarian thrust across the Vistula into Russian Poland and joint command arrangements all received attention.

Nor did Conrad neglect his relationship with General von Moltke. The two men continued to exchange letters, to offer assessments of the future (usually gloomy) and to reinforce each other's fears. Not surprisingly, Rumania's military defection got frequent mention from Conrad. Without Rumania, Vienna faced losing sixteen and a half Rumanian divisions against Russia. Furthermore, a Rumanian defection could mean a Rumanian attack in Transylvania. Even with German help, Austria–Hungary would encounter a potentially larger and better financed Russia. Only if Vienna acted quickly and decisively in any military crisis could the Russian advantages be minimized. The only way to give the Danubian monarchy a margin of security would be for Germany to devote more divisions to the eastern campaign. Conrad returned repeatedly to this point with Moltke, but the German general offered no concessions.[31]

The two men met for a final, sober session at Karlsbad on 12 May. Both considered Rumania lost, though Moltke had no high regard for Bulgaria as a replacement. He did, however, still nourish the hope for Italian assistance and significantly Conrad did not contest the idea. Instead, the feisty Austrian general concentrated on the dangers posed by the one hundred Russian divisions, against which he believed the forty Habsburg and the twelve German ones would be seriously at risk after the initial advantages conferred by faster mobilization. Still Moltke refused to promise more initial German help. He assured Conrad, however, that victory in the west would release enough troops to take care of the eastern front before Russia could win. Beyond this the chief of the German General Staff made no commitment. Conrad's persistent worries about the Balkans, even more than Russia, made Moltke's offer disappointing.[32]

Still, Conrad had since the initial staff talks of January 1909 achieved some coordination with German strategy, won agreement on liaison and reconnaissance functions and shared some intelligence data. Both generals, moreover, recognized their interdependence for the military success of either state. Austria would have to deter Russia long enough to allow the Germans to win in the west; the Germans would have to win quickly in the west to keep Austria–Hungary from being overrun by the Russians. In almost a prisoner's dilemma, the two sides were bound to each other. One important difference between them persisted. Conrad really preferred to attack Serbia — a step that did not help Germany, that could provoke Russia and that would leave Austria–Hungary sorely exposed if St Petersburg subsequently intervened once the Habsburgs were committed in the south. Yet the staff talks and the Moltke–Conrad discussions never adequately addressed this possibility. It was the crucial variation in joint planning and the most likely scenario from Vienna's point of view. Military leaders, always self-congratulatory about their realism, often shy away from an examination of the actual worst case. In July–August 1914 both Moltke and Conrad would pay heavily for this failure.[33]

The details of the Habsburg war plans on the eve of Sarajevo are well known. Both Plan R and Plan B called for defensive forces along the Russian and/or the Serbian frontiers. (See Map 4.) Their deployments would require thirty-six and a half divisions (twenty-eight and a half against Russia and eight against Serbia). To these would be added another twelve divisions that constituted a self-contained offensive force. The deployment of these latter divisions would convert either scheme into Plan R or Plan B. If added to the twenty-eight and a half divisions in the north, Plan R became operational with an Austro-Hungarian offensive scheduled for two directions: one northward toward Lublin, the other eastward and then north. Although Russia would have about thirty-five divisions mobilized after the twentieth day and sixty divisions after the thirtieth day, Conrad and Moltke believed these plans would work.

If Conrad deployed the twelve divisions in the south, Plan B went into effect. In this case, twenty Habsburg divisions would confront up to twelve Serbian first and second-line units. The Habsburg goal was to drive south and eastward and entrap the Serbian army in the area between Šabac and the Kolubara River valley. The plan would work well if Serbia moved into the Austro-Hungarian trap. If Serbia did not attack, then a war of attrition would begin, a war that left Austria–Hungary increasingly vulnerable to Russian intervention. Conrad never overcame the dilemma of attacking Serbia without the threat of Russian intervention. This dilemma would, of course, be the one that actually confronted him in July 1914.

During early 1914 Conrad had, however, moved closer to admitting that the monarchy's military forces would not be adequate for its strategic needs. The threat posed by Russia's accelerated mobilization schedule especially worried him. In fact, in March he even considered a major revision of Plan R, placing his initial deployments well back of the Russian frontier lest they be attacked too quickly. But Conrad's railway planners had argued that the current plans could not be changed so quickly and thus persuaded him to leave the original deployment intact. But when the July crisis came, Conrad in fact made this very change — in an ad hoc fashion. On the other hand, while Conrad worried anew about Russia, especially given the problem of Bucharest, he did not alter his two fundamental war plans: Plan R and Plan B. Nor did he ever consider

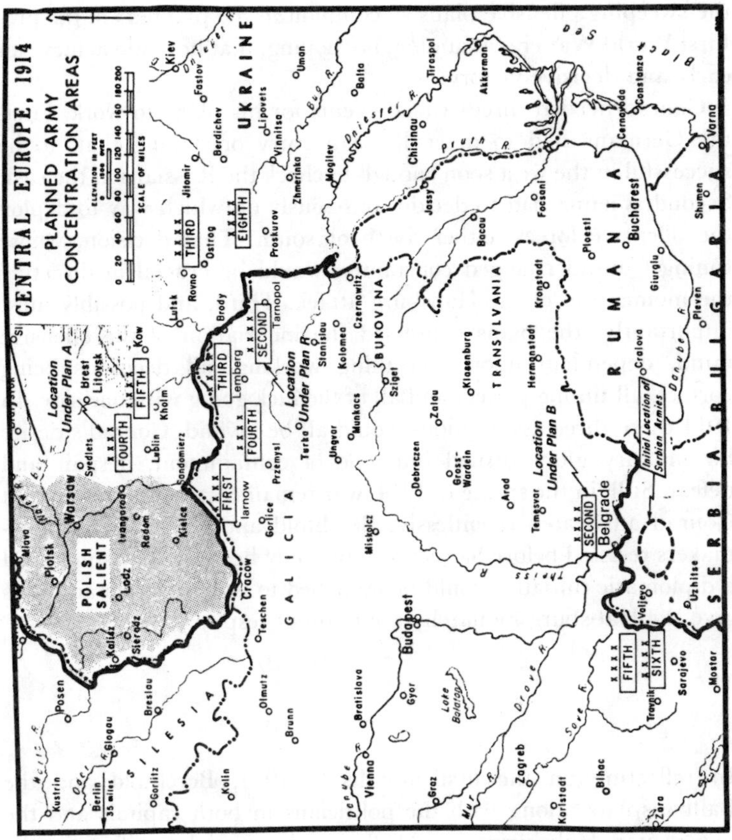

Map 4
Central Europe, 1914:
Planned Army
Concentration Areas

or plan to seize Belgrade as a hostage city. Rather, he stayed with the sweeping offensive plans so common to the planners of the pre-First World War era, assuming, no, hoping, that he could achieve an early and decisive victory.

Conrad needed three crucial events for his plans to work. First, the Germans had to deter Russian entry or, failing that, to be successful in the west soon enough to check the Russians in the east. Second, Vienna had to decide consciously on which way to deploy the offensive forces, either north or south. That decision, whose timing Conrad changed constantly, would be crucial in directing the momentum of the Habsburg attack. Third, and possibly most importantly, the plans expressed the inebriation of the offensive mind, dependent upon everything working, all decisions being correct, all timing perfect and all of the luck going with one side. In 1914 these three assumptions would all be invalid. Conrad's desire for military glory turned into one of containment, despair and defeat. Still, in the spring of 1914, war remained a policy option that Conrad advocated relentlessly. Berchtold and the civilian policy-makers resisted before Sarajevo — but only because they still hoped a diplomatic initiative could be launched to isolate Serbia and thus give the Habsburg monarchy a margin of respite.

V

In reflecting on the first months of 1914, Berchtold and the Ballhausplatz, along with the politicians in both capitals and the two senior Habsburgs, could find only partial comfort in the domestic political life of the monarchy. If there were serious, possibly fatal foreign policy problems that touched upon crucial aspects of the monarchy's domestic agenda, there were also fundamental domestic questions that appeared unsolvable. Two examples each from the Austrian and Hungarian halves of the monarchy illustrate this.

Throughout 1913, during the successive crises over the Balkans, the Czech and German parties in the Bohemian Diet had battled. All of their squabbles ultimately dealt with one central question: could a peaceful balance between Czechs and Germans be achieved? Stürgkh, the bureaucrat turned prime minister, laboured to keep the Diet functioning and to mediate the almost unbridgeable differences.

Threats of dissolving the Diet had had momentary positive effect, but quickly the acrimony and chaos started anew. Eventually, he suspended the Bohemian constitution in the summer of 1913. He had reverted to the older Habsburg policy of employing administrative law to rule.

The failure to resolve the Prague conflict was matched by failure in Vienna a few months later. Denied their Prague arena, the Czech-German politicians merely switched locales to the Austrian Reichsrat. In that setting Stürgkh soon found business almost impossible to conduct. Yet at the same time he desperately needed legislative approval for the new budgets and for the long-delayed Bosnian railway project. Ruthenian demands that aggravated the Polish Club were coupled with the Czech-German clashes, just to complicate matters further. A desperate Stürgkh sought to negotiate among four different nationality groups, to reach a compromise and to make the political process function. He had only marginal success. In January 1914 the Poles granted new political and cultural rights to the Ruthenians, and Stürgkh thus eased the turmoil in Galicia. In fact, his success helped to deflect the appeal of Russian propaganda aimed at discontented Ruthenians. In this instance, successful domestic politics eased an international agenda.

But Stürgkh was not so lucky with the Czech-German clashes. Repeated efforts to mediate got nowhere. Then, in December 1913 the Czech politicians resorted to a policy of legislative obstruction. The Reichsrat's effectiveness simply disappeared. The longer the obstruction persisted, the more the German parties became obdurant. Finally Stürgkh, thoroughly despairing of the situation, asked Emperor Franz Joseph to allow him to prorogue the Reichsrat and rule by Paragraph 14. On 16 March Franz Joseph agreed. From that date until 21 October 1916 no Austrian parliament met, no Austrian prime minister faced parliamentary critics, and all administrative action and taxation issues were authorized under the emergency provisions of Paragraph 14.

Contemporaries commented frequently about this cessation of parliamentary life, for it constituted a major setback for the political development of the monarchy. Domestic instability in Austria had waxed and waned since the 1890s. Now new domestic tension at a time of recurring international crisis and of waning self-confidence about the economy did not bode well for the future. While stumbling through might yet work as a policy process, even as a policy structure, the depth of nationality differences between the Czechs and Germans proved paralysing and debilitating. Furthermore, these internal conflicts weakened Austria's hand when dealing with Budapest.[34]

In the Magyar capital parliamentary life continued, in part because the Hungarian legal system did not have a clause similar to Paragraph 14. Tisza in any case did not need much help in dominating the Hungarian government since he still possessed a working majority in the parliament. Yet there were problems. His efforts, whether genuinely intended to ease the plight of the Rumanians in Transylvania or not, had exposed him to daily attacks from his parliamentary critics led by Count Apponyi. The critics wanted no concessions of any kind to Bucharest. Tisza parried these threats, yet could not achieve enough flexibility to make any concession palatable to the Rumanian National Party. He did manage to conduct budget discussions and to discuss administrative reform. But the Rumanian issue dogged him every week, right up to the first weeks of June. Few issues, as events ever since 1914 have reaffirmed, remain so volatile as the Magyar-Rumanian relationship over co-nationals living together in Transylvania.[35]

From Budapest's point of view, the future after King Franz Joseph was equally unpredictable. With the monarch's serious illness during the spring, so serious that Franz Ferdinand had a train kept ready at Konopischt in case he became the new monarch, the Magyar leadership had to consider how to handle Franz Ferdinand. In particular, as Berlin recognized, how would Tisza and the new monarch cooperate? Neither man showed much willingness to initiate a *modus vivendi*. Even during the William II–Franz Ferdinand meeting at Konopischt, the German ruler found the *Thronfolger* resistant to improving his relationship with Tisza. So long as Tisza and the archduke could not agree to cooperate, the monarchy's overall future looked unpromising, a fact publicists and editorial writers had no difficulty in discerning. A crisis over succession appeared an ever increasing probability.[36]

In the third political arena — the two provinces of Bosnia and Herzegovina — General Potiorek enjoyed a bit more success. After months of wrangling, the Common Ministerial Council moved to sanction the Bosnian railway projects. This construction would greatly facilitate economic development in the two provinces. While efforts at land reform remained sporadic, Potiorek could assert that the Landtag had functioned and that Muslims, Serbs and Croats enjoyed benefits conferred by Habsburg rule, which lessened the appeals for South Slav unity. Other observers had offsetting perceptions. Writer, political figure and sometime minister, J. M. Baernreither visited Sarajevo in the autumn of 1913 and left profoundly depressed. He especially disliked Potiorek's military style and the attitudes of the Serb politicians. Yet the Bosnian Landtag functioned in contrast to its counterparts in Prague and Vienna. At least there was a forum for open political debate. General Potiorek could hope his enlightened autocratic rule might yet prompt improved conditions. Or put another way, Potiorek wished that kindness and benefits might soften the appeal of the propaganda coming from Serbia.[37]

The Delegations deserve attention as the final political forum within the monarchy. Opened by Franz Ferdinand in May 1914 because of Franz Joseph's illness, the sessions in Budapest were subdued, cautious. The military budget for 1914–15 called for more expenditures and new capital outlays for a naval squadron. The increased expenses sparked comment, but no major clashes. Berchtold faced attacks, but managed to survive without undue harm. His own pronouncements spoke of the need for peace, of the desire for better relations with Serbia, of the preservation of the monarchy as a conservative force and of economic prosperity. Tisza, who had spared Berchtold from the Magyar attacks in the earlier Delegations, did not have to worry this time. No tempest developed; only a few questioned Tisza about his role in the Rumanian negotiations. Otherwise the Delegations, probably chastened by Franz Joseph's illness, met, talked, dined and departed. The monarchy's only quasi-imperial parliament reflected little of the uncertainty of the Ballhausplatz and of the senior decision-making elites.[38]

In mid-1914, when juxtaposed, the domestic and foreign policy problems of the Austro-Hungarian monarchy were cause for concern. Parliamentary government in Austria was paralysed, the Rumanians were defecting from the Triple Alliance, the Albanian government was in shambles, the Russians were more aggressive and the Serbians continued to agitate. Each of these considerations had shaped and influenced Matscheko's analysis. But his proposed response, though urgent and desperate, centred upon aggressive diplomacy, not upon aggressive military action. This diplomatic effort would be coordinated with Berlin and would require the support of all the Habsburg foreign policy-makers: Franz Joseph,

Franz Ferdinand, Tisza and senior officials at the Ballhausplatz. On the eve of Sarajevo, Vienna contemplated a new, more assertive diplomatic policy. After Sarajevo, Matscheko's analysis would become the basis for a military solution instead of militant diplomacy. Conrad's values would become those of the government; war, not peace, would be the result.

VI

In Belgrade during the months of May and June, Prime Minister Pašić and his senior associates continued to clash with the military party. As they did, information reached them of Bosnian youths being smuggled from Serbia back into Bosnia. Pašić and Protić sought an explanation from Apis, only to be 'stonewalled'. Apis and his colleagues were too powerful for Pašić to thwart; the conspiracy proceeded.

Without recounting the details of the assassination plot, a series of observations help put the terrorist plot into perspective. However assessed, Vienna and the officials in Sarajevo failed to take adequate security measures. While Pašić gave no formal warning to Vienna of possible trouble, enough hints of danger existed for precautions to have been in place. For that failure, Potiorek's overweening arrogance was the chief culprit. In charge of security and treating the entire visit as a military exercise, the general neglected a series of military axioms including the danger of surprise. Potiorek's misjudgements were compounded by his failure, even after the initial bomb attack on that Sunday, to curtail the visit and thereby avoid further risk. The hubris of command became the death sentence for Franz Ferdinand and Sophie.[39]

The assassins' link with Belgrade would be clearly established after their arrest, and by 2 July. What remained unclear but suspected would be the role of any ranking Serbian officials. Evidence of low-level ties was discovered almost immediately. The link to Apis, the head of Serbian military intelligence, would only emerge after the war began. In July 1914 Vienna kept hoping to find the ultimate, 'smoking gun' connection to Belgrade but could not do so. Still, the residual connection had quickly become apparent.[40]

In Belgrade in the late spring of 1914, three Bosnian students — Gavrilo Princip, Trifko Grabež and Nedeljko Čabrinović —

discussed the possible assassination of Franz Ferdinand. Assisted by Milan Ciganović, a low-ranking Serbian governmental employee, the group made contact with individuals who were or had been members of the Black Hand. Trained by the Black Hand in the use of weapons, the three youths would be carefully smuggled back into Bosnia in late May. There, three other active conspirators would be recruited — Mehmed Mehmedbašić, Vasa Čubrilović and Cvetko Popović — and all of them assisted by Danilo Ilić. Determined to assert the cause of Bosnian and Serbian nationalism and given tacit encouragement by Apis (who could also see advantages in his struggle with Pašić), the conspirators refused to be deterred despite later misgivings. On Sunday morning, 28 June, the conspirators took their posts.

As the archducal couple rode along Apel Quai, toward the centre of Sarajevo, Čabrinović stepped forward and tossed a bomb. Bouncing off the canvas of the touring car, the bomb exploded and injured, though not seriously, two of Franz Ferdinand's aides. The royal couple proceeded to the town hall. After an awkward reception and grim, prophetic comments by the archduke, the couple got back into the car to travel to the military hospital and check on the condition of the injured.

At this point the accidental occurred. Potiorek failed to inform the driver of the first car of the change in programme, going to the hospital instead of the planned trip through the narrow streets of Sarajevo. When Potiorek realized that the driver of his own car, in which Franz Ferdinand and Sophie were also riding, was turning into the side street as previously scheduled, the general ordered the driver to stop, back up and continue toward the hospital. In that moment of pause, Gavrilo Princip stepped forward and fired two shots. The Archduke Franz Ferdinand and Sophie, Duchess of Hohenburg, were dead within minutes. They were the first victims of what became the First World War.

10 Vienna and the July Crisis

At Bad Ischl on 28 July 1914, eighty-four year old Franz Joseph signed the declaration of war against Serbia. Seated at a small writing table, with a view of his favourite hunting terrain and far removed from the pressures of the capital cities, the monarch reluctantly agreed to replace diplomacy with military action. He did so, moreover, with the clear realization that any war might not remain localized. Russia might intervene and a local war thus become a European struggle. Nevertheless, Franz Joseph, like his senior advisers and generals, did not waiver. Each believed the Serbian problem could only be resolved by military action. To delay further would not only increase the danger but fritter away the strong German support that had been assured. The orders thus went out. Later that same day Austro-Hungarian artillery batteries at Semlin (Zemun) engaged in some sporadic shelling of nearby Belgrade. The Third Balkan War had begun; soon it would become the First World War.

Given the voluminous literature on the Habsburg decision in 1914, this chapter will be limited to the principal issues for Austria–Hungary. It will focus on the major steps that led to Franz Joseph's declaration of war, the immediate consequences of that decision and briefly sketch where those decisions fit into the larger context of the European plunge to war.[1]

I

Word of the Sarajevo assassination on 28 June had to reach a Habsburg leadership scattered across the monarchy. Quickly, the common and Austrian ministers and Franz Joseph returned to Vienna, with Prime Minister Tisza paying a visit to the capital two days later. Shock, dismay, bitterness, fear, revenge and anger left the senior figures more troubled possibly than the general populace,

whose initial reactions to the murders had been one of acknowledge-
ment but not of deep mourning or even a curtailment of regular
activities.[2]

Publicly Franz Joseph and the monarchy prepared to render
modest honours to the archduke and his wife. The ceremonies were
in fact so limited that Franz Joseph had to take the unusual step
of publicly defending the actions of his court chamberlain, Prince
Montenuovo, who admittedly was no friend of the couple. Yet
evidence suggests that Franz Joseph himself was deeply troubled by
the assassinations and expressed a personal sadness to Berchtold
when he saw the foreign minister on 30 June. The ageing monarch
did not have to like his nephew. But Franz Joseph could not fail to
appreciate the leadership experience which the *Thronfolger* had
gained or the dangers that his death suggested about future relations
with neighbouring Serbia. Franz Joseph hoped to discuss those
dangers with Kaiser William II when he came to Vienna for the
funeral services. But rumours of a possible Serb attack on the
German ruler led the German monarch to abandon his visit, forcing
the leadership in Vienna to utilize a special emissary to negotiate
with Berlin.[3]

While the public mourning continued, senior officials at the
Ballhausplatz, the War Ministry and the civilian ministries in
Vienna and Budapest urgently considered the Habsburg response to
the murders. Count Leopold Berchtold, the Austro-Hungarian
foreign minister, dominated this process. Unlike his earlier performances, which could be seen as vacillating and uncertain, Berchtold
on this occasion commanded and managed the process as he dealt
with Conrad on the one hand and Tisza on the other. Personally
deeply grieved by the murders, the foreign minister's initial reaction
was one of caution mixed with firm resolve. Berchtold wanted to
know more about the assassinations, to gauge his emperor's reaction
and to assess the international response. And, since he believed
William II would be coming to Vienna for the funeral, Berchtold
moved carefully in the first days after Sarajevo.[4]

Far less calculated were Austrian Prime Minister Stürgkh's and
Common Finance Minister Biliński's calls for immediate action
against Serbia. Both men wanted to deal directly with Serbia and
put an end to the South Slav menace. Their desire required no
German pressure. They had held the same conviction in the May
1913 crisis and now returned to it forcefully after the murders. Not

surprisingly, Biliński also wanted to erase the affront of having the murders occur in the two provinces under his control. In fact, Biliński engaged in private (and not so private) recriminations with General Potiorek over who had been responsible for the security failure in the Bosnian capital. Biliński did not, however, accept Potiorek's sweeping recommendations for political repression in Bosnia–Herzegovina; rather the common finance minister's perspective remained an imperial and not military one.[5]

Joining Stürgkh and Biliński in calls for immediate action were the two senior Habsburg generals, War Minister Krobatin and Chief of the General Staff, Conrad von Hötzendorf. Krobatin pressed repeatedly for action. His responsibility for the quality of Habsburg security forces — military and naval — forced him to deal less with strategic questions than with the need to restore credibility to the monarchy. Far more didactic and specific were Conrad's demands for action. When he met with Berchtold on Monday, 29 June, he called for an immediate attack on Serbia and frequently repeated this demand. As Berchtold later wrote, Conrad's views could be summarized as: 'Krieg, Krieg, Krieg'. But the foreign minister resisted the demand, pleading for more time to assess the situation.[6]

The next day, 30 June, Berchtold saw Franz Joseph for the first time since Sarajevo. He found Franz Joseph shaken, with moistened eyes and anxious to be reassured about the future of Habsburg rule. His personal gestures, including offering his hand and asking Berchtold to sit next to him, were unusual and revealing. The ruler doubted that Vienna could afford to appear weak towards Serbia. Franz Joseph observed Berchtold's determination to act, a determination that the ruler shared. But both men wanted to know more about the judicial investigation and to assess Tisza's views, while they awaited a report on Berlin's attitude. Nevertheless, when Berchtold left Schönbrunn, he believed Franz Joseph would support a policy of action against Serbia.[7]

István Tisza remained Berchtold's key protagonist in the decision process. The Magyar leader visited Franz Joseph and Berchtold on Tuesday, 30 June. Each found Tisza opposed to a military confrontation with Belgrade. Instead, Tisza argued for a policy of diplomatic encirclement of Serbia with the possibility of war retained as an option. Berchtold disagreed with Tisza's analysis and insisted there could be no further delay. When the two men parted, the political and bureaucratic message was unmistakable: Berchtold would have to overcome Tisza's position if he wanted a policy of action against Belgrade. That task, along with the question of what Berlin would do if Austria–Hungary decided to act, formed the major segment of the foreign minister's agenda for the next two weeks.[8]

Reports from the Bosnian capital, meanwhile, helped to galvanize the Habsburg policy process. By 2 July the police investigation had identified the seven major conspirators; all save Mehmedbašić were in custody. In the interrogations new, incriminating evidence linked the conspirators with Čiganović in Belgrade and with a Serbian Major Vojin Tankosić. More importantly, the major had apparently supervised target practice in a Belgrade park, with Princip an apt pupil. From Belgrade the Habsburg military attaché, Otto Gellinek, sent reports of rumours linking a Major Milan Pribićević with the *Narodna Odbrana*; he also confirmed the name of Tankosić as one of the military plotters. Further, Gellinek later sent information that appeared to implicate Dragutin Dimitrević (Apis), the head of Serbian military intelligence. Gellinek's assessment, which came close to the heart of the conspiracy, apparently never left the Habsburg War Ministry. Still, the evidence from Sarajevo, buttressed by information coming from Belgrade, correctly reinforced Vienna's initial assumptions that some elements of the Serbian government had been involved in the assassination plot. Not only did the information help solidify the emerging consensus for action against Belgrade, the intelligence provided details for treating the murders as an international issue, as a foreign policy problem and not just a domestic concern.[9]

Yet Potiorek also sought to utilize the domestic argument to compel action by Vienna. From early July until the delivery of the ultimatum to Belgrade on 23 July, the Governor-General badgered his civilian masters to take action. To justify his proposal he exaggerated the degree of unrest in the two provinces and declared that failure to act might make it impossible to govern the areas. Potiorek wanted to dissolve the Landtag, arrest the most outspoken Serbian deputies, close down Serbian associations and move promptly to defend Bosnia–Herzegovina by attacking Serbia.

In essence, Potiorek advocated a blatant variation of save the domestic situation by attacking a foreign enemy. The Sarajevo outrages fitted perfectly into this strategy, as did Potiorek's own distortion of the degree of unrest in Bosnia and Herzegovina. With this argument the general provided Conrad with a powerful tool to pressure the civilians for war; in the process, the argument also became one that Berchtold could use against Tisza. Protecting Bosnia–Herzegovina against Serbia was an argument that could not easily be brushed aside. Moreover, because of Potiorek's alarmist reports, Berchtold scheduled a Common Ministerial Council for 7 July to discuss what further steps should be taken to restore order and defend the provinces. Bosnia and Herzegovina became the pawns in a larger power struggle over the future of Habsburg policy towards Serbia.[10]

While the police continued their investigations in the Bosnian capital, Berchtold had his associates at the Ballhausplatz rework the Matscheko memorandum for use with the German leaders. When it became apparent that Kaiser William would not come to Vienna, the minister had a private letter from Franz Joseph to the German emperor also drafted. The changes in Matscheko's June memorandum placed more urgency upon action without, however, incorporating the word 'war' into the text. In the revision, Franco-Russian aggressiveness was emphasized and Rumanian fickleness given additional attention. The Austro-German alliance was, in the words of the document, in a life or death struggle with Russia and, by association, France.

Franz Joseph's personal letter stressed the Russian danger and blamed the assassination on Russian and Serbian Pan-Slavists. Declaring that the plot had been hatched in Belgrade, Franz Joseph in his letter wanted Bulgarian help and yet still hoped for Rumanian loyalty. The venerable monarch also avoided using the word 'war', though he clearly stated that the 'band of criminal agitators in Belgrade' could not go 'unpunished'. Taken together, the memorandum and the private letter could have left little doubt in Berlin that this time Vienna would act.[11]

The same message had already reached Berlin from Ambassador Tschirschky's reports of conversations with the Habsburg elite. In meetings with Berchtold on 30 June and again two days later, the Habsburg foreign minister talked of a *final and fundamental reckoning* with Belgrade. In the second encounter, which Tschirschky may not have reported to Berlin, Berchtold spoke of forceful actions and wondered if Germany would back such a step since it had been evasive in previous crises. But in those, Tschirschky had retorted, the Habsburgs had not presented a written proposal for action. The

German representative suggested if such a request did come, this time Berlin would respond favourably.[12]

The stage was now set for the famous Hoyos mission to Berlin. The funeral ceremonies for the archduke and Sophie took place on 3 July. Since William II had not come to Vienna, he now planned to leave Berlin on 6 July for his scheduled North Sea cruise — one of his annual fixtures. At this point and still without the 'smoking gun' evidence to link the Belgrade government with the murders, Berchtold decided to seek a formal declaration of German support. Mindful of Tschirschky's injunction about a written request, he polished the memorandum and asked the aged kaiser to sign the letter to his German counterpart.

Late on 4 July Berchtold telegraphed Ambassador Szögyény that Count Hoyos, his thirty-six year old *chef de cabinet* and personal friend of Chancellor Bethmann Hollweg's nephew, would arrive in Berlin the next day. The ambassador was to request an interview with the kaiser and the chancellor. The selection of Hoyos, advanced by the aggressive subordinate himself, would bring to Berlin one of the most articulate 'hawks' in Berchtold's intimate circle, so assertive that contemporaries would saddle him with much of the blame for Habsburg policy in the July crisis. By picking Hoyos, Berchtold did three things: assured himself that the Germans would hear of Vienna's determination to act; reduced Ambassador Szögyény's role; and forestalled a further intrusion by Tisza into the diplomatic process.[13]

Hoyos shared the Ballhausplatz documents with Szögyény upon his arrival in Berlin. They then met with part of the German leadership, the ambassador having lunch with the German kaiser and Hoyos with Arthur Zimmermann, the under-secretary of the German Foreign Office. Both conversations went well. While saying he would have to consult Bethmann Hollweg before giving a final decision, William II agreed to back Vienna in any action that it took. His only request was that the action be prompt. In giving his approval, the German ruler explicitly recognized the risk of Russian intrusion, yet accepted this possibility. He even agreed to a diplomatic overture to Bulgaria. The fifty-five year old monarch said he would deplore the situation if Vienna did not exploit 'the present moment which is so favourable to us'. Zimmermann echoed the same aggressive sentiments with Hoyos. But Zimmermann also said that Bethmann Hollweg would have to concur. Each man would preserve constitutional scruples even though the emperor's decided opinion would be difficult to overturn.[14]

Szögyény and Hoyos returned to the Habsburg embassy to cable the thrust of their discussion to Berchtold. William II and Zimmermann met with the German chancellor at 5:00 p.m. that same afternoon, along with Moritz von Lyncker, chief of the kaiser's military cabinet and Erich von Falkenhayn, Prussian minister of war. Quickly, the men covered the discussion with the Austrian envoys, considered the question of Russian intervention and accepted the risk of a general war. At the end of the meeting they agreed that Bethmann Hollweg and Zimmermann would meet Szögyény and Hoyos the next day, 6 July.[15]

That meeting ratified the commitments made by William II the previous day. Bethmann Hollweg, for reasons including a sense of isolation for Germany in the world arena and concern about Anglo-Russian attempts to encircle the Reich, agreed to support Berlin's longtime ally. The chancellor even offered the major concession, indicating that Berchtold would not have to alert Bucharest or Rome in advance about any pending action. In short, the German chancellor, like his royal master, endorsed prompt Habsburg action. Unlike the tenuous German support in the previous three Balkan crises, Vienna now had an unequivocal statement of support from Germany.[16]

The German 'blank cheque' gave Vienna the assurance it needed to opt for decisive action against Serbia. Berchtold hoped that early and decisive support would deter Russian intervention. A firm German declaration might keep the war local. If the action were not localized, the Austro-Hungarian flank with Russia would be protected. From Berlin's standpoint, it had agreed to Vienna's request. But the initiative had been Vienna's not Berlin's. The steps that pushed Europe toward war were taken in Vienna. The support given by Berlin simply confirmed and assured that the Habsburg decision to settle accounts would this time be a military solution rather than a diplomatic one.

Leaders in both countries had assessed Russia's recent role in European affairs. What they had seen did not please them. Thanks to French funds and British permissiveness, St Petersburg had engaged in an aggressive policy in the Balkans, had clashed with Germany over Constantinople and had begun secret naval talks with London. Nor could Vienna or Berlin ignore the probable fact that Russia had had some knowledge of the plot, or at least had helped to foster a climate that made such a terrorist act an acceptable state policy. The Russian threat played a far greater role, one could argue, in shaping the two allies' reactions to Sarajevo than the Anglo-German naval race or even the Austro-Serbian antagonism.[17]

Would Vienna have acted without Berlin's strong support? The answer is probably not. Yet one must remember that Vienna had been willing to act in October 1913 with only minimal notification to Berlin. This procedure might have been repeated in July 1914. Furthermore, given Conrad's fulminations, he could have staged a border incident that would have escalated. Or the Habsburg general could have proposed to seize Serbian territory in lieu of a major fight. What would have been difficult without Berlin's support and thus unlike October 1913 would have been the problem of convincing Tisza of the need for military action. With German assurances of support, Berchtold could address the question of Tisza far more effectively.

Germany, by its pledges, had surrendered the direction and the pace of the July crisis to Habsburg hands. In a monarchy where promptitude was not a trait and where a major political leader still opposed action, Berlin's anticipation of a quick Habsburg response was to be disappointed. The Germans gave a blank cheque on 5 July; Vienna took more than two weeks to deliver the ultimatum. The reasons for the delay constitute the next phase of the July crisis.

II

Strengthened by the robust declaration of German backing, Foreign Minister Berchtold now plotted to move against Serbia. Still, he had to convince Tisza. The foreign minister tried when the Common Ministerial Council met on 7 July, ostensibly to review measures to restore law and order in Bosnia–Herzegovina. In fact the ministers convened to assess the monarchy's overall strategic situation. When the meeting adjourned, there could be little doubt that if Tisza could be convinced, then Austria–Hungary would send an unacceptable ultimatum to Serbia and that war would almost certainly follow. For over four hours the ministers in Vienna carefully and deliberately examined each option. The decisions taken were not 'spasm ones', but carefully evaluated choices. Each option had been addressed and considered. But a single, overriding theme dominated: settle accounts with Serbia. Placed within that perceptual framework, peace did not have much of a chance in July 1914.[18]

Except for Tisza, the ministers who gathered had confronted war or peace decisions three times in the last twenty months. Prisoners of their own experience, each also knew where the other stood on the question of war. On this occasion Krobatin, Biliński, Tisza, Stürgkh and Berchtold were later joined by Conrad and Admiral Kailer in the afternoon session for a discussion of the military options. Hoyos served as a rapporteur. The discussion quickly revealed that all the ministers, except Tisza, wanted a diplomatic confrontation with Serbia that would risk war. Only Tisza held out for a purely diplomatic approach, although even he had to consider the military options and to comment upon them. The net result was a frank set of exchanges which posed hard questions. If Tisza's desire for a diplomatic option failed, so also did Krobatin's and Conrad's pleas for a surprise attack upon Serbia. The ministers felt that without diplomatic preparation, such a move would isolate the monarchy among the other European governments. Instead, a broad consensus emerged for a strongly worded ultimatum to Belgrade, one which the ministers believed would be rejected, to be followed by a localized war. When Tisza resisted this proposal, Berchtold argued that Vienna must exploit Germany's support — a point Tisza brushed aside. The Magyar leader was less successful in dismissing Stürgkh's contention, supported by Biliński, that Austria–Hungary had to act to protect the two provinces. The greater Serbian threat challenged the government internationally, as well as domestically. Anything short of force would be unacceptable. Still Tisza resisted; he even threatened to invoke his constitutional right to veto steps that were likely to lead to war. But Tisza was on the defensive with a phalanx of determined colleagues confronting him. When the morning session ended, all save Tisza had agreed upon a diplomatic confrontation which they fully expected would lead to war.[19]

In the afternoon, with Conrad and Kailer present, the ministers reviewed the military plans. Conrad, displaying more candour than any of his counterparts elsewhere in Europe during the July crisis, reviewed each of his war plans. While the general downplayed the Rumanian problem, he confronted the question of Russia directly: if St Petersburg intervened, the principal military sector would shift from the south to the north and east. He hoped that he would know what Russia would do by the fifth day of Habsburg mobilization. Russian intervention, Conrad frankly conceded, could force Austria–Hungary initially to concede some territory in Galicia. To Tisza's scepticism about a war, Conrad reiterated his familiar dirge: better now than later. In short, the general outlined Plan B and Plan R, sharing the strategic details while minimizing the overall risk. Once informed, the ministers were not deterred by what they heard. After they considered what measures to take in Bosnia–Herzegovina and when, the meeting adjourned. If Franz Joseph agreed to these actions and Tisza accepted that decision, the ministers believed that a diplomatic and military confrontation with Serbia was not far off. The session was a watershed; peace had little chance once the meeting ended.[20]

Because of the pivotal role of this session, four points must be remembered. First, German support was appreciated by those present, but none felt pressured by Berlin to act. Second, reasonably detailed and convincing evidence linked Belgrade with the conspiracy; even Tisza was swayed on this. Third, the Italians were virtually ignored in the discussion. This suggests both their place in Habsburg thinking and helps explain the later trouble that Austro-Hungarian policy-makers had in negotiating with their ally/neighbour/enemy. Finally, the probability of Russian intervention got attention, but there was no discussion of whether St Petersburg might be persuaded to stand aside. The risks of a wider war were clear, yet the casual response toward St Petersburg remains puzzling. This attitude reveals how determined most of the Habsburg ministers were to strike at Serbia regardless of the consequences.

When the meeting ended, Berchtold still had not convinced the Magyar leader of the need for action. For the next seven days, until 14 July, the foreign minister worked assiduously to achieve that task. At the same time his staff drafted an ultimatum, sought more evidence to link Belgrade with the murders and considered how to explain Habsburg actions to Europe.

Berlin had expected 'prompt' action and complained about Vienna's inactivity. The explanation for the delay rests in part with Tisza, but a second matter was more important. Conrad had earlier instituted a policy of harvest-leaves to appease the agrarian interests in the monarchy. The policy allowed military troops to return home temporarily to help harvest the crops. The soldiers would then return to their units for the annual summer manoeuvres. On 6 July

Conrad discovered that units at Agram (Zagreb), Graz, Pressburg (Bratislava), Cracow, Temesvár (Timişoara), Innsbruck and Budapest were on leave, and not scheduled to return until 25 July. Although he cancelled future leaves, the general decided not to revoke those already granted. To do so would hamper the harvest, threaten to overload the railway schedules and most important of all, alert Europe to Vienna's possible military intentions. Thus Conrad's organizational arrangements prevented a 'surprise' attack, once advocated by him and desired by Berlin. To complicate things further, the end of the harvest-leaves criss-crossed the long-scheduled state visit of French President Raymond Poincaré and Prime Minister René Viviani to St Petersburg. As a result, 22–23 July was the earliest date Vienna could consider for delivery of an ultimatum to Belgrade. Ironically, the Habsburg resolve to act decisively demanded delay, not expedition.[21]

Berchtold, meanwhile, continued his efforts to sway Tisza. But the Magyar leader remained impervious to all arguments. Even after he knew of Franz Joseph's desire to proceed, Tisza was reluctant. What finally convinced him was the argument advanced by Count Burián, his own envoy in Vienna and an experienced foreign policy adviser. Burián warned Tisza that failure to resolve the Serbian problem might exacerbate the Rumanian issue in Transylvania. The fact that the Germans were now prepared to intervene in Bucharest was one consideration. More important, failure to act against Serbia might encourage Rumanian agitation in Transylvania. Burián surmised that action now might forestall subsequent Rumanian demands for Hungarian territory. Or, as was so often the case, domestic considerations led to a foreign policy conclusion. By 14 July Tisza had agreed to accept a militant confrontation with Serbia. A day later he hinted in the Hungarian House of Deputies that the monarchy might take action. With Tisza in agreement and a date set for the delivery of the ultimatum, one problem remained — lulling Europe until the eight days had elapsed. This Berchtold proceeded to do with great skill.[22]

Vienna's policy of deception had several features. In both capital cities, the press was asked to curtail comments about Serbia. Abroad, the Ballhausplatz sought help with the foreign press in reporting news more favourable to the monarchy. General Krobatin and Conrad departed from Vienna, ostensibly on leave, with conspicuous fanfare. No military moves were undertaken and Habsburg officers on leave were left undisturbed. The Literary Bureau of the Foreign Ministry sought to assure journalists that all was well, in part to calm the Vienna stockmarket that showed signs of collapse. Save for intermittent contact with the embassy in St Petersburg, Vienna directed no questions toward Russia and even made some efforts to reassure — if not mislead — the Italians.

Somewhat surprisingly, Berchtold became extremely reluctant to share information about Habsburg intentions with Berlin. The caution stemmed in part from his fear that the more information that was exchanged, the greater the danger of a leak. But Jagow's decision on 11 July to inform German Ambassador Flotow in Rome of the general thrust of Habsburg intentions also shaped Berchtold's conduct. The German ambassador had mentioned Jagow's message to San Giuliano, the Italian foreign minister. The latter had then sent telegrams to the Italian embassies in St Petersburg, Vienna and Belgrade with this information. In Vienna the Austrian code experts, who had broken the Italian ciphers, discovered the Italian knowledge of Habsburg intentions and knew that this knowledge had also gone to two unfriendly capitals. Thereafter, Berchtold shared little information with Berlin until he sent the draft of the ultimatum to Germany on 22 July — just one day before its delivery.[23]

The discovery of the German indiscretions led to other operational consequences. The Russian code experts, among Europe's most sophisticated, had also almost certainly broken the Italian code. Berchtold had to assume this and subsequent Russian behaviour appeared to justify his assumption. He could also surmise that St Petersburg might have alerted Belgrade to Vienna's intentions. While neither the recently published Serbian documents nor the Russian documents give any indication of messages from St Petersburg, indirect evidence from the Serbian documents suggests that Belgrade learned of the Habsburg intentions.

In any event, the Serbians would not misread this intelligence, for by 7 July Minister Jovanović was warning Belgrade that strong Habsburg action might be forthcoming. Further, he had detected the Ballhausplatz's conscious manipulation of the monarchy's press and feared what that meant. From this information and probably intelligence from Russia and possibly Rome, Pašić resolved on 18 July to alert all Serbian missions (except Vienna) that Belgrade would resist any Habsburg demand that infringed upon its sovereignty. Thus even before the crisis reached its critical stage, Pašić had adopted a tough, unyielding line. The German indiscretion to the Italians was probably responsible for this stance. Thus, Berchtold had reason to fear the worst from Berlin's carelessness and he limited the information reaching his closest ally.[24]

Berchtold could also blame himself. The delay in the delivery of the ultimatum inevitably opened officials to indiscretions. Berchtold, for instance, had described the monarchy's intentions to Heinrich Lützow, the former Habsburg ambassador to Rome. The ex-official subsequently hinted at this to the British ambassador who in turn told his French colleague. By 20 July, speculation was widespread within and outside the monarchy that Vienna intended to send a stiff note to Belgrade.[25]

The Habsburg leadership nevertheless continued to move stealthily. The Common Ministerial Council reassembled on 19 July at Berchtold's private residence and all the members came in unmarked vehicles. The usual group, joined by Conrad and Kailer, had an additional member on this occasion: Count Burián. The agenda was straightforward: to agree upon the terms of the ultimatum and to review what would happen if Serbia did not accept it. The ultimatum, as drafted, linked the Belgrade government with the assassinations, demanded a joint committee to investigate the murder, wanted an army order published that condemned the Serbian military involvement with the murders and required strict pledges of future good behaviour from Serbia. No Serbian government would likely accept this set of demands. Thus the meeting focused upon what would follow after Serbia had rejected the terms. Again Conrad surveyed the military situation and assured Tisza that enough troops were available to protect Transylvania should Rumania decide to attack. As before, the discussion concentrated on Serbia and Plan B rather than Plan R. Yet the ministers did not probe further.[26]

One issue remained unresolved: would there be any territorial adjustments if the monarchy defeated Serbia? Tisza had demanded as his price for agreeing to act that the monarchy pledge to take no territory. The Magyar leader wanted no more Slavs in the monarchy. His fellow ministers accepted this restraint; there would only be strategic border rectifications. Otherwise, no territory would be annexed from Serbia. Although Conrad was pleased that war was in sight, after the meeting he expressed consternation at the territorial self-limitation. But he also noted sardonically to Krobatin: 'We will see. Before the Balkan Wars, the powers also talked of the status quo; after the war no one concerned himself with it.'[27]

Now that the ministers had accepted the terms of the ultimatum, Berchtold travelled to Bad Ischl on 21 July to give Franz Joseph a final briefing. The emperor/king assented to the ultimatum. With his ministers resolutely united for this course of action, the emperor accepted their judgement that the monarchy had to defend itself against the threat of a greater Serbia. Belgrade's failure to abide by its earlier pledges, coupled with evidence that some groups in the Serbian capital had been involved in the plot, provided a powerful impetus to act. That the war would be won or even remain localized was far from certain. Nor were the leaders even clear what a war would achieve beyond punishing Serbia. Still, the Habsburg leadership pressed ahead, even an ageing emperor who, Berchtold later wrote, was fully aware of the 'tragedy of that contemporary moment'. The ultimatum would be delivered in Belgrade late in the afternoon of 23 July; the Serbian government would have forty-eight hours in which to respond.[28]

While Berchtold completed the final preparations for the ultimatum, discordant information reached him from St Petersburg. This news should possibly have prompted some reconsideration of Habsburg policy. At a reception for visiting French President Poincaré, the Habsburg Ambassador Friedrich Szápáry had had a lengthy discussion with the president. At one point, Poincaré emphatically rejected the argument that a government could be responsible for acts plotted on its territory. He warned, ominously, that Serbia 'had friends'. These words, which Szápáry interpreted as threatening, reached Vienna by cable later that same evening. This new information did not deter Berchtold. Rather, it almost certainly confirmed his assumptions about German indiscretions and Russian knowledge of Habsburg intentions. Since the Russian ambassador in Vienna had gone on leave, lulled by Berchtold, the intercepts could have been the trigger for Poincaré's warning. Further, the French admonition suggested that French and Russian statesmen were discussing in detail how the two governments would respond to any Habsburg *démarche* at Belgrade. The unity of the Franco-Russian governments during the crisis, including Russia's acceleration of the crisis, buttress this belief. Nevertheless the warning from St Petersburg had come and would be ignored. The ultimatum was delivered as scheduled.[29]

San Giuliano also cautioned Berchtold on 21 July. While the Italian foreign minister said he would support Austria–Hungary if trouble came with Serbia, no territorial changes, including any idea of the Habsburgs gaining the Lovčen heights in Montenegro, could be considered. Nor did Italy want to see Serbia reduced territorially. On this point Rome would give Belgrade diplomatic support. Thus, Vienna had qualified Italian backing. Italian ambivalence did not, of course, slow the momentum toward confrontation.[30]

Wladimir Giesl, the Austro-Hungarian minister in Belgrade, delivered the ultimatum at 6:00 p.m. on 23 July to the Serbian foreign ministry. Received by a senior official rather than Pašić, who was away campaigning for re-election, the ultimatum had a forty-eight-hour deadline. In that interval Pašić and his colleagues drafted a masterful response that amazed even the leadership in Vienna. Serbia's reply was conciliatory, open, almost apologetic, but unyielding on the fundamental question of a joint investigation of the conspiracy. As Pašić had indicated to the Serbian missions abroad on 18 July, Belgrade would not allow its sovereignty to be infringed. Thus, when Giesl received the Serbian response late on the afternoon of 25 July, he glanced at it, termed it unacceptable, broke diplomatic relations and travelled from Belgrade to nearby Habsburg territory at Semlin.[31]

Even as the countries moved from peace toward war, Tisza still had hopes for a diplomatic solution. Writing to his daughter in tones that revealed both his religious faith and his tender love for her, he said:

> These days, as you know, I must visit Vienna quite often. We must react seriously to the insolence of the Serbs; we cannot simply swallow it. The business may come to an end without war; and I pray to God that it will; but I cannot give you full assurance that we shall not end up in a war. You know, my little angel, with what loving and understanding sympathy we would surround you in that case. Let us trust in God that such a trial will be avoided; but if it is His will to visit it upon us, we shall have to trust in His help with double faith.

But as Tisza's colleague Burián said of the delivery of the ultimatum: 'The wheel of history rolls.' Now the hand of diplomacy would give way to the wheel of war.[32]

III

With the break of diplomatic relations on 25 July, Franz Joseph ordered the partial mobilization of Habsburg troops to start three days later on 28 July. The order meant that two-fifths of the monarchy's forces would be called to duty, with defensive forces placed along the Serbian-Montenegrin frontier and the reserve forces — the units that constituted the offensive attack — held in place until a further decision. Conrad had already indicated that the decision on the offensive direction had to come within five days of mobilization. Franz Joseph had, at this point, ordered no measures of any kind along the Russian frontier. The Habsburgs made every effort to keep the war localized and to deny Russia any pretext for intervention. To allow the maximum flexibility to Habsburg planners, Conrad even wanted to delay a declaration of war until the partial mobilization was completed.

But other developments were confounding Conrad's plans for the Serbian war. Dismayed at the hiatus between mobilization and the actual start of fighting, the diplomats feared that international efforts to force Austria–Hungary to negotiate would intensify. Thus Berchtold and Hoyos pressed for a declaration of war against Serbia. Conrad reluctantly accepted the idea on 27 July. Franz Joseph assented a day later. Still, aside from some limited firing on the night of 28–29 July, no significant fighting between Austria and Serbia would come for nearly two weeks.[33]

Confusing but unsettling information about Russian military activity also helped pressure Vienna into a declaration of war. Reports reached Vienna and Berlin indicating that St Petersburg had ordered extensive mobilization measures in four military districts: Kiev, Warsaw, Odessa and Moscow. These so-called 'preparatory to war' steps meant that the Austro-Hungarian monarchy faced the real prospect of Russian military intervention. In fact, the Russians on 25 July had initiated the practical equivalent of a partial mobilization even before the Serbian response was known. In taking this action the Russians honoured their pledge to Serbia. St Petersburg also hoped to dissuade Vienna from taking military action against the neighbouring kingdom. To add to confusion, however, Russian diplomats vehemently denied that any Russian military preparations were under way. Although intelligence sources discounted these assurances, Berlin in particular wanted to avoid premature action that could make Germany appear the aggressor. Amid this welter of conflicting intelligence, the senior Habsburg leadership met again on 27 July. Conrad did not ignore the intelligence data; rather, he asked that Berchtold seek German help in coercing the Russians to take no further steps. The general was still determined to act against Serbia; he continued to hope that Germany would deter Russian involvement.[34]

During the next three days the chances for a localized war diminished. Each report from the east indicated further Russian preparations. Each report from the south indicated the Serbs were mobilizing effectively. More alarming, diplomatic efforts to contain the crisis intensified as London worked to forestall a further widening of the war. Conrad was forced to wonder if Berlin would relent in its commitment to Austria–Hungary. Berchtold faced strong pressure to reconsider Habsburg policy. But he resisted any alternative course, including the idea of a 'halt in Belgrade' that Berlin seemed to favour. When the Common Ministerial Council met on 31 July, following news of the Russian mobilization, the ministers reaffirmed their intention to fight Serbia. They consciously risked war with Russia; the ministers insisted on military action against Serbia.[35]

At this point, Conrad, the veteran of many crises and the prime agitator for a military solution, committed a major strategic error. From the start of the crisis he had informed the civilians that he had to know by 1 August what Russia would do. With this knowledge he could then direct the offensive forces in the direction of Russia and thus set in motion Plan R. Otherwise he would move to implement Plan B. Yet, in effect, he allowed the troops from the offensive force to begin moving southward on 30 July, despite evidence of possible Russian intervention and two days ahead of his own schedule. Not until word reached Vienna on 31 July of the czar's order for general mobilization did Conrad begin to contemplate a change in the direction of the troops. Then his railway authorities urged him to let the troops continue southward rather than split the units. The soldiers could better go south, then upon arrival re-embark and move northward. Conrad did not immediately communicate this abrupt shift in plans to General Potiorek. Conrad's confusing deployment complicated both the fighting against Serbia and the later fighting against Russia.[36]

Conrad subsequently gave many excuses for his actions: the Russian situation had been unclear; he believed Berlin would deter

St Petersburg; Moltke had failed to place enough troops in the east and to put them on the offensive, in keeping with his earlier promises. Conrad even hinted that his own staff had let him down. A more straightforward explanation may be the correct one: Conrad wanted war and it would come sooner in the south than in the north. To commit the troops against Serbia ensured fighting; it would also entrap the Germans into fulfilling their part of the alliance commitment. The Russian sector was dangerous, but he expected the German help there — plus Plan R — to be adequate. His first task was to thwart the diplomats. An early military clash in the south would subvert a diplomatic solution. The first clashes were indeed in the south, but the occurred only days before the initiation of the struggle in Galicia. In any case, Conrad got his war. But he had exhausted his troops and confused the Austrian high command in the process.

Conrad continued to freelance with his prepared plans. Following Russian and German mobilizations, the Habsburg monarchy initiated full mobilization on 4 August. This in turn set in motion Plan R and directed the swing troops north after they had completed their unnecessary train ride south. Conrad had already committed one error. Now he proceeded to alter the deployments long associated with Plan R. Instead of putting the troops immediately along the Galician border, he stationed them back from the border, so that they then had to march forward to their originally planned deployment areas. Again, the troops suffered and command problems were exacerbated. The dapper general proved that he could shrewdly manoeuvre the country into war. Whether he could effectively fight a war was already coming into question.

There is a further observation about Russia's intervention. Since 1912 Vienna had confronted Russian activism in the Balkans. During the course of the First Balkan War, for nearly six months their forces had faced each other. St Petersburg's obvious patronage of Pašić and the South Slavs was evident everywhere. Matscheko's analysis in June for Berchtold had repeatedly stressed the threat posed by France and Russia. The papers Conrad prepared for Berchtold in early July stressed the Russian danger. Further, in the Common Ministerial Council on 7 July, the issue had been addressed. At each point Habsburg leaders explored Russian intentions and the probability of Russian interference in a Balkan conflict. Conrad's own analysis in early July had been sober, pessimistic; even in subsequent discussions he took that pose.[37]

But paralleling this realism ran another, almost fantasy approach. Conrad hoped that Berlin's unequivocal support would forestall Russian intervention. Perhaps Russia would not violate the principle of monarchical solidarity. Perhaps the Willy–Nicky relationship between Queen Victoria's descendants would be effective. For whatever reason, Conrad paid less and less attention to the Russian problem in the later stages of the July crisis. At the same time he urged the militarized civilians to reject every opportunity to negotiate a way out of the crisis or accept a German cover for a retreat. Despite the evidence reaching him, Conrad kept his attention riveted on Serbia and Plan B. Possibly surprised by the extent of Russia's military preparations and the activism of St Petersburg, the general reacted in an almost classical fashion by ignoring the information that contradicted what he wanted most — war with Serbia.

The Russian problem also concerned the German high command as well. Berlin had also assumed Russia would stand aside, that the czar would permit Serbia's chastisement and back away as he had in earlier crises. But the successes of an assertive Balkan policy (dating from the spring of 1912) gave St Petersburg no incentives to relent now. When St Petersburg surprised Berlin by its July actions, the German diplomats and the German military found their own safety margins for decision-making severely reduced.

Russian actions during the July crisis contributed to the escalation of the affair; indeed, converted a local war into wider conflagration. However gauged, St Petersburg's actions had the effect of reducing the chances for peace in Europe. Those same measures also put Vienna into the dreaded prospect of a two-front war. Throughout, the Habsburg preparations rested upon hopes and illusions rather than realistic chances for success. The illusions of the short war and the power of the offensive, so thoroughly a part of pre-1914 European military doctrine, had far less relevance for campaigns in eastern Europe. Conrad warmly embraced both fallacies. Finally, his views had seduced the monarchy's civilian leadership as well. The war to save the monarchy destroyed it.[38]

IV

As the monarchy moved to war with Serbia, Berchtold and his associates sought to buttress Vienna's diplomatic position.

Surprisingly, their efforts had a fair degree of success. Berlin's sudden willingness to pressure Rumania to abide by its secret agreement with the Triple Alliance helped, as did the loan to Bulgaria. Almost immediately, after the 5–6 July conferences in the German capital, Bethmann Hollweg had sought to convince King Carol that Austria–Hungary faced a major challenge from Serbia. Having avoided tough talk earlier with the Rumanian leader, the German diplomats now abruptly told Carol that Berlin backed a Triple Alliance overture to Rumania's rival: Bulgaria. Faced with this sober news and with the prospect of diplomatic isolation, Carol promised to be more conciliatory toward Vienna. More importantly, he pledged that Bucharest would not join with Serbia in any move against Austria–Hungary. Then, in mid-July, the Ballhausplatz briefed Ottokar Czernin, who had been consistently excluded to this point, on the forthcoming ultimatum. Ordered to inform King Carol on the afternoon of 23 July about Habsburg plans, Czernin was to state unequivocally that Vienna had no territorial ambitions. In this fashion the Ballhausplatz, helped along by Berlin, hoped to rescue the errant Rumanian ally. Some hefty pressure from Berlin transformed the would-be defector of June into a neutral.[39]

Vienna had similar success with Sofia. The German loan culminated months of prolonged negotiation. The funds also signalled Berlin's willingness to seek a fresh approach to the Balkans. Berchtold, meanwhile, sought to build King Ferdinand's confidence. He ordered Minister Tarnowski to approach Sofia about the Triple Alliance. Berchtold wanted the Bulgarian leaders to be assured that their interests in territorial adjustments would be considered. Yet Berchtold refrained from encouraging a Bulgarian attack on Serbia that would threaten the Rumanians and worry the Germans. Instead, he preferred a friendly, neutral Sofia. He managed to get his wish as the July crisis unfolded.[40]

Vienna's efforts to win Italian assistance were less satisfactory. From the start of the July crisis Berchtold had sought to curtail Rome's involvement. He won German agreement for this with the Hoyos mission. Then, as we have seen, the Habsburg foreign minister discovered — through the code intercepts — that Flotow had informed San Giuliano of Vienna's belligerent intentions. As the delivery date for the ultimatum neared, the question of how to handle a questionable ally resurfaced. In fact, on 15 July, German Secretary of State Jagow even bruited with Ambassador Tschirschky the idea of Vienna surrendering Valona to Rome, possibly even Trentino, or simply letting the Italians become deeply embroiled in Albania. Berlin did not, however, actually make these proposals to Berchtold who would have been mortified. In any event, German hints to Berchtold that some territorial concession would be necessary to keep the Italians loyal got nowhere. Berchtold told Tschirschky on 20 July that the Austro-Hungarian pledge not to annex territory in the Balkans should be sufficient to assuage Italy. The most the Habsburg foreign minister would promise was to notify San Giuliano ahead of time about the ultimatum.

Berchtold's perspective toward Rome shifted somewhat after 31 July, when the localized war was clearly becoming a European affair. He then received instructions from the Common Ministerial Council to offer Valona to Italy, if Rome met its obligations as an ally and if the Habsburgs actually occupied Serbia. Beyond this concession Vienna would not go. If Italy remained neutral, as it in fact did, Berchtold could feel that he had achieved — for the moment — the minimum goal of his diplomacy.[41]

Finally, Berchtold sought to induce King Nikita of Montenegro to remain neutral. Disavowing territorial ambitions and offering money, always needed by the Montenegrin monarch, Vienna sought to drive a wedge between Belgrade and Cetinje. Eventually Nikita refused all of the blandishments and joined the war. Berchtold's efforts to limit his losses in the south were thus only partly successful.[42]

By Sunday, 2 August 1914, while the British government debated whether to intervene and German troops prepared to seize Luxembourg and move into Belgium, Habsburg statesmen could not be comfortable with the European strategic situation. Their earlier confident hopes of a local war with Serbia had dissolved. Russia had intervened, prompting German mobilization and a wider war. Plan R, not Plan B, became the Habsburg plan of attack. Serbia, the real enemy, was replaced by its ally/protector as the enemy. In this transposition the two great eastern powers, fencing in the shadows at least since the 1850s for control over the Balkans, now confronted each other directly. The long-deferred struggle between Russia and Austria–Hungary for mastery of eastern Europe had begun. In the initial line-up, the odds still looked at least no worse than Conrad and the Habsburg ministers had expected: Italy, Bulgaria and Rumania were neutral, Montenegro aligned with Serbia. If Conrad had stumbled badly in allowing Plan B to proceed, then abruptly ordering Plan R, the ramifications of those decisions were not yet apparent.

Multinational and anachronistic, the Danubian monarchy had resolved to confront and defeat modern nationalism by blunting the destructive appeals of the South Slavs. But alliance obligations forced Austria–Hungary to defeat Russia first. Victory over this great power ensured success over the smaller power; the reverse was not true. Consequently, Plan R had to be a prelude to Plan B. Conrad had his long-desired war. Franz Joseph entered the war he had endeavoured so long to avoid. Berchtold encountered the war he had so skilfully postponed until Franz Ferdinand's murder. And Tisza was cajoled into the war he feared but later zealously embraced. Contradictory to its dissolution, the Habsburg monarchy went to war not for territory or glory but to save itself. How war would achieve that goal the policy-makers never really examined. War was merely assumed to address the problem. Peace gave way to the grim, hard logic of war.

V

As peace faded and the sombre decisions of war emerged, the issue of war aims also surfaced. The monarchy had pledged no territorial annexations, though Conrad thought this would be unlikely in reality. Nonetheless, in the first weeks of war — before defeat replaced victory — Habsburg statesmen allowed their imaginations to think of precise territorial goals. For a few weeks acquisitions supplanted survival as the motif. Vienna's ambitions show that Berlin was not alone in its rapacity nor that the Habsburg elite was so wedded to the notion of no territorial benefits. By 12 August, for example, the Ballhausplatz had advanced plans to join Russian Poland to the monarchy. When Prime Minister Tisza learned of this, he naturally protested and effectively vetoed the scheme. Still, this proposal indicates some of the changing Habsburg assumptions. Initially Vienna did not address what might happen to the Ukraine in a victorious struggle. But later, as the autumn progressed, bureaucrats would think in more comprehensive terms and of a significant expansion of Habsburg and German influence in eastern Europe.[43]

In the south the policy-makers had to be more circumspect, since territorial goals might drive Italy and Rumania from their neutrality. Initial confidence about a quick victory over Serbia prompted plans for the economic integration of the region. For instance, a 10 August memorandum speculated on whether Serbia should become a part of a customs union with the monarchy or be left as an independent trading partner under Habsburg sway. For his part, Conrad always thought in terms of territorial gains at Serbian expense, arguing that some Serbian territory be partitioned among Albania, Bulgaria and even Rumania. Yet beyond these generalized expectations, Conrad did not press these matters in early August — that would have created new trouble with Tisza. In any event, Vienna expected the war to foster better relations with Rumania and Bulgaria. Not surprisingly, each Habsburg scenario depicted Austria–Hungary as the dominant political force in the Balkans, supplanting Russia and excluding Germany. In this way, the monarchy would have reinvigorated itself and acquired a new historic mission. Such success would guarantee the future of the Danubian state.

The defeats of autumn and winter replaced the dreams of summer. Habsburg war aims quickly became more modest. Already in early 1915, the return to the status quo in the south appeared acceptable, even to Conrad. Others talked of bringing the war to a close. Desperation emerged as the Italians now threatened to intervene against Austria–Hungary unless the monarchy surrendered Trentino. What had begun as a war to preserve the monarchy now required a surrender of precious territory merely to keep an ostensible ally from becoming an enemy. By the spring of 1915, survival with dignity had become Vienna's central war aim. Later that year hopes would rise again, along with military successes, but survival — not victory — was never thereafter distant from Habsburg thinking.[44]

VI

In July 1914 Austria–Hungary declared war on Serbia to avenge the Sarajevo murders and to put an end to the perceived greater Serbian threat. This decision by a seasoned set of policy-makers had unusually complete and united backing. Convinced that diplomatic and military intimidation had not worked earlier, the statesmen, including Franz Joseph, concluded that only militant diplomacy remained an option. Three times since 1912, Vienna had come to the brink of war; this time, assured of strong German support, the Habsburg leadership took the plunge.[45]

In that decision a series of factors, fatefully and almost inevitably, converged to propel the decision for war. Among them the threat of Pan-Slavic nationalism cannot be underestimated. Harassed by Serbia and the Balkan League since early 1912, Vienna had watched Belgrade defy its neighbour, spurn Habsburg offers and exploit Russian support. The conspiracy's link with the Serbian military, if not conclusively implicating the senior rank of the Serbian government, nonetheless could not be turned aside. Habsburg failure to act to crush Serbian nationalism would presumably only inflame the situation in Bosnia–Herzegovina. Convinced that continued Serbian agitation would undermine the domestic peace in the two provinces, the leaders exploited foreign policy to resolve a domestic political problem. In doing so, Tisza and the others hoped to stem the problem of Rumanian nationalism in Transylvania. Failure to act against Serbia would, they now believed, also increase the assertiveness of Bucharest. Nationalism constituted a powerful motive force in their decisions in the summer of 1914.

The sense of losing the military advantage, the worry that the Austro-German military position was in fact deteriorating *vis-à-vis* the Triple Entente, also contributed to despair in 1914. Moltke and Conrad believed that the Triple Entente was becoming relatively stronger. While the feisty Habsburg general continued to lament the monarchy's earlier failures to act, his refrain of better now than later fed the general perceptions of July 1914. Hoping that German support would deter Russia, the time to reduce the Serbian capacity for later mischief had arrived. Conrad assumed that he and the Austrian generals controlled the initiative. In this instance, the Habsburg military's lethargic movements and inadequate railway system made the pace so deliberate that Germany despaired. In 1914 the Habsburg military pressed for war and controlled the momentum. Yet Conrad erred repeatedly in his estimates and in his deployments. Although the military calculated carefully, the leaders were simply wrong.

Alliance politics were also influential in the choice of Habsburg options. Italy and Rumania remained neutral; Berchtold could hardly have expected more, especially given the way he neglected their leadership in the crisis. Germany proved more compliant now than at any time in the previous two years. William II and his subordinates had their own reasons for supporting prompt action by Vienna. Russian assertiveness alarmed them, as did signs that the Triple Entente was growing stronger and more coherent. Chancellor Bethmann Hollweg evaluated the benefits of backing his Danubian ally and resolved to act. Germany, dependent upon the Habsburgs to make the Schlieffen Plan work, hoped its unambiguous stance would keep Russia on the sidelines. Austria–Hungary, dependent upon the Germans for protection against Russia, hoped the deterrence theory would be effective. This fateful interdependence, stemming from geography, attitudes and military planning over three decades, now linked the fortunes of the two countries together. In plunging into war, the Danubian government also ensured — if the war was enlarged — that its conduct would be dominated by Berlin. No one in Vienna thoroughly appreciated that prospect. But the continuation of the war ultimately reduced Vienna's independence and caused its demise.

The July decisions also involved personal fortunes. Franz Ferdinand's death had altered the policy process. Not only did his absence give Conrad a new lease in office, but Franz Joseph and Berchtold were deprived of a consistent advocate for peace. Without the *Thronfolger*, Franz Joseph had to face his advisers and generals alone. Perfectly willing to fight if necessary, the emperor nonetheless confronted the policy process as an old man who did not want to be the last Habsburg. The foreign minister struggled to shape the monarchy's future in July. His decisiveness, even if prompted in part by his subordinates, amazed those who watched him. Berchtold dominated the process, out-manoeuvred Tisza and kept the direction of Habsburg activity firmly in his hands until war became a reality. In this process he found support from Biliński and Stürgkh, who wanted revenge, and from Conrad and Krobatin, who advanced the military option. At the top of this small decision-making hierarchy, Berchtold kept his position secure. For some he became the villain of 1914. For others he was another statesman seeking to rescue the fortunes of a monarchy that, by its own definition, was anachronistic in the early twentieth century.

No aspect of the monarchy's foreign relations so complicated its fortunes as did the nearly constant interplay between external and domestic factors. Whether the terms of the *Ausgleich*, the problems of compensation to Italy, the Transylvanian issue or the future of

Bosnia–Herzegovina were in question, the monarchy's international agenda always had an internal component. But the administrative structure of the Dual Monarchy, its multinational population and the artificial, even accidental, boundaries were integral components of the Danubian regime. The Germans and Magyars might control the chief levers of political power, but other nationality groups determined much of the domestic and foreign agendas. In a maelstrom in which external and internal factors are forever jumbled, power calculations of ends and means are difficult. Indeed, issues are seldom resolved, because the context remains in flux. In this ambiguous setting, Austria–Hungary had acquired Bosnia–Herzegovina and then attempted to govern the two colonial provinces. As the Habsburg share of the Ottoman legacy, the two provinces guaranteed clashes with Serbia and Montenegro, trouble with the Croats and other South Slavs and, invariably, conflict with the Russians who also wanted to dominate the Balkans. The assassinations at Sarajevo galvanized the Habsburg monarchy to defend its control of the provinces. The leadership in Vienna and Budapest finally believed that this required war with Serbia. That war did not remain local, becoming almost instantly a general war.

Having declared war, the Habsburg monarchy had to fight that war and survive. It did so for four years despite appalling military leadership and the efforts of its enemies to dismantle Austria–Hungary. Far more than Berchtold had realized in 1914, the Austro-Hungarian government had staying power. Paradoxically, the monarchy lost its existence in proving that point. Yet policy-makers in Vienna in July 1914 believed that any measure short of war would lead to a loss of credibility and of control over the monarchy's future.

In Vienna in July 1914 a set of leaders experienced in statecraft, power and crisis management consciously risked a general war to fight a local war. Battered during the Balkan Wars by Serbian expansion, Russian activism and now by the loss of Franz Ferdinand, the Habsburg leaders desperately desired to shape their future, rather than let events destroy them. The fear of domestic disintegration made war an acceptable policy option. The Habsburg decision, backed by the Germans, gave the July crisis a momentum that rendered peace an early casualty. Ironically, the most assertive phase of Berchtold's diplomacy was also its most dangerous. In July 1914, desperation, blind faith, hope, ambition and exhaustion overcame prudence, experience and caution. The Habsburg monarchy opted for a Draconian, military solution. The results were equally Draconian and militarily devastating. War brought not victory or a solution to the Slav problem, but rather defeat and dissolution. From those results momentous consequences still flow.

Abbreviations

Austria, Protokolle	Austria, *Stenographische Sitzungs-Protokolle der Delegation des Reichsrathes: Neunundvierzigste Session: Budapest 1914*
Berchtold Diary	'Memoiren des Grafen Leopold Berchtold'
Conrad	Franz Conrad von Hötzendorf, *Aus meiner Dienstzeit*
Documents Serbie	*Documents sur la politique exterieure du Royaume de Serbie, 1903–1914 [Documenti o spoljnoj politici Kraljevine Srbije, 1903–1914]*
GP	*Die grosse Politik der europäischen Kabinette, 1871–1914*
HHStA	Haus-, Hof- und Staatsarchiv, Vienna
JMH	*Journal of Modern History*
KA	Kriegsarchiv, Vienna
KD	*Outbreak of the World War: German Documents Collected by Karl Kautsky (Kautsky Documents)*
KM Präs	Kriegsminsterium Präsidial Series
MKFF	Militärkanzlei des Generalinspektors der gesamten bewaffneten Macht (Franz Ferdinand), Kriegsarchiv, Vienna
MKSM	Militärkanzlei Seiner Majestät des Kaisers (Franz Joseph), Kriegsarchiv, Vienna
MÖS	*Mitteilungen des Österreichischen Staatsarchivs*
NFF	Nachlass Franz Ferdinand, Haus-, Hof- und Staatsarchiv, Vienna
PA	Politisches Archiv, Haus-, Hof- und Staatsarchiv, Vienna
ÖUA	*Österreich-Ungarns Aussenpolitik von der Bosnischen Krise 1908 bis zum Kriegsausbruch 1914*
VA	Verwaltungsarchiv, Vienna

Notes and References

1. AUSTRIA–HUNGARY AND THE INTERNATIONAL SYSTEM: GREAT POWER OR DOOMED ANACHRONISM?

1. The quotes are from Joachim Remak, 'The Healthy Invalid: How Doomed the Habsburg Monarchy?', *Journal of Modern History* [hereafter *JMH*], XLI (June 1969) 131–2. On the history of the monarchy, these works remain standard: A. J. May, *The Hapsburg Monarchy, 1867–1914* (Cambridge, Mass., 1951); A. J. P. Taylor, *The Habsburg Monarchy, 1809–1918* (London, 1948); C. A. Macartney, *The Habsburg Empire, 1790–1918* (London, 1968); Robert A. Kann, *A History of the Habsburg Empire, 1526–1918* (Berkeley, Calif., 1974); József Galántai, *Die Österreichisch-Ungarische Monarchie und der Weltkrieg* (Budapest, 1979); and two recent surveys, John W. Mason, *The Dissolution of the Austro-Hungarian Empire, 1867–1918* (New York, 1985) and Alan Sked, *The Decline and Fall of the Habsburg Empire, 1815–1918* (London, 1989). For a contemporary account, now much neglected, see Heinrich Kanner, *Kaiserliche Katastrophenpolitik* (Leipzig, 1922); and for a dashing account, Winston S. Churchill, *The Unknown War: The Eastern Front* (New York, 1932).

2. For an overall survey of the monarchy's foreign policy, see F. R. Bridge, *From Sadowa to Sarajevo: The Foreign Policy of Austria–Hungary, 1866–1914* (London, 1972); also Luigi Albertini, *The Origins of the War of 1914*, trans. and ed. Isabella Massey, 3 vols (London, 1952–7), I, pp. 1–64. A scathing indictment is Anton Mayr-Harting, *Der Untergang: Österreich–Ungarn, 1848–1922* (Vienna, 1988).

3. On the intellectual atmosphere of the monarchy during these years, see William M. Johnston, *The Austrian Mind: An Intellectual and Social History, 1848–1938* (Berkeley, Calif., 1972) pp. 45–75; John Lukacs, *Budapest 1900: A Historical Portrait of a City and its Culture* (New York, 1988); Peter Gay, *Freud: A Life for Our Time* (New York, 1988); Edward Timms, *Karl Kraus: Apocalyptic Satirist: Culture and Catastrophe in Habsburg Vienna* (New Haven, Conn., 1986). Also see the very important article by R. J. W. Evans, 'The Habsburg Monarchy and the Coming of the War', in *The Coming of the First World War*, eds R. J. W. Evans and Hartmut Pogge von Strandmann (Oxford, 1988) pp. 33–55.

4. The following assessment draws heavily upon *Schicksalsjahre Österreichs, 1908–1919: Das politische Tagebuch Josef Redlichs*, ed. Fritz Fellner, 2 vols (Graz, 1953–4); Joseph M. Baernreither, *Fragments of a Political Diary*, ed. Josef Redlich (London, 1930); Franz Conrad von Hötzendorf, *Aus meiner Dienstzeit, 1906–1918*, 5 vols (Vienna, 1921–5) [hereafter, Conrad].

5. S. R. Williamson, 'The Origins of World War I', *Journal of Interdisciplinary History*, XVIII (Spring 1988) 795–818.

6. Leslie C. Tihany, 'The Austro-Hungarian Compromise, 1867–1918: A Half Century of Diagnosis; Fifty Years of Post-Mortem', *Central European History*, II (1969) 114–38.

7. Frederic Morton, *Thunder at Twilight: Vienna 1913/1914* (New York, 1989) p. 19; Morton's volume is entertaining but not reliable. Also see Andrew G. Whiteside, *The Socialism of Fools: Georg Ritter von Schönerer and Austrian Pan-Germanism* (Berkeley, Calif., 1975); John W. Boyer, *Political Radicalism in Late Imperial Vienna: Origins of the Christian Social Movement, 1848–1897* (Chicago, 1981).

8. Baernreither worried about the South Slav question in detail; also see the letters of R. W. Seton-Watson to political figures inside the monarchy, *R. W. Seton-Watson and the Yugoslavs: Correspondence, 1906–1941*, ed. Hugh Seton-Watson et al., 2 vols (London, 1976).

9. Josef Redlich, *Austrian War Government* (New Haven, Conn., 1929) stresses this point. Also see Carl E. Schorske, *Fin-de-Siècle Vienna: Politics and Culture* (New York, 1980); David S. Luft, *Robert Musil and the Crisis of European Culture, 1880–1942* (Berkeley, Calif., 1980); Solomon Wank, 'The Austrian Peace Movement and the Habsburg Ruling Elite, 1906–1914', in *Peace Movements and Political Cultures*, eds Charles Chatfield and Peter van den Dungen (Knoxville, Tenn., 1988) pp. 40–63.

10. Andrew Rossos, *Russia and the Balkans: Inter-Balkan Rivalries and Russian Foreign Policy, 1908–1914* (Buffalo, NY, 1981).

11. On society and the military, see Joseph Roth's powerful novel, *The Radetzky March*, trans. Eva Tucker (Woodstock, NY, 1983).

12. On the impact of domestic pressures on foreign policy, see Oscar Jászi, *The Dissolution of the Habsburg Monarchy* (Chicago, 1929) and Arno J. Mayer, *The Persistence of the Old Regime: Europe to the Great War* (New York, 1981).

2. THE DOMESTIC CONTEXT OF HABSBURG FOREIGN POLICY

1. On the struggle between Austria and Prussia for the domination of Germany, see Heinrich Lutz, *Zwischen Habsburg und Preussen: Deutschland, 1815–1866* (Berlin, 1985) and *Österreich–Ungarn und die Gründung des Deutschen Reiches: Europäische Entscheidungen, 1867–1871* (Frankfurt, 1979); and the essays in Heinrich Lutz and Helmut Rumpler (eds), *Österreich und die deutsche Frage im 19. und 20. Jahrhundert: Probleme der politisch-staatlichen und soziokulturellen Differenzierung im deutschen Mitteleuropa* (Munich, 1982).

2. Anton Vantuch and L'udovit Holotik (eds), *Der österreichisch-ungarische Ausgleich 1867* (Bratislava, 1971); Peter Berger (ed.), *Der österreichisch-ungarische Ausgleich von 1867: Vorgeschichte und Wirkungen* (Vienna, 1967); and Tihany, 'The Austro-Hungarian Compromise', analyse these arrangements. But two older works are also valuable; Louis Eisenmann, *Le Compromis austro-hongrois de 1867: Étude sur le dualisme* (Paris,

1904); Edmund Bernatzik, *Die österreichischen Verfassungsgesetze mit Erläuterungen*, 2nd ed. (Vienna, 1911).

3. A brief summary of the arrangements is found in Kann, *History*, pp. 331–42: also Adam Wandruszka and Peter Urbanitsch (eds), *Die Habsburgermonarchie, 1848–1918*, vol. II: *Verwaltung und Rechtswesen* (Vienna, 1975); Redlich, *War Government*; Péter Hanák, *Ungarn in der Donaumonarchie* (Vienna, 1984).

4. Henry Wickham Steed, *The Times* of London correspondent in Vienna from 1902 to 1913, gave a harsh assessment at the time in *The Hapsburg Monarchy*, 2nd ed. (London, 1914).

5. There is no comprehensive study of Austrian domestic politics for the last years before the war; but see William A. Jenks, *The Austrian Electoral Reform of 1907* (New York, 1950), and the sarcastic assessment in Mayr-Harting, *Der Untergang*, pp. 616–95. Alexander Fussek has written frequently about Stürgkh; e.g., 'Graf Stürgkh und Graf Tisza', *Österreich in Geschichte und Literatur*, VIII (1964) 427–31.

6. Miklós Komjáthy has written extensively about the Common Ministerial Council; see his introduction to *Protokolle des Gemeinsamen Ministerrates der Österreichisch–Ungarischen Monarchie, 1914–1918* (Budapest, 1966) pp. 1–137. Publication of the minutes of the Council is now underway. A few of the more important sets of minutes for the years after 1908 may be found in Ludwig Bittner and Hans Übersberger (eds), *Österreich-Ungarns Aussenpolitik von der Bosnischen Krise 1908 bis zum Kriegsausbruch 1914*, 9 vols (Vienna, 1930) [hereafter *ÖUA*]. The original minutes are in the Politisches Archiv, Haus-, Hof- und Staatsarchiv, Vienna, XL/278–315 [hereafter PA].

7. The minutes of the Austrian Cabinet were almost completely destroyed in the Justice Palace fire in Vienna in 1927; scattered fragments may be found, including an index, in the Verwaltungsarchiv, Vienna, [hereafter VA].

8. For a lively, perceptive analysis of the Hungarians and foreign policy; see István Diószegi, *Hungarians in the Ballhausplatz: Studies on the Austro-Hungarian Common Foreign Policy*, trans. Kornél Balás and Mary Boros (Budapest, 1983). Also see Gabor Vermes, *István Tisza: The Liberal Vision and Conservative Statecraft of a Magyar Nationalist* (New York, 1985).

9. German translations of the Hungarian Cabinet minutes may be found in 'Ungarische Ministerrats-Protokolle', Haus-, Hof- und Staatsarchiv, Vienna [hereafter HHStA].

10. On Burián's role, see part of his diary edited by István Diószegi, 'Aussenminister Stephan Graf Burián: Biographie und Tagebuchstelle', *Annales Universitatis Scientiarum Budapestinensis de Kolando Eötvös Nominate: Sectio Historica*, VIII (Budapest, 1966) pp. 161–208; also Galántai, *Monarchie*, pp. 154–6.

11. Eisenmann thought the Delegations the most original of the constitutional arrangements legitimized by the *Ausgleich*; see *Le Compromis*, pp. 602–8.

12. Minutes of the Delegations and copies of documents submitted to them are found in the stenographic records prepared by each government.

See, for example, Austria, *Stenographische Sitzungs-Protokolle der Delegation des Reichsrathes: Neunundvierzigste Session: Budapest 1914* [hereafter Austria, *Protokolle*] (Vienna, 1914).

13. The foreign minister and his staff at the Ballhausplatz prepared the material for the Delegations and ensured that the Common Ministerial Council had agreed to the budget proposals before the Delegations actually convened.

14. No comparative assessment of parliamentary control of foreign policy in the years before 1914 exists. Critics of the 'Old Diplomacy' talked much about the absence of such control but their expectations were excessive, as later practice has shown. For a helpful study on the problem in France, see Thomas H. Conner, 'Parliament and the Making of Foreign Policy: France under the Third Republic, 1875–1914', diss. (Chapel Hill, N. Carol., 1983).

15. No adequate biography of Franz Joseph exists, but the following offer insights: Josef Redlich, *Emperor Francis Joseph of Austria: A Biography* (New York, 1929); Egon Corti and Hans Sokol, *Der alte Kaiser: Franz Joseph I. vom Berliner Congress bis zu seinem Tod* (Graz, 1955); Alexander Novotny, 'Der Monarch und seine Ratgeber', in Wandruszka and Urbanitsch (eds), *Verwaltung und Rechtswesen*, pp. 57–99; Franz Herre, *Kaiser Franz Joseph von Österreich. Sein Leben, seine Zeit* (Cologne, 1978). The recent work by Heinrich Drimmel, *Franz Joseph: Biographie einer Epoche* (Vienna, 1983), adds little that is new. But the study by Jean-Paul Bled, *François-Joseph* (Paris, 1987) is helpful.

16. For an introduction to the Habsburg military, see Gunther Rothenberg, *The Army of Francis Joseph* (West Lafayette, Ind., 1976); Johann C. Allmayer-Beck, 'Das Heerwesen', in Friedrich Engel–Janosi and Helmut Rumpler (eds), *Probleme der Franzisko-Josephinischen Zeit, 1848–1916* (Vienna, 1967) pp. 67–78; Edmund Glaise von Horstenau, *Franz Josephs Weggefährte: Das Leben des Generalstabschefs Grafen Beck* (Vienna, 1930); Redlich, *Francis Joseph*, pp. 20–1, 45, 33–72, 318–33. The most comprehensive study of the Habsburg army is found in the recently published Adam Wandruszka and Peter Urbanitsch (eds), *Die Habsburgermonarchie, 1848–1918*, vol. V: *Die Bewaffnete Macht* (Vienna, 1987).

17. On the work of the Civil Chancellory, see Fritz Reinöhl, *Geschichte der k.u.k. Kabinettskanzlei, Mitteilungen des Österreichischen Staatsarchivs*, Ergänzungsband VII, (Vienna, 1963); on the Military Chancellory, the unpublished mss by Maj. Gen. Egon von Pauppert, 'Aus der Militärkanzlei des Kaisers und Königs Franz Joseph: vom Kriegsbeginn 1914 bis zum Tode des Monarchen 1916', (Vienna, 1950), in the Kriegsarchiv [hereafter KA], Vienna. The files of both chancellories are voluminous. On monarchical work habits in Germany and Russia see Isabel V. Hull, *The Entourage of Kaiser Wilhelm II, 1888–1918* (Cambridge, 1982); Lamar Cecil, *Wilhelm II: Prince and Emperor, 1859–1900* (Chapel Hill, N. Carol., 1989); D. C. B. Lieven, *Russia and the Origins of the First World War* (New York, 1983); Harrison E. Salisbury, *Black Night, White Snow: Russia's Revolutions, 1905–1917* (New York, 1978).

18. The quote is from Maurice Muret, *L'archiduc François-Ferdinand* (Paris, 1932) p. 172. The literature on Franz Ferdinand is copious and

helpful. A chatty, recent study that matches the sources well, despite its grasping title, is Gordon Brook-Shepherd, *Archduke of Sarajevo: The Romance and Tragedy of Franz Ferdinand of Austria* (Boston, 1984); also see Gerd Holler, *Franz Ferdinand von Österreich-Este* (Vienna, 1982); Lavender Cassels, *The Archduke and the Assassin: Sarajevo, June 28th 1914* (New York, 1984); Rudolf Kiszling, *Erzherzog Franz Ferdinand* (Graz, 1953); Leopold von Chlumecky, *Erzherzog Franz Ferdinands Wirken und Wollen* (Berlin, 1929); Robert A. Kann, *Erzherzog Franz Ferdinand Studien* (Vienna, 1976). Karl Renner told the Austrian Reichsrat on March 16, 1910: 'We no longer have a monarchy, a single authority; we have a dyarchy, a state of competition between Schönbrunn and Belvedere....', quoted in Vladimir Dedijer, *The Road to Sarajevo*, (New York, 1966) p. 116. On this see S. R. Williamson, 'Influence, Power, and the Policy Process: The Case of Franz Ferdinand, 1906–1914', *The Historical Journal*, XVII (1974) 417–34.

19. On the nationality issue, see Robert A. Kann, *The Multinational Empire: Nationalism and National Reform in the Habsburg Monarchy, 1848–1918*, 2 vols (New York, 1950); Adam Wandruszka and Peter Urbanitsch (eds), *Die Habsburgermonarchie, 1848–1918*, vol. III (2 pts): *Die Völker des Reiches* (Vienna, 1980); Solomon Wank, 'Foreign Policy and the Nationality Problem in Austria–Hungary, 1867–1914', *Austrian History Yearbook*, III (1967) 37–56; Leo Valiani, *The End of Austria–Hungary* (New York, 1973) pp. 1–47; and Steed, *The Hapsburg Monarchy*, pp. 282–96.

20. The figures come from 'Tabelle 1: Die Bevölkerung der Kronländer Cisleithaniens nach der Nationalität und nach der Umgangssprach 1851–1910 (absolut und in Prozenten)', in Adam Wandruszka and Peter Urbanitsch (eds), *Die Habsburgermonarchie, 1848–1918*, vol. III, (2 pts): *Die Völker des Reiches*, (Vienna, 1980) pt 1, pp. 33–153.

21. An excellent recent study that probes this issue is Whiteside, *The Socialism of Fools*.

22. Kann, *The Multinational Empire*, I, pp. 222–32.

23. For example, see Jászi, *Dissolution*, pp. 403–11.

24. Jászi, *Dissolution*, pp. 274–345; Lászlo Katus, 'Die Magyaren', in *Die Völker des Reiches*, pp. 410–88; Julius Miskolczy, *Ungarn in der Habsburger Monarchie* (Vienna, 1959).

25. On the Russian activity in both Hungary and Austria, see Z. A. B. Zeman, *The Break-Up of the Habsburg Empire, 1914–1918* (London, 1961).

26. Keith Hitchins, 'The Nationality Problem in Hungary: István Tisza and the Rumanian National Party, 1906–1914', *JMH*, LIII (Dec. 1981) 619–51; F. Pölöskei, 'István Tisza's Policy toward the Romanian Nationalities on the Eve of World War I', *Acta Historica: Academiae Scientiarum Hungaricae*, XVIII (1972) 267–90; Gheorghe Nicolae Căzan and Şerban Rădulescu-Zoner, *Români si Tripla Alianţă, 1878–1914* (Bucharest, 1979) pp. 355–403; Galántai, *Monarchie*, pp. 183–94.

27. For a polemical view, yet not always amiss, see R. W. Seton-Watson's contemporary indictment, *Racial Problems in Hungary* (London, 1908); Barbara Jelavich, *History of the Balkans*, 2 vols (Cambridge, 1983), II, pp. 63–76; Jászi, *Dissolution*, pp. 366–75. Also Péter Hanák (ed.), *Die Nationale Frage in der Österreichisch-Ungarischen Monarchie, 1900–1918*

(Budapest, 1966); Valiani, *The End of Austria–Hungary*, chap. 1; Wolf Dietrich Behschnitt, *Nationalismus bei Serben und Kroaten, 1830–1914* (Munich, 1980).

28. On this see John W. Boyer, 'The End of the Old Regime: Visions of Political Reform in Late Imperial Austria', *JMH*, LVIII (March 1986) 159–93: Solomon Wank, 'Pessimism in the Austrian Establishment at the Turn of the Century', in *The Mirror of History: Essays in Honor of Fritz Fellner*, ed. Solomon Wank et al. (Santa Barbara, Calif., 1988) pp. 295–314; Hanák, *Ungarn in der Donaumonarchie*; Jászi, *Dissolution*.

29. On Franz Ferdinand's views, see Kann, *Franz Ferdinand*; Redlich, *War Government*, pp. 65–76.

30. On the Russian activity, see Zeman, *The Break-Up of the Habsburg Empire*.

31. Jelavich, *Balkans*, II, pp. 59–63; Theodor von Sosnosky, *Die Balkanpolitik Österreich-Ungarns seit 1866*, 2 vols (Vienna, 1913–14); Peter F. Sugar, *Industrialization of Bosnia–Herzegovina, 1878–1918* (Seattle, Wash., 1963); Robert J. Donia, *Islam under the Double Eagle: The Muslims of Bosnia and Hercegovina, 1878–1914* (New York, 1981).

32. For the Serbian perspective, see Dedijer, *Sarajevo*; Behschnitt, *Nationalismus bei Serben und Kroaten*.

33. Brook-Shepherd, *Archduke of Sarajevo*, pp. 125–51.

34. The most recent works include Alois Brusatti (ed.), *Die Wirtschaftliche Entwicklung*, vol. I of *Die Habsburgermonarchie, 1848–1918* (Vienna, 1973); David F. Good, *The Economic Rise of the Habsburg Empire, 1750–1914* (Berkeley, Calif., 1984); Eduard März, *Austrian Banking and Financial Policy: Creditanstalt at a Turning Point, 1913–1923*, trans. Charles Kessler (New York, 1984); Richard L. Rudolph, *Banking and Industrialization in Austria–Hungary: The Role of Banks in the Industrialization of the Czech Crownlands, 1873–1914* (Cambridge, 1976); Bernard Michel, *Banques & Banquiers en Autriche au début du 20e Siècle* (Paris, 1976); John Komlos, *The Habsburg Monarchy as a Customs Union: Economic Development in Austria–Hungary in the Nineteenth Century* (Princeton, New Jersey, 1983); I. T. Berend and György Ránki, *Hungary: A Century of Economic Development* (New York, 1974).

35. On state finances, see Akos Paulinyi, 'Die sogenannte gemeinsame Wirtschaftspolitik Österreich-Ungarns', in Brusatti (ed.), *Die Wirtschaftliche Entwicklung*, pp. 567–604; I. T. Berend and György Ránki, 'Ungarns wirtschaftliche Entwicklung 1849–1918', in ibid., pp. 520–7; März, *Austrian Banking* , pp. 26–35.

36. In 1910 the imbalance was 304.3 million crowns: in 1911, 601.1 million; in 1912, 584.6 million.

37. See Bridge's perceptive comments, *From Sadowa*, pp. 22–9. There is no detailed study of the press or public opinion as such for this period in Habsburg history. But see Peter Schuster's analysis of an astute foreign observer: *Henry Wickham Steed und Die Habsburgermonarchie* (Vienna, 1970).

38. For instance, the Hungarian ministers made clear their perception of what the 'public' would tolerate about taxes when discussing the 1912 and

1913 military budgets; minutes of the Common Ministerial Council, 10 July 1912, PA XL/310. Reports from the respective Ministries of Interior also offered assessments of public opinion and especially of nationality agitation.

39. Franz Ferdinand appreciated the value of a press claque better than many of his contemporaries. Among those who helped him were Leopold von Chlumecky and Friedrich Funder, editor of the *Reichspost*; see Funder's memoirs, *Vom Gestern ins Heute* (Vienna, 1952).

3. DYNASTY, GENERALS, DIPLOMATS: THE INSTRUMENTS OF HABSBURG FOREIGN POLICY

1. Stanley Hoffmann's *The State of War: Essays in the Theory and Practice of International Relations* (New York, 1965) remains a vivid portrait of the lawlessness of the international system; of course, Niccolò Machiavelli and Thomas Hobbes described its brutality earlier.

2. For an excellent summation as it applied to the Habsburgs, Steed, *The Hapsburg Monarchy*, chap. 4; also Reinhard Bendix, *Kings or People: Power and the Mandate to Rule* (Berkeley, Calif., 1978).

3. For a critical view of these common elements, see Jászi, *Dissolution*; compare his assessment with May, *The Hapsburg Monarchy*.

4. Bridge, *From Sadowa*, describes the main events of Franz Joseph's foreign policy.

5. Hugo Hantsch's biography of Berchtold, drawing upon the foreign minister's diary, provides insights into the foreign minister's relationship with his sovereign: *Leopold Graf Berchtold: Grandseigneur und Staatsmann*, 2 vols (Graz, 1963).

6. Conrad's memoirs record the topics of his discussions, often heated, with Franz Joseph; see Conrad, III, pp. 622–8.

7. A brief survey of the Habsburg navy is found in Paul Halpern, *The Mediterranean Naval Situation, 1908–1914* (Cambridge, Mass., 1971) pp. 150–86.

8. Kann's essays in *Franz Ferdinand* describe the archduke's involvement in foreign policy.

9. On the London visit, see Brook-Shepherd, *Archduke of Sarajevo*, pp. 205–10; also F. R. Bridge, *Great Britain and Austria–Hungary, 1906–1914: A Diplomatic History* (London, 1972) pp. 204–12.

10. Franz Ferdinand's espousal of the monarchy's military and naval forces led many, inside and out of the monarchy, to view him as a belligerent militarist. Nowhere was this perception more widespread than in St Petersburg, with harsh results.

11. On Franz Ferdinand's relations with Berchtold, see Kann, *Franz Ferdinand*, pp. 206–40; Hugo Hantsch, 'Erzherzog Thronfolger Franz Ferdinand und Graf Leopold Berchtold', in *Historica* (Vienna, 1965), pp. 175–98; Williamson, 'The Case of Franz Ferdinand', pp. 427–34.

12. For thoughtful comments about the Franz Joseph–Franz Ferdinand relationship, see Rudolf Sieghart, *Die letzten Jahrzehnte einer Grossmacht: Menschen, Völker, Probleme des Habsburger-Reiches* (Berlin, 1932).

13. For an introduction to the Foreign Ministry, see Helmut Rumpler, 'The Foreign Ministry of Austria and Austria–Hungary, 1848 to 1918', in Zara Steiner (ed.), *The Times' Survey of Foreign Ministries of the World* (London, 1982) pp. 49–59.

14. Ibid., p. 54; also Ludwig Bittner, 'Das österreichisch-ungarische Ministerium des Aussen. Seine Geschichte und Organisation', *Berliner Monatshefte*, XV (2) (1937) 819–43; Erwin Matsch, *Geschichte des Auswärtigen Dienstes von Österreich–Ungarn, 1720–1920* (Vienna, 1980).

15. The information on titles is taken from the official rank list published by the Foreign Ministry, *Jahrbuch des k.u.k. auswärtigen Dienstes: 1913* (Vienna, 1914); cf. Nikolaus von Preradovich, *Die Führungsschichten in Österreich und Preussen, 1804–1918* (Wiesbaden, 1955). For samples of typical careers, see Graf Heinrich von Lützow, *Im diplomatischen Dienst der k.u.k. Monarchie*, ed. Peter Hohenbalken (Vienna, 1971) and Erwin Matsch (ed.), *November 1918 auf dem Ballhausplatz: Erinnergungen Ludwigs Freiherrn von Flotow des letzten Chefs des Österreichischen-Ungarischen Auswärtigen Dienstes* (Vienna, 1982).

16. On the issue of Hungarian influence, see Diószegi, *Hungarians*; James A. Treichel, 'Magyars at the Ballplatz: A Study of the Hungarians in the Austro-Hungarian Diplomatic Service, 1906–1914', diss. (Georgetown, Wash. D.C., 1971).

17. On the administrative arrangements see Robert Stropp, 'Die Akten des k.u.k. Ministeriums des Aussern 1848–1918', *Mitteilungen des Österreichischen Staatsarchivs*, XX (1970) 389–506.

18. For a survey of Aehrenthal's and Berchtold's policies, see Bridge, *From Sadowa*, pp. 310–89.

19. Hantsch's biography of Berchtold provides a useful set of insights into the multiple duties of a foreign minister. The files of the Foreign Ministry in the HHStA are indispensable for understanding the range of duties assigned to the minister. Also see Friedrich Engel-Janosi, *Geschichte auf dem Ballhausplatz: Essays zur österreichischen Aussenpolitik, 1830–1945* (Graz, 1963) pp. 9–28. There is no equivalent to Zara Steiner's *The Foreign Office and Foreign Policy, 1898–1914* (Cambridge, 1969) for the Habsburg Foreign Ministry. But Diószegi, *Hungarians*, and Galántai, *Monarchie*, offer glimpses into its operations; also see Lützow, *Im diplomatischen Dienst*. Helmut Rumpler is currently preparing an overall assessment of the Foreign Ministry.

20. There is no adequate biography of Aehrenthal, but Solomon Wank (who is preparing one) has written often about him. See, for example, 'A Note on the Genealogy of a Fact: Aehrenthal's Jewish Ancestry', *JMH*, XLI (Sept. 1969) 319–26 which denies Aehrenthal was Jewish. For summaries of Aehrenthal's career, see Bridge, *From Sadowa*, pp. 288–340; G. P. Gooch, *Before the War: Studies in Diplomacy*, 2 vols (London, 1936–8), I, pp. 367–438. For insights into Aehrenthal's earlier career and attitudes, see his letters to his father in Ernst Rutkowski (ed.), *Briefe und Dokumente zur Geschichte der österreichisch-ungarischen Monarchie unter besonderer Berücksichtigung des böhmisch-mährischen Raumes*, vol. I (Vienna, 1983).

21. Diószegi, *Hungarians*, pp. 203–10.

22. On Berchtold's career, see Hantsch, *Berchtold*; also Gooch, *Before the War, II*, pp. 373–447; Bridge, *From Sadowa*, pp. 340–89; Solomon Wank, 'The Appointment of Count Berchtold as Austro-Hungarian Foreign Minister', *Journal of Central European Affairs*, XXIII (July 1963) 143–51.

23. The most recent studies are in the multi-volume work of Wandruszka and Urbanitsch (eds), *Die Bewaffnete Macht*; see especially Johann C. Allmayer-Beck, 'Die Bewaffnete Macht in Staat und Gesellschaft', ibid., pp. 88–141; also his *Die k.u.k. Armee, 1848–1914* (Vienna, 1974); Norman Stone, 'Army and Society in the Habsburg Monarchy, 1900–1914', *Past and Present*, XXXIII (1966) 95–111. The memoirs of General Edmund Glaise von Horstenau are also very valuable; see Peter Broucek (ed.), *Ein General im Zwielicht: Die Erinnerungen Edmund Glaises von Horstenau*, vol. I (Vienna, 1980).

24. The War Ministry moved in 1913 to more spacious quarters on the Stubenring; the building is now occupied by the various Austrian ministries.

25. These figures are compiled from *Militär-Adressbuch für Wien und Umgebung 1914: Zusammengestellt beim k.u.k. Platzkommando in Wien* (Vienna, 1913). These were the personnel assigned to the Kriegsministerium, not the General Staff nor the separate Austrian or Hungarian defence staffs.

26. Rothenberg provides a succinct summary of some of the problems; *Army*, pp. 159–65.

27. Samuel Huntington, *The Soldier and the State: The Theory and Politics of Civil–Military Relations* (Cambridge, Mass., 1957) presents a classic formulation of relationships between the war ministry/war department and general staff leaderships. On the early evolution of this relationship in Vienna, see Walter Wagner, *Geschichte des k.k. Kriegsministerium*, 2 vols (Vienna, 1966–71), and his section, 'Die k.u.k. Armee-Gliederung und Aufgabenstellung', in Wandruszka and Urbanitsch (eds), *Die Bewaffnete Macht*, pp. 351–89.

28. The files of the two chancellories are nearly complete in the KA. See Rainer Egger, 'Die Militärkanzlei des Erzherzog Franz Ferdinand und ihr Archiv im Kriegsarchiv Wien', *Mitteilungen des Österreichischen Staatsarchivs*, XXVIII (1975) 141–63. There is no adequate study on Bolfras. On Brosch, see Martha Sitte, 'Alexander von Brosch, der Flügeladjutant und Vorstand der Militärkanzlei des Thronfolgers Franz Ferdinand', diss. (Vienna, 1961). On Karl von Bardolff, see his memoirs, *Soldat im alten Österreich* (Jena, 1938).

29. There is no monograph on the budget process. This description is based on the files of the Kriegsministerium and the records of the Common Ministerial Council in PA XL/310.

30. See Auffenberg's memoirs, *Aus Österreichs Höhe und Niedergang* (Munich, 1921); also Josef Ullreich, 'Moritz von Auffenberg-Komarów. Leben und Wirken, 1911–1918', diss. (Vienna, 1961). On Auffenberg's views, see 'Geist und Innere Verfassung der Armee, 1910', [n.d. but July 1910], Nachlass Franz Ferdinand [hereafter NFF], HHStA, carton 'Denkschrift'.

31. On the numbers, see Rothenberg, *Army*, p. 165; Karl Gluckmann, *Das Heerwesen der österreichisch-ungarischen Monarchie*, 12th ed. (Wien,

1911) pp. 58–61; also Auffenberg to Common Finance Minister Leon von Biliński, 3 July 1912, Militärkanzlei des Generalinspektors der gesamten bewaffneten Macht (Franz Ferdinand) [hereafter MKFF], KA, Fasz. 188. Austria: Österreichischen Bundesminsterium für Heereswesen und vom Kriegsarchiv, *Österreich-Ungarns Letzter Krieg, 1914–1918*, 7 vols and 10 suppls (Vienna, 1930–8), I, pp. 28–32; Oskar Regele, *Feldmarschall Conrad: Auftrag und Erfüllung, 1906–1918* (Vienna, 1955) pp. 155–66, 182–8, 225.

32. On Auffenberg's efforts, see *Aus Österreichs Höhe und Niedergang*, pp. 195–213 and the minutes of the Common Ministerial Council meetings 8–9 July and 3, 8–9 Oct. 1912, PA XL/310.

33. There is no comprehensive study of the General Staff, but see Wandruszka and Urbanitsch (eds), *Die Bewaffnete Macht*, pp. 373–89; Oskar Regele, *Generalstabschefs aus vier Jahrhunderten* (Vienna, 1966); Glaise von Horstenau, *Franz Josephs Weggefährte*; and Conrad's memoirs.

34. For a general survey, see Norman Stone, 'Austria–Hungary', in Ernest R. May (ed.), *Knowing One's Enemies: Intelligence Assessment Before the Two World Wars* (Princeton, 1984) pp. 37–61. On the work of the intelligence section, see the manuscript by August Urbanski von Ostrymiecz, 'Das Tornisterkind: Lebenserinnerungen des Feldmarschalleutnants August von Urbanski', Nachlass Urbanski, KA, B/58; Urbanski headed the intelligence section for Conrad. On counter-intelligence, see Max Ronge, *Kriegs-und Industrie-Spionage: Zwölf Jahre Kundschaftsdienst* (Vienna, 1930).

35. Assessments of the damage done by Redl still differ; see for example, Stone, 'Austria–Hungary', pp. 42–3, and William C. Fuller, Jr, 'Russia', pp. 115 in May, *Knowing One's Enemies*; cf. Georg Markus, *Der Fall Redl: Mit unveröffentlichten Geheimdokumenten zur folgenschwersten Spionage-Affaire des Jahrhunderts* (Vienna, 1984). Robert B. Asprey, *The Panther's Feast* (New York, 1959) remains useful. See also Ian D. Armour, 'Colonel Redl: Fact and Fantasy', *Intelligence and National Security*, II (Jan. 1987) 170–83.

36. Conrad still lacks an adequate biography, though the literature on him is extensive. See the bibliography in Franz Conrad von Hötzendorf, *Private Aufzeichnungen*, ed. Kurt Peball (Vienna, 1977) pp. 337–9. Also see Regele, *Conrad*; August Urbanski von Ostrymiecz, *Conrad von Hötzendorf: Soldat und Mensch* (Vienna, 1938); Rothenberg, *Army*, chaps 10–14.

37. For a summary of his views, see Hans Angermeier, 'Der österreichische Imperialismus des Generalfeldmarschalls Conrad von Hötzendorf', in Dieter Albrecht (ed.), *Festschrift für Max Spindler zum 75. Geburtstag* (Munich, 1969) pp. 777–92; Rothenberg, *Army*, pp. 142–8. A recent work studying Conrad's plans for an attack on Italy is Hans Jürgen Pantenius, *Der Angriffsgedanke gegen Italien bei Conrad von Hötzendorf*, 2 vols (Vienna, 1984).

38. See Gina Conrad von Hötzendorf, *Mein Leben mit Conrad von Hötzendorf* (Leipzig, 1935); also see various entries for 1913–14 in Josef Redlich's *Tagebuch*, I, pp. 191, 194, 197, 199, 209, 226, 253–4.

39. Conrad's plans are summarized in Norman Stone, 'Die Mobilmachung

der österreichisch-ungarischen Armee 1914', *Militärgeschichtliche Mitteilungen*, II (1974) 67–95 and his essay, 'Austria–Hungary', in May, *Knowing One's Enemies*, pp. 39–61; also Rothenberg, *Army*, pp. 176–184. On the Russian issues, see S. R. Williamson, 'Military Dimensions of Habsburg–Romanov Relations during the Era of the Balkan Wars', in Béla K. Király and Dimitrije Djordevic (eds) *East Central European Society and the Balkan Wars* (New York, 1987) pp. 318–37.

40. The budget figures are found in Wandruszka and Urbanitsch (eds), *Die Bewaffnete Macht*, pp. 590–1; on the Habsburg navy, see the section by Lothar Höbelt, 'Die Marine', ibid, pp. 687–763. The study by Milan N. Vego, 'The Anatomy of Austrian Sea Power, 1904–1914', diss. (Georgetown, Wash. D.C., 1981) is a major contribution. Also see Halpern, *Naval Situation*, chaps 6, 9; Anthony Sokol, *The Imperial and Royal Austro-Hungarian Navy* (Annapolis, Maryland, 1968); Hans Hugo Sokol, *Österreich-Ungarns Seekrieg, 1914–1918*, 2 vols (Vienna 1933) and *Geschichte der k.u.k. Kriegsmarine*, vol. III (Vienna, 1980).

41. Peter Handel-Mazzetti, 'Admiral Rudolf Graf Montecuccoli degli Erri', *Neue Österreichische Biographie*, XIV (Vienna, 1960) 89–95; Vego, 'Anatomy', pp. 153–191. Louis A. Gebhard, Jr, 'Austro–Hungary's Dreadnought Squadron: The Naval Outlay of 1911', *Austrian History Yearbook*, IV–V (1968–69) 245–58; Sokol, *Geschichte*, pp. 197–238.

42. On Montecuccoli's efforts, see the minutes of the Common Ministerial Council meetings of 14 Sept., 3, 8–9 Oct. 1912, PA XL/310. Also Vego, 'Anatomy', pp. 250–9, 271–6, 301–4.

43. On Haus's efforts at the Common Ministerial Council, see minutes for the meetings of 3 Oct., 14 Dec. 1913, PA XL/310. On Haus's tenure, see Vego, 'Anatomy', pp. 320–2, 376–86. See Sokol, *Geschichte*, pp. 239–42; Horst Friedrich Mayer, 'Die k.u.k. Kriegsmarine unter dem Kommando von Admiral Anton Haus', diss. (Vienna, 1962).

44. Halpern, *Naval Situation*, provides an excellent summary of the strategic arguments and the Triple Alliance arrangements for naval cooperation; chaps 6–9.

45. Vego, 'Anatomy', pp. 556–79.

46. A. Sokol, *Imperial and Royal Navy*, pp. 75–76.

47. On the monarchy's economic life after 1900, see the articles in Brusatti (ed.), *Die Wirtschaftliche Entwicklung*; Rudolph, *Banking and Industrialization*; Michel, *Banques*; März, *Austrian Banking*; 'The Economic Development of Austria–Hungary, 1850–1914', in Alan S. Milward and S. B. Saul, *The Development of the Economies of Continental Europe, 1850–1914* (Cambridge, Mass., 1977) pp. 271–331; Komlos, *Habsburg Monarchy*; Good, *Economic Rise*. On Berchtold's belated attention to economic policy, see the minutes of a meeting of the Foreign Office staff on this issue, 16 Oct. 1912, *OÜA*, IV, no. 4118.

48. For an excellent survey of this competition in the context of the larger Anglo-German rivalry, see Richard J. Crampton, *The Hollow Detente: Anglo-German Relations in the Balkans, 1911–1914* (London, 1979).

49. März, *Austrian Banking*, surveys some of the impact, pp. 30–1, 42–6, 54–7, 100–4.

50. No study of the Common Ministerial Council as such exists, but Miklos Komjáthy's introduction to the Council minutes for 1914–18 is especially helpful; see *Protokolle des Gemeinsamen Ministerrates*, pp. 1–137. The full minutes for the Council from 1912 through 1914 are in PA XL/310 and 311.

4. AEHRENTHAL'S LEGACY: BOSNIAN COLONIAL SUCCESS AND THE ITALO-TURKISH WAR

1. For example, D. K. Fieldhouse, *Economics and Empire, 1830–1914* (London, 1973) makes no mention of Austria–Hungary. The concept of Austria–Hungary as a colonial power appeared in descriptions of the two provinces before 1914; see the especially valuable Ferdinand Schmid, *Bosnien und die Herzegowina unter der Verwaltung Österreich-Ungarns* (Leipzig, 1914). On the concept of the 'official mind' and strategic necessity, see the magisterial work by Ronald Robinson and John Gallagher with Alice Denny, *Africa and the Victorians: The Official Mind of Imperialism* (London, 1961); Gustav Schmidt, *Der europäische Imperialismus* (Munich, 1985).

2. For an excellent general survey, see Dwight E. Lee, *Europe's Crucial Years: The Diplomatic Background of World War I, 1902–1914* (Hanover, New Hampshire, 1974); also Paul Kennedy, *The Rise of the Anglo-German Antagonism, 1860–1914* (London, 1980).

3. Albertini's coverage of Austro-Italian relations is superb; also see Richard Bosworth, *Italy and the Approach of the First World War* (New York, 1983) and *Italy, the Least of the Great Powers: Italian Foreign Policy before the First World War* (Cambridge, 1979).

4. John D. Treadway, *The Falcon and the Eagle: Montenegro and Austria–Hungary* (West Lafayette, Ind., 1982); Alexander Dragnich, *Serbia, Nikola Pašić, and Yugoslavia* (New Brunswick, New Jersey, 1974); Michael Petrovich, *A History of Modern Serbia, 1804–1918*, 2 vols (New York, 1976).

5. Volker Berghahn, *Germany and the Approach of War in 1914* (New York, 1973); Fritz Fischer, *Krieg der Illusionen: Die deutsche Politik von 1911 bis 1914* (Düsseldorf, 1969) pp. 17–144 [the English version is *War of Illusions: German Policies from 1911 to 1914*, trans. Marian Jackson (New York, 1975)]; Zara S. Steiner, *Britain and the Origins of the First World War* (New York, 1977).

6. On foreign policy issues as decisive, see Remak, 'The Healthy Invalid', pp. 141–3.

7. On Andrássy, the older biography by Eduard Wertheimer, *Graf Julius Andrássy*, 3 vols (Stuttgart, 1910) remains useful. For a convenient summary of Andrássy's policies, see Bridge, *From Sadowa*, chap. 3 and Diószegi, *Hungarians*, pp. 60–72. Still valuable for its information and for the attitude it conveys is Sosnosky, *Balkanpolitik*. Also see Sked, *The Decline and Fall*, pp. 239–46; Mayr-Harting, *Der Untergang*, pp. 327–54.

8. Rothenberg, *Army*, chap. 7; also Glaise von Horstenau, *Franz Josephs Weggefährte*, pp. 179–217.

9. These studies offer insight into Habsburg rule in Bosnia–Herzegovina; Schmid, *Bosnien*; Sugar, *Industrialization*, chap. 2; Donia, *Islam*, pp. 8–36; also May, *Hapsburg*, pp. 133–6. For a colourful description of the two provinces, see Rebecca West, *Black Lamb and Grey Falcon: A Journey through Yugoslavia* (New York, 1943).

10. Sugar, *Industrialization*, is very helpful on this, as is John R. Lampe and Marvin R. Jackson, *Balkan Economic History, 1550–1950: From Imperial Borderlands to Developing Nations* (Bloomington, Ind., 1982) pp. 284–7, 301–10. Also see Kurt Wesseley, 'Die wirtschaftliche Entwicklung von Bosnien–Herzegowina (1978–1918)', *Der Donauraum*, XIX (1974) 182–8.

11. Schmid, *Bosnien*, pp. 695–742.

12. Sugar, *Industrialization*, pp. 137–8, 231.

13. This discussion draws on Schmid, *Bosnien*, chap. 9; Sugar, *Industrialization*, pp. 6–15; Lampe and Jackson, *Balkan Economic History*, pp. 284–7.

14. Sugar, *Industrialization*, pp. 71–88, 233–4; Schmid, *Bosnien*, pp. 582–612.

15. On Conrad's analysis, see his memoirs, I, pp. 99–102, 656–61.

16. For an excellent account of the negotiation of the Anglo-Russian accord, see Lee, *Crucial Years*, chap. 6; also W. M. Carlgren, *Iswolsky und Aehrenthal vor der bosnichen Annexionskrise* (Uppsala, 1955).

17. On the trade dispute, Wayne S. Vucinich, *Serbia Between East and West: The Events of 1903–1908* (Stanford, Calif., 1954) remains valuable; also Lampe and Jackson, *Balkan Economic History*, pp. 175–83. On Serbian politics, see Dragnich, *Serbia*.

18. Conrad reprinted a number of these overtures in his memoirs; see, e.g., I, pp. 513–33; also Rothenberg, *Army*, pp. 152–4.

19. Excellent accounts of the crisis are found in Bernadotte Schmitt, *The Annexation of Bosnia* (Cambridge, 1937); Albertini, *Origins*, I, chaps 4–5; Bridge, *From Sadowa*, pp. 301–9; Stephan Verosta, *Theorie und Realität von Bündnissen* (Vienna, 1971) chap. 13.

20. See the important, path-breaking article by F. R. Bridge, 'Izvolsky, Aehrenthal, and the End of the Austro-Russian Entente, 1906–08', *Mitteilungen des Österreichischen Staatsarchivs* XXIX (1976) 315–62, which utilizes new Russian materials. The essential Austrian documents are found in *ÖUA*, I; also see Hantsch, *Berchtold*, I, chap. 3.

21. Partial records of the Common Ministerial Council for 19 Aug. and 10 Sept. 1908 are found in *ÖUA*, I, nos. 40, 75.

22. Schmitt, *Annexation*, is useful on the negotiations among the powers; on Montenegro, see Treadway, *Montenegro*. Also Bridge, *Great Britain and Austria–Hungary*, pp. 126–34; and Keith Wilson, 'Isolating the Isolator: Cartwright, Grey and the Seduction of Austria–Hungary, 1908–12', *Mitteilungen des Österreichischen Staatsarchivs*, XXXV (1982) 169–98.

23. On the creation of the *Narodna Odbrana*, see Behschnitt, *Nationalismus*, pp. 108–26.

24. On the military measures, see Conrad, I, pp. 116–63; Rothenberg, *Army*, pp. 154–6. On Aehrenthal's many moods, see Redlich, *Tagebuch*, I,

pp. 6–11; Redlich favoured a war and later defended the annexations with great skill.

25. On the military conversations with Moltke, see Norman Stone, 'Moltke-Conrad: Relations between the Austro-Hungarian and German General Staffs, 1909–14', *The Historical Journal*, IX (1966) 201–28 and reprinted in *The War Plans of the Great Powers, 1880–1914*, ed. Paul Kennedy (London, 1979) pp. 222–51. [Later references to this article are to the reprint in the Kennedy volume.]

26. Albertini is very critical of Aehrenthal's withdrawal from the Sanjak, *Origins*, I, pp. 301–6.

27. For revealing insights into the domestic scene in the wake of the Friedjung trial and on South Slav matters generally, see Baernreither, *Fragments*, pp. 40–108.

28. Schmid, *Bosnien*, chronicles some of these efforts.

29. There is no biography of Potiorek, an important and puzzling figure who allegedly was a homosexual. See Franz Weinraum, 'FZM Oskar Potiorek: Leben und Wirken als Chef der Landesregierung für Bosnien und der Herzegowina in Sarajevo, 1911–1914', diss. (Vienna, 1964). Potiorek's bi-weekly reports to Vienna are extremely instructive and allow the reader to follow the political life in the two provinces very carefully; they are found in the Nachlass Potiorek, KA, A13:C–D.

30. On relations with Constantinople, see F. R. Bridge, 'Austria–Hungary and the Ottoman Empire in the Twentieth Century', *Mitteilungen des Österreichischen Staatsarchivs*, XXXIV (1981) 234–71.

31. On the reconstruction of the Russian military during these years, see Norman Stone, *The Eastern Front, 1914–1917* (London, 1975), chap. 1; William C. Fuller, Jr, *Civil–Military Conflict in Imperial Russia, 1881–1914* (Princeton, New Jersey, 1985), chap. 7; Jack Snyder, *The Ideology of the Offensive: Military Decision Making and the Disasters of 1914* (Ithaca, NY, 1984), chaps 6–7. On Berchtold's efforts to restore relations, see Hantsch, *Berchtold*, I, chap. 4.

32. On Serbian activities, see Behschnitt, *Nationalismus*, pp. 116–132, 305–18; David MacKenzie, 'Serbian Nationalist and Military Organizations and the Piedmont Idea, 1844–1914', *East European Quarterly*, XVI (1982) 323–44; Dedijer, *Sarajevo*, chaps 10–11.

33. On Italian diplomacy, the two works by Richard Bosworth are indispensable: *Italy, the Least of the Great Powers* and *Italy and the Approach of the First World War*. Michael Behnen gives copious details of the relations between the two rivals in *Rüstung—Bündnis—Sicherheit: Dreibund und informeller Imperialismus* (Tübingen, 1985), including a section on Conrad's plans against Italy, pp. 159–64; a more detailed study of those plans is in Pantenius, *Conrad*. Albertini, a major political figure in Italy before 1914 and editor of the famous Milan paper, *Corriere della Sera*, offers a full account of this era, *Origins*, I, pp. 257–68. Also see the memoirs of Ambassador Lützow who served in Rome from 1904 to 1910, *Im diplomatischen Dienst*, pp. 135–71.

34. Bosworth, *Italy, the Least of the Great Powers*, chap. 5.

35. Ibid., p. 163.

232 AUSTRIA–HUNGARY AND THE ORIGINS OF THE FIRST WORLD WAR

36. Ibid., chap. 6; Albertini, *Origins*, I, pp. 340–9, 352–63.

37. Edward C. Thaden, *Russia and the Balkan Alliance of 1912* (University Park, Penn., 1965). On the Russian efforts to create the Balkan League, see Hans Übersberger, *Österreich zwischen Russland und Serbien* (Graz, 1958) pp. 59–73.

38. See Conrad, II, pp. 218–69; also Conrad to Aehrenthal, 3 Jan. 1911, *ÖUA*, III, no. 2404; Mérey to Aehrenthal, 31 Jan. 1911, ibid., no. 2438. On Conrad's meddling, see Aehrenthal to Franz Joseph, 4 March 1911, ibid., no. 2475; Conrad to Franz Joseph, 10 March 1911, ibid., no. 2480. On the Serbian threat, Conrad to Aehrenthal, 17 March 1911, ibid., no. 2487. There are numerous other examples of Conrad's aggressive stance toward the minister.

39. Aehrenthal's memorandum of 22 Oct. 1911 is reprinted in *OUA*, III, no. 2809; also see the footnotes following that document. On the final clashes, see Conrad, II, pp. 267–84.

40. Gooch gives a useful assessment of Aehrenthal's final months in office; *Before the War*, I, pp. 429–38.

41. On the British efforts to assess and then to dismiss Habsburg independence, see Wilson, 'Isolating'; on the momentum among the Triple Entente states and the role of the military discussions between them, see S. R. Williamson, *The Politics of Grand Strategy: Britain and France Prepare for War, 1904–1914* (Cambridge, Mass., 1969).

5. THE MONARCHY'S ALLIES: AGGRESSIVE BERLIN, DUBIOUS ROME, UNCERTAIN BUCHAREST

1. Bridge, *From Sadowa*, provides a convenient overview of the alliance scene; also see Gordon Martel, *The Origins of the First World War* (London, 1987); Fritz Fellner, *Der Dreibund: Europäische Diplomatie vor dem Ersten Weltkrieg*, 2nd ed. (Munich, 1960).

2. On Bismarck's diplomacy see the recent study by Lothar Gall, *Bismarck: The White Revolutionary*, vol. II: *1871–1898*, trans. J. A. Underwood (London, 1986); also William L. Langer, *European Alignments and Alliances, 1871–1890*, 2nd ed. (New York, 1956); George F. Kennan, *The Decline of Bismarck's Order: Franco-Russian Relations, 1875–1890* (Princeton, New Jersey, 1979).

3. The texts of the treaties are found in Alfred F. Pribram, *The Secret Treaties of Austria–Hungary, 1879–1914*, vol. I, ed. Archibald Cary Coolidge, trans. Denys P. Myers and J. G. D'Arcy Paul (Cambridge, Mass., 1920).

4. For a recent discussion of the alliance relationship, see Lothar Höbelt, 'Österreich–Ungarn und das Deutsche Reich als Zweibundpartner', in Lutz and Rumpler, *Österreich und die deutsche Frage*, pp. 255–81.

5. For a thoughtful study on the changes, see Verosta, *Theorie und Realität*.

6 On this, see Lutz, *Österreich–Ungarn und die Gründung des Deutschen Reiches*.

7. On William, see Lamar Cecil, *Wilhelm II: Prince and Emperor, 1859–1900* (Chapel Hill, N. Carol., 1989) pp. 82, 85, 131, 170, 268. For an example of their later communications, see Franz Joseph to William, 29 Sept. 1908, in Johannes Lepsius et al., (eds) *Die grosse Politik der europäischen Kabinette, 1871–1914*, 40 vols (Berlin, 1922–7) [hereafter *GP*], XXVI (1), no. 8978; William to Franz Joseph, 14 Oct. 1908, ibid., no. 9006. For colourful glimpses into the royal world of the monarchs, see Gordon Brook-Shepherd, *Royal Sunset: The European Dynasties and the Great War* (Garden City, NY, 1987).

8. Brook-Shepherd, *Archduke of Sarajevo*, pp. 166–70, provides a good summary of the relationship. On their correspondence, see Kann, 'Kaiser Wilhelm II und der Thronfolger Erzherzog Franz Ferdinand in ihrer Korrespondenz', reprinted in Kann, *Franz Ferdinand*, pp. 47–85.

9. For a critical assessment of Tschirschky, see the diary entry for 29 Jan. 1913, Baernreither, *Fragments*, pp. 158–9.

10. On Berchtold's visit to Berlin in mid-1912, see Hantsch, *Berchtold*, I, pp. 271–4. On the impressions made upon William by Tisza, see Vermes, *Tisza*, pp. 213–14.

11. Though dated, Oswald Henry Wedel, *Austro-German Diplomatic Relations, 1908–1914* (Stanford, Calif., 1932) remains a useful chronicle of the relationship.

12. On German economic penetration in the Balkans, see Dörte Löding, 'Deutschlands und Österreich-Ungarns Balkanpolitik von 1912 bis 1914 unter besonderer Berücksichtigung ihrer Wirtschaftsinteressen', diss. (Hamburg, 1967); also Crampton, *Hollow Detente*; Lampe and Jackson, *Balkan Economic History*, pp. 228–36, 260–4; Fritz Klein, 'Die Rivalität zwischen Deutschland und Österreich–Ungarn in der Türkei am Vorabend des ersten Weltkrieges', in Fritz Klein (ed.), *Politik im Krieg: 1914–1918* (Berlin, 1964) pp. 1–21.

13. On the earlier relations, see Lothar Höbelt, 'Schlieffen, Beck, Potiorek und das Ende der gemeinsamen deutsch-österreichisch-ungarischen Aufmarschpläne im Osten', *Militärgeschichtliche Mitteilungen*, XXXVI (1984) 7–30. Also Ronald Louis Ernharth, 'The Tragic Alliance: Austro-German Military Cooperation, 1871–1918', diss. (Columbia University, 1970).

14. On the evolution of German plans, see Behnen, *Dreibund*, pp. 119–164; also Gerhard Ritter, *Staatskunst und Kriegshandswerk: Das Problem des 'Militarismus' in Deutschland*, vol. II: *Die Hauptmächte Europas und das wilhelminische Reich, 1890–1914* (Munich, 1960), chap. 9.

15. Norman Stone's article remains the best summary of the renewed conversations, 'Moltke–Conrad', pp. 222–51; Horst Brettner-Messler, 'Die militärische Absprachen zwischen den Generalstäben Österreich-Ungarns und Italiens vom Dezember 1912 bis Juni 1914', *Mitteilungen des Österreichischen Staatsarchivs*, XXIII (1970) 225–49.

16. The best survey of the strategic dilemma is Stone, 'Die Mobilmachung', pp. 67–95. Also see Rothenberg, *Army*, chaps 10–12; Gordon A. Craig, 'The World War I Alliance of the Central Powers in Retrospect: The Military Cohesion of the Alliance', *JMH*, XXXVII (Sept. 1965) 336–40.

17. See, for example, Fischer, *Krieg*, chap. 10.

18. On these assumptions, see L. L. Farrar, Jr, *Arrogance and Anxiety: The Ambivalence of German Power, 1848–1914* (Iowa City, Iowa, 1981); Hull, *Entourage*, pp. 248–65.

19. Ivan Scott, 'The Making of the Triple Alliance in 1882', *East European Quarterly*, XII (1978) 399–423.

20. See Bosworth, *Italy, the Least of the Great Powers* and *Italy and the Approach of the First World War*. Behnen, *Dreibund*, offers valuable new information on the economic relationships.

21. On the Italian royal family, see Brook-Shepherd, *Royal Sunset*, pp. 157–80.

22. On Berchtold's view in mid-1912 about Italy, see Hantsch, *Berchtold*, I, pp. 252–78. For comments on the Lützow and Mérey eras, see the memoirs of Lützow, *Im diplomatischen Dienst*. On the Italian side, the memoirs of Giovanni Giolitti, *Memoirs of My Life*, trans. Edward Storer (London, 1923) provide interesting insights on Italian attitudes toward the alliance.

23. For a full discussion of these issues, see Friedrich Engel-Janosi, *Österreich und der Vatikan, 1846–1918*, vol. II (Graz, 1960) pp. 126–89. Franz Ferdinand's Catholic views were also a factor in these relations, as Engel-Janosi makes clear.

24. See Bosworth, *Italy, the Least of the Great Powers*, pp. 196–254.

25. Behnen, *Dreibund*, pp. 124–64; also Pantenius, *Conrad*.

26. Paul Halpern summarizes the arguments in *Naval Situation*, pp. 150–219; Vego, 'Anatomy', pp. 82–125.

27. On Nikita's ambitions, see Treadway, *Montenegro*; on Nikita and his court, see Brook-Shepherd, *Royal Sunset*, pp. 3–17.

28. Pribram, *Secret Treaties*, contains the texts of the agreements. On the Rumanian court, see Brook-Shepherd, *Royal Sunset*, pp. 69–80. On the broader issues see Căzan and Rădulescu-Zoner, *România*.

29. Fischer, *Krieg*, pp. 417–9.

30. The works by Keith Hitchins are crucial to understanding these issues: see his *The Nationality Problem in Austria–Hungary: The Reports of Alexander Vaida to Archduke Franz Ferdinand's Chancellery* (Leiden, 1974); and 'The Nationality Problem in Hungary'.

31. On Bulgarian diplomacy, see Richard J. Crampton, *Bulgaria, 1878–1918: A History* (New York, 1983) and his *A Short History of Modern Bulgaria* (Cambridge, 1987) pp. 57–64.

32. On the earlier military considerations of Bucharest, see, for example, Rothenberg, *Army*, pp. 114–7; Conrad, I, pp. 61–2.

33. R. W. Seton-Watson's *A History of the Roumanians* (Cambridge, 1934) pp. 432–7 remains a valuable guide to Rumanian domestic politics from 1908 to 1914.

34. Hitchins, *The Nationality Problem*, pp. ix–xvii.

35. Hitchins, 'The Nationality Problem', pp. 610–32; Vermes, *Tisza*, pp. 138–42.

36. Richard Neustadt first popularized the term in *Alliance Politics* (New York, 1970).

6. THE MONARCHY'S ENEMIES: SERBIA, MONTENEGRO AND THE
TRIPLE ENTENTE

1. Christopher Andrew and David Dilks (eds), *The Missing Dimension: Governments and Intelligence Communities in the Twentieth Century* (Urbana and Chicago, 1984) pp. 1–16; May, *Knowing One's Enemies*, pp. 11–36; Heinz Höhne, *Der Krieg im Dunkeln: Macht und Einfluss des deutschen und russichen Geheimdienstes* (Munich, 1985) pp. 36–7, 96–135.

2. Bridge, *From Sadowa*, pp. 19–22. On life in Cetinje, see Wladimir von Giesl, *Zwei Jahrzehnte im nahen Orient* (Berlin, 1927) pp. 238–49. For a sample of Ugron's reporting, see his dispatch of 30 Sept. 1912 in *ÖUA*, IV, no. 3873.

3. E.g., Leopold von Andrian (Warsaw) to Vienna, 18 Nov. 1912, *ÖUA*, IV, no. 4488; for a surveillance report on Žvivojin Dačić, 20 May 1912, see ibid., no. 3528.

4. Urbanski, *Conrad*, pp. 177–208, and his unpublished memoirs, 'Das Tornisterkind'; Ronge, *Kriegs*; Norman Stone, 'Austria–Hungary', in May, *Knowing One's Enemies*, pp. 37–61. On Figl's work, see August Urbanski's memorandum, 'Wie unsere Chiffren-Gruppe entstand', Oct. 1924, Nachlass Urbanski, B/58; Josef Reifberger, 'Die Entwicklung des militärischen Nachrichtenwesens in der k.u.k. Armee', *Österreichische Militärische Zeitschrift*, XIV (3, 1976) 213– 23.

5. On Gellinek's reporting, see his dispatch of 5 June 1912 on the Black Hand, *ÖUA*, IV, no. 3552; on Hubka's reporting, see, e.g., his report to Conrad, 18 Feb. 1914, ibid., VII, no. 9386. The full records from Belgrade are in 'Militär Attaché, Belgrade', KA.

6. On Ronge's assessment, see *Kriegs*, pp. 60–92.

7. On the Redl case, see Stone, 'Austria–Hungary', in May, *Knowing One's Enemies*, p. 43; Fuller, 'Russia', ibid., pp. 115–116; Höhne, *Der Krieg im Dunkeln*, pp. 100–110; Markus, *Der Fall Redl*.

8. For a sample of Conrad's own efforts to collate material, see his memorandum of 31 October 1910 in Conrad, II, pp. 74–91. Also see the annual reports compiled as 'Jahresberichte', cited in Stone, 'Austria–Hungary', in May, *Knowing One's Enemies*, fn. 9, p. 43.

9. Charles and Barbara Jelavich, *The Establishment of the Balkan National States, 1804–1920* (Seattle, Wash., 1977) pp. 185–92, 207–16, 254–65; Dedijer, *Sarajevo*, pp. 68–87; Vladimir Dedijer, Ivan Božič, Sima Čirković, and Milorad Ekmečić, *History of Yugoslavia* (New York, 1974) pp. 333–452; Ivo Banac, *The National Question in Yugoslavia: Origins, History, Politics* (Ithaca, NY, 1984) pp. 80–115; Vucinich, *Serbia*, pp. 1–59, 165–230; Petrovich, *Serbia*, II, pp. 402–533, 544–54; Brook-Shepherd, *Royal Sunset*, pp. 22–33.

10. Bridge, *From Sadowa*, pp. 277–280; Vucinich, *Serbia*, pp. 165–230; Petrovich, *Serbia*, II, pp. 544–554; Dragnich, *Serbia*, pp. 61–73, 93–5.

11. Rossos, *Russia*, pp. 26–27. On Hartwig's early influence, see Forgách to Vienna, 12 Dec. 1910, *ÖUA*, III, no. 2369. MacKenzie, 'Serbian Nationalist', pp. 334–5; Dedijer, *Sarajevo*, pp. 377–8; Behschnitt, *Nationalismus*, pp. 108–113.

12. Dedijer provides a convenient summary of these efforts, *Sarajevo*, pp. 236–77.

13. Baernreither, *Fragments*, pp. 96–108.

14. Behschnitt, *Nationalismus*, pp. 114–132; David MacKenzie, *Apis: The Congenial Conspirator* (Boulder, Col., 1989) chap. 7.

15. Rossos, *Russia*, pp. 34–52; Ernst C. Helmreich, *The Diplomacy of the Balkan Wars, 1912–1913* (Cambridge, Mass., 1938) pp. 36–8; Lee, *Crucial Years*, pp. 275–81, 302–7; Thaden, *Russia and the Balkan Alliance*, pp. 58–98.

16. Hantsch, *Berchtold*, I, pp. 268–73, 277–85; Baernreither, *Fragments*, pp. 109–122; Mayr-Harting, *Der Untergang*, pp. 649–64.

17. Rothenberg, *Army*, pp. 155–60, 164–6; also see Conrad's assessment of 31 Oct. 1910, Conrad, II, pp. 74–91; Stone, 'Moltke and Conrad', pp. 222–31.

18. Treadway, *Montenegro*, is now the standard work; also Brook-Shepherd, *Royal Sunset*, pp. 3–17.

19. Treadway, *Montenegro*, pp. 72–97; Helmreich, *Diplomacy*, pp. 81–6.

20. Treadway, *Montenegro*, pp. 79–97.

21. Conrad, I, pp. 612–13, II, pp. 436–52.

22. Treadway, *Montenegro*, pp. 91, 101.

23. Lee, *Crucial Years*, pp. 209–300, for a good summary.

24. Bridge, *Great Britain and Austria–Hungary*, pp. 21–3, 180–200; Keith M. Wilson, *Empire and Continent: Studies in British Foreign Policy from the 1880s to the First World War* (London, 1987) pp. 73–88.

25. Bridge, *Great Britain and Austria–Hungary*, pp. 36–40; Harry Hanak, *Great Britain and Austria–Hungary during the First World War: A Study in the Formation of Public Opinion* (London, 1962) pp. 1–35; Steed, *The Hapsburg Monarchy*; Peter Schuster, *Steed*, pp. 123–60; *The History of 'The Times'*, vol. III: *The Twentieth Century Test, 1884–1912* (New York, 1947) pp. 688–91, 726–33, and vol. IV: *The 150th Anniversary and Beyond, 1912–1948* (part I, New York, 1952) pp. 73–5.

26. Wilson, *Empire and Continent*, pp. 82–6; Keith Neilson, ' "My Beloved Russians": Sir Arthur Nicolson and Russia, 1906–1916', *The International History Review*, IX (Nov. 1987) 521–54; Zara Steiner, *Britain and the Origins of the First World War* (New York, 1977) pp. 42–93.

27. Halpern, *Naval Situation*, pp. 13–46, 86–110; Williamson, *Politics*, pp. 264–83; Vego, 'Anatomy', pp. 240–50.

28. John F. V. Keiger, *France and the Origins of the First World War* (New York, 1983) pp. 44–116.

29. Jack Snyder, *Ideology*, pp. 90–106; Williamson, *Politics*, pp. 205–226; Dietrich Geyer, *Russian Imperialism: The Interaction of Domestic and Foreign Policy, 1860–1914*, trans. Bruce Little (New Haven, Conn., 1987) pp. 287–92; May, *Knowing One's Enemies*, p. 45. René Girault, *Emprunts Russes et Investissements Français en Russie, 1887–1914* (Paris, 1973).

30. Keiger, *France*, pp. 88–116; Halpern, *Naval Situation*, pp. 304–8.

31. Kiszling, *Franz Ferdinand*, pp. 126–9; Hantsch, *Berchtold*, I, pp. 242–9, 263–6; Bridge, *From Sadowa*, pp. 340–2.

32. Zeman, *The Break-Up of the Habsburg Monarchy* offers a quick survey; also Hans Kohn, *Pan Slavism: Its History and Ideology*, 2nd ed. (New York, 1960) pp. 231–54.

33. Quoted in Lee, *Europe's Crucial Years*, p. 296, also pp. 275–81, 301–7; Rossos, *Russia*, pp. 34–69; Thaden, *Russia and the Balkan Alliance*, pp. 38–136; Übersberger, *Österreich*, pp. 72–89.

34. Risto Ropponen, *Die Kraft Russlands* (Helsinki, 1968) pp. 241–5; Conrad, I, pp. 384–93; May, *Knowing One's Enemies*, pp. 50–2; Stone, 'Die Mobilmachung', pp. 68–77.

35. On perceptions of Russian military strength, see William C. Wohlforth, 'The Perceptions of Power: Russia in the Pre-1914 Balance', *World Politics*, XXXIX (April 1987) 353–81; also Pertti Luntinen, *French Information on the Russian War Plans, 1880–1914* (Helsinki, 1984); Keith Neilson, 'Watching the "Steamroller": British Observers and the Russian Army before 1914', *Journal of Strategic Studies*, VIII (June 1985), 199–217.

36. On the general climate of opinion about offensive strategy, see Stephen Van Evera, 'The Cult of the Offensive and the Origins of the First World War', in Steven Miller (ed.) *Military Strategy and the Origins of the First World War* (Princeton, New Jersey, 1985) pp. 58–107.

37. Hantsch, *Berchtold*, I, pp. 287–322.

7. MILITANT DIPLOMACY: THE HABSBURGS AND THE FIRST BALKAN WAR, AUGUST 1912–MAY 1913

1. On the Balkan Wars, see Helmreich, *Diplomacy*; Lee, *Crucial Years*; and the essays in Béla K. Király and Dimitrije Djordevic (eds), *East Central European Society and the Balkan Wars* (Boulder, Col., 1987).

2. On Berchtold's efforts, see Hantsch, *Berchtold*, I, pp. 287–311; also Übersberger, *Österreich*, chaps 10–15.

3. Schemua memorandum, 28 Sept. 1912, in *ÖUA*, IV, no. 3869; also see Berchtold's reply of 2 Oct. 1912, ibid., no. 3928; Helmreich, *Diplomacy*, pp. 157–64.

4. For a scathing assessment of Germany's failure to back its ally, see Szápáry's memorandum of 7 Oct. 1912, *ÖUA*, IV, no. 3991.

5. Berchtold had expressed these views to Chancellor Bethmann Hollweg when they met on 7–8 Sept. 1912 at Buchlau; see the memorandum of the conversation, ibid., no. 3771; also the memorandum of a conversation with Prince Stolberg, the German chargé d'affaires, 26 Sept. 1912, ibid., no. 3850; Stolberg to the German Foreign Office, 27 Sept. 1912, in *GP*, XXXIII, no. 12172.

6. On this see Berchtold's memoranda of 2, 7, 9, 10 Oct. 1912, *ÖUA*, IV, nos. 3900, 3987, 4017, 4032.

7. For a different view of Habsburg diplomacy, see Albertini, *Origins*, I, pp. 375–97; cf. Bridge, *From Sadowa*, pp. 343–9.

8. For examples of the pressure, see Potiorek to Schemua, 23 Sept. 1912, Generalstab: Operations Büro, KA, Fasz. 61; Potiorek to Schemua, 1, 2, 3 Oct. (tels) 1912, MKFF, series 1912, Mb/11. On the broader issues, see Helmreich, *Diplomacy*, pp. 185–92; Williamson, 'Military Dimensions', pp. 316–37.

9. The best summaries of the military action are those prepared by Col. Karl Bardolff, the head of Franz Ferdinand's military chancellory, for use

by the archduke; e.g., MKFF, Fasz. 193 and 194. For a wholly different point of view of the war, see George Weissman and Duncan Williams (eds), trans. Brian Pearce, *The War Correspondence of Leon Trotsky: The Balkan Wars, 1912–13* (New York, 1980).

10. The minutes of the Common Ministerial Council are in PA XL/310; for a chronicle of subsequent military measures, see Wilhelm Deutschmann, 'Die militärischen Massnahmen in Österreich–Ungarn während der Balkankriege, 1912/13', diss., (Vienna, 1965); also Berchtold's diary entry for 29 Oct. 1912, 'Memoiren des Grafen Leopold Berchtold', PA I/524a [hereafter Berchtold Diary].

11. Josef Redlich served as the intermediary with Belgrade; on his efforts, see his diary entries for 2, 4–7 Nov. 1912, in Redlich, *Tagebuch*, I, pp. 166–76. Also see Ugron to Berchtold, 10 Nov. 1912 (tel.), *ÖUA*, IV, no. 4351 and Berchtold's record of his conversation with the Serbian minister (Georg Simić), 11 Nov. 1912, ibid., no. 4365. On Redlich's trip, also see Mayr-Harting, *Der Untergang*, pp. 657–64.

12. On the Montenegrin position, see Treadway, *Montenegro*, pp. 121–9.

13. Kageneck to Berlin, 23, 25–6 Nov. 1912, *GP*, XXXIII, nos. 12422, 12434–5. On the Franz Ferdinand–Schemua visit to Berlin, see Williamson, 'The Case of Franz Ferdinand', pp. 428–9; on the naval measures, Vego, 'Anatomy', pp. 276–82.

14. Helmreich, *Diplomacy*, remains the best guide, pp. 221–248.

15. On Berchtold's diplomatic efforts, Hantsch, *Berchtold*, I, pp. 350–60.

16. On the military pressures, see Potiorek memorandum, 24 Nov. 1912, MKFF, 1912, Mb/11; Bardolff to Franz Ferdinand, 4 Dec. 1912, ibid., Fasz. 194/2; Hoyos's memorandum, 7 Dec. 1912, PA I/658; Auffenberg to Franz Joseph, 5 Dec. and 6 Dec. 1912, Militärkanzlei Seiner Majestät des Kaisers [hereafter MKSM], KA, 1912, 82–1/8–8 and 8–10.

17. On Conrad's return to power, see his own account: Conrad, II, pp. 373–9.

18. Hantsch reprints Berchtold's diary entry for 11 Dec. 1912 in *Berchtold*, I, pp. 360–4.

19. Three days later, on 14 Dec. 1912, the Austrian government refused to agree to the call-up of additional troops in Dalmatia; see Austrian Cabinet minutes, 14 Dec. 1912, VA, Österreich Protokolle, 1912. That same day Berchtold refused Conrad's request to close the Montenegrin frontier; Berchtold to Conrad, 14 Dec. 1912, *ÖUA*, V, no. 4922.

20. Conrad's memoirs recount his pressures on Berchtold; Conrad II, pp. 380–96. The meeting on 23 Dec. 1912 is listed as a meeting of the Common Ministerial Council, though neither the Austrian nor the Magyar premier was present. The discussion here follows the notes kept by Alex Hoyos, dated 24 Dec. 1912, reprinted in *ÖUA*, V, no. 5059, and from telegrams from Merizzi (Potiorek's adjutant) to Potiorek, 23–4 Dec. 1912, Nachlass Potiorek, KA, A/3: A: 1914: 323B. On Berchtold's session with the monarch, see diary entry for 27 Dec. 1912, Berchtold Diary.

21. The minutes of this meeting are in PA XL/311.

22. The troop totals remain hard to compute accurately; but see Deutschmann, 'Massnahmen', pp. 67–130; Helmreich, *Diplomacy*, p. 462.

23. For examples of Schemua's assessments, see Schemua to Berchtold, 7 Oct. 1912, Operations Büro, KA Fasz. 61; and Schemua's memorandum, 'Allgemeiner Zustand der russischen Armee im Vergleich mit unserer Wehrmacht', 13 Oct. 1912, ibid. On the German assessments, see Jack R. Dukes, 'Militarism and Arms Policy Revisited: The Origins of the German Army Law of 1913', in Jack R. Dukes and Joachim Remak (eds), *Another Germany: A Reconsideration of the Imperial Era* (Boulder, Col., 1988) pp. 28–33. On the overall problem, see Rudolf Kiszling, 'Russlands Kriegsvorbereitungen im Herbst 1912 und ihre Rückwirkungen auf Österreich–Ungarn', *Berliner Monatshefte*, XIII (March 1935) 181–92; Williamson, 'Military Dimensions', pp. 316–28.

24. On the Russian decisions, see Vladimir Kokovtsov, *Out of My Past: The Memoirs of Count Kokovtsov*, trans. Laura Matvev, ed. H. H. Fisher (Stanford, Calif., 1935) pp. 344–56; May, *Knowing One's Enemies*, pp. 17–26. On Sazonov's change of position, see Thurn to Berchtold, 25–26 Nov. (tels) 1912, *ÖUA*, IV, nos. 4620, 4639–41. Also Rossos, *Russia*, pp. 101–6.

25. The Austrian documents are curiously silent on this trip. On it, see Berchtold to Franz Ferdinand, 13–14 Jan. 1913, NFF, carton 9; Conrad to Berchtold, 20 Jan. 1913, Berchtold Archiv, HHStA, no. 9; Conrad, III, pp. 77–81; Tschirschky to Foreign Office, 14 Jan. (tel.) 1913, *GP*, XXXIV (1), no. 12679; Zimmermann to Tschirschky, 16 Jan. 1913, ibid., no. 12691.

26. Julius Szilassy, *Der Untergang der Donau-Monarchie* (Berlin, 1921) pp. 209–10, 222–50; Conrad, III, pp. 113–7; Übersberger, *Österreich*, pp. 111–8; Franz Ferdinand to Berchtold, 1 Feb. 1913, quoted in Kann, *Franz Ferdinand*, p. 219.

27. On the trip, Berchtold to Thurn, 28 Jan. 1913, *ÖUA*, V, nos. 5583–4; Franz Joseph to Nicholas II, 1 Feb. 1913, ibid., no. 5653; and Hoyos's memorandum of his debriefing of Hohenlohe, 10 Feb. 1913, ibid., no. 5751.

28. Jagow to Moltke, 6 Feb. 1913, *GP*, XXXIV (1), no. 12793; Bethmann Hollweg to Berchtold, 10 Feb. 1913, ibid., no. 12818; Moltke to Conrad, 10 Feb. 1913, quoted in Conrad, III, pp. 144–7; Conrad to Moltke, 15 Feb. 1913, ibid., pp. 147–51. On Franz Joseph's views, see the diary entries for 10, 21, 25, 27 Feb. 1913, Schiessl Diary, Nachlass Schiessl, HHStA; and Franz Ferdinand to Nicholas II, 20 Mar. 1913, quoted in Milos Boghitschewitsch (ed.), *Die Auswärtige Politik Serbiens, 1903–1914*, vol. II (Berlin, 1929), no. 785.

29. The quote is from William to Franz Ferdinand, 28 Feb. 1913, quoted in Kann, *Franz Ferdinand*, p. 80; Hantsch, *Berchtold*, I, pp. 392–4; Helmreich *Diplomacy*, pp. 288–90.

30. Williamson, 'Military Dimensions', pp. 329–32.

31. Diary entries, 2, 6, 7, 8, 18 March 1913, Berchtold Diary; Conrad, III, pp. 157–79, 227–30; diary entry, 21 March 1913, Redlich, *Tagebuch*, I, pp. 192–3; Vego, 'Anatomy', pp. 307–18.

32. Thurn to Berchtold, 24 March (tel.) 1913, *ÖUA*, V, nos. 6291, 6293; Pourtales to the German Foreign Office, 25 March (tel.) 1913, *GP*, XXXIV (2), no. 13017.

33. On the demonstration, see Conrad, III, pp. 186–97; diary entries for 27, 29, 31 March 1913, Berchtold Diary; Berchtold to Franz Joseph,

1 April 1913, *ÖUA*, VI, no. 6413; also Treadway, *Montenegro*, pp. 135–43; Helmreich, *Diplomacy*, pp. 310–11.

34. On the Serbian decision, see Treadway, *Montenegro*, pp. 137–40.

35. Despite pressure from Conrad, Berchtold had the strong support of Franz Joseph and the two national governments for his European policy; see diary entry, 17 April 1913, Redlich, *Tagebuch*, I, p. 197; also Tschirschky to Bethmann Hollweg, 4 April 1913, *GP*, XXXIV (2), no. 13087. When the Common Ministerial Council met on 21 April, the Balkan crisis was not on the agenda; see minutes, PA XL/311. On Conrad's demands, see his memoirs, III, pp. 252–66.

36. On the German view, see Jagow to Tschirschky, 28 April (tel.) 1913, *GP*, XXXIV (2), no. 13226; also a letter of that same date, quoted extensively in Fischer, *Krieg der Illusionen* , pp. 297–8. On Franz Ferdinand's view, see Hantsch, *Berchtold* , I, pp. 407–8, 411–2. On the details of Plan M, see Kageneck to Berlin, 30 April 1913, *GP*, XXXIV (2), no. 13247; also Potiorek to Conrad, 26 April (tel.) 1913, Operations Büro, Fasz. 27, KA.

37. On the general situation at this point, see Treadway, *Montenegro*, pp. 143–56; also Richard Crampton, 'The Decline of the Concert of Europe in the Balkans, 1913–1914', *Slavonic and East European Review*, LII (1974) 393–419 and his *Hollow Detente*, pp. 88–96.

38. The complete minutes of the meeting are in *ÖUA*, VI, no. 6870; brief summaries are found in Hantsch, *Berchtold*, I, pp. 413–7, and Helmreich, *Diplomacy*, pp. 320–2.

39. On Berchtold's views, see his diary entry, 2 May 1913, Berchtold Diary.

40. Diary entries, 2, 3, 5 May 1913, Berchtold Diary; Hantsch, *Berchtold*, I, p. 420. Conrad met with Franz Joseph on 9 May 1913 and complained about there being no war; Operations Büro, Fasz. 91, KA.

8. DIPLOMATIC OPTIONS RECONSIDERED: THE SECOND BALKAN WAR AND AFTER, JUNE–DECEMBER 1913

1. Bridge, *From Sadowa*, pp. 353–67; Lee, *Crucial Years*, pp. 334–41; Albertini, *Origins*, I, pp. 448–9; Hantsch, *Berchtold*, I, pp. 419–520.

2. Helmreich, *Diplomacy*, pp. 341–406.

3. Crampton, *Bulgaria*, pp. 418–23; Wolfgang-Uwe Friedrich, *Bulgarien und Die Mächte, 1913–1915* (Stuttgart, 1985) pp. 2–19.

4. Rossos, *Russia*, pp. 179–206.

5. Crampton, *Hollow Detente*, pp. 112–13.

6. Crampton, *Bulgaria*, pp. 415–27.

7. Conrad, III, pp. 338–80; diary entries, 13, 16, 21, 22 May 1913, Berchtold Diary; Krobatin to Tisza, 17 June 1913, MKFF, 1913, 14–24/5.

8. Conrad to Moltke, 5 July 1913, Conrad, III, pp. 426–7; Conrad to Berchtold, 2 July 1913, Berchtold Archiv, no. 9; same to same, 12 July 1913, Operations Büro, Fasz. 91, KA; Krobatin to Berchtold, 5, 22 July 1913, PA I/658.

9. Franz Ferdinand to Berchtold, 4 July 1913, Berchtold Archiv, no. 9; Kann, *Franz Ferdinand*, pp. 223–4.

10. Franz Ferdinand to Berchtold, 6, 24 July 1913, Berchtold Archiv, no. 9; also extracts in Kann, *Franz Ferdinand*, pp. 224–8; Hantsch, *Berchtold*, II, pp. 447–8.

11. Franz Ferdinand to Berchtold, 24 July 1913, Berchtold Archiv, no. 9. Franz Joseph even sent the Court Chamberlain, Prince Montenuovo, to see Franz Ferdinand in an effort to reconcile him with Tisza, diary entries, 14, 16 June 1913, Berchtold Diary. On Tisza, see Vermes, *Tisza*, pp. 177–90.

12. On Burián's role, see Diószegi, 'Aussenminister Burián', pp. 168–84; Galántai, *Monarchie*, pp. 132–57.

13. On Berlin and Rome, see Tschirschky to Berlin, 1 July (tel.), 2 July 1913, *GP*, XXXV, nos. 13475, 13477; Berchtold to Szögyény, 1 July 1913, *ÖUA*, VI, no. 7566; Szögyény to Berchtold, 4 July (tel.) 1913, ibid., no. 7614; Mérey to Berchtold, 12 July (tel.), 12 July 1913, ibid., nos. 7747–8; Albertini, *Origins*, I, pp. 457–59, 466–71.

14. Helmreich, *Diplomacy*, pp. 390–406; Hantsch, *Berchtold*, II, pp. 475–6; Bridge, *From Sadowa*, pp. 356–9; Albertini, *Origins*, I, pp. 460–6.

15. Memorandum of Berchtold conversation with Tschirschky, 21 July 1913, *ÖUA*, VI, no. 7889; diary entry, 21 July 1913, Berchtold Diary; Berchtold to Szögyény, 1 Aug. 1913, *ÖUA*, VII, nos. 8157–59; Hantsch, *Berchtold*, II, pp. 460–76.

16. Memoranda by Tisza, 11, 25 Aug. 1913, *ÖUA*, VII, nos. 8343, 8474; Berchtold to Franz Joseph, 13, 28 Aug. 1913, ibid., nos. 8376, 8498; diary entries, 11, 14 Aug. 1913, Diósezgi, 'Aussenminister Burián', pp. 188–9; Hantsch, *Berchtold*, II, pp. 471–80.

17. Conrad, III, pp. 431–41; Kiszling, *Franz Ferdinand*, pp. 264–9; Gina von Hötzendorf, *Mein Leben*, pp. 70–81, 122–7; Albertini, *Origins*, I, pp. 471-3; 22 Sept. 1913, *Neue Freie Presse*.

18. On the September crisis, see Gellinek to Conrad, 24 Sept. (tel.), 1913, Conrad, III, pp. 443; same to same, 24 Sept. 1913, *ÖUA*, VII, no. 8694; Evidenz Bureau summaries, 1, 2 Oct. 1913, MKFF, Fasz. 192.

19. Berchtold memorandum, 10–11 Oct. 1913, *ÖUA*, VII, no. 8813; Hantsch, *Berchtold*, II, pp. 489–91; Griesinger to Bethmann Hollweg, 7 Oct. 1913, *GP*, XXXVI (1), no. 14157; Hartwig to Sazonov, 9 Oct. 1913, *Die Auswärtige Politik Serbiens*, II, no. 861; diary entry, 3 Oct. 1913, Diószegi, 'Aussenminister Burián', p. 190; diary entry, 3 Oct. 1913, Berchtold Diary.

20. Part of the minutes are in *ÖUA*, VII, no. 8779; a full copy is in Conrad, III, pp. 724–46. Also see József Galántai, 'Austria–Hungary and the War: The October 1913 Crisis — Prelude to July 1914', *Etudes Historiques Hongroises 1980* (Budapest, 1980) pp. 62–89.

21. Berchtold to Ambrózy, 9 Oct. (tel.) 1913, *ÖUA*, VII, no. 8810; Berchtold to Flotow, 10 Oct. (tel.), 1913, ibid., no. 8816; Franz Ferdinand to Berchtold, 12 Oct. 1913, in Kann, *Franz Ferdinand*, pp. 231–2; diary entries, 11–12 Oct. 1913, Berchtold Diary.

22. Tisza to Berchtold, 9 Oct. 1913, in Hantsch, *Berchtold*, II, pp. 498–9; Conrad to Berchtold, 8 Oct. 1913, II, pp. 463–4.

23. There is no official record of the meeting; see Conrad, III, pp. 464–6, 474–5; diary entries, 12–14 Oct. 1913, Berchtold Diary; diary entry, 13 Oct. 1913, Diósezgi, 'Aussenminister Burián', p. 191. The recently published Serbian documents reveal Belgrade's understanding of Vienna's intentions and of German support; see Jovanović to Pašić, 14, 17, 18 Oct. 1913, in Kliment Džambazovski (ed.), *Documents sur la politique exterieure du Royaume de Serbie, 1903–1914 [Dokumenti o spoljnoj politici Kraljevine Srbije, 1903–1914]* (Belgrade, 1983), tome VI, vol. III [hereafter *Documents Serbie*] nos. 373, 386, 394. I am grateful to Professor Dragan Živojinović of the University of Belgrade for help with the Serbian documents.

24. Berchtold to Storck, 14 Oct. (tel.) 1913, *ÖUA*, VII, no. 8828; Storck to Berchtold, 15 Oct. (tels) 1913, ibid., nos. 8834–5; Berchtold to Berlin, Bucharest, Rome, 15 Oct. (tel.) 1913, ibid., no. 8837; Stolberg to Berlin, 15 Oct. (tel.) 1913, *GP*, XXXVI (1), no. 14160. The ultimatum is in Berchtold to Storck, 17 Oct. (tel.) 1913, *ÖUA*, no. 8850; Albertini, *Origins*, I, pp. 480–2.

25. Diary entries, 16–17, 19 Oct. 1913, Berchtold Diary; also see entries for 15–16, 18 Oct. 1913, Redlich, *Tagebuch*, I, pp. 210–12.

26. On the Serbian decision, see Storck to Berchtold, 20 Oct. (tels) 1913, *ÖUA*, VII, nos. 8880–2; Pašić to Vienna, Rome, Berlin, 19 Oct. 1913, *Documents Serbie*, tome VI, vol. III, no. 399; Jovanović to Pašić, 20 Oct. 1913, ibid., nos. 404–5.

27. Berchtold memorandum, 20 Oct. 1913, *ÖUA*, VII, no. 8934; Hantsch, *Berchtold*, II, pp. 502–6; Sosnosky, *Balkanpolitik*, II, pp. 381–92; Fischer, *Krieg der Illusionen*, pp. 310–17; Helmreich, *Diplomacy*, pp. 427–8.

28. Albertini, *Origins*, I, pp. 481–7.

29. E.g., Zimmermann to Tschirschky, 22 Oct., 11 Nov. 1913, *GP*, XXXVI (1), nos. 14193, 14202; Otto Czernin to Berchtold, 24 Oct., 28 Oct. (tel.) 1913, *ÖUA*, VII, nos. 8911–14, 8936–7; Albertini, *Origins*, I, 485–7.

30. Storck to Berchtold, 22 Oct. 1913, PA XIX/65; Gellinek to Conrad, 15 Nov. 1913, Kriegsminsterium Präsidial Series, KA, 1913, 47–7/152 [hereafter, KM Präs].

31. Franz Ferdinand to Berchtold, 21 Oct. 1913, quoted in Kann, *Franz Ferdinand*, pp. 232–3; cf. with original in Berchtold Archiv, no. 9.

32. These and the succeeding paragraphs are drawn from the minutes of the Delegations; see Austria, *Stenographische Sitzungs-Protokolle der Delegation des Reichsrathes. Achtundvierzigste Session: Vienna* (Vienna, 1914). Also see Kanner, *Katastrophenpolitik*, pp. 142–50; Frank E. Norgate, 'The Internal Policies of the Stürgkh Government, November 1911-March 1914: A Study in a Holding Action', diss. (New York University, 1978) pp. 245–72; Hantsch, *Berchtold*, II, pp. 511–14.

33. On Habsburg economic policy, see Brusatti (ed.), *Die Wirtschaftliche Entwicklung*; also Good, *Economic Rise*, pp. 186–236, 257–260; März, *Austrian Banking*, pp. 3–107, passim.

34. Stock values are computed from the weekly summaries in *Volkswirtschaftliche Chronik* (Vienna, 1912–14); diary entry, 1 Oct. 1912, Redlich, *Tagebuch*, I, p. 154.

35. März, *Austrian Banking*, pp. 26–35.

36. Herbert Feis, *Europe: The World's Banker, 1870–1914*, (New Haven, Conn., 1930) pp. 306–10; Michel, *Banques*, pp. 274–9; Crampton, *Hollow Detente*, pp. 159–60. After August 1913 the track was distributed as follows: 430.107 km in Turkey; 380 km in Serbia; 84.685 km in Bulgaria; and 68 km in Greece.

37. Feis, *Europe: The World's Banker*, pp. 306–10. The published Habsburg documents offer no help on this. But see, for example, Pašić to Jovanović, 14 May 1914, in Vladimir Dedijer and Života Anić (eds), *Documents Serbie* (Belgrade, 1980), tome VII, vol. II, no. 1.

38. Kann, *Franz Ferdinand*, pp. 156–205; Ottokar Czernin, *In the World War* (London, 1919) pp. 77–86; Căzan and Rădulescu-Zoner, *Români*, pp. 355–425; Berchtold, *Hantsch*, II, pp. 495–7; Vermes, *Tisza*, pp. 208–10.

39. Hitchins, 'The Nationality Problem in Hungary', pp. 619–51.

40. Instructions to Grafen Ottokar Czernin, 26 Nov. 1913, *ÖUA*, VII, no. 9032; also Tschirschky to Jagow, 29 Nov. 1913, *GP*, XXXIX, no. 15803.

41. Czernin to Berchtold, 5 Dec. (tel.), 5 Dec. 1913, *ÖUA*, VII, nos. 9051–2; Czernin to Franz Ferdinand, 4 Dec. 1913, NFF, carton 13.

42. Berchtold to Czernin, 18 Dec. 1913, *ÖUA*, VII, no. 9103; diary entry, 18 Dec. 1913, Berchtold Diary; also Hantsch, *Berchtold*, II, p. 520.

43. Czernin to Berchtold, 30 Dec. (tel.), 30 Dec. 1913, *ÖUA*, VII, nos. 9137–8; Czernin to Franz Ferdinand, 30 Dec. 1913, MKFF, Fasz. 203/9; Czernin to Berchtold, 30 Dec. 1913, Berchtold Archiv, no. 9; Williamson, 'The Case of Franz Ferdinand', pp. 431–33.

9. AUSTRIA–HUNGARY AND THE LAST MONTHS BEFORE SARAJEVO: JANUARY–JUNE 1914

1. Entry, 14 June 1914, Berchtold Diary; Hantsch, *Berchtold*, II, pp. 544–5; Fischer, *Krieg*, pp. 608–10; Albertini, *Origins*, I, pp. 533–4; Lee, *Crucial Years*, pp. 336–69.

2. Galántai, *Monarchie*, pp. 200–3.

3. Hantsch, *Berchtold*, II, pp. 545–51; Bridge, *From Sadowa*, pp. 367–8; M. B. A. Peterson, 'Das österreichisch-ungarische Memorandum an Deutschland vom 5 Juli 1914', *Scandia*, XXX (1964) 138–90; the original is in *ÖUA*, VIII, no. 9918.

4. Crampton, *Hollow Detente*, pp. 154–62; Albertini, *Origins*, I, pp. 524–7.

5. Bosworth, *Italy, the Least of the Great Powers*, pp. 240–6, 249–54; Zimmermann to Tschirschky, 3 July 1914, *GP*, XXXIX, no. 14526.

6. George B. Leon, 'Greece and the Central Powers, 1913–1914: The Origins of the National Schism', *Südostforschung*, XXXIX (1980) 156–67; Fischer, *Krieg*, pp. 594–5.

7. Crampton, *Bulgaria*, pp. 429–35.

8. Albertini, *Origins*, I, pp. 492–7; Feis, *Europe: The World's Banker*, pp. 277–83; Friedrich, *Bulgarien*, pp. 20–105.

9. Vermes, *Tisza*, pp. 213–5; Galántai, *Monarchie*, pp. 194–9; Hantsch, *Berchtold*, II, pp. 529–31; memorandum by Tisza, 15 March 1914, *ÖUA*, VII, no. 9482.

10. Bethmann Hollweg to Jagow, 8 May 1914, *GP*, XXXVIII, no. 15549; Tschirschky to Jagow, 10, 22 May 1914, *GP*, XXXIX, nos. 15732, 15734.

11. Memorandum by Matscheko, 24 June 1914, *ÖUA*, VIII, no. 9918.

12. Friedrich, *Bulgarien*, pp. 73–90.

13. Hitchins, 'The Nationality Problem in Hungary', pp. 642–3.

14. Hungarian House of Deputies, 20 Feb. 1914, *Parlamentarische Chronik, 1914* (Vienna, 1914) pp. 160–4.

15. Baernreither, *Fragments*, pp. 294–5.

16. Czernin to Franz Ferdinand, 16 May, 14 June 1914, NFF, carton 13; Czernin to Berchtold, 12 June 1914, *ÖUA*, VIII, nos. 9845–7.

17. Serge Sazonov, *Fateful Years, 1909–1916* (New York, 1918) pp. 103–15; Egon Gottschalk, 'Die Entrevue von Constanza', *Berliner Monatshefte*, XII (June 1934) 466–85.

18. Krobatin to Franz Joseph, 25 May 1914, KM Präs, 1914, 40–11/1–5.

19. Hans Heilbronner, 'The Merger Attempts of Serbia and Montenegro, 1913–1914', *Journal of Central European Affairs*, XVIII (1958) 288–91; Treadway, *Montenegro*, pp. 177–81; Mark Cornwall, 'Between the Two Wars: King Nikola of Montenegro and the Great Powers, August 1913–August 1914', *The South Slav Journal*, IX (1986) 59–74.

20. Dragnich, *Serbia*, pp. 75–79; MacKenzie, *Apis: The Congenial Conspirator*, chap. 11.

21. See, for example, Giesl to Berchtold, 5 June (tel.), 6, 12, June 1914, *ÖUA*, VIII, nos. 9809, 9819, 9844; Dedijer, *Sarajevo*, 386–96.

22. Matscheko memorandum, *ÖUA*, VIII, no. 9918.

23. Risto Ropponen, *Die russische Gefahr* (Helsinki, 1976) pp. 173–80.

24. Memorandum by Szápáry, 20 Jan. 1914, *ÖUA*, VII, no. 9219.

25. Albertini, *Origins*, I, pp. 509–23; Zeman, *The Break-Up of the Habsburg Monarchy*, pp. 3–23.

26. On the shift in German thinking, see Holger H. Herwig, 'Imperial Germany', in May, *Knowing One's Enemies*, pp. 62–97.

27. Bosworth, *Italy, the Least of the Great Powers*, pp. 246–54.

28. F. R. Bridge, ' "Tarde venientibus ossa:" Austro-Hungarian Colonial Aspirations in Asia Minor (1913–14)', *Middle Eastern Studies*, VI (1970) 319–330; Bosworth, *Italy, the Least of the Great Powers*, pp. 363–72.

29. Jagow to Tschirschky, 15 May 1914, in German Foreign Ministry Archives, Botschaft Wien: Jagow–Tschirschky Korrespondenz, on microfilm, National Archives, T-120, roll 3785, frames H 316872-75; also see Tschirschky to Jagow, 22 May 1914, *GP*, XXXIX, no. 15734.

30. Fischer, *Krieg*, chaps. 12, 14, 16, passim.

31. Conrad, III, pp. 601–3, 609–12; Brettner-Messler, 'Die militärische Absprachen zwischen den Generalstäben', pp. 238–42.

32. Conrad, III, pp. 667–73; Fischer, *Krieg*, p. 582.

33. This and succeeding paragraphs are based on material in Stone, 'Die Mobilmachung', pp. 67–77; Rothenberg, *Army*, pp. 172–9.

34. A concise history of the domestic politics of Austria before 1914

remains to be written. But see Norgate, 'The Internal Policies of the Stürgkh Government', chaps 5–6; also the diary entries, Jan.–June 1914, Redlich, *Tagebuch*, I, pp. 213–33.

35. Vermes, *Tisza*, pp. 207–10.
36. Ibid., pp. 213–19.
37. Baernreither, *Fragments*, pp. 243–7.
38. Hantsch, *Berchtold*, II, pp. 537–9.
39. Studies of the conspiracy to assassinate the archduke are abundant. The most recent is MacKenzie, *Apis: The Congenial Conspirator*, but Galántai and Albertini are also useful, as is Sidney B. Fay, *The Origins of the World War*, 2nd ed. (New York, 1930) and Bernadotte E. Schmitt, *The Coming of the War 1914*, 2 vols (Chicago, 1930). Dedijer in *Sarajevo* makes use of the Serbian documents; also see Friedrich Würthle, *Die Spur führt nach Belgrad* (Vienna, 1975) and his *Dokumente zum Sarajevoprozess: Ein Quellenbericht*, ed. Kurt Peball (Vienna, 1978).
40. The recently published Serbian documents are especially helpful in establishing what the Serbian officials knew and how Apis managed to evade the efforts of Pašić to ferret out the truth of the situation.

10. VIENNA AND THE JULY CRISIS

1. The literature on Austria–Hungary and the start of the July crisis is extensive. The following are especially helpful: Albertini, *Origins*; James Joll, *The Origins of the First World War* (London, 1984); Galántai, *Monarchie*; Lee, *Crucial Years*, pp. 376–427; Bridge, *From Sadowa*, pp. 373–9; Erwin Hölzle, *Die Selbstentmachtung Europas: Das Experiment des Friedens vor und im Ersten Weltkrieg* (Frankfurt, 1975) pp. 246–392; Fischer, *Krieg*, pp. 686–720; Willibald Gutsche, *Sarajevo 1914: Vom Attentat zum Weltkrieg* (Berlin, 1984); Mayr-Harting, *Der Untergang*, pp. 704–38; Williamson, 'Origins'; William Jannen, Jr, 'The Austro-Hungarian Decision for War in July 1914' and S. R. Williamson, 'Vienna and July 1914: The Origins of the Great War Once More', in S. R. Williamson and Peter Pastor (eds), *Essays on World War I: Origins and Prisoners of War* (New York, 1983).
2. Hantsch, *Berchtold*, II, pp. 541–82; Conrad, IV, pp. 13–18; Vermes, *Tisza*, pp. 217–33; Robert A. Kann, *Kaiser Franz Joseph und der Ausbruch des Weltkrieges* (Vienna, 1971); Kanner, *Katastrophenpolitik*, pp. 192–241.
3. Brook-Shepherd, *Archduke of Sarajevo*, pp. 253–70.
4. Conrad, IV, pp. 13–36; Hantsch, *Berchtold*, II, pp. 557–69; Leon von Biliński, *Wspomnienia i dokumenty, 1846–1922 [Memoirs and Documents, 1846–1922]*, 2 vols (Warsaw, 1924–5), I, pp. 274–8; Tisza to Franz Joseph, 1 July 1914, *ÖUA*, VIII, no. 9978; Franz Joseph to William II, 2 July 1914, ibid., no. 9984; Diószegi, 'Aussenminister Burián', pp. 204–05; Karl von Macchio, 'Momentbilder aus der Julikrise 1914', *Berliner Monatshefte*, XIV (Oct. 1936) 765–6.
5. The Biliński–Potiorek exchanges are in vol. VIII of *ÖUA*; see, for example, Biliński to Potiorek, 30 June (tel.) 1914, ibid., no. 9962.
6. Hantsch, *Berchtold*, II, pp. 558–9.

7. Ibid., pp. 559–60.

8. Galántai, *Monarchie*, pp. 251–55; Hantsch, *Berchtold*, II, pp. 560–1; Tisza to Franz Joseph, 1 July 1914, *ÖUA*, VIII, no. 9978.

9. Würthle, *Die Spur*, traces the plot. Albertini, *Origins*, II, chaps 2–3 remain valuable. On the later investigation, see W. A. Dolph Owings, Elizabeth Pribic and Nikola Pribic (trans. and eds), *The Sarajevo Trial*, 2 vols (Chapel Hill, N. Carol., 1984) which is a transcript of the trial of the conspirators. The reports from Gellinek to Conrad, 3–6 July 1914 are in Militärattaché: Belgrade, KA, Fasz. 8. The Habsburg archives for the administration of Bosnia and Herzegovina, now located in the Archiv Bosne i Hercegovine in Sarajevo, contain valuable additional information. See, e.g., Potiorek to Biliński, 10 July 1914, with extensive details of the plot, Gemeinsames Finanzministerium, Präs. 1914, no. 919; also Potiorek to Biliński, 16 July (tel.), 1914, ibid., no. 955. I am especially indebted to Professor Milorad Ekmečić of the University of Sarajevo and to Director Dr Božidar Madžar of the archives for help with these documents.

10. See, e.g., Potiorek to Biliński, 1 July (tel.) 1914, *ÖUA*, VIII, no. 9974.

11. The completed memorandum, dated 1 July 1914, and Franz Joseph's letter to William II, 2 July 1914, are in ibid., no. 9984. They are also in the published German documents on July 1914, reprinted in *Outbreak of the World War: German Documents Collected by Karl Kautsky*, eds Max Montgelas and Walther Schüking (New York, 1924), known as the *Kautsky Documents* [hereafter *KD*] nos. 13–4.

12. Tschirschky to Bethmann Hollweg, 30 June, 2 July (tel.) 1914, *KD*, nos. 7, 9, 11; Berchtold's memorandum, 3 July 1914, *ÖUA*, VIII, no. 10006; also see Hoyos's report of his talk with Viktor Naumann, 1 July 1914, ibid., no. 9966.

13. Fritz Fellner, 'Die "Mission Hoyos"' in Vasa Čubrilović (ed.), *Recueil des travaux aux assises scientifiques internationales: Les grandes puissances et la Serbie à la veille de la Première guerre mondiale* (Belgrade, 1976), IV, pp. 387–418.

14. Szögyény to Berchtold, 5 July (tel.) 1914, *ÖUA*, no. 10058.

15. Konrad Jarausch, *The Enigmatic Chancellor: Bethmann Hollweg and the Hubris of Imperial Germany* (New Haven, Conn., 1973) pp. 155–9; Bethmann Hollweg to Tschirschky, 6 July (tel.) 1914, *KD*, no. 15; Albertini, *Origins*, II, pp. 143–50.

16. Szögyény to Berchtold, 6 July (tel.) 1914, *ÖUA*, VIII, no. 10076; Fischer, *Krieg*, pp. 478–80.

17. Manfred Rauh, 'Die britisch-russische Marinekonvention von 1914 und der Ausbruch des Ersten Weltkrieges', *Militärgeschichtliche Mitteilungen*, XLI (1987) 37–62; Hölzle, *Die Selbstentmachtung Europas*, pp. 241–55.

18. The minutes of the meeting are reprinted in part in Imanuel Geiss (ed.), *July 1914: The Outbreak of the First World War: Selected Documents* (New York, 1967) pp. 80–7; the full record is in *ÖUA*, VIII, no. 10118.

19. Galántai, *Monarchie*, pp. 251–8; Vermes, *Tisza*, pp. 222–3.

20. Conrad, IV, pp. 53–7; Rothenberg, *Army*, pp. 176–84.

21. General Staff memorandum, 'Vorbereitende Massnahmen', no date

but seen by Conrad on 6 July 1914, Generalstab: Operations Büro, Fasz. 43, KA.

22. Galántai, *Monarchie*, pp. 264–71; Norman Stone, 'Hungary and the Crisis of July 1914', *Journal of Contemporary History*, I (1966) 153–70.

23. See Mérey to Berchtold, 18 July (tel.) 1914, *ÖUA*, VIII, no. 10364 and the lengthy footnotes on pp. 494–5; Berchtold to Mérey, 20 July (tel.) 1914, ibid., no. 10418; San Giuliano to Berlin, St Petersburg, Vienna, and Belgrade, 16 July (tels) 1914, in Italian Foreign Ministry, *I Documenti Diplomatici Italiani*, 4th ser. 1908–14, vol. XII (Rome, 1964), no. 272. Also see Bosworth, *Italy, the Least of the Great Powers*, pp. 380–6; Albertini, *Origins*, II, pp. 223–41.

24. Jovanović to Pašić, 7 July (rec. 10 July), 15 July 1914, *Documents Serbie*, VII (2), nos. 355, 431, 433; Pašić to all missions (except Vienna), 18 July (tels) 1914, ibid., no. 462.

25. Lützow, *Im diplomatischen Dienst*, pp. 218–22; Christopher H. D. Howard, 'The Vienna Diary of Berta de Bunsen, 28 June–17 August 1914', *Bulletin of the Institute of Historical Research*, LI (1978) 214.

26. Albertini reprints the ultimatum, *Origins*, II, pp. 286–9; the minutes of the meeting are in *ÖUA*, VIII, no. 10393.

27. Conrad, IV, p. 92.

28. Hantsch, *Berchtold*, II, pp. 602–3.

29. Szápáry to Berchtold, 21 July (tel.) 1914, *ÖUA*, VIII, no. 10461; Spalajković to Pašić, 22 July (tels), 24 July 1914, *Documents Serbie*, VII (2), nos. 477, 484, 520; Albertini, *Origins*, II, pp. 188–203.

30. Bosworth, *Italy, the Least of the Great Powers*, pp. 385–9; Albertini, *Origins*, II, pp. 235–41.

31. The Serbian documents reveal a strong Serbian determination to resist from the start; no Russian pressure was needed. See, e.g., Pašić to London, 24 July (tel.) 1914, *Documents Serbie*, VII (2), no. 502; Regent Alexander to Nicholas II, 24 July (tel.) 1914, ibid., no. 505. On Russia, see Spalajković to Pašić, 24 July (tel.) 1914, ibid., no. 527. Also see the memoirs of Giesl, *Zwei Jahrzehnte*, pp. 264–70. On the question of Russian pressure, see Gale Stokes, 'The Serbian Documents from 1914: A Preview', *JMH*, XXXXVI (1976), microform; also see the abbreviated Nazi edition of the captured Serbian documents, *Serbiens Aussenpolitik, 1908–1918*, ed. by Hans Uebersberger et al., vol. III (Vienna, 1945).

32. Tisza to Zeyk, 21 July 1914, in *Gróf Tisza István összes munkai*, vol. V (Berlin, 1924) pp. 49–50; diary entry, 24 July 1914, Diószegi, 'Aussenminister Burián', p. 207.

33. On the Habsburg military in 1914, see Stone, *The Eastern Front*, pp. 73–89; Rothenberg, *Army*, pp. 177–86; Galántai, *Monarchie*, pp. 344–55; Churchill, *The Unknown War*, pp. 63–144. A comprehensive monograph remains to be written.

34. The Serbian documents shed valuable insights into the extent of the Russian measures which began on 25 July 1914; see Spalajković to Pašić, 24 July (tel.), 25 July (tels.), 26 July (tels.), 27 July (tel.), 29 July (tels.) 1914, *Documents Serbie*, VII (2), nos. 503, 559, 570, 584–5, 598, 663, 673. Also Albertini, *Origins*, II, pp. 304–6; Ulrich von Trumpener, 'War Premeditated?

248 AUSTRIA–HUNGARY AND THE ORIGINS OF THE FIRST WORLD WAR

German Intelligence Operations in July 1914', *Central European History*, IX (March 1976) 66–85; Höhne, *Der Krieg im Dunkeln*, pp. 32–5.

35. The minutes for the Common Ministerial Council for 31 July 1914 are in *ÖUA*, VIII, no. 11203; also reprinted in Geiss, *July 1914*, pp. 318–22; Galántai, *Monarchie*, pp. 359–65; Hantsch, *Berchtold*, II, pp. 632–47.

36. Stone, 'Die Mobilmachung', pp. 77-95.

37. See Conrad's memorandum of 2 July 1914, *ÖUA*, VIII, no. 9995.

38. Albertini, *Origins*, II, pp. 528–81; Fischer, *Krieg*, pp. 704–29. Cf. Lieven, *Russia*, pp. 146–51.

39. Galántai, *Monarchie*, pp. 266–71; also see Gary W. Shanafelt, 'Activism and Inertia: Ottokar Czernin's Mission to Romania', *Austrian History Yearbook*, XXXIX–XL (1983-4) 202–5.

40. Crampton, *Bulgaria*, pp. 431–6.

41. Bosworth, *Italy, the Least of the Great Powers*, pp. 381–88; Albertini, *Origins*, II, pp. 226–41, III, pp. 254–363; William A. Renzi, *In the Shadow of the Sword: Italy's Neutrality and Entrance into the Great War, 1914–1915* (New York) pp. 59–82.

42. Treadway, *Montenegro*, pp. 182–99.

43. Wolfdieter Bihl, 'Zu den Österreichisch-ungarischen Kriegszielen 1914', *Jahrbücher für die Geschichte Österreuropas*, XVI (1968) 505–30.

44. Fritz Fellner, 'Zwischen Kriegsbegeisterung und Resignation — ein Memorandum des Sektionschef Graf Forgách vom Januar 1915', in *Beiträge zur allgemeinen Geschichte: Alexander Novotny zur Vollendung seiner 70. Lebensjahre* (Graz, 1975) pp. 152–62.

45. For perspectives about Austria–Hungary, the following provide helpful insights: Bridge, *From Sadowa*, pp. 380–9; Taylor, *Habsburg Monarchy*, pp. 229–32, 252–61; May, *Hapsburg Monarchy*, pp. 476–492; Mason, *The Dissolution of the Austro-Hungarian Empire*; Sked, *The Decline and Fall of the Habsburg Monarchy*, pp. 246–69; Evans, 'The Habsburg Monarchy and the Coming of the War'; Galánti, *Monarchie*, pp. 366–85; and Robert Kann's masterful reflections, 'Die Habsburgermonarchie und das Problem des übernationalen Staates', in Wandruszka and Urbanitsch (eds), *Verwaltung und Rechtswesen*, pp. 1–56.

Note After this study was in final proof, the long-awaited volume on foreign policy in the series edited by Adam Wandruszka and Peter Urbanitsch, *Die Habsburgermonarchie, 1848–1918* was published. Volume VI, pt 1, *Die Habsburgermonarchie im System der internationalen Beziehungen* (Vienna, 1989) adds much detail to this study. For F. R. Bridge's analysis of July 1914, see pp. 329–38.

Bibliography

BASIC BACKGROUND READING

LUIGI ALBERTINI, *The Origins of the War of 1914*, trans. and ed. Isabella Massey, 3 vols (London, 1952–7)

F. R. BRIDGE, *From Sadowa to Sarajevo: The Foreign Policy of Austria–Hungary, 1866–1914* (London, 1972)

SIDNEY B. FAY, *The Origins of the World War*, 2nd ed. (New York, 1930)

JAMES JOLL, *The Origins of the First World War* (London, 1984)

DWIGHT E. LEE, *Europe's Crucial Years: The Diplomatic Background of World War I, 1902–1914* (Hanover, New Hampshire, 1974)

ARTHUR J. MAY, *The Hapsburg Monarchy, 1867–1914* (Cambridge, Mass., 1951)

GUNTHER ROTHENBERG, *The Army of Francis Joseph* (West Lafayette, Ind., 1976)

ALAN SKED, *The Decline and Fall of the Habsburg Empire, 1815–1918* (London, 1989)

A. J. P. TAYLOR, *The Habsburg Monarchy, 1809–1918* (London, 1948)

L. F. C. TURNER, *Origins of the First World War* (New York, 1970)

GENERAL BIBLIOGRAPHY

JOHANN C. ALLMAYER-BECK, *Die k.u.k. Armee, 1848–1914* (Vienna, 1974)

CHRISTOPHER ANDREW AND DAVID DILKS (eds), *The Missing Dimension: Governments and Intelligence Communities in the Twentieth Century* (Urbana and Chicago, 1984)

ROBERT B. ASPREY, *The Panther's Feast* (New York, 1959)

MORTIZ VON AUFFENBERG-KOMARÓW, *Aus Österreichs Höhe und Niedergang* (Munich, 1921)

JOSEPH BAERNREITHER, *Fragments of a Political Diary*, ed. Josef Redlich (London, 1930)

IVO BANAC, *The National Question in Yugoslavia: Origins, History, Politics* (Ithaca, NY, 1984)

KARL VON BARDOLFF, *Soldat im alten Österreich* (Jena, 1938)

MICHAEL BEHNEN, *Rüstung — Bündnis — Sicherheit: Dreibund und informeller Imperialismus* (Tübingen, 1985)

WOLF DIETRICH BEHSCHNITT, *Nationalismus bei Serben und Kroaten, 1830–1914* (Munich, 1980)

REINHARD BENDIX, *Kings or People: Power and the Mandate to Rule* (Berkeley, Calif., 1978)

I. T. BEREND AND GYÖRGY RÁNKI (eds), *Economic Development in East–Central Europe in the 19th and 20th Centuries* (New York, 1974)
——, *Hungary: A Century of Economic Development* (New York, 1974)
PETER BERGER (ed.), *Der österreichisch-ungarisch Ausgleich von 1867: Vorgeschichte und Wirkungen* (Vienna, 1967)
VOLKER BERGHAHN, *Germany and the Approach of War in 1914* (New York, 1973)
EDMUND BERNATZIK, *Die österreichischen Verfassungsgesetze mit Erläuterungen*, 2nd ed. (Vienna, 1911)
LEON VON BILIŃSKI, *Wspomnieńia i dokumenty, 1846–1922 [Memoirs and Documents, 1846–1922]*, 2 vols (Warsaw, 1924–5)
JEAN-PAUL BLED, *François-Joseph* (Paris, 1987)
RICHARD BOSWORTH, *Italy and the Approach of the First World War* (New York, 1983)
——, *Italy, the Least of the Great Powers: Italian Foreign Policy Before the First World War* (Cambridge, 1979)
JOHN W. BOYER, *Political Radicalism in Late Imperial Vienna: Origins of the Christian Social Movement, 1848–1897* (Chicago, 1981)
F. R. BRIDGE, *Great Britain and Austria–Hungary, 1906–1914: A Diplomatic History* (London, 1972)
GORDON BROOK-SHEPHERD, *Archduke of Sarajevo: The Romance and Tragedy of Franz Ferdinand of Austria* (Boston, 1984)
——, *Royal Sunset: The European Dynasties and the Great War* (Garden City, NY, 1987)
ALOIS BRUSATTI (ed.), *Die Wirtschaftliche Entwicklung*, vol. I of *Die Habsburgermonarchie, 1848–1918* (Vienna, 1973)
STEPHAN BURIÁN, *Drei Jahre aus der Zeit meiner Amtsführung im Kriege* (Berlin, 1923)
W. M. CARLGREN, *Iswolsky und Aehrenthal vor der bosnischen Annexionskrise* (Uppsala, 1955)
LAVENDER CASSELS, *The Archduke and the Assassin: Sarajevo, June 28th, 1914* (New York, 1984)
GHEORGHE NICOLAE CĂZAN AND ȘERBAN RĂDULESCU-ZONER, *Români si Tripla Alianță, 1878–1914* (Bucharest, 1979)
LAMAR CECIL, *Wilhelm II: Prince and Emperor, 1859–1900* (Chapel Hill, N. Carol, 1989)
LEOPOLD VON CHLUMECKY, *Erzherzog Franz Ferdinands Wirken und Wollen* (Berlin, 1929)
WINSTON S. CHURCHILL, *The Unknown War: The Eastern Front* (New York, 1932)
FRANZ CONRAD VON HÖTZENDORF, *Aus meiner Dienstzeit, 1906–1916*, 5 vols (Vienna, 1921–5)
——, *Private Aufzeichnungen*, ed. Kurt Peball (Vienna, 1977)
GINA CONRAD VON HÖTZENDORF, *Mein Leben mit Conrad von Hötzendorf* (Lepzig, 1935)
EGON CORTI AND HANS SOKOL, *Der alte Kaiser: Franz Joseph I. vom Berliner Congress bis zu seinem Tod* (Graz, 1955)
RICHARD J. CRAMPTON, *Bulgaria, 1878–1918: A History* (New York, 1983)

——, *The Hollow Detente: Anglo–German Relations in the Balkans, 1911–1914* (London, 1979)

——, *A Short History of Modern Bulgaria* (Cambridge, 1987)

VASA ČUBRILOVIĆ (ed.), *Recueil des trauvaux aux assises scientifiques internationales: Les grandes puissances et la Serbie à la veille de la Première mondiale* (Belgrade, 1976)

OTTOKAR CZERNIN, *In the World War* (London, 1919)

VLADIMIR DEDIJER, *The Road to Sarajevo* (New York, 1960)

VLADIMIR DEDIJER, IVAN BOŽIČ, SIMA ČIRKOVIĆ AND MILORAD EKMEČIĆ, *History of Yugoslavia* (New York, 1974)

ISTVÁN DIÓSZEGI, *Hungarians in the Ballhausplatz: Studies on the Austro-Hungarian Common Foreign Policy*, trans. Kornél Balás and Mary Boros (Budapest, 1983)

ROBERT J. DONIA, *Islam under the Double Eagle: The Muslims of Bosnia and Herzegovina, 1878–1914* (New York, 1981)

GEOFFREY DRAGE, *Austria–Hungary* (London, 1909)

ALEXANDER DRAGNICH, *Serbia, Nikola Pašić, and Yugoslavia* (New Brunswick, New Jersey, 1974)

HEINRICH DRIMMEL, *Franz Joseph: Biographie einer Epoche* (Vienna, 1983)

LOUIS EISENMANN, *Le Compromis austro-hongrois de 1867: Étude sur le dualisme* (Paris, 1904)

FRIEDRICH ENGEL-JANOSI, *Geschichte auf dem Ballhausplatz: Essays zur österreichischen Aussenpolitik, 1830–1945* (Graz, 1963)

——, *Österreich und der Vatikan, 1846–1918*, vol. II (Graz, 1960)

—— AND HELMUT RUMPLER (eds), *Probleme der Franzisko-Josephinischen Zeit, 1848–1916* (Vienna, 1967)

L. L. FARRAR, Jr, *Arrogance and Anxiety: The Ambivalence of German Power, 1848–1914* (Iowa City, Iowa, 1981)

HERBERT FEIS, *Europe: The World's Banker, 1870–1914* (New Haven, Conn., 1930)

FRITZ FELLNER, *Der Dreibund: Europäische Diplomatie vor dem Ersten Weltkrieg*, 2nd ed. (Munich, 1960)

D. K. FIELDHOUSE, *Economics and Empire, 1830–1914* (London, 1973)

FRITZ FISCHER, *Krieg der Illusionen: Die deutsche Politik von 1911 bis 1914* (Düsseldorf, 1969); the English version is *War of Illusions: German Policies from 1911 to 1914*, trans. Marian Jackson (New York, 1975)

WOLFGANG-UWE FRIEDRICH, *Bulgarien und Die Mächte, 1913–1915* (Stuttgart, 1985)

WILLIAM C. FULLER, Jr, *Civil–Military Conflict in Imperial Russia, 1881–1914* (Princeton, New Jersey, 1985)

FRIEDRICH FUNDER, *Vom Gestern ins Heute* (Vienna, 1952)

JÓSEF GALÁNTAI, *Die Österreichisch–Ungarische Monarchie und der Weltkrieg* (Budapest, 1979)

LOTHAR GALL, *Bismarck: The White Revolutionary, 1871–1898*, vol. II: *1871–1898*, trans. J. A. Underwood (London, 1986)

PETER GAY, *Freud: A Life for Our Time* (New York, 1988)

IMANUEL GEISS (ed.), *July 1914: The Outbreak of the First World War: Selected Documents* (New York, 1967)

DIETRICH GEYER, *Russian Imperialism: The Interaction of Domestic and Foreign Policy, 1860–1914*, trans. Bruce Little (New Haven, Conn., 1987)

WLADIMIR VON GIESL, *Zwei Jahrzehnte im nahen Orient* (Berlin, 1927)

GIOVANNI GIOLITTI, *Memoirs of My Life*, trans. Edward Storer (London, 1923)

RENÉ GIRAULT, *Emprunts Russes et Investissements Français en Russie, 1887–1914* (Paris, 1973)

EDMUND GLAISE VON HORSTENAU, *Ein General im Zwielicht: Die Erinnerungen Edmund Glaises von Horstenau*, ed. Peter Broucek, vol. I (Vienna, 1980)

——, *Franz Josephs Weggefährte: Das Leben des Generalstabschefs Grafen Beck* (Vienna, 1930)

KARL GLUCKMANN, *Das Heerwesen der österreichisch-ungarischen Monarchie*, 12th ed. (Wien, 1911)

G. P. GOOCH, *Before the War: Studies in Diplomacy*, 2 vols (London, 1936–8)

DAVID F. GOOD, *The Economic Rise of the Habsburg Empire, 1750–1914* (Berkeley, Calif., 1984)

RODERICH GOOSS, *Das Wiener Kabinett und die Entstehung des Weltkrieges* (Vienna, 1919)

WILLIBALD GUTSCHE, *Sarajevo 1914: Vom Attentat zum Weltkrieg* (Berlin, 1984)

PAUL HALPERN, *The Mediterranean Naval Situation, 1908–1914* (Cambridge, Mass., 1971)

HARRY HANAK, *Great Britain and Austria–Hungary during the First World War: A Study in the Formation of Public Opinion* (London, 1962)

PÉTER HANÁK(ed.), *Die Nationale Frage in der Österreichisch-Ungarischen Monarchie, 1900–1918* (Budapest, 1966)

——, *Ungarn in der Donaumonarchie: Probleme der bürgerlichen Umgestaltung eines Vielvölkerstaates* (Vienna, 1984)

HUGO HANTSCH, *Leopold Graf Berchtold: Grandseigneur und Staatsmann*, 2 vols (Graz, 1963)

ERNST C. HELMREICH, *The Diplomacy of the Balkan Wars, 1912–1913* (Cambridge, Mass., 1938)

FRANZ HERRE, *Kaiser Franz Joseph von Österreich. Sein Leben, seine Zeit* (Cologne, 1978)

KEITH HITCHINS, *The Nationality Problem in Austria–Hungary: The Reports of Alexander Vaida to Archduke Franz Ferdinand's Chancellery* (Leiden, 1974)

STANLEY HOFFMANN, *The State of War: Essays in the Theory and Practice of International Relations* (New York, 1965)

HEINZ HÖHNE, *Der Krieg im Dunkeln: Macht und Einfluss des deutschen und russischen Geheimdienstes* (Munich, 1985)

GERD HOLLER, *Franz Ferdinand von Österreich-Este* (Vienna, 1982)

ERWIN HÖLZLE, *Die Selbstentmachtung Europas: Das Experiment in des Friedens vor und im Ersten Weltkrieg* (Frankfurt, 1975)

ISABEL V. HULL, *The Entourage of Kaiser Wilhelm II, 1888–1918* (Cambridge, 1982)

SAMUEL HUNTINGTON, *The Soldier and the State: The Theory and Politics of Civil–Military Relations* (Cambridge, Mass., 1957)

KONRAD JARAUSCH, *The Enigmatic Chancellor: Bethmann Hollweg and the Hubris of Imperial Germany* (New Haven, Conn., 1973)

OSCAR JÁSZI, *The Dissolution of the Habsburg Monarchy* (Chicago, 1929)

BARBARA JELAVICH, *History of the Balkans*, 2 vols (Cambridge, 1983)

——, *Modern Austria: Empire and Republic, 1815–1986* (New York, 1987)

CHARLES AND BARBARA JELAVICH, *The Establishment of the Balkan National States, 1804–1920* (Seattle, Wash., 1977)

WILLIAM A. JENKS, *The Austrian Electoral Reform of 1907* (New York, 1950)

WILLIAM M. JOHNSTON, *The Austrian Mind: An Intellectual and Social History, 1848–1938* (Berkeley, Calif., 1972)

ROBERT A. KANN, *Erzherzog Franz Ferdinand Studien* (Vienna, 1976)

——, *A History of the Habsburg Empire, 1526–1918* (Berkeley, Calif., 1974)

——, *Kaiser Franz Joseph und der Ausbruch des Weltkrieges* (Vienna, 1971)

——, *The Multinational Empire: Nationalism and National Reform in the Habsburg Monarchy, 1848–1918*, 2 vols (New York, 1950)

——, and Zdeněk V. David, *The Peoples of the Eastern Habsburg Lands, 1526–1918* (Seattle, Wash., 1984)

HEINRICH KANNER, *Kaiserliche Katastrophenpolitik* (Leipzig, 1922)

JOHN F. V. KEIGER, *France and the Origins of the First World War* (New York, 1983)

GEORGE F. KENNAN, *The Decline of Bismarck's Order: Franco–Russian Relations, 1875–1890* (Princeton, New Jersey, 1979)

PAUL KENNEDY, *The Rise of the Anglo–German Antagonism, 1860–1914* (London, 1980).

——, *The Rise and Fall of the Great Powers* (New York, 1987)

BÉLA K. KIRÁLY AND DIMITRIJE DJORDEVIC (eds), *East Central European Society and the Balkan Wars* (Boulder, Col., 1987)

RUDOLF KISZLING, *Erzherzog Franz Ferdinand* (Graz, 1953)

HANS KOHN, *Pan Slavism: Its History and Ideology*, 2nd ed. (New York, 1960)

VLADIMIR KOKOVTSOV, *Out of My Past: The Memoirs of Count Kokovtsov*, trans. Laura Matvev, ed. H. H. Fisher (Stanford, Calif., 1935)

JOHN KOMLOS, *The Habsburg Monarchy as a Customs Union: Economic Development in Austria–Hungary in the Nineteenth Century* (Princeton, New Jersey, 1983)

JOHN R. LAMPE AND MARVIN R. JACKSON, *Balkan Economic History, 1550–1950: From Imperial Borderlands to Developing Nations* (Bloomington, Ind., 1982)

WILLIAM L. LANGER, *European Alignments and Alliances, 1871–1890*, 2nd ed. (New York, 1956)

D. C. B. LIEVEN, *Russia and the Origins of the First World War* (New York, 1983)

DAVID S. LUFT, *Robert Musil and the Crisis of European Culture, 1880–1942* (Berkeley, Calif., 1980)

JOHN LUKACS, *Budapest 1900: A Historical Portrait of a City and its Culture* (New York, 1988)

PERTTI LUNTINEN, *French Information on the Russian War Plans, 1880–1914* (Helsinki, 1984)

HEINRICH LUTZ, *Österreich-Ungarn und die Gründung des Deutschen Reiches: Europäische Entscheidungen, 1867–1871* (Frankfurt, 1979)

——, *Zwischen Habsburg und Preussen: Deutschland, 1815–1866* (Berlin, 1985)

HEINRICH LUTZ AND HELMUT RUMPLER (eds), *Österreich und die deutsche Frage im 19. und 20. Jahrhundert: Probleme der politisch-staatlichen und soziokulturellen Differenzierung im deutschen Mitteleuropa* (Munich, 1982)

HEINRICH VON LÜTZOW, *Im diplomatischen Dienst der k.u.k. Monarchie*, ed. Peter Hohenbalken (Vienna, 1971)

C. A. MACARTNEY, *The Habsburg Empire, 1790–1918* (London, 1968)

DAVID MACKENZIE, *Apis: The Congenial Conspirator* (Boulder, Col., 1989)

GEORG MARKUS, *Der Fall Redl: Mit unveröffentlichten Geheimdokumenten zur folgenschwersten Spionage-Affaire des Jahrhunderts* (Vienna, 1984)

GORDON MARTEL, *The Origins of the First World War* (London, 1987)

EDUARD MÄRZ, *Austrian Banking and Financial Policy: Creditanstalt at a Turning Point, 1913–1923*, trans. Charles Kessler (New York, 1984)

JOHN W. MASON, *The Dissolution of the Austro-Hungarian Empire, 1867–1918* (New York, 1985)

ERWIN MATSCH, *Geschichte des Auswärtigen Dienstes von Österreich–Ungarn, 1720–1920* (Vienna, 1980)

——, (ed.), *November 1918 auf dem Ballhausplatz: Erinnerungen Ludwigs Freiherrn von Flotow des letzten Chefs des Österreichischen-Ungarischen Auswärtigen Dienstes* (Vienna, 1982)

ERNEST R. MAY (ed.), *Knowing One's Enemies: Intelligence Assessment Before the Two World Wars* (Princeton, New Jersey, 1984)

ARNO J. MAYER, *The Persistence of the Old Regime: Europe to the Great War* (New York, 1981)

ANTON MAYR-HARTING, *Der Untergang: Österreich–Ungarn, 1848–1922* (Vienna, 1988)

BERNARD MICHEL, *Banques & Banquiers en Autriche au début du 20e Siècle* (Paris, 1976)

STEVEN MILLER (ed.), *Military Strategy and the Origins of the First World War* (Princeton, New Jersey, 1985)

ALAN S. MILWARD AND S. B. SAUL, *The Development of the Economies of Continental Europe, 1850–1914* (Cambridge, Mass., 1977)

JULIUS MISKOLCZY, *Ungarn in der Habsburger Monarchie* (Vienna, 1959)

FREDERIC MORTON, *Thunder at Twilight: Vienna 1913/1914* (New York, 1989)

MAURICE MURET, *L'archiduc François-Ferdinand* (Paris, 1932)

RICHARD NEUSTADT, *Alliance Politics* (New York, 1970)

W. A. DOLPH OWINGS, ELIZABETH PRIBIC and NIKOLA PRIBIC (trans. and eds), *The Sarajevo Trial*, 2 vols (Chapel Hill, N. Carol. 1984)

HANS JÜRGEN PANTENIUS, *Der Angriffsgedanke gegen Italien bei Conrad von Hötzendorf*, 2 vols (Vienna, 1984)

RAYMOND PEARSON, *National Minorities in Eastern Europe, 1848–1945* (London, 1983)

MICHAEL PETROVICH, *A History of Modern Serbia, 1804–1918*, 2 vols (New York, 1976)

NIKOLAUS VON PRERADOVICH, *Die Führungsschichten in Österreich und Preussen, 1804–1918* (Wiesbaden, 1955)

JOSEF REDLICH, *Austrian War Government* (New Haven, Conn., 1929)

——, *Emperor Francis Joseph of Austria: A Biography* (New York, 1929)

——, *Schicksalsjahre Österreich, 1908–1919: Das Politische Tagebuch Josef Redlichs*, ed. Fritz Fellner, 2 vols (Graz, 1953–4)

OSKAR REGELE, *Feldmarschall Conrad: Auftrag und Erfüllung, 1906–1918* (Vienna, 1955)

——, *Generalstabschefs aus vier Jahrhunderten* (Vienna, 1966)

FRITZ REINÖHL, *Geschichte der k.u.k. Kabinettskanzlei, Mitteilungen des Österreichischen Staatsarchivs*, Ergänzungsband VII (Vienna, 1963)

WILLIAM A. RENZI, *In the Shadow of the Sword: Italy's Neutrality and Entrance into the Great War, 1914–1915* (New York, 1987)

GERHARD RITTER, *Staatskunst und Kriegshandwerk: Das Problem des 'Militarismus' in Deutschland*, vol. II: *Die Hauptmächte Europas und das wilhelminische Reich, 1890–1914* (Munich, 1960)

RONALD ROBINSON AND JOHN GALLAGHER WITH ALICE DENNY, *Africa and the Victorians: The Official Mind of Imperialism* (London, 1961)

MAX RONGE, *Kriegs- und Industrie-Spionage: Zwölf Jahre Kundschaftsdienst* (Vienna, 1930)

RISTO ROPPONEN, *Die Kraft Russlands* (Helsinki, 1968)

——, *Die russische Gefahr* (Helsinki, 1976)

ANDREW ROSSOS, *Russia and the Balkans: Inter-Balkan Rivalries and Russian Foreign Policy, 1908–1914* (Buffalo, NY, 1981)

JOSEPH ROTH, *The Radetzky March*, trans. Eva Tucker (Woodstock, NY, 1983)

RICHARD L. RUDOLPH, *Banking and Industrialization in Austria–Hungary: The Role of Banks in the Industrialization of the Czech Crownlands, 1873–1914* (Cambridge, 1976)

ERNST RUTKOWSKI (ed.), *Briefe und Dokumente zur Geschichte der österreichisch-ungarischen Monarchie unter besonderer Berücksichtigung des böhmisch-mährischen Raumes*, vol. I (Vienna, 1983)

HARRISON E. SALISBURY, *Black Night, White Snow: Russia's Revolutions, 1905–1917* (New York, 1978)

SERGE SAZONOV, *Fateful Years, 1909–1916* (New York, 1918)

FERDINAND SCHMID, *Bosnien und die Herzegowina unter der Verwaltung Österreich–Ungarns* (Leipzig, 1914)

GUSTAV SCHMIDT, *Der europäische Imperialismus* (Munich, 1985)

BERNADOTTE E. SCHMITT, *The Annexation of Bosnia* (Cambridge 1937)

——, *The Coming of the War 1914*, 2 vols (Chicago, 1930)

CARL E. SCHORSKE, *Fin-de-Siècle Vienna: Politics and Culture* (New York, 1980)

PETER SCHUSTER, *Henry Wickham Steed und Die Habsburgermonarchie* (Vienna, 1970)

HUGH SETON-WATSON and CHRISTOPHER SETON-WATSON, *The Making of the New Europe: R. W. Seton-Watson and the Last Years of Austria–Hungary* (London, 1981)

R. W. SETON-WATSON, *A History of the Roumanians* (Cambridge, 1934)

——, *Racial Problems in Hungary* (London, 1908)

——, R. W. Seton-Watson and the Yugoslavs: Correspondence, 1906–1941, ed. Hugh Seton-Watson et al., 2 vols (London, 1976)

RUDOLF SIEGHART, Die letzten Jahrzehnte einer Grossmacht: Menschen, Völker, Probleme des Habsburger-Reiches (Berlin, 1932)

JACK SNYDER, The Ideology of the Offensive: Military Decision Making and the Disasters of 1914 (Ithaca, NY, 1984)

ANTHONY SOKOL, The Imperial and Royal Austro-Hungarian Navy (Annapolis, Maryland, 1968)

HANS HUGO SOKOL, Geschichte der k.u.k. Kriegsmarine, vol. III: Die k.k. österreichische Kriegsmarine in dem Zeitraum von 1848 bis 1914 (Vienna, 1980)

——, Österreich-Ungarns Seekrieg, 1914–1918, 2 vols (Vienna 1933)

THEODOR VON SOSNOSKY, Die Balkanpolitik Österreich-Ungarns seit 1866, 2 vols (Stuttgart, 1913)

HENRY WICKHAM STEED, The Hapsburg Monarchy, 2nd ed. (London, 1914)

ZARA S. STEINER, Britain and the Origins of the First World War (New York, 1977)

——, The Foreign Office and Foreign Policy, 1898–1914 (Cambridge, 1969)

NORMAN STONE, The Eastern Front, 1914–1917 (London, 1975)

PETER F. SUGAR, Industrialization of Bosnia–Herzegovina, 1878–1918 (Seattle, Wash., 1963)

JULIUS SZILASSY, Der Untergang der Donau-Monarchie (Berlin, 1921)

EDWARD C. THADEN, Russia and the Balkan Alliance of 1912 (University Park, Penn., 1965)

The Times (London), The History of 'The Times', vol. III: The Twentieth Century Test, 1884–1912, (New York, 1947)

——, vol. IV: The 150th Anniversary and Beyond, 1912–1948, part 1 (New York, 1952)

EDWARD TIMMS, Karl Kraus: Apocalyptic Satirist: Culture and Catastrophe in Habsburg Vienna (New Haven, Conn., 1986)

ISTVÁN TISZA, Gróf Tisza István összes Munkai, vol. V (Berlin, 1924)

JOHN D. TREADWAY, The Falcon and the Eagle: Montenegro and Austria–Hungary (West Lafayette, Ind., 1982)

LEON TROTSKY, The War Correspondence of Leon Trotsky: The Balkan Wars, 1912–13, trans. Brian Pearce, eds George Weissman and Duncan Williams (New York, 1980)

HANS ÜBERSBERGER, Österreich zwischen Russland und Serbien (Cologne, 1958)

AUGUST URBANSKI VON OSTRYMIECZ, Conrad von Hötzendorf: Soldat und Mensch (Vienna, 1938)

LEO VALIANI, The End of Austria–Hungary (New York, 1973)

ANTON VANTUCH AND L'UDOVIT HOLOTIK (eds), Der österreichisch-ungarische Ausgleich 1867 (Bratislava, 1971)

GABOR VERMES, István Tisza: The Liberal Vision and Conservative Statecraft of a Magyar Nationalist (New York, 1985)

STEPHAN VEROSTA, Theorie und Realität von Bündnissen (Vienna, 1971)

WAYNE S. VUCINICH, Serbia Between East and West: The Events of 1903–1908 (Stanford, Calif., 1954)

WALTER WAGNER, *Geschichte des k.k. Kriegsministerium*, 2 vols (Vienna, 1966–71)

ADAM WANDRUSZKA AND PETER URBANITSCH (eds), *Die Habsburger-monarchie, 1848–1918*: vol. II: *Verwaltung und Rechtswesen* (Vienna, 1975); vol. III (2 parts): *Die Völker des Reiches* (Vienna, 1980); vol. V: *Die Bewaffnete Macht* (Vienna, 1987)

OSWALD HENRY WEDEL, *Austro-German Diplomatic Relations, 1908–1914* (Stanford, Calif., 1932)

EDUARD VON WERTHEIMER, *Graf Julius Andrássy*, 3 vols (Stuttgart, 1910)

REBECCA WEST, *Black Lamb and Grey Falcon: A Journey through Yugoslavia* (New York, 1943)

ANDREW G. WHITESIDE, *The Socialism of Fools: Georg Ritter von Schönerer and Austrian Pan-Germanism* (Berkeley, Calif., 1975)

S. R. WILLIAMSON, *The Politics of Grand Strategy: Britain and France Prepare for War, 1904–1914* (Cambridge, Mass., 1969)

——, AND PETER PASTOR (eds), *Essays on World War I: Origins and Prisoners of War* (New York, 1983)

KEITH M. WILSON, *Empire and Continent: Studies in British Foreign Policy from the 1880s to the First World War* (London, 1987)

FRIEDRICH WÜRTHLE, *Die Spur führt nach Belgrad* (Vienna, 1975)

——, *Dokumente zum Sarajevoprozess: Ein Quellenbericht*, ed. Kurt Peball (Vienna, 1978)

Z. A. B. ZEMAN, *The Break-Up of the Habsburg Empire, 1914–1918* (London, 1961)

ARTICLES AND DISSERTATIONS

JOHANN C. ALLMAYER-BECK, 'Das Heerwesen' in Friedrich Engel-Janosi and Helmut Rumpler (eds), *Probleme der Franzisko-Josephinischen Zeit, 1848–1916* (Vienna, 1967)

——, 'Die Bewaffnete Macht in Staat und Gesellschaft' in Wandruszka and Urbanitsch (eds), *Die Bewaffnete Macht*

HANS ANGERMEIER, 'Der österreichische Imperialismus des Generalfeldmarschalls Conrad von Hötzendorf' in Dieter Albrecht (ed.), *Festschrift für Max Spindler zum 75. Geburtstag* (Munich, 1969)

I. T. BEREND AND GYÖRGY RÁNKI, 'Ungarns wirtschaftliche Entwicklung, 1849–1918' in Brusatti (ed.), *Die Wirtschaftliche Entwicklung*

WOLFDIETER BIHL, 'Zu den österreichisch-ungarischen Kriegszielen 1914', *Jahrbücher für Geschichte Osteuropas*, XVI (1968)

LUDWIG BITTNER, 'Das österreichisch-ungarische Ministerium des Aussen. Seine Geschichte und Organisation', *Berliner Monatshefte*, XV (2) (1937)

JOHN W. BOYER, 'The End of the Old Regime: Visions of Political Reform in late Imperial Austria', *JMH*, LVIII (March 1986)

HORST BRETTNER-MESSLER, 'Die Balkanpolitik Conrad von Hötzendorf von seiner Wiederernennung zum Chef des Generalstabes bis Oktober–Ultimatum 1913', *Mitteilungen des österreichischen Staatsarchivs* (hereafter cited as *MÖS*), XX (1967)

——, 'Die militärische Absprachen zwischen den Generalstäben Österreich-Ungarns und Italiens vom Dezember 1912 bis Juni 1914', *MÖS*, XXIII (1970)

F. R. BRIDGE, 'Austria–Hungary and the Ottoman Empire in the Twentieth Century', *MÖS*, XXXIV (1981)

——, 'Izvolsky, Aehrenthal, and the End of the Austro-Russian Entente, 1906–08', *MÖS*, XXIX (1976)

——, '"Tarde venientibus ossa"': Austro-Hungarian Colonial Aspirations in Asia Minor (1913–14)', *Middle Eastern Studies*, VI (1970)

THOMAS H. CONNER, 'Parliament and the Making of Foreign Policy: France under the Third Republic, 1875–1914', diss. (Chapel Hill, N. Carol., 1983)

MARK CORNWALL, 'Between the Two Wars: King Nikola of Montenegro and the Great Powers, August 1913–August 1914', *The South Slav Journal*, IX (1986)

GORDON A. CRAIG, 'The World War I Alliance of the Central Powers in Retrospect: The Military Cohesion of the Alliance', *JMH*, XXXVII (Sept. 1965)

RICHARD J. CRAMPTON, 'The Balkans as a Factor in German Foreign Policy, 1912–1914', *Slavonic and East European Review*, LV (1977)

——, 'The Decline of the Concert of Europe in the Balkans, 1913–1914', *Slavonic and East European Review*, LII (1974)

WILHELM DEUTSCHMANN, 'Die militärischen Massnahmen in Österreich-Ungarn während der Balkankriege, 1912/13', diss. (Vienna, 1965)

ISTVÁN DIÓSZEGI, 'Aussenminister Stephan Graf Burián: Biographie und Tagebuchstelle', *Annales Universitatis Scientiarum Budapestinensis de Kolando Eötvös: Sectio Historica*, VIII (Budapest, 1966)

JACK R. DUKES, 'Militarism and Arms Policy Revisited: The Origins of the German Army Law of 1913', in Jack R. Dukes and Joachim Remak (eds), *Another Germany: A Reconsideration of the Imperial Era* (Boulder, Col., 1988)

RAINER EGGER, 'Die Militärkanzlei des Erzherzog Franz Ferdinand und ihr Archiv im Kriegsarchiv Wien', *MÖS*, XXVIII (1975)

RONALD LOUIS ERNHARTH, 'The Tragic Alliance: Austro-German Military Cooperation, 1871–1918', diss. (Colombia University, 1970)

R. J. W. EVANS, 'The Habsburg Monarchy and the Coming of the War', in *The Coming of the First World War*, eds R. J. W. Evans and Hartmut Pogge von Strandmann (Oxford, 1988)

FRITZ FELLNER, 'Die "Mission Hoyos"' in Vasa Čubrilović (ed.), *Recueil des trauvaux aux assises scientifiques internationales: Les grandes puissances et la Serbie à la veille de la Première guerre mondiale* (Belgrade, 1976)

——, 'Zwischen Kriegsbegeisterung und Resignation — ein Memorandum des Sektionschef Graf Forgách vom Januar 1915', in *Beiträge zur allgemeinen Geschichte: Alexander Novotny zur Vollendung seiner 70. Lebensjahre* (Graz, 1975)

WILLIAM C. FULLER, Jr, 'Russia', in May, (ed.), *Knowing One's Enemies*

ALEXANDER FUSSEK, 'Graf Stürgkh und Graf Tisza', *Österreich in Geschichte und Literatur*, VIII (1964)

JÓZSEF GALÁNTAI, 'Austria–Hungary and the War: The October 1913 Crisis — Prelude to July 1914', *Etudes Historiques Hongroises 1980* (Budapest, 1980)
——, 'István Tisza und der Erste Weltkrieg', *Annales Universitatis Scientarum Budapestinensis: Sectio Historica*, V (1963)
LOUIS A. GEBHARD, Jr, 'Austria–Hungary's Dreadnought Squadron: The Naval Outlay of 1911', *Austrian History Yearbook*, IV–V (1968–69)
EGON GOTTSCHALK, 'Die Entrevue von Constanza', *Berliner Monatshefte*, XII (June 1934)
PETER HANDEL-MAZZETTI, 'Admiral Rudolf Graf Montecuccoli degli Erri', *Neue Österreichische Biographie*, XIV (Vienna, 1960)
HUGO HANTSCH, 'Erzherzog Thronfolger Franz Ferdinand und Graf Leopold Berchtold', *Historica* (Vienna, 1965)
HANS HEILBRONNER, 'The Merger Attempts of Serbia and Montenegro, 1913–1914,' *Journal of Central European Affairs*, XVIII (1958)
HOLGER H. HERWIG, 'Imperial Germany', in May (ed.), *Knowing One's Enemies*
KEITH HITCHINS, 'The Nationality Problem in Hungary: István Tisza and the Rumanian National Party, 1906–1914', *JMH*, LIII (Dec. 1981)
LOTHAR HÖBELT, 'Die Marine' in Wandruszka and Urbanitsch (eds), *Die Bewaffnete Macht*
——, 'Österreich-Ungarn und das Deutsche Reich als Zweibundpartner', in Lutz and Rumpler (eds), *Österreich und die deutsche Frage im 19. und 20. Jahrundert: Probleme der politisch-staatlichen und soziokulturellen Differenzierung im deutschen Mitteleuropa*
——, 'Schlieffen, Beck, Potiorek und das Ende der gemeinsamen deutsch-österreichisch-ungarischen Aufmarschpläne im Osten', *Militärgeschichtliche Mitteilungen*, XXXVI (1984)
CHRISTOPHER H. D. HOWARD, 'The Vienna Diary of Berta de Bunsen, 28 June–17 August 1914', *Bulletin of the Institute of Historical Research*, LI (1978)
WILLIAM JANNEN, Jr, 'The Austro-Hungarian Decision for War in July 1914', in Williamson and Pastor (eds), *Essays on World War I: Origins and Prisoners of War*
DAVID E. KAISER, 'Germany and the Origins of the First World War', *JMH*, LV (Sept. 1983)
ROBERT A. KANN, 'Die Habsburgermonarchie und das Problem des übernationalen Staates', in Wandruszka and Urbanitsch (eds), *Verwaltung und Rechtswesen*
LÁSZLO KATUS, 'Die Magyaren' in Wandruskza and Urbanitsch (eds), *Die Völker des Reiches*
RUDOLF KISZLING, 'Russlands Kriegsvorbereitungen im Herbst 1912 und ihre Rückwirkungen auf Österreich–Ungarn', *Berliner Monatshefte*, XIII (March 1935)
FRITZ KLEIN, 'Die Rivalität zwischen Deutschland und Österreich–Ungarn in der Türkei am Vorabend des ersten Weltkrieges', in Fritz Klein (ed.), *Politik im Krieg: 1914–1918* (Berlin, 1964)

GEORGE B. LEON, 'Greece and the Central Powers, 1913–1914: The Origins of the National Schism', *Südostforschung*, XXXIX (1980)

DÖRTE LÖDING, 'Deutschlands und Österreich-Ungarns Balkanpolitik von 1912 bis 1914 unter besonderer Berücksichtigung ihrer Wirtschaftsinteressen', diss. (Hamburg, 1967)

KARL VON MACCHIO, 'Momentbilder aus der Julikrise 1914', *Berliner Monatshefte*, XIV (Oct. 1936)

DAVID MACKENZIE, 'Serbian Nationalist and Military Organizations and the Piedmont Idea, 1844–1914', *East European Quarterly*, XVI (1982)

JOSEF MANN, 'Feldmarschalleutant Blasius Schemua. Chef des Generalstabes am Vorabend des Weltkrieges, 1911–1912', diss. (Vienna, 1978)

HORST FRIEDRICH MAYER, 'Die k.u.k. Kriegsmarine unter dem Kommando von Admiral Anton Haus', diss. (Vienna, 1962)

KEITH NEILSON, '"My Beloved Russians", Sir Arthur Nicolson and Russia, 1906–1916', *The International History Review*, IX (Nov. 1987)

——, 'Watching the "Steamroller": British Observers and the Russian Army before 1914', *Journal of Strategic Studies*, VIII (June 1985)

FRANK E. NORGATE, 'The Internal Policies of the Stürgkh Government, November 1911–March 1914: A Study in a Holding Action', diss. (New York University, 1978)

ALEXANDER NOVOTNY, 'Der Monarch und seine Ratgeber' in Wandruszka and Urbanitsch (eds), *Verwaltung und Rechtswesen*

AKOS PAULINYI, 'Die sogenannte gemeinsame Wirtschaftspolitik Österreich–Ungarns' in Brusatti (ed.), *Die Wirtschaftliche Entwicklung*

EGON VON PAUPPERT, 'Aus der Militärkanzlei des Kaisers und Konigs Franz Joseph: vom Kriegsbeginn 1914 bis zum Tode des Monarchen 1916', unpubl. ms. (Vienna, 1950); copy in the Kriegsarchiv, Vienna

M. B. A. PETERSON, 'Das österreichisch-ungarische Memorandum an Deutschland vom 5 Juli 1914', *Scandia*, XXX (1964)

F. PÖLÖSKEI, 'István Tisza's Policy toward the Romanian Nationalities on the Eve of World War I', *Acta Historica: Academiae Scientiarum Hungaricae*, XVIII (1972)

MANFRED RAUH, 'Die britisch-russische Marinekonvention von 1914 und der Ausbruch des Ersten Weltkrieges', *Militärgeschichtliche Mitteilungen*, XLI (1987)

JOSEF REIFBERGER, 'Die Entwicklung des militärischen Nachrichtenwesens in der k.u.k. Armee', *Österreichische Militärische Zeitschrift*, XIV (3, 1976)

JOACHIM REMAK, 'The Healthy Invalid: How Doomed the Habsburg Monarchy?', *JMH*, (June 1969)

HELMET RUMPLER, 'The Foreign Ministry of Austria and Austria–Hungary, 1848 to 1918' in Zara Steiner (ed.), *'The Times' Survey of Foreign Ministries of the World* (London, 1982)

IVAN SCOTT, 'The Making of the Triple Alliance in 1882', *East European Quarterly*, XII (1978)

GARY W. SHANAFELT, 'Activism and Inertia: Ottokar Czernin's Mission to Romania', *Austrian History Yearbook*, XXXIX-XL (1983–4)

MARTHA SITTE, 'Alexander von Brosch, der Flügeladjutant und Vorstand der Militärkanzlei des Thronfolgers Franz Ferdinand', diss. (Vienna, 1961)

GALE STOKES, 'The Serbian Documents from 1914: A Preview', *JMH*, XXXXVI (1976), microform

NORMAN STONE, 'Army and Society in the Habsburg Monarchy, 1900–1914', *Past and Present*, XXXIII (1966)

——, 'Austria–Hungary', in May (ed.), *Knowing One's Enemies*

——, 'Moltke-Conrad: Relations between the Austro–Hungarian and German General Staffs, 1909–14', *The Historical Journal*, IX (1966); repr. in *The War Plans of the Great Powers, 1880–1914*, ed. Paul Kennedy (London, 1979)

——, 'Hungary and the Crisis of July 1914', *Journal of Contemporary History*, I (1966)

——, 'Die Mobilmachung der österreichisch–ungarischen Armee 1914', *Militärgeschichtliche Mitteilungen*, II (1974)

ROBERT STROPP, 'Die Akten des k.u.k. Ministeriums des Aussern 1848–1918', *MÖS*, XX (1970)

LESLIE C. TIHANY, 'The Austro-Hungarian Compromise, 1867–1918: A Half Century of Diagnosis; Fifty Years of Post-Mortem', *Central European History*, II (1969)

JAMES A. TREICHEL, 'Magyars at the Ballplatz: A Study of the Hungarians in the Austro-Hungarian Diplomatic Service, 1906–1914', diss. (Georgetown, Wash. D.C., 1971)

ULRICH VON TRUMPENER, 'War Premeditated? German Intelligence Operations in July 1914', *Central European History*, IX (March 1976)

L. F. C. TURNER, 'The Russian Mobilization in 1914', *Journal of Contemporary History*, III (1968)

JOSEF ULLREICH, 'Moritz von Auffenberg-Komarów. Leben und Wirken, 1911–1918', diss. (Vienna, 1961)

STEPHEN VAN EVERA, 'The Cult of the Offensive and the Origins of the First World War', in Steven Miller (ed.), *Military Strategy and the Origins of the First World War* (Princeton, New Jersey, 1985)

MILAN N. VEGO, 'The Anatomy of Austrian Sea Power, 1904–1914', diss. (Georgetown, Wash. D.C., 1981)

WALTER WAGNER, 'Die k.u.k. Armee-Gliederung und Aufgabenstellung', in Wandruszka and Urbanitsch (eds), *Die Bewaffnete Macht*

SOLOMON WANK, 'The Appointment of Count Berchtold as Austro-Hungarian Foreign Minister', *Journal of Central European Affairs*, XXIII (July 1963)

——, 'The Austrian Peace Movement and the Habsburg Ruling Elite, 1906–1914', in Charles Chatfield and Peter van den Dungen (eds) *Peace Movements and Political Cultures*

——, 'Foreign Policy and the Nationality Problem in Austria–Hungary, 1867–1914', *Austrian History Yearbook*, III (1967)

——, 'The Growth of Nationalism in the Habsburg Monarchy, 1848–1918', *East Central Europe/L'Europe du Centre-Est*, X, pts 1–2 (1983)

——, 'A Note on the Genealogy of a Fact: Aehrenthal's Jewish Ancestry', *JMH*, XLI (Sept. 1969)

——, 'Pessimism in the Austrian Establishment at the Turn of the Century', in Solomon Wank et al, (eds), *The Mirror of History: Essays in Honor of Fritz Fellner*, (Santa Barbara, Calif., 1988)

FRANZ WEINRAUM, 'FZM Oskar Potiorek: Leben und Wirken als Chef der Landesregierung für Bosnien und der Herzegowina in Sarajevo, 1911– 1914', diss. (Vienna, 1964)

KURT WESSELEY, 'Die wirtschaftliche Entwicklung von Bosnien– Herzegowina (1878–1918)', *Der Donauraum*, XIX (1974)

S. R. WILLIAMSON, 'Influence, Power, and the Policy Process: The Case of Franz Ferdinand, 1906–1914', *The Historical Journal*, XVII (1974)

——, 'Military Dimensions of Habsburg–Romanov Relations during the Era of the Balkan Wars', in Király and Djordevic (eds), *East Central European Society and the Balkan Wars*

——, 'The Origins of World War I', *Journal of Interdisciplinary History*, XVIII (Spring 1988)

——, 'Theories of Organizational Process and Foreign Policy Outcomes', in Paul G. Lauren (ed.), *Diplomacy: New Approaches in History, Theory, and Policy* (New York, 1979)

——, 'Vienna and July 1914: The Origins of the Great War Once More', in Williamson and Pastor (eds), *Essays on World War I*

KEITH M. WILSON, 'Isolating the Isolator: Cartwright, Grey and the Seduction of Austria–Hungary, 1908–12', *MÖS*, XXXV (1982)

WILLIAM C. WOHLFORTH, 'The Perceptions of Power: Russia in the Pre-1914 Balance', *World Politics*, XXXIX (April 1987)

ARCHIVES AND PUBLISHED DOCUMENTS

ARCHIVES

AUSTRIA–HUNGARY

● Haus-, Hof-, und Staatsarchiv,
   Vienna:

Manuscript Collections:	*Official Documents:*
Berchtold Archiv	Politisches Archiv, including:
Franz Ferdinand Nachlass	Memorien des Grafen Leopold Berchtold,
Schiessl Nachlass	PA 1/524a and 524b
	Gemeinsame Ministerratsprotokolle,
	PA XL/310–11
	Ungarische Ministerratsprotokolle

● Kriegsarchiv, Vienna:

Manuscript Collections:	*Official Documents:*
Bardolff Nachlass	Generalstab: Operations Büro
Conrad Archiv	Generalstab: Evidenz Büro
Potiorek Nachlass	Generalstab: Militär Attaché
Urbanski Nachlass	Militärkanzlei des Generalinspektors des gesamten bewaffneten Macht (Franz Ferdinand)
	Militärkanzlei des Seiner Majestät des Kaisers (Franz Joseph)

● Verwaltungsarchiv, Vienna:
Austrian cabinet papers, 1912–14

GERMANY
Politisches Archiv des Auswärtigen Amtes, on microfilm in the National Archives, Washington:
Botschaft Wien: Jagow–Tschirschky Korrespondenz, reel T–120/3785

YUGOSLAVIA
Gemeinsames Finanzministerium: files relating to the Habsburg administration of Bosnia and Herzegovina; now located in the Archiv Bosne i Hercegovine, Sarajevo

PUBLISHED DOCUMENTS

AUSTRIA–HUNGARY
Jahrbuch des k.u.k. Auswärtigen Dienstes: 1913 (Vienna, 1914)
Militär-Adressebuch für Wien und Umgebung 1914: Zusammengestellt beim k.u.k. Platzkommando in Wien (Vienna, 1913)
ALFRED F. PRIBRAM, *The Secret Treaties of Austria–Hungary, 1879–1914*, vol. I, ed. Archibald Cary Coolidge; trans. Denys P. Myers and J. G. D'Arcy Paul (Cambridge, Mass., 1920)
Protokolle des Gemeinsamen Ministerrates der Österreichisch-Ungarischen Monarchie, 1914–1918, ed. Miklós Komjáthy (Budapest, 1966)
Österreich-Ungarns Aussenpolitik von der bosnischen Krise 1908 bis zum Kriegsausbruch 1914, eds Ludwig Bittner and Hans Übersberger, 9 vols (Vienna, 1930)
Österreich-Ungarns Letzter Krieg, 1914–1918, 7 vols and 10 supplements (Vienna, 1930–8)
Stenographische Sitzungsprotokolle der Delegation des Reichsrathes:
Siebenundvierzigste Session. Budapest 1912 (Vienna, 1913)
Achtundvierzigste Session. Vienna 1913 (Vienna, 1914)
Neunundvierzigte Session. Budapest (Vienna, 1914)
Volkswirtschaftliche Chronik (Vienna, 1912–14)

GERMANY
Die grosse Politik der europäischen Kabinette, 1871–1914, eds Johannes Lepsius, Albrecht Mendelssohn Bartholdy and Friedrich Thimme, 40 vols (Berlin, 1922–27)
Outbreak of the World War: German Documents Collected by Karl Kautsky, (the *Kautsky Documents*) eds Max Montgelas and Walther Schüking (New York, 1924)

ITALY
I Documenti Diplomatici Italiani, 4th ser., 1908–1914, vol. XII (Rome, 1964)

RUSSIA
Die internationalen Beziehungen im Zeitalter des Imperialismus, ed. Otto Hoetzsch, 1st ser., 5 vols (Berlin, 1931–34); 3rd ser. 4 vols to date, (Berlin, 1939–)

SERBIA

Die Auswärtige Politik Serbiens, 1903–1914, ed. Milos Boghitschewitsch, 3 vols (Berlin, 1928–31)

Documents sur la politique exterieure du Royaume de Serbie, 1903–1914 [Dokumenti o spoljnoj politici Kraljevine Srbije, 1903–1914]
tome VI, vol. III, ed. Kliment Džambazovski (Belgrade, 1983)
tome VII, vol. II, eds Vladimir Dedijer and Života Anić (Belgrade, 1980)
Serbiens Aussenpolitiak₂ 1908–1918, vol. III, eds Ludwig Bittner, Alois Hajek, and Hans Übersberger (Vienna, 1945)

Index